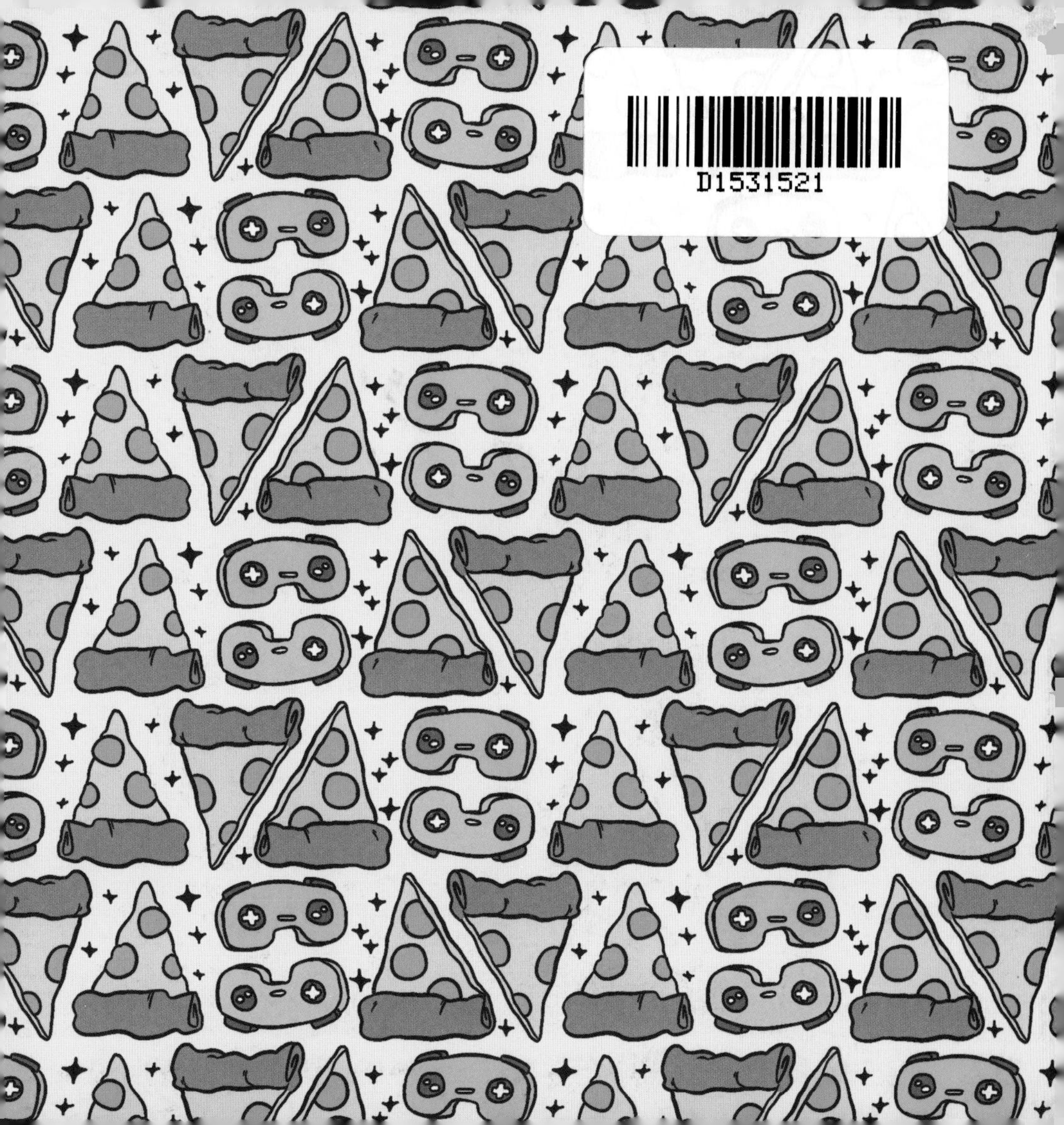

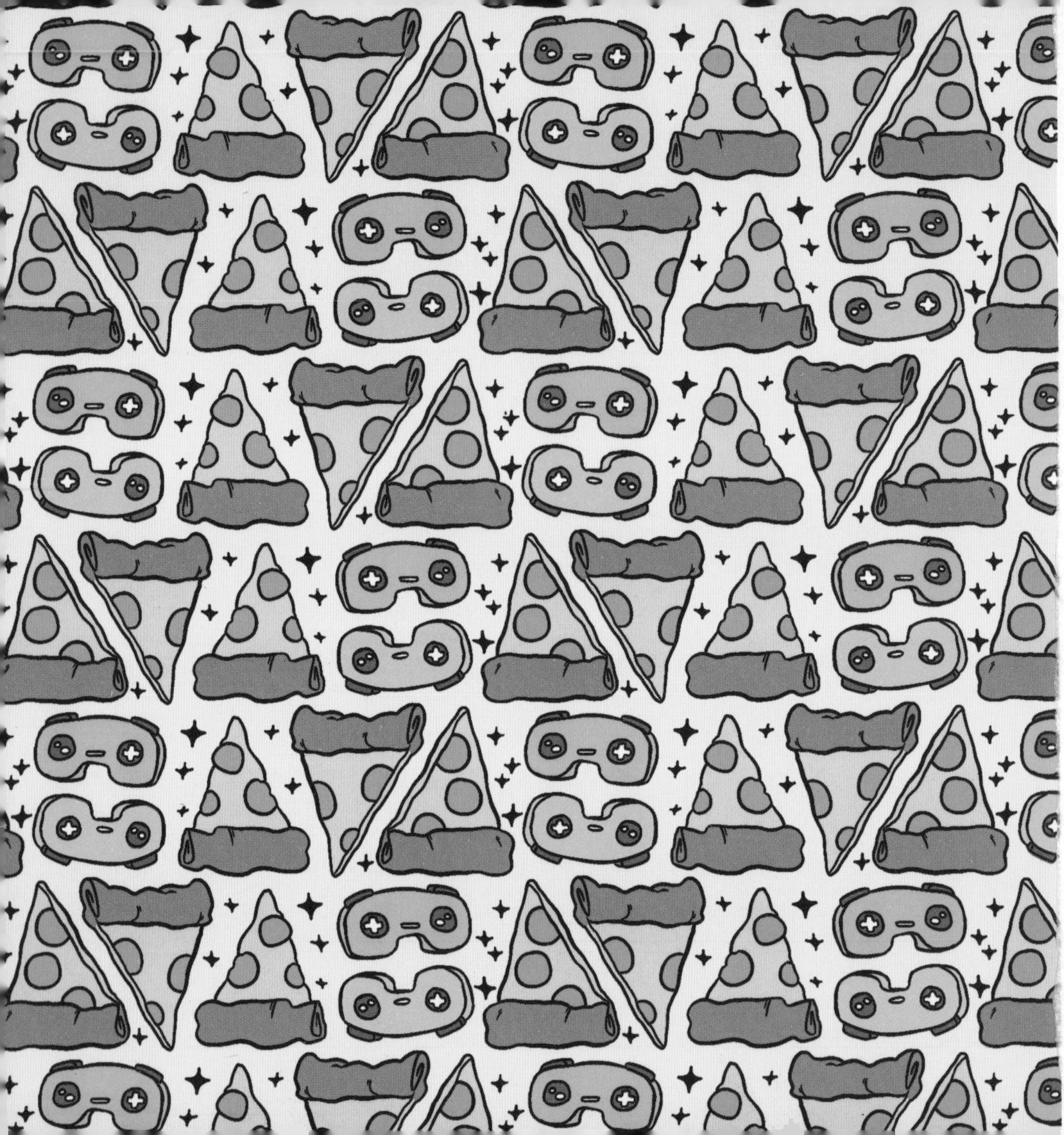

OUR SUPER ADVENTURE

VIDEO GAMES AND PIZZA PARTIES

by Sarah Graley and Stef Purenins

AN ONI PRESS
PUBLICATION

Edited by **Ari Yarwood**
Book Design by **Sarah Graley** & **Stef Purenins**

Published by **Oni Press, Inc.**
Joe Nozemack, Founder & Chief Financial Officer × **James Lucas Jones**, Publisher
Sarah Gaydos, Editor in Chief × **Charlie Chu**, V.P. of Creative & Business Development
Brad Rooks, Director of Operations × **Melissa Meszaros**, Director of Publicity
Margot Wood, Director of Sales × **Sandy Tanaka**, Marketing Design Manager
Amber O'Neill, Special Projects Manager × **Troy Look**, Director of Design & Production
Kate Z. Stone, Senior Graphic Designer × **Sonja Synak**, Graphic Designer
Angie Knowles, Digital Prepress Lead × **Robin Herrera**, Senior Editor
Ari Yarwood, Senior Editor × **Desiree Wilson**, Associate Editor × **Kate Light**, Editorial Assistant
Michelle Nguyen, Executive Assistant × **Jung Lee**, Logistics Associate

Originally self-published by **Shiny Sword Press**

1319 SE Martin Luther King, Jr. Blvd.
Suite 240
Portland, OR 97214

onipress.com
facebook.com/onipress
twitter.com/onipress
onipress.tumblr.com
instagram.com/onipress

oursuperadventure.com
sarahgraley.com
@sarahgraleyart

First Edition: July 2019
Retail Edition ISBN: 978-1-62010-646-4   **Artist Edition ISBN:** 978-1-62010-647-1

Printed in China.

Library of Congress Control Number: 2018967239

1 2 3 4 5 6 7 8 9 10

OUR SUPER ADVENTURE

VIDEO GAMES AND PIZZA PARTIES

by Sarah Graley and Stef Purenins

Written by **Sarah Graley** and **Stef Purenins**
Art and Colouring by **Sarah Graley**
Lettering, Colour Assisting and Design by
Stef Purenins

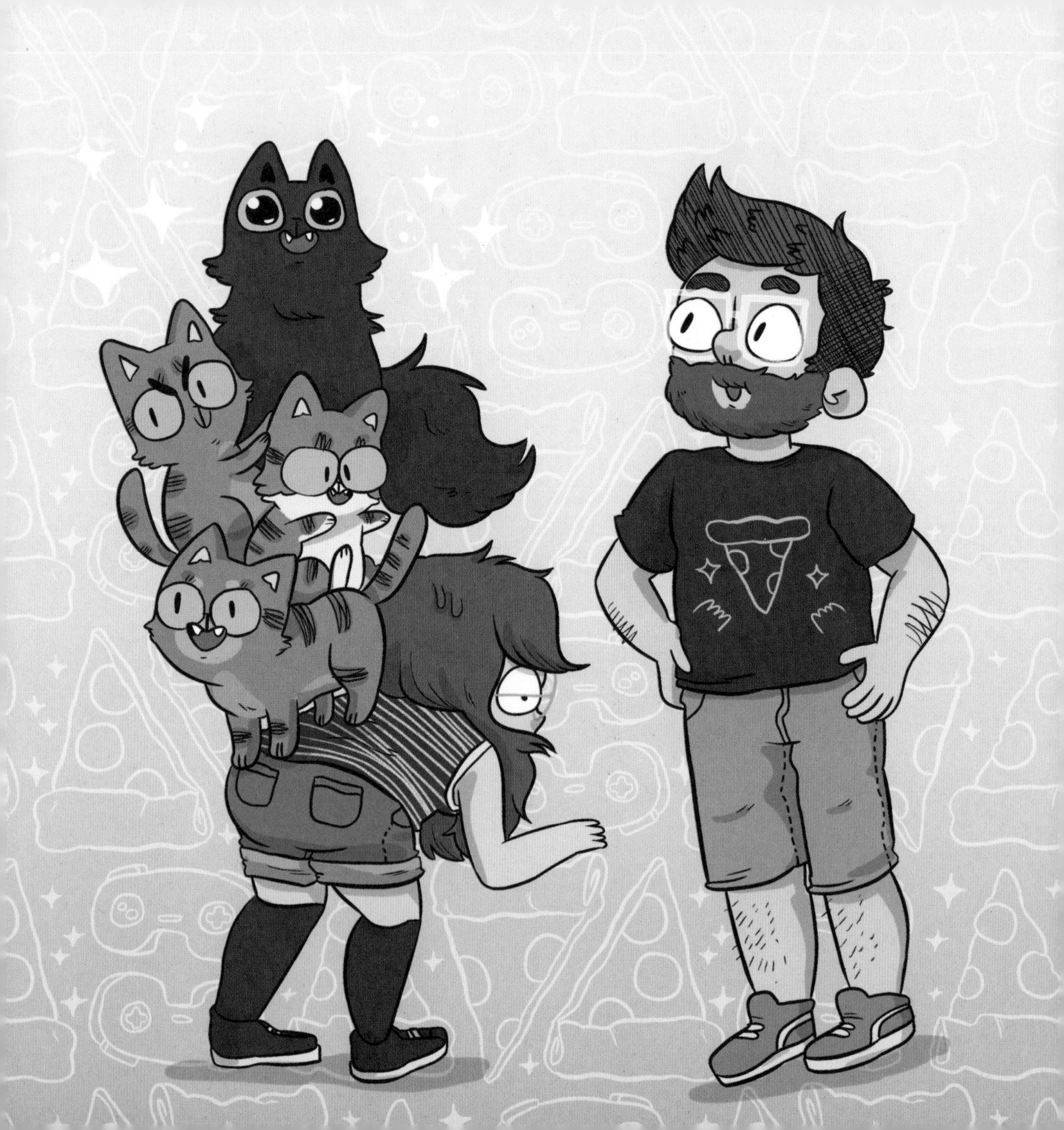

INTRODUCTION

Welcome to *Video Games and Pizza Parties* - the second *Our Super Adventure* collection! This book collects comics posted online between 2015 and 2018, as well as a bunch of new ones!

If you're new to all of this, *Our Super Adventure* is my diary comic all about the life that I share with my partner Stef, and our four cats: Pesto, Toby, Pixel and Wilson! I've been making them since 2012 and they've acted as a really great way to keep track of the weird, cute and funny moments in our relationship. Stef now works with me on the comics doing all of the lettering and colour assisting, and he helps out with writing too!

The first *Our Super Adventure* book came out in 2015, and since then I've been working on comics like *Rick and Morty: Lil' Poopy Superstar* (Oni Press), *Invader Zim* (Oni Press), *Minecraft Volume 1* (Dark Horse Comics), and my original titles, *Kim Reaper* (Oni Press) and *Glitch* (Scholastic Graphix). Working on these books has been amazing! Me and Stef have also been able to travel out to a whole bunch of American and Canadian comic shows and meet so many awesome people! It really has been a dream come true, and it all started with *Our Super Adventure: Press Start To Begin*, a book that I'm still incredibly proud of!

The entire time, we've still been creating and posting *Our Super Adventure* comics online, but a large amount had to exist on little scraps of paper and old notebooks until I found the time to draw and colour them properly, and thankfully, that time is now! This book manages to contain a whole bunch of weird little snapshots into our lives during the last three years, and we hope you find something to enjoy in these pages.

Thank you for picking up this book!

- Sarah and Stef (and Pesto, Toby, Wilson and Pixel too!)

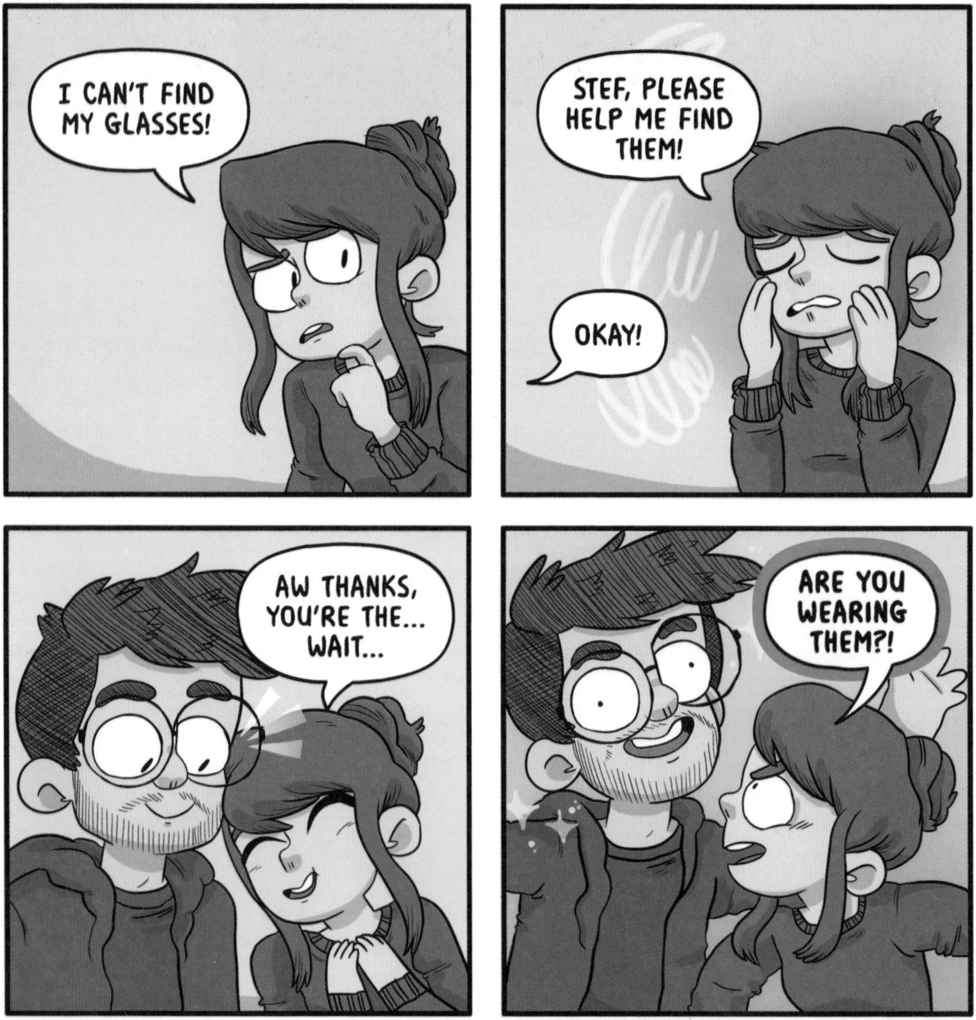
I CAN'T FIND MY GLASSES!
STEF, PLEASE HELP ME FIND THEM!
OKAY!
AW THANKS, YOU'RE THE... WAIT...
ARE YOU WEARING THEM?!

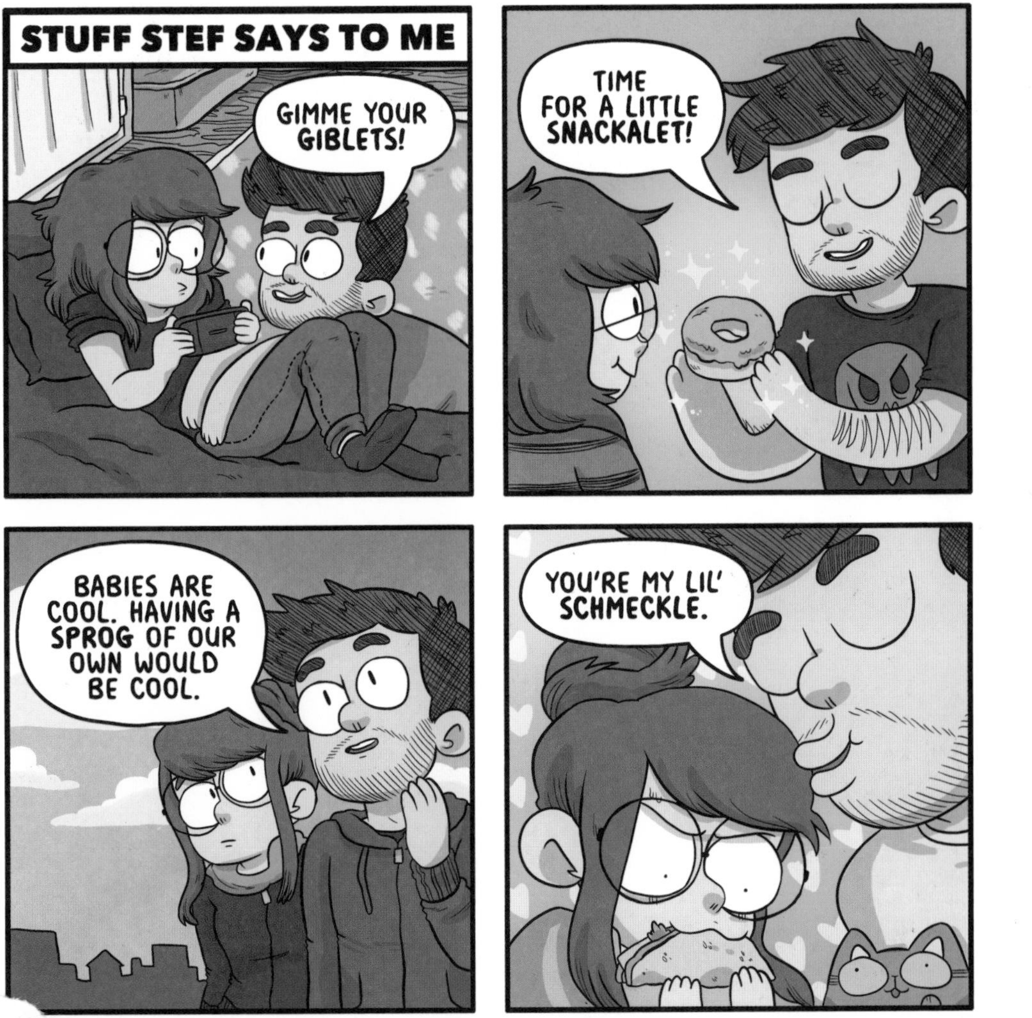
STUFF STEF SAYS TO ME
GIMME YOUR GIBLETS!
TIME FOR A LITTLE SNACKALET!
BABIES ARE COOL. HAVING A SPROG OF OUR OWN WOULD BE COOL.
YOU'RE MY LIL' SCHMECKLE.

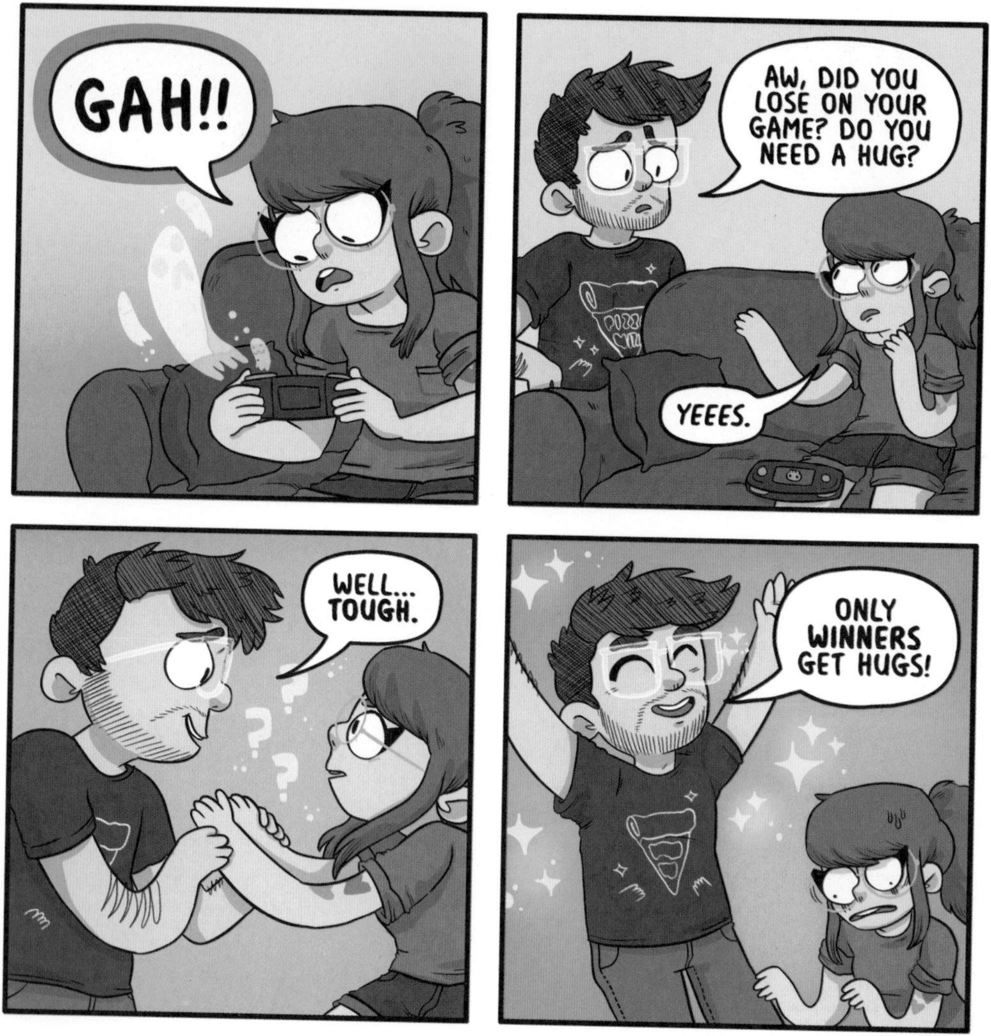
GAH!!
AW, DID YOU LOSE ON YOUR GAME? DO YOU NEED A HUG?
YEEES.
WELL... TOUGH.
ONLY WINNERS GET HUGS!

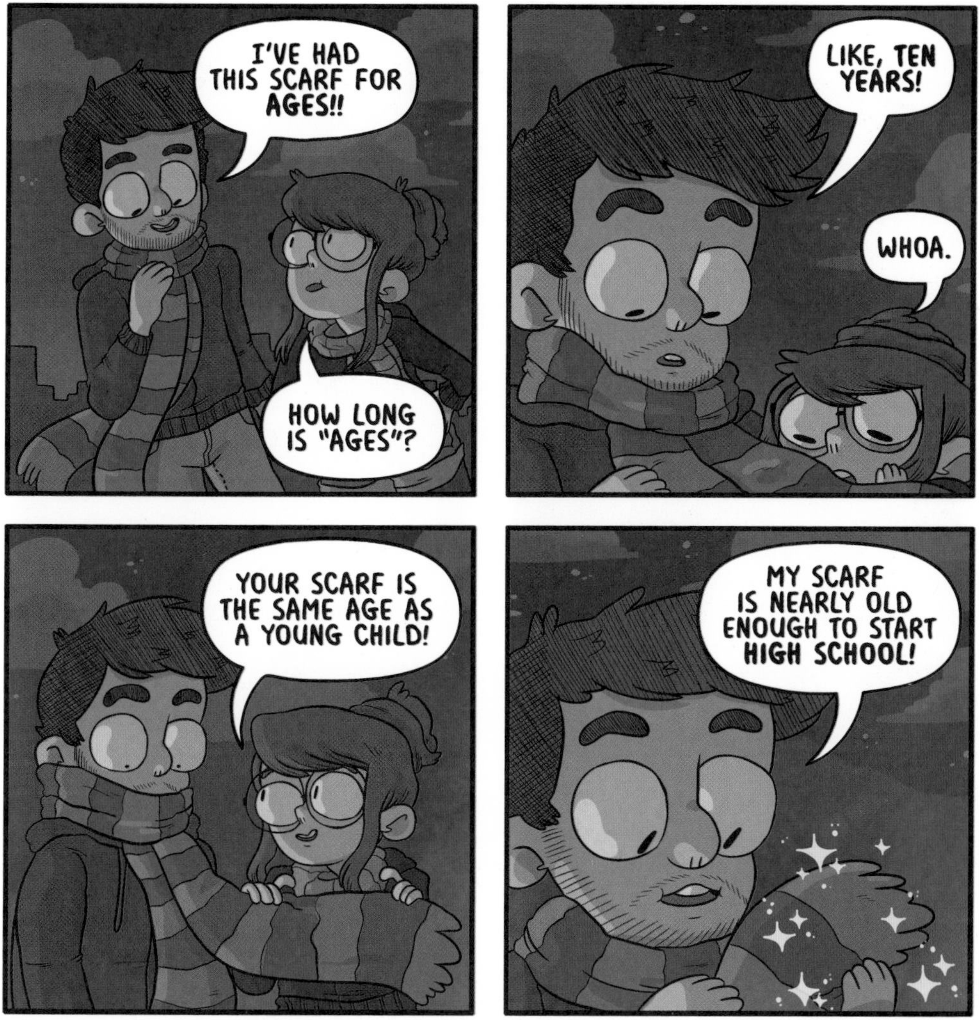
I'VE HAD THIS SCARF FOR AGES!!
HOW LONG IS "AGES"?
LIKE, TEN YEARS!
WHOA.
YOUR SCARF IS THE SAME AGE AS A YOUNG CHILD!
MY SCARF IS NEARLY OLD ENOUGH TO START HIGH SCHOOL!

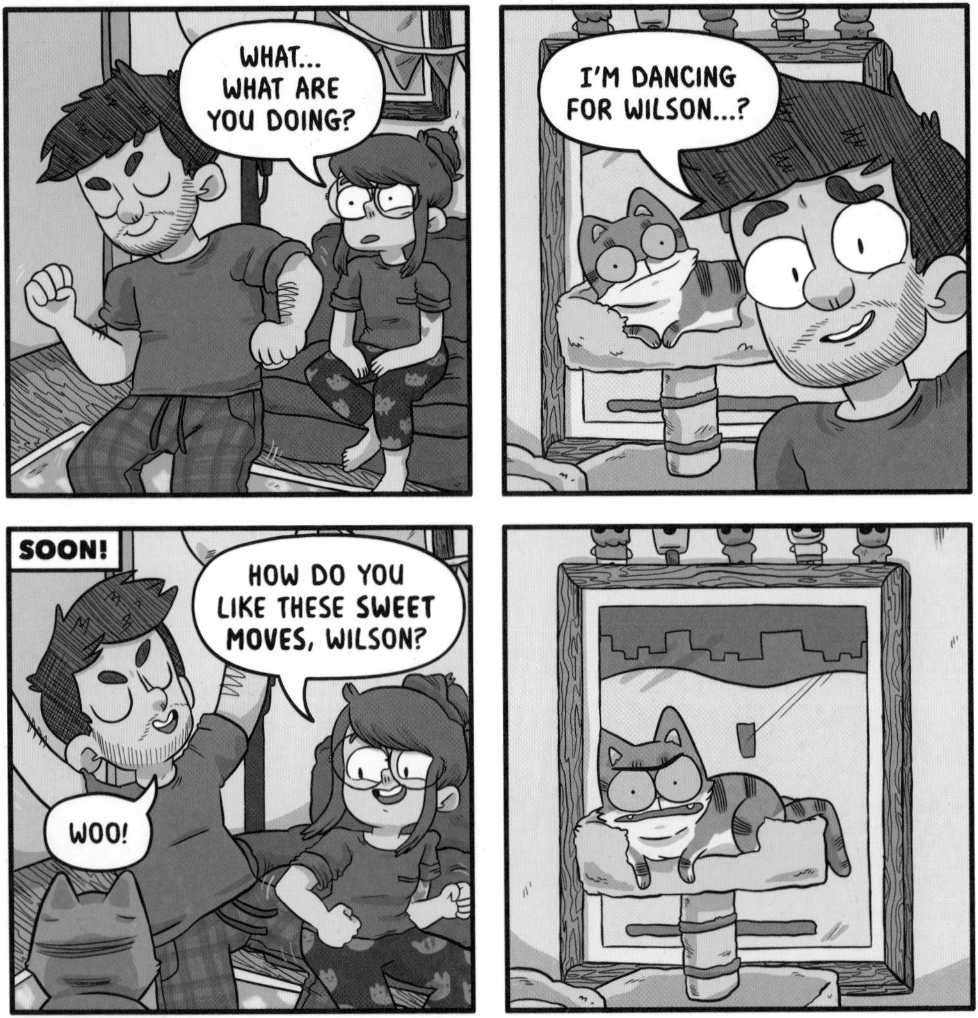
WHAT... WHAT ARE YOU DOING?
I'M DANCING FOR WILSON...?
SOON!
HOW DO YOU LIKE THESE SWEET MOVES, WILSON?
WOO!

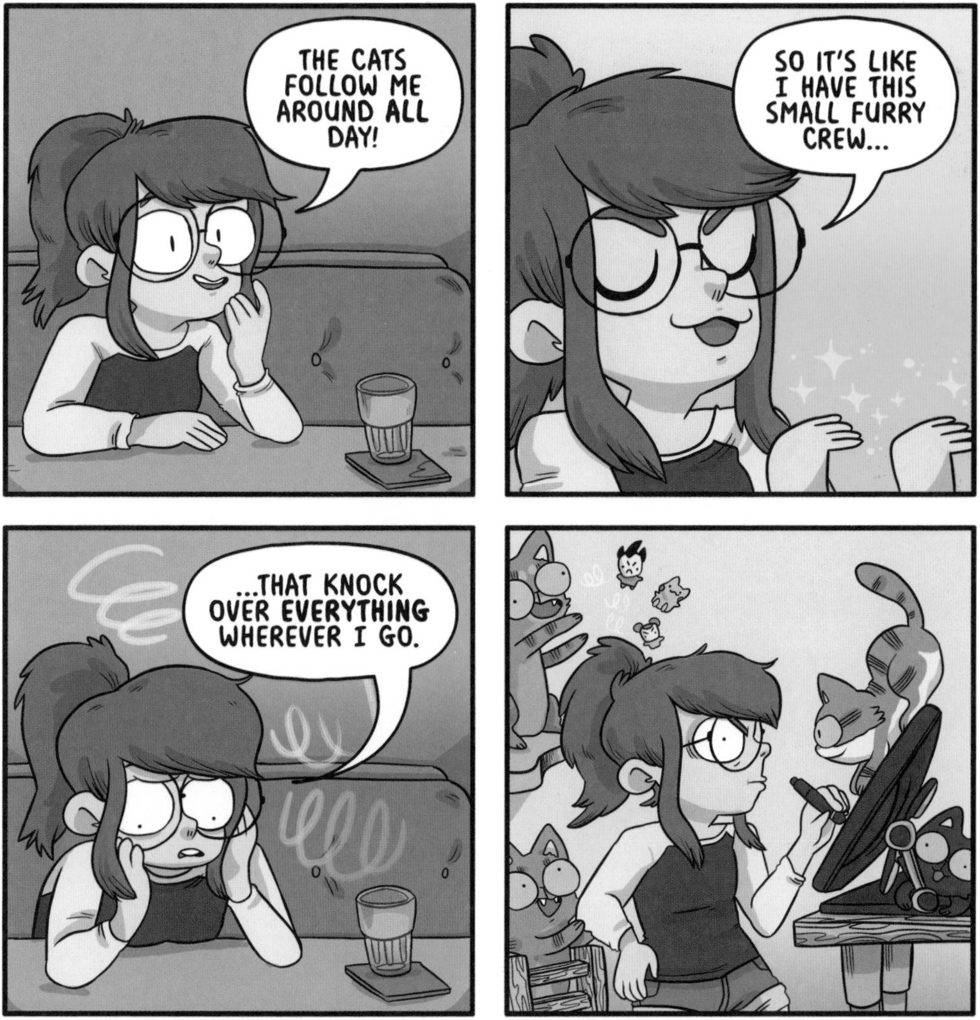
THE CATS FOLLOW ME AROUND ALL DAY!
SO IT'S LIKE I HAVE THIS SMALL FURRY CREW...
...THAT KNOCK OVER EVERYTHING WHEREVER I GO.

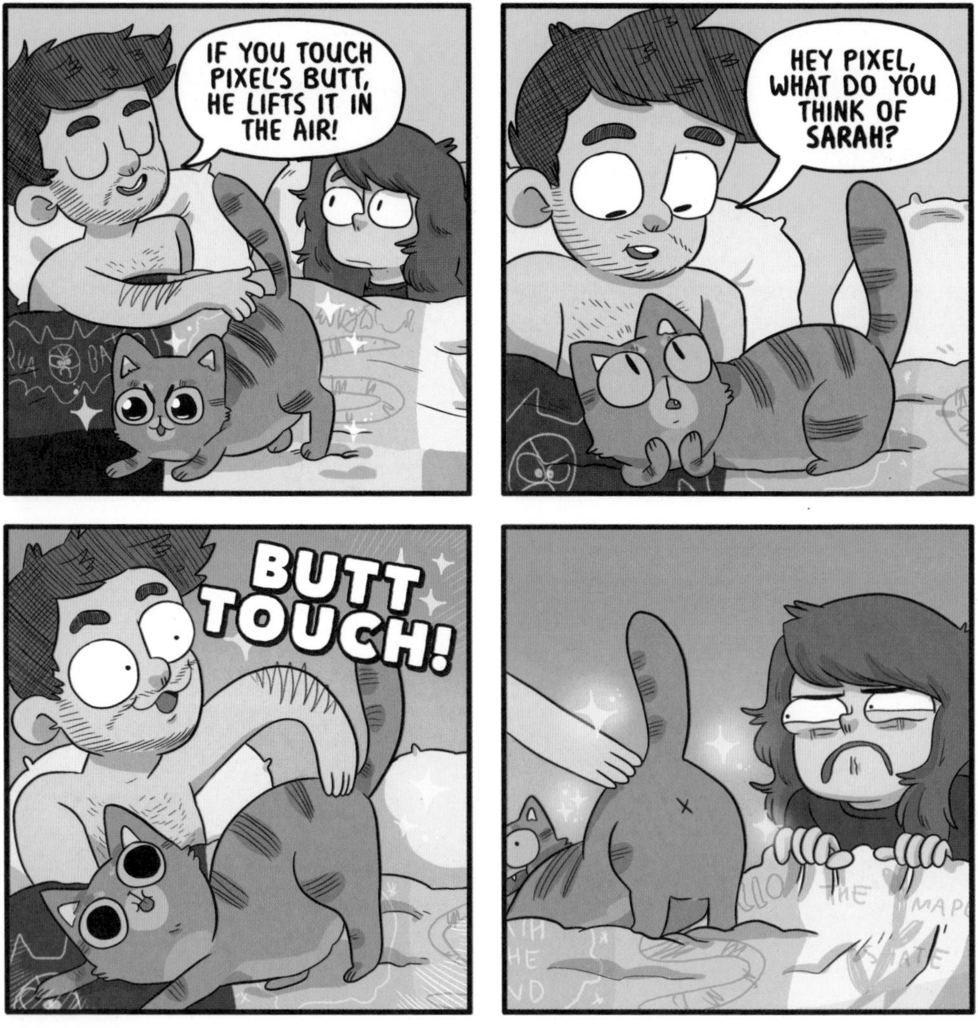
IF YOU TOUCH PIXEL'S BUTT, HE LIFTS IT IN THE AIR!
HEY PIXEL, WHAT DO YOU THINK OF SARAH?
BUTT TOUCH!

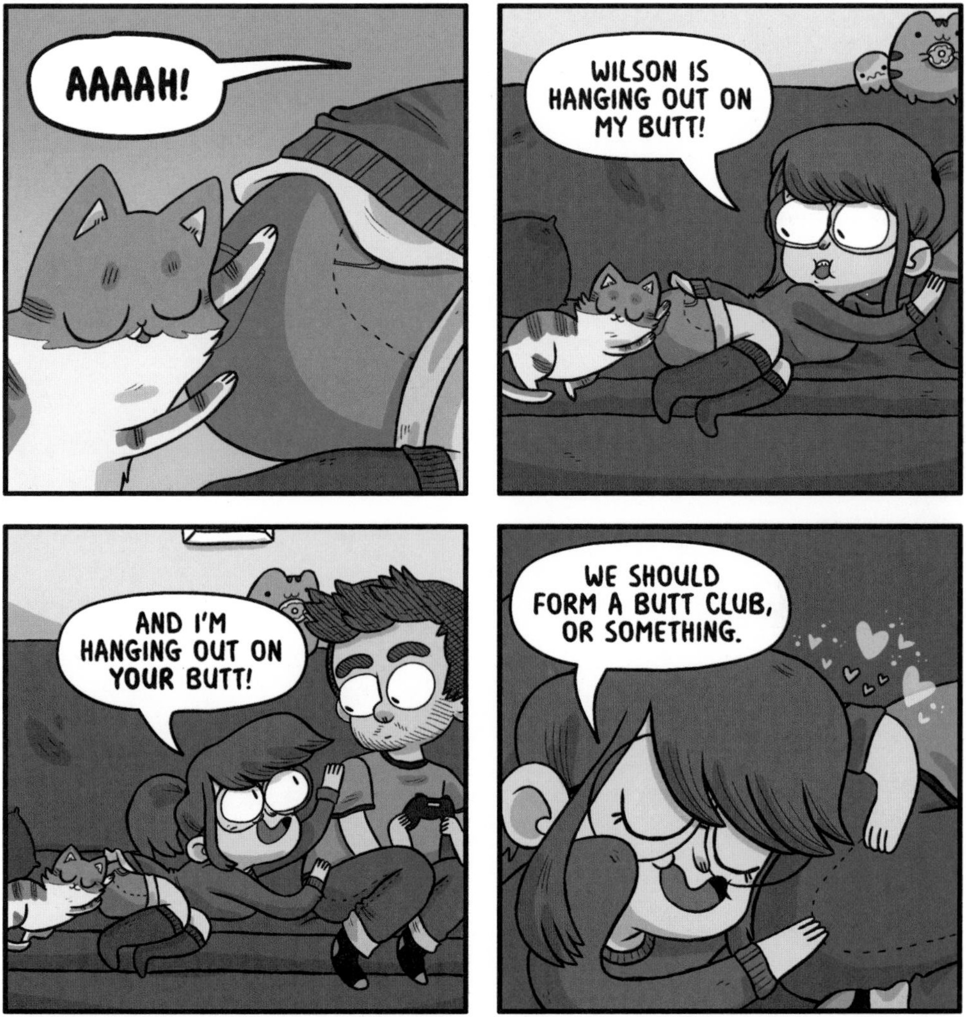
AAAAH!
WILSON IS HANGING OUT ON MY BUTT!
AND I'M HANGING OUT ON YOUR BUTT!
WE SHOULD FORM A BUTT CLUB, OR SOMETHING.

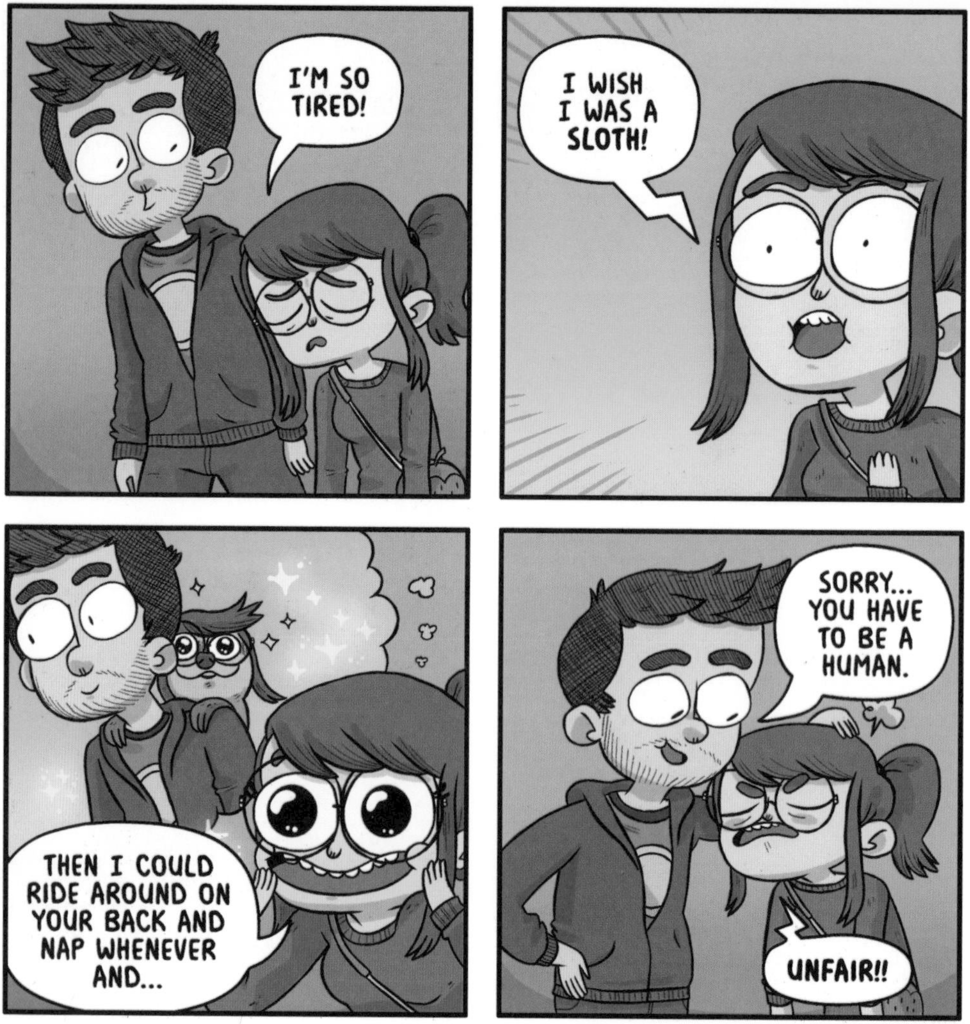
I'M SO TIRED!
I WISH I WAS A SLOTH!
THEN I COULD RIDE AROUND ON YOUR BACK AND NAP WHENEVER AND...
SORRY... YOU HAVE TO BE A HUMAN.
UNFAIR!!

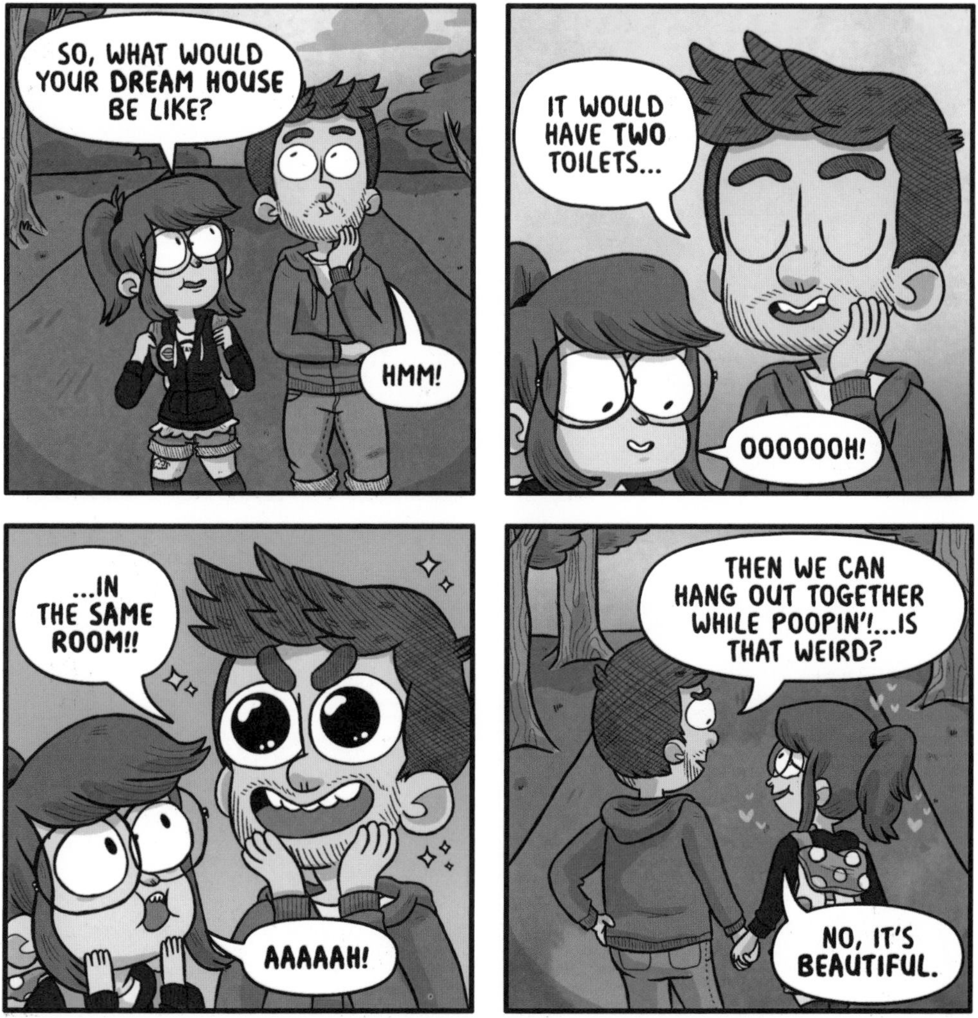
SO, WHAT WOULD YOUR DREAM HOUSE BE LIKE?
HMM!
IT WOULD HAVE TWO TOILETS...
OOOOOOH!
...IN THE SAME ROOM!!
AAAAAH!
THEN WE CAN HANG OUT TOGETHER WHILE POOPIN'!...IS THAT WEIRD?
NO, IT'S BEAUTIFUL.

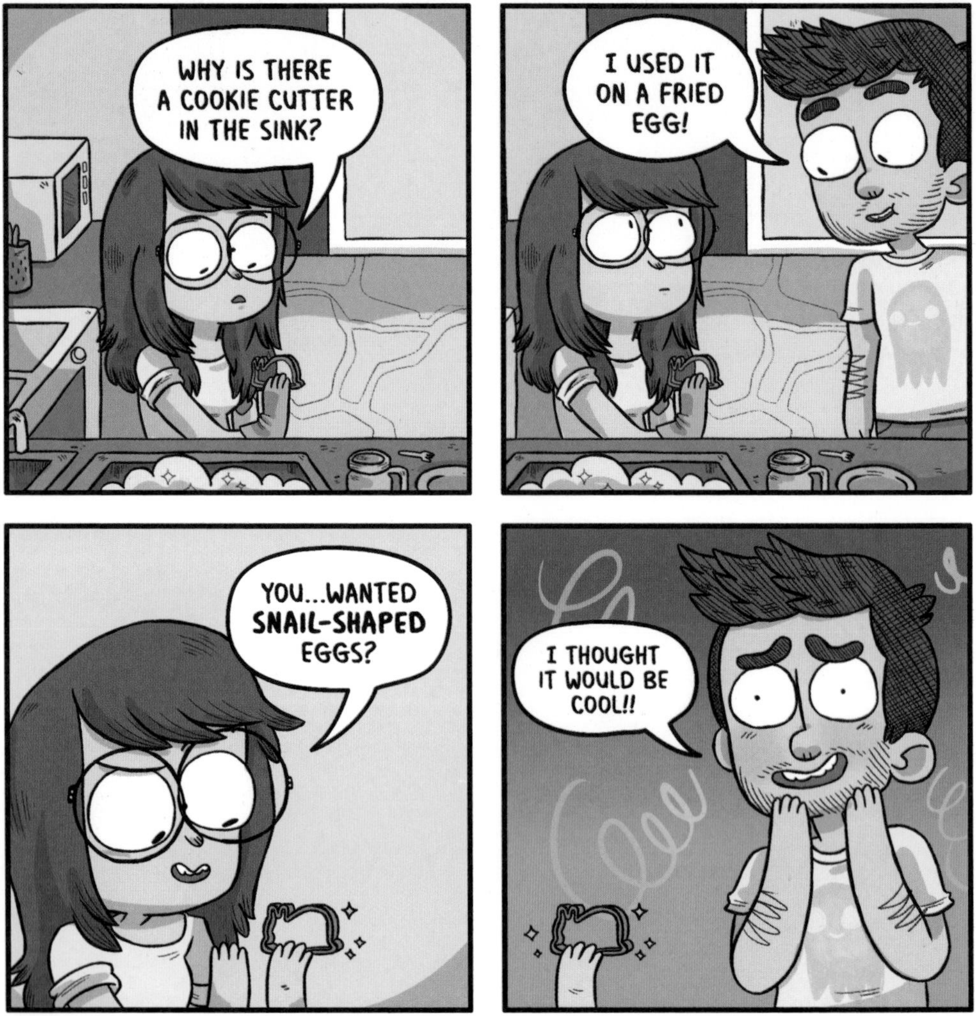
WHY IS THERE A COOKIE CUTTER IN THE SINK?
I USED IT ON A FRIED EGG!
YOU...WANTED SNAIL-SHAPED EGGS?
I THOUGHT IT WOULD BE COOL!!

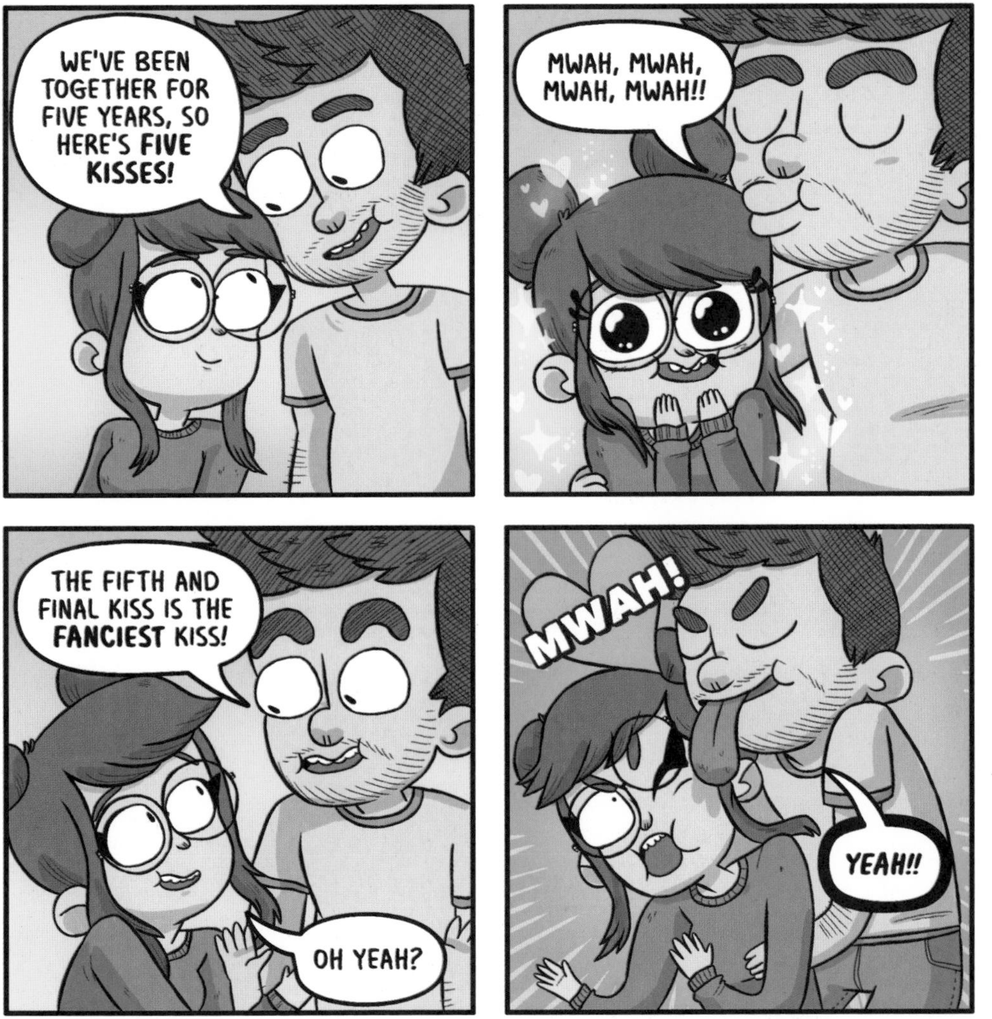
WE'VE BEEN TOGETHER FOR FIVE YEARS, SO HERE'S FIVE KISSES!
MWAH, MWAH, MWAH, MWAH!!
THE FIFTH AND FINAL KISS IS THE FANCIEST KISS!
OH YEAH?
MWAH!
YEAH!!

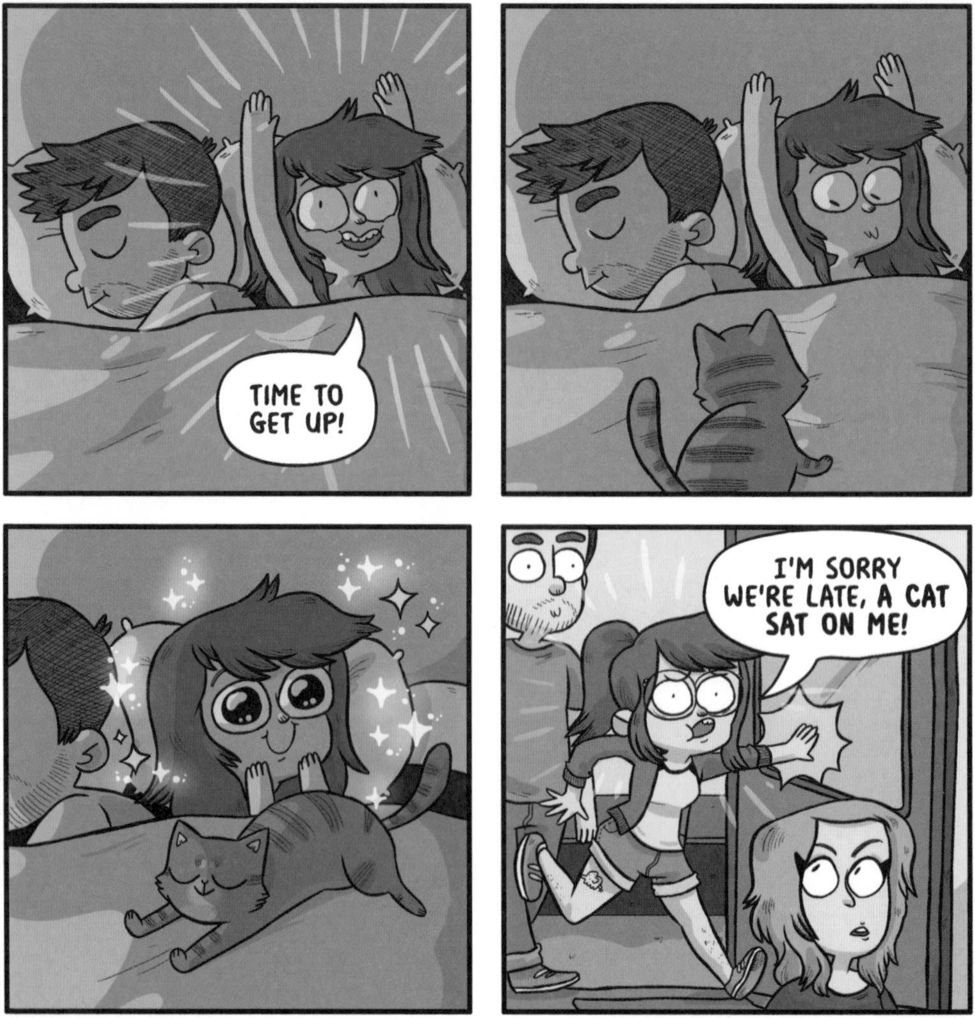
TIME TO GET UP!
I'M SORRY WE'RE LATE, A CAT SAT ON ME!

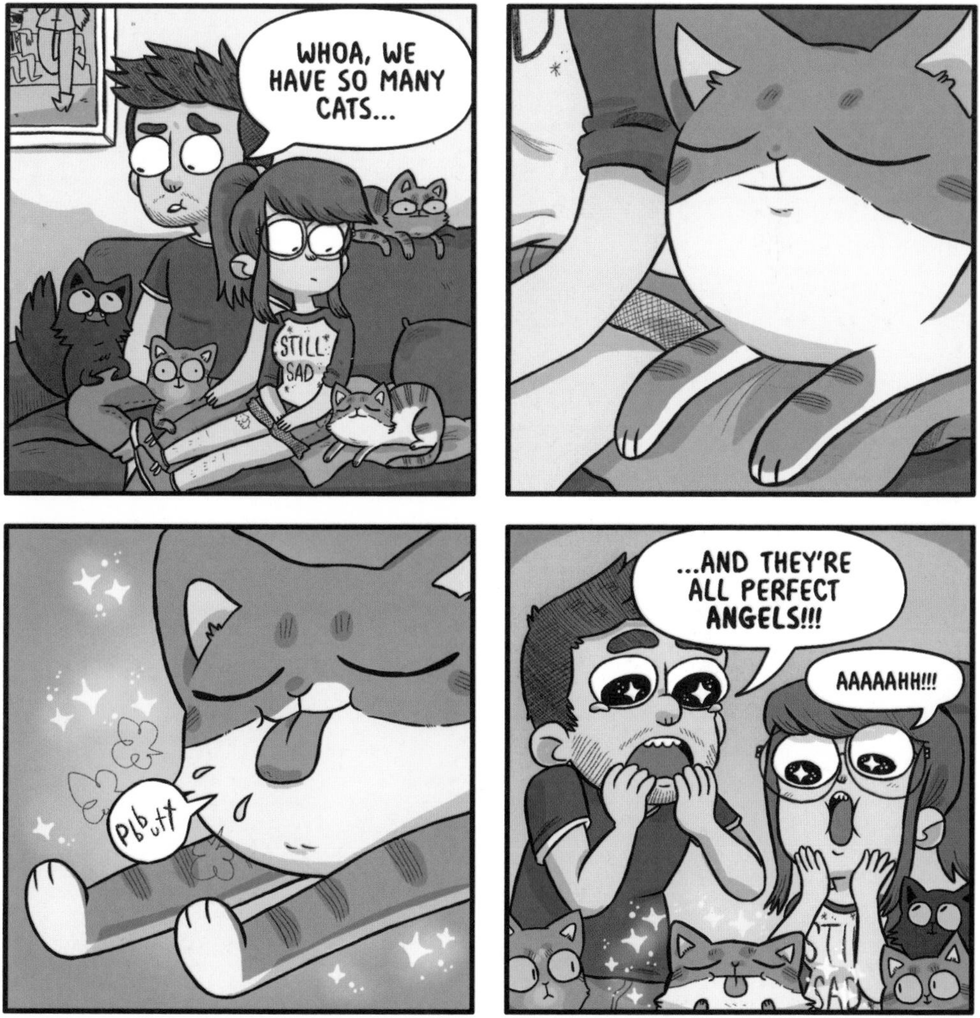
WHOA, WE HAVE SO MANY CATS...
STILL SAD
Pbbutt
...AND THEY'RE ALL PERFECT ANGELS!!!
AAAAAHH!!!

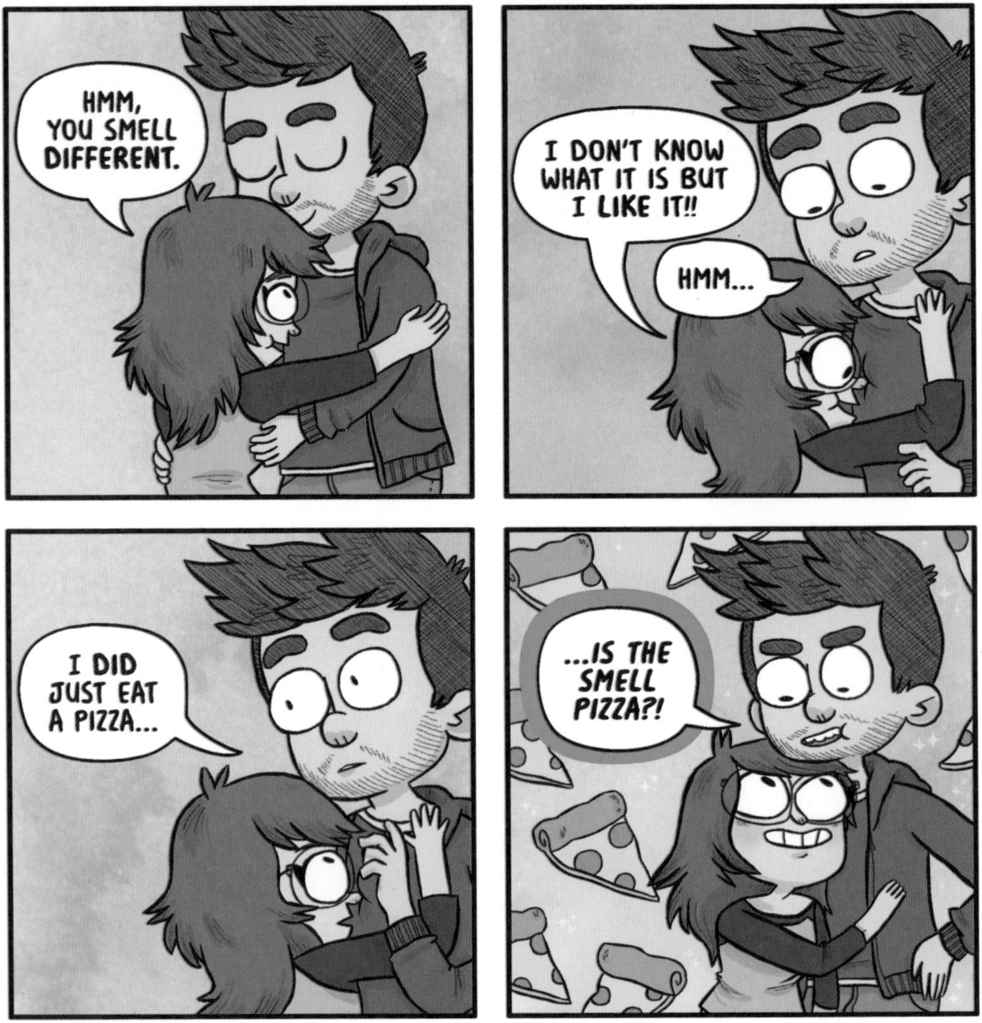
HMM, YOU SMELL DIFFERENT.
I DON'T KNOW WHAT IT IS BUT I LIKE IT!!
HMM...
I DID JUST EAT A PIZZA...
...IS THE SMELL PIZZA?!

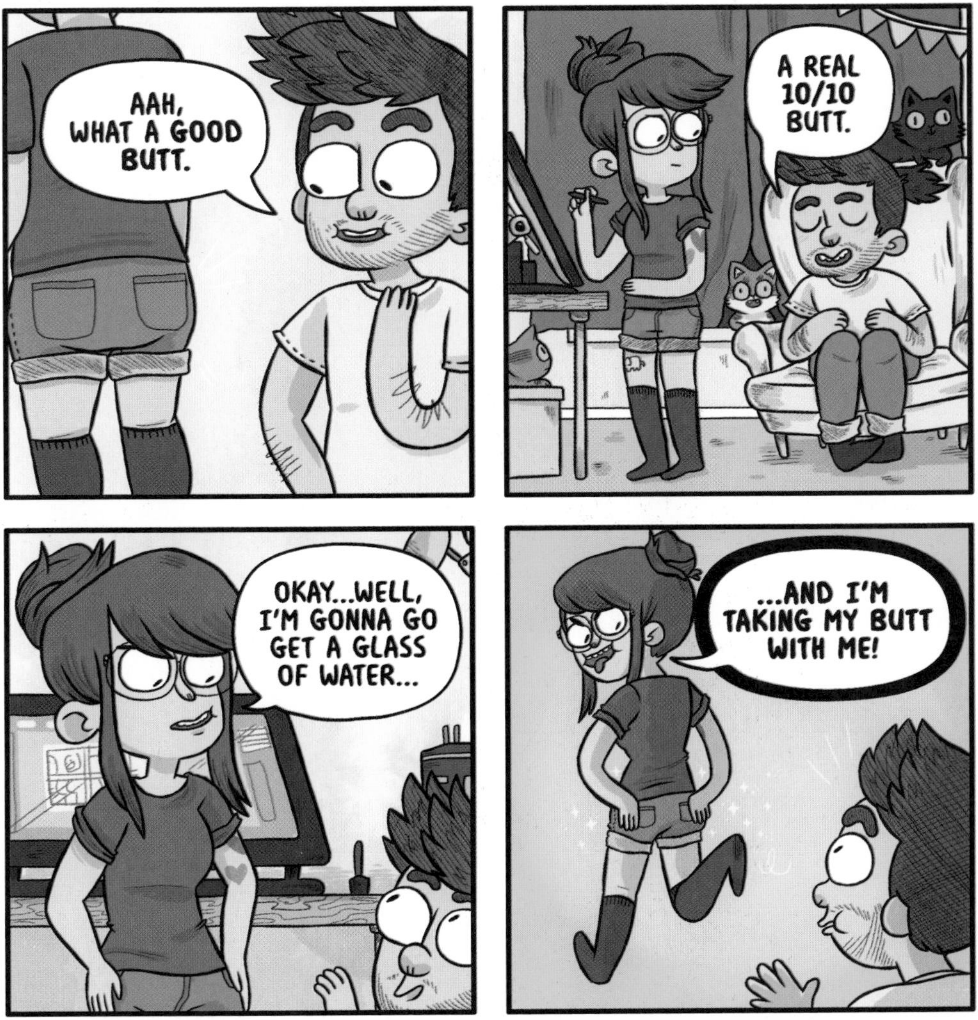
AAH, WHAT A GOOD BUTT.
A REAL 10/10 BUTT.
OKAY...WELL, I'M GONNA GO GET A GLASS OF WATER...
...AND I'M TAKING MY BUTT WITH ME!

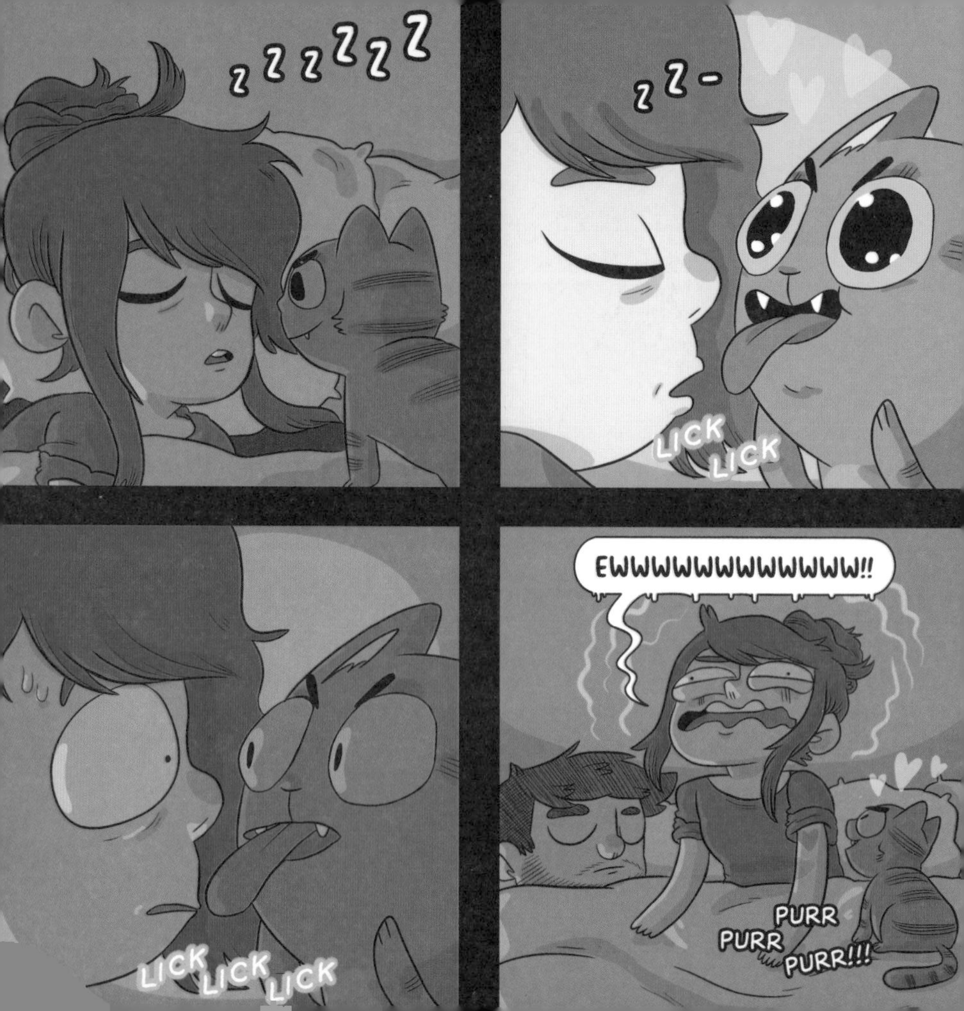
Z Z Z Z Z Z Z
Z Z -
LICK
LICK
LICK
LICK
LICK
EWWWWWWWWWWWW!!
PURR
PURR
PURR!!!

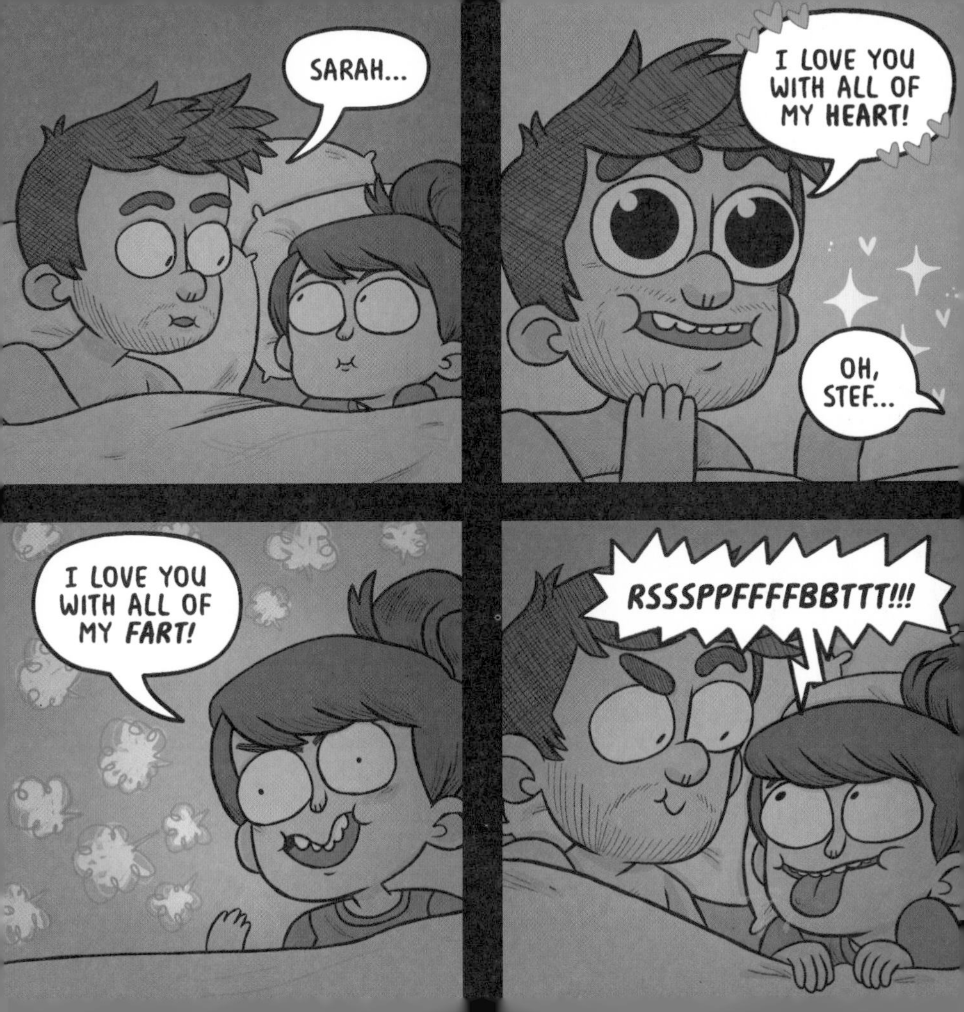
SARAH...
I LOVE YOU WITH ALL OF MY HEART!
OH, STEF...
I LOVE YOU WITH ALL OF MY FART!
RSSSPPFFFFBBTTT!!!

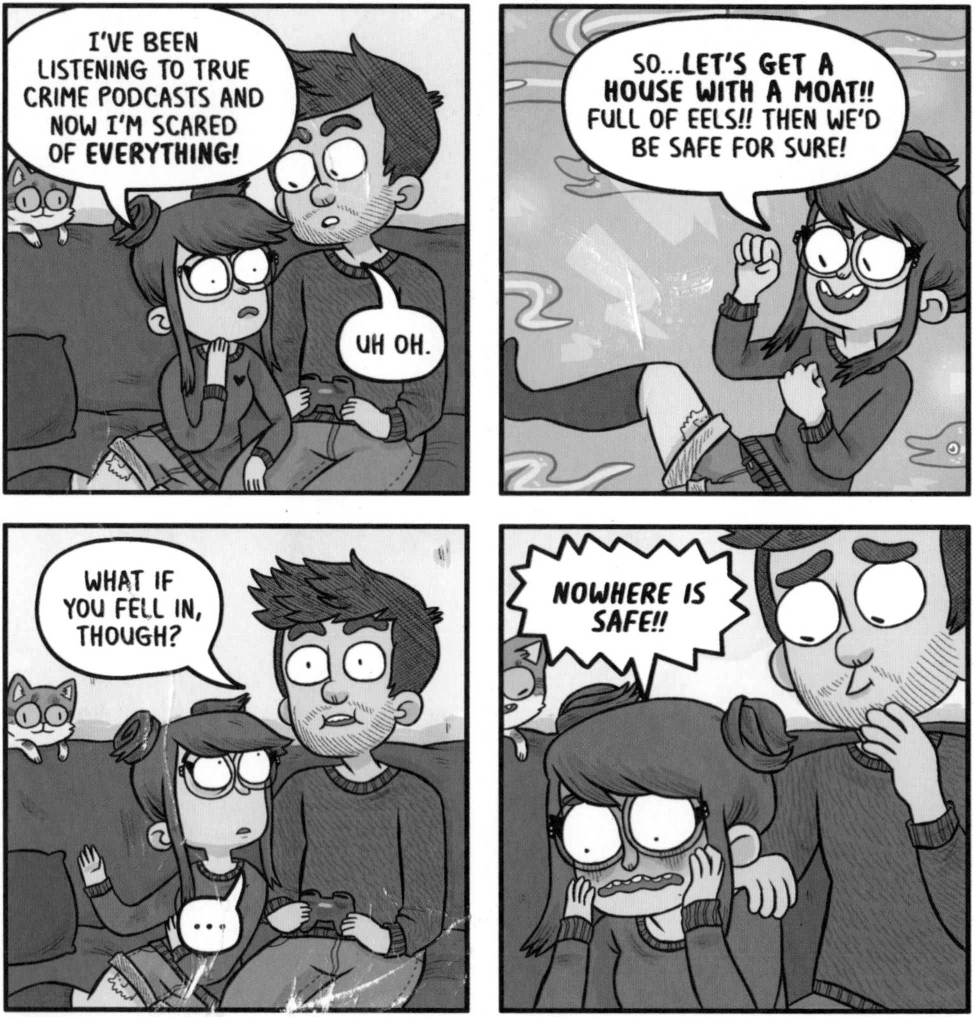
I'VE BEEN LISTENING TO TRUE CRIME PODCASTS AND NOW I'M SCARED OF **EVERYTHING!**
UH OH.
SO...**LET'S GET A HOUSE WITH A MOAT!!** FULL OF EELS!! THEN WE'D BE SAFE FOR SURE!
WHAT IF YOU FELL IN, THOUGH?
...
NOWHERE IS SAFE!!

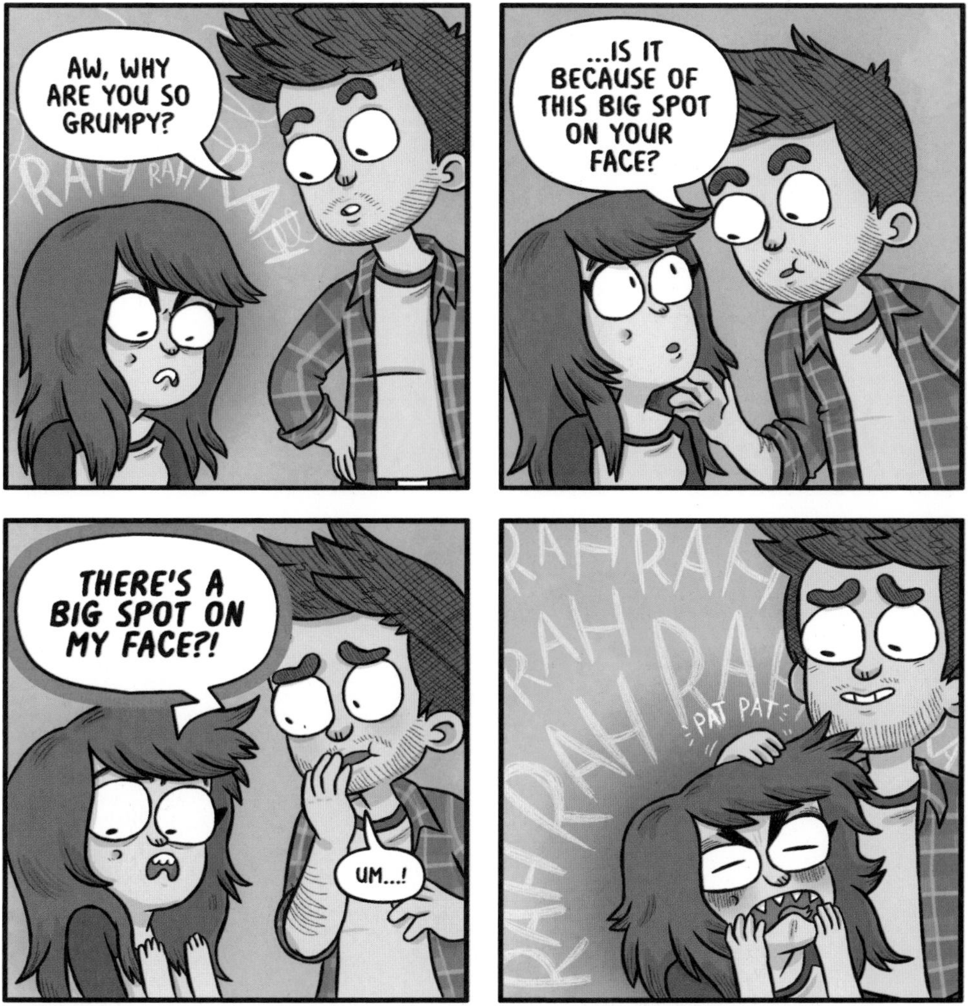
AW, WHY ARE YOU SO GRUMPY?
RAH RAH
...IS IT BECAUSE OF THIS BIG SPOT ON YOUR FACE?
THERE'S A BIG SPOT ON MY FACE?!
UM...!
RAH RAH RAH RAH RAH
PAT PAT

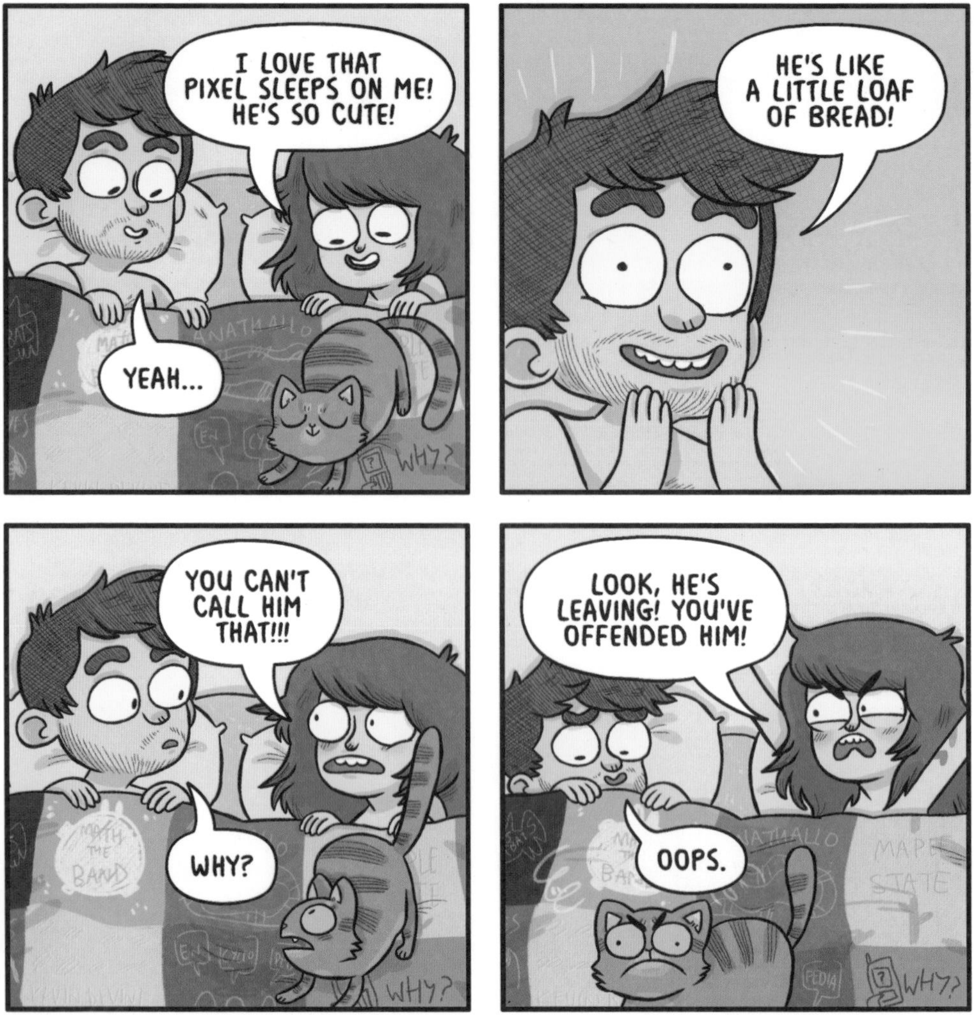
I LOVE THAT PIXEL SLEEPS ON ME! HE'S SO CUTE!
YEAH...
HE'S LIKE A LITTLE LOAF OF BREAD!
YOU CAN'T CALL HIM THAT!!!
WHY?
LOOK, HE'S LEAVING! YOU'VE OFFENDED HIM!
OOPS.

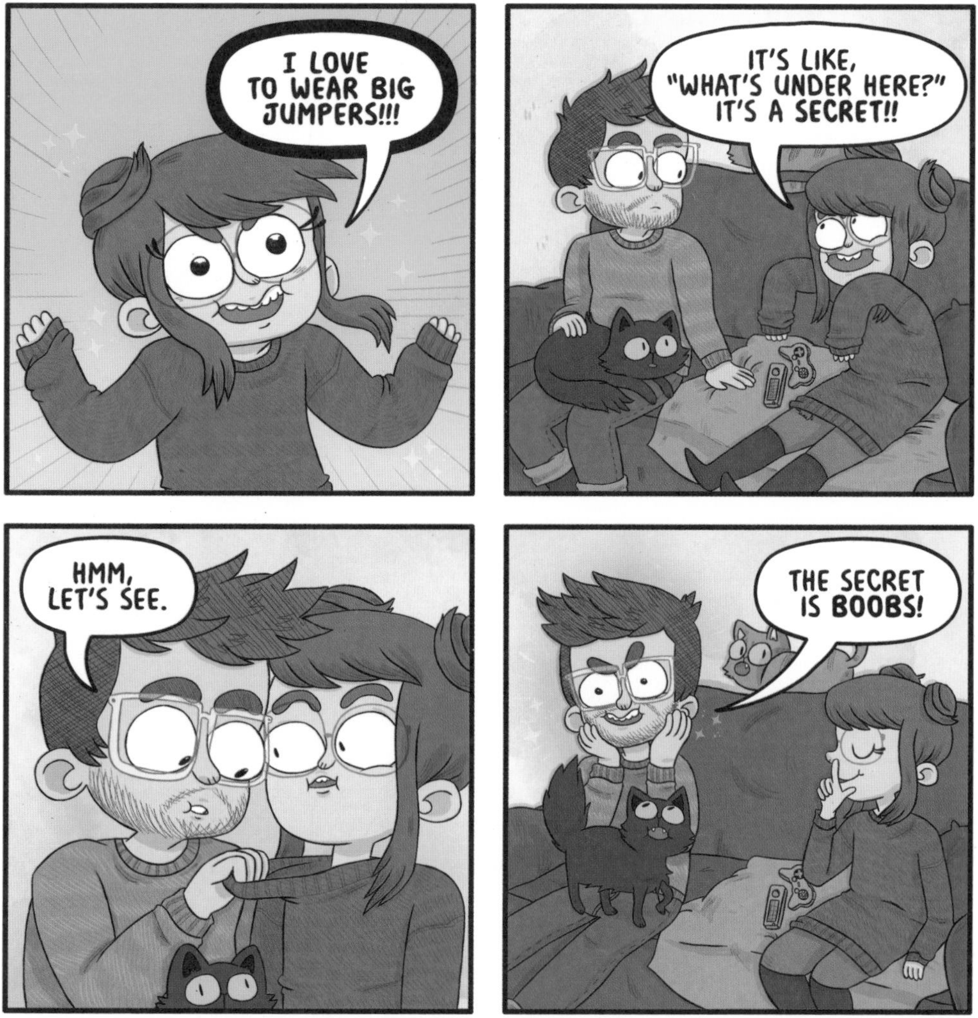
I LOVE TO WEAR BIG JUMPERS!!!
IT'S LIKE, "WHAT'S UNDER HERE?" IT'S A SECRET!!
HMM, LET'S SEE.
THE SECRET IS **BOOBS**!

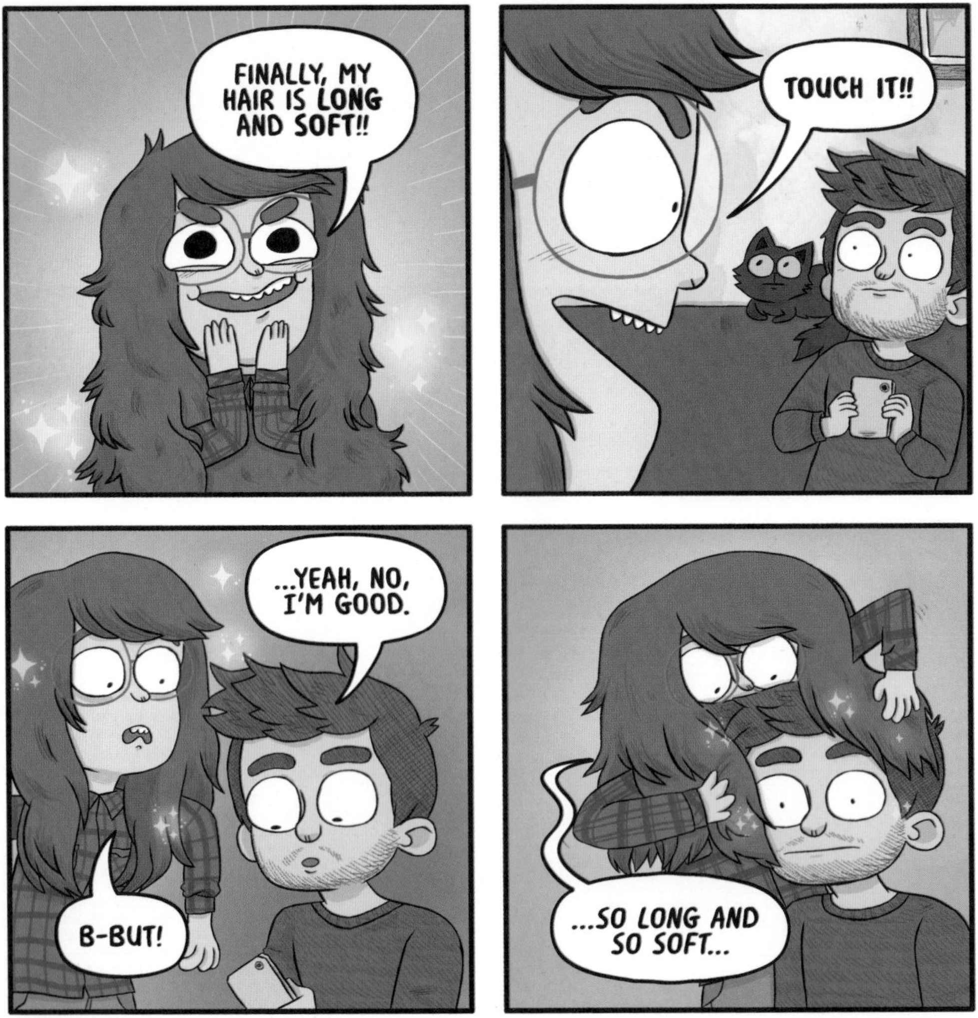
FINALLY, MY HAIR IS LONG AND SOFT!!
TOUCH IT!!
...YEAH, NO, I'M GOOD.
B-BUT!
...SO LONG AND SO SOFT...

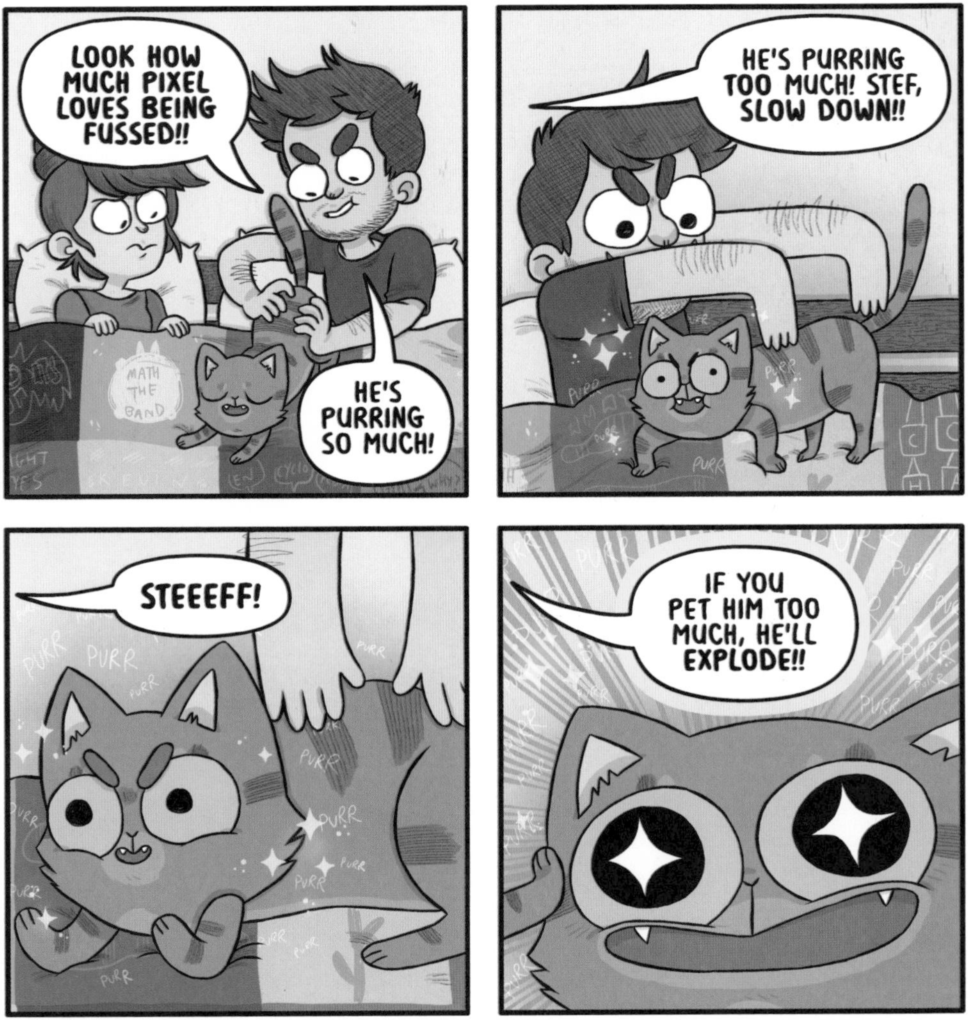
LOOK HOW MUCH PIXEL LOVES BEING FUSSED!!
HE'S PURRING SO MUCH!
HE'S PURRING TOO MUCH! STEF, SLOW DOWN!!
STEEEFF!
IF YOU PET HIM TOO MUCH, HE'LL EXPLODE!!

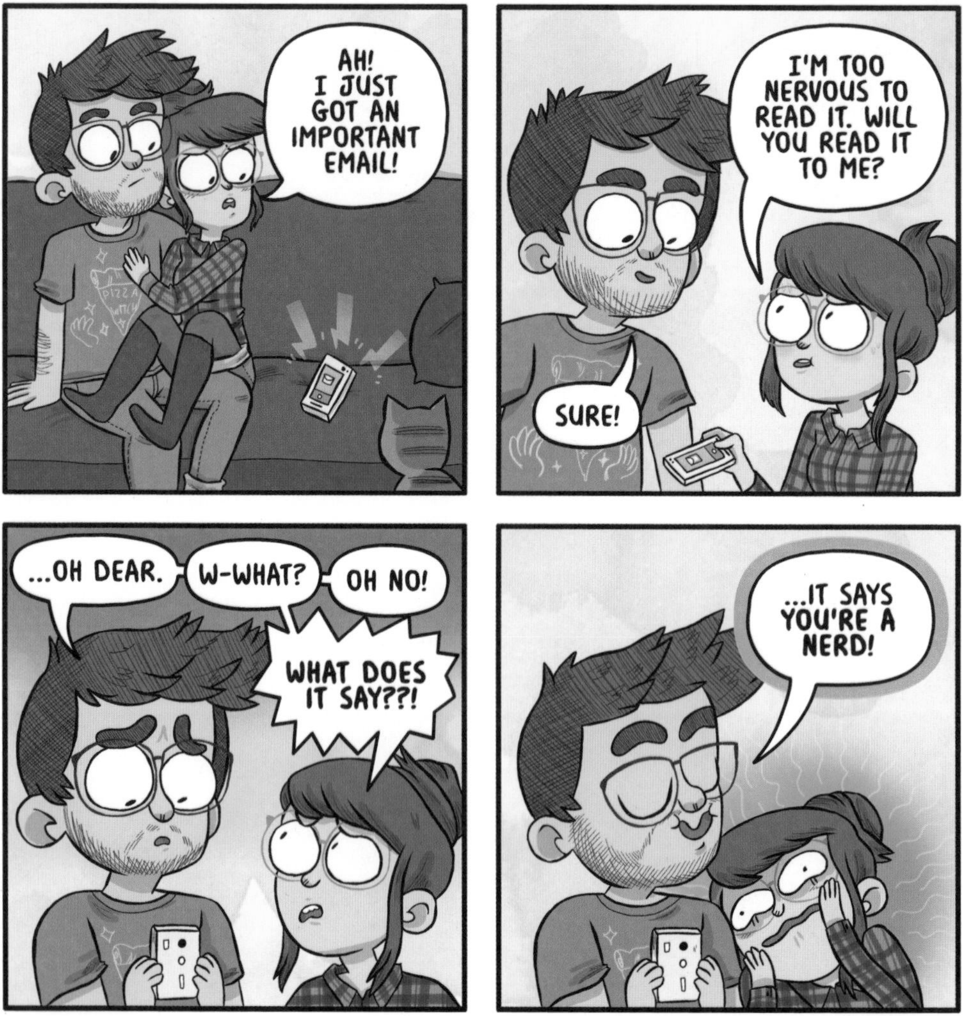
AH! I JUST GOT AN IMPORTANT EMAIL!
PIZZA
I'M TOO NERVOUS TO READ IT. WILL YOU READ IT TO ME?
SURE!
...OH DEAR.
W-WHAT?
OH NO!
WHAT DOES IT SAY??!
...IT SAYS YOU'RE A NERD!

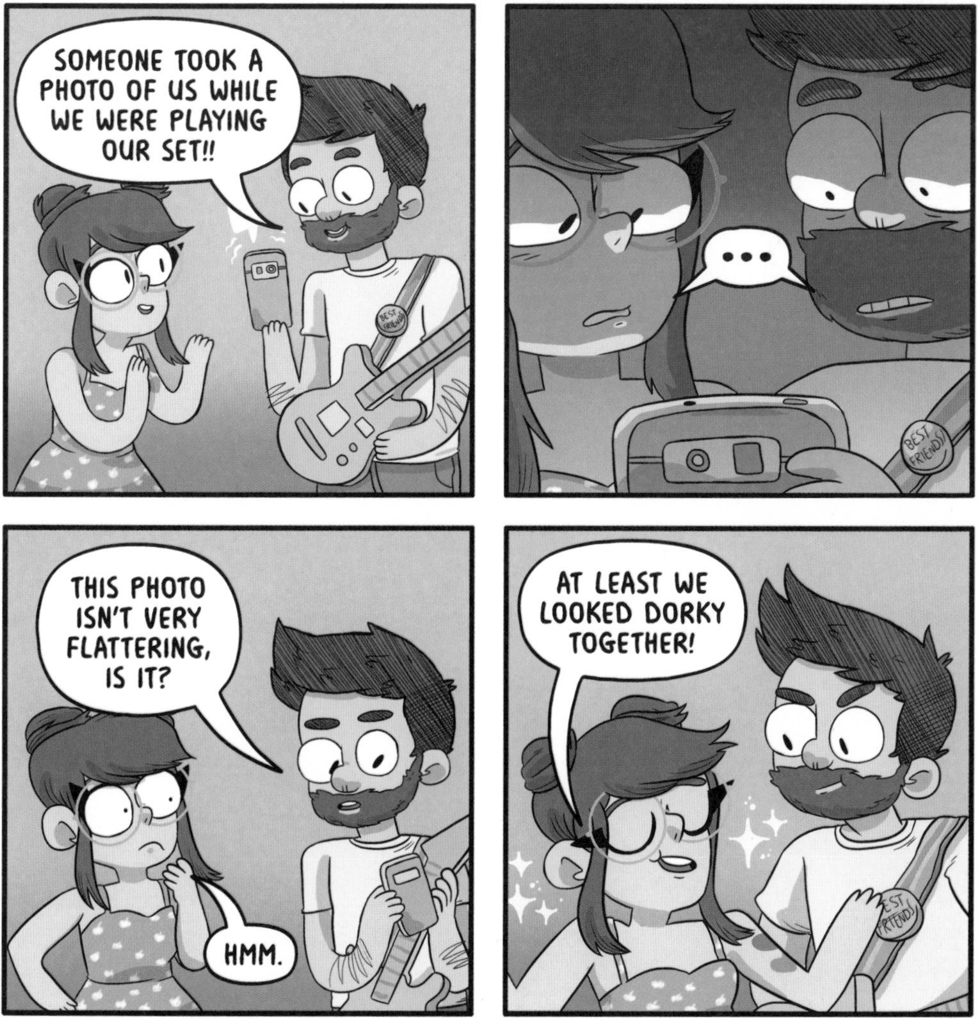
SOMEONE TOOK A PHOTO OF US WHILE WE WERE PLAYING OUR SET!!
...
THIS PHOTO ISN'T VERY FLATTERING, IS IT?
HMM.
AT LEAST WE LOOKED DORKY TOGETHER!

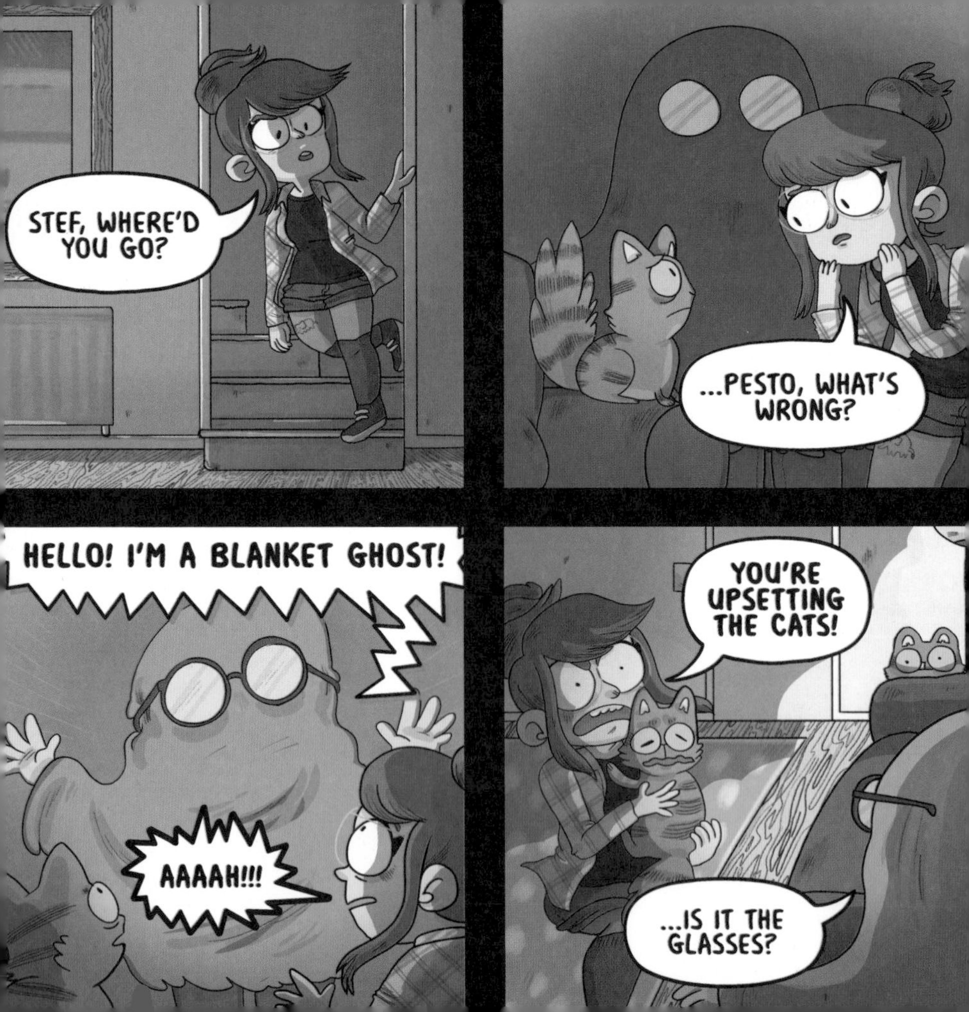
STEF, WHERE'D YOU GO?
...PESTO, WHAT'S WRONG?
HELLO! I'M A BLANKET GHOST!
AAAAH!!!
YOU'RE UPSETTING THE CATS!
...IS IT THE GLASSES?

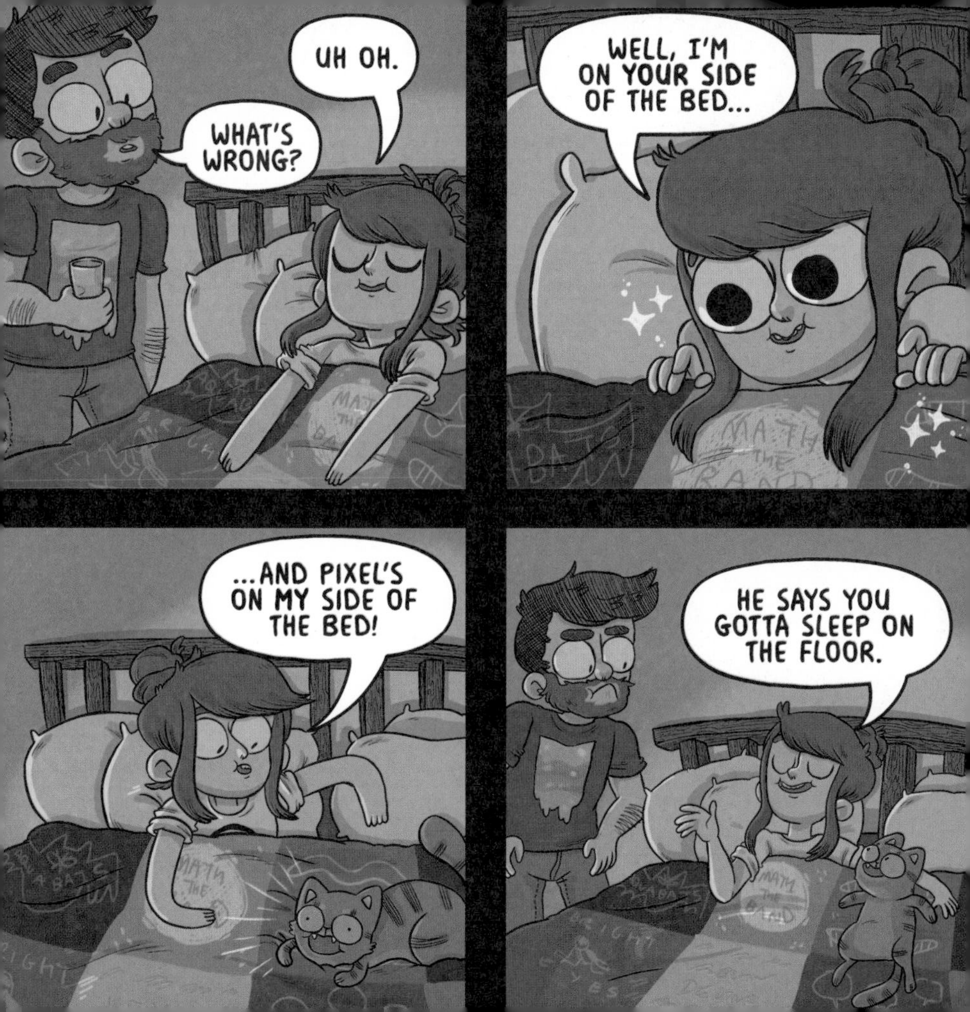
UH OH.
WHAT'S WRONG?
WELL, I'M ON YOUR SIDE OF THE BED...
...AND PIXEL'S ON MY SIDE OF THE BED!
HE SAYS YOU GOTTA SLEEP ON THE FLOOR.

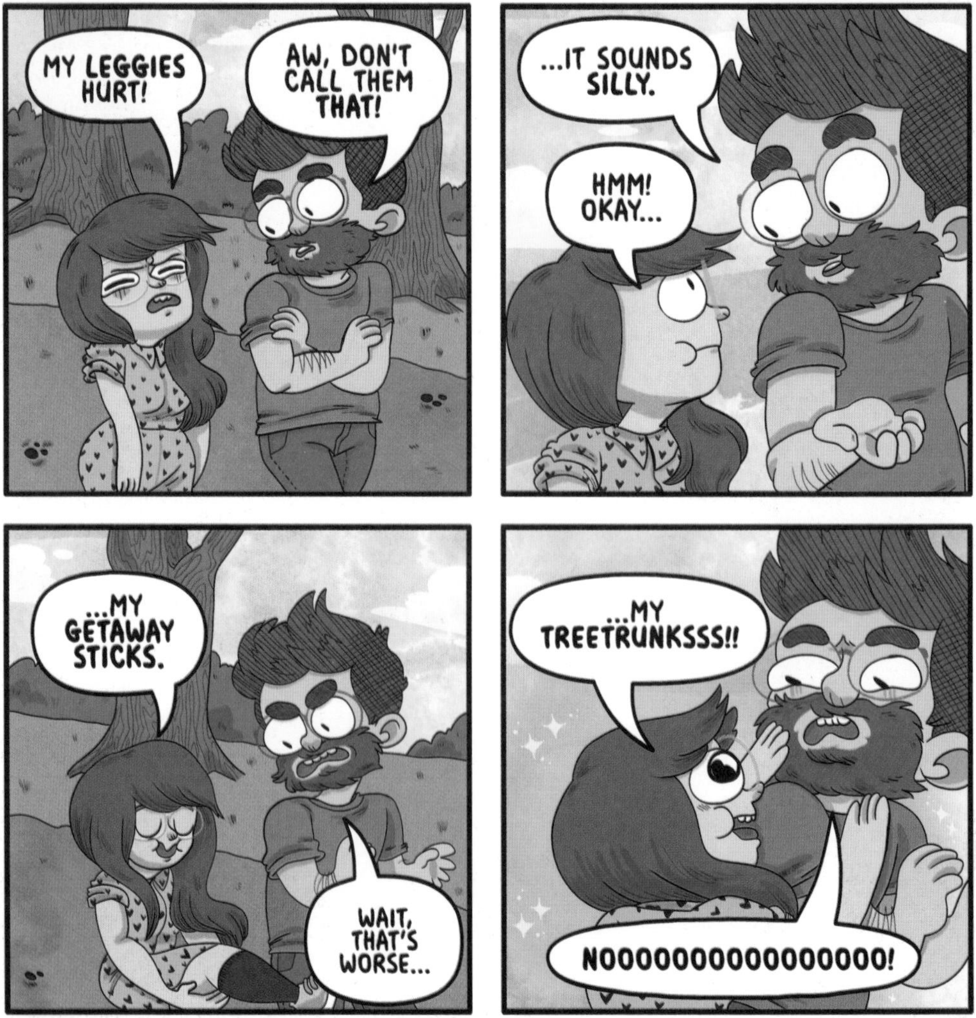
MY LEGGIES HURT!
AW, DON'T CALL THEM THAT!
...IT SOUNDS SILLY.
HMM! OKAY...
...MY GETAWAY STICKS.
WAIT, THAT'S WORSE...
...MY TREETRUNKSSS!!
NOOOOOOOOOOOOOOOOO!

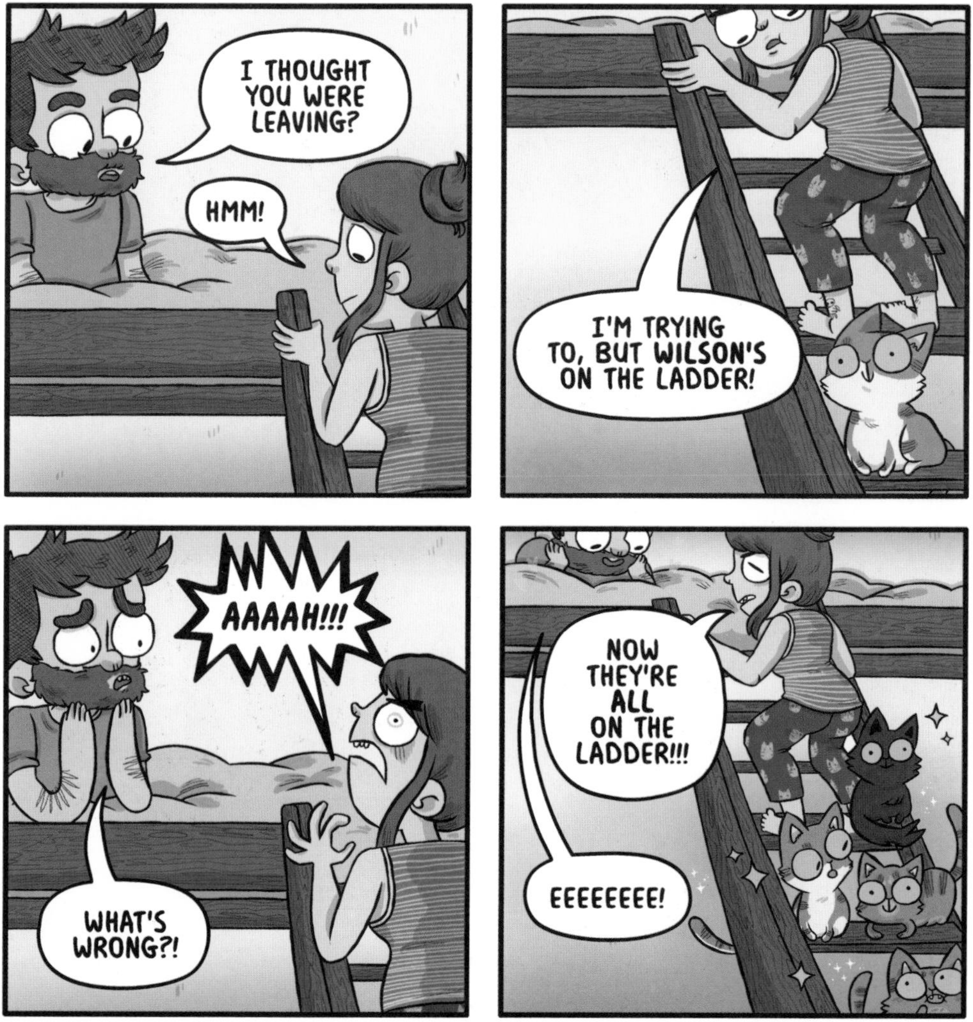
I THOUGHT YOU WERE LEAVING?
HMM!
I'M TRYING TO, BUT WILSON'S ON THE LADDER!
AAAAH!!!
WHAT'S WRONG?!
NOW THEY'RE ALL ON THE LADDER!!!
EEEEEEEE!

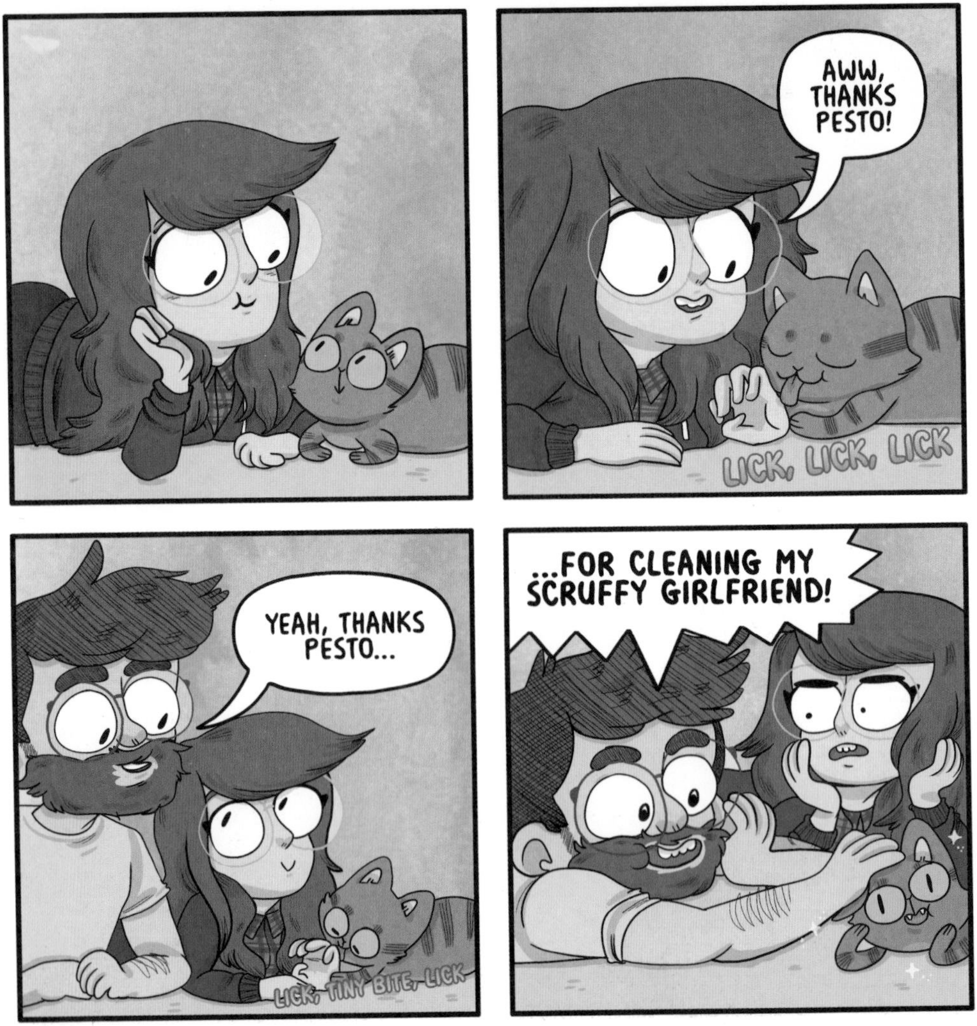
AWW, THANKS PESTO!
LICK, LICK, LICK
YEAH, THANKS PESTO...
LICK, TINY BITE, LICK
...FOR CLEANING MY SCRUFFY GIRLFRIEND!

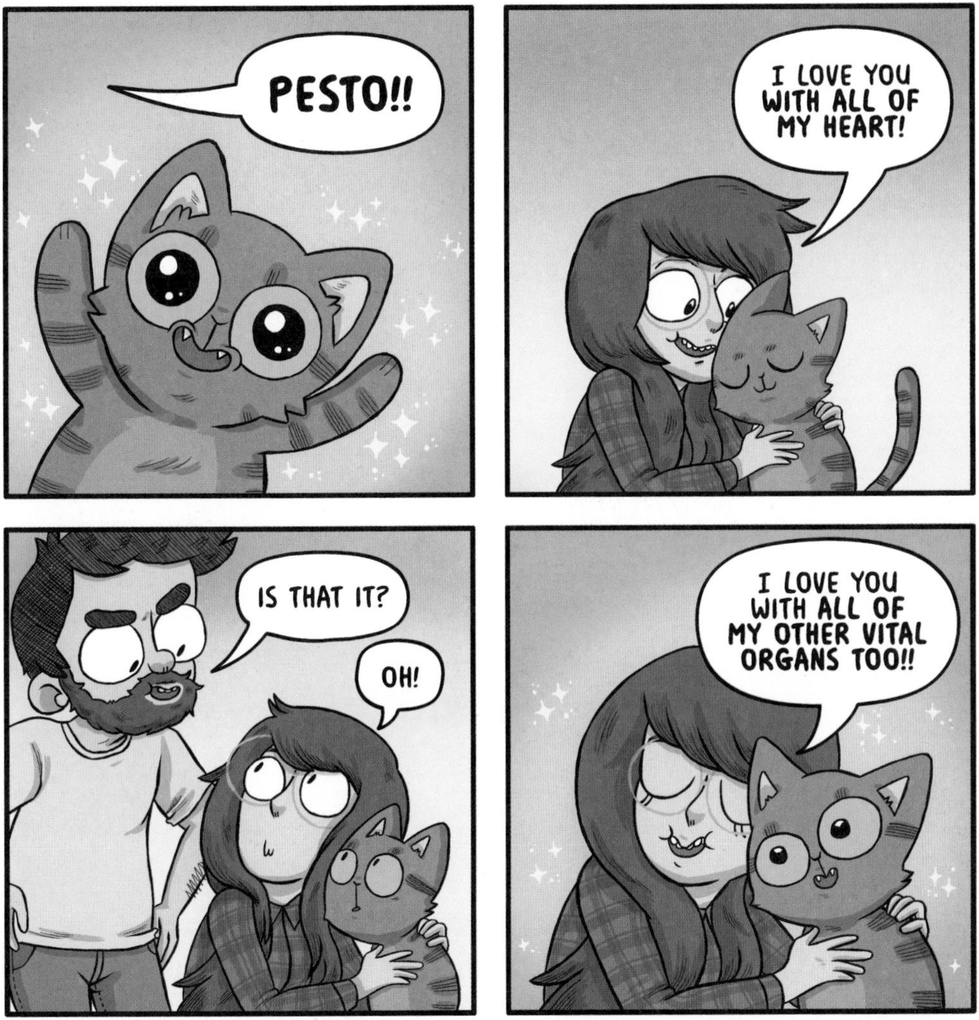
PESTO!!
I LOVE YOU WITH ALL OF MY HEART!
IS THAT IT?
OH!
I LOVE YOU WITH ALL OF MY OTHER VITAL ORGANS TOO!!

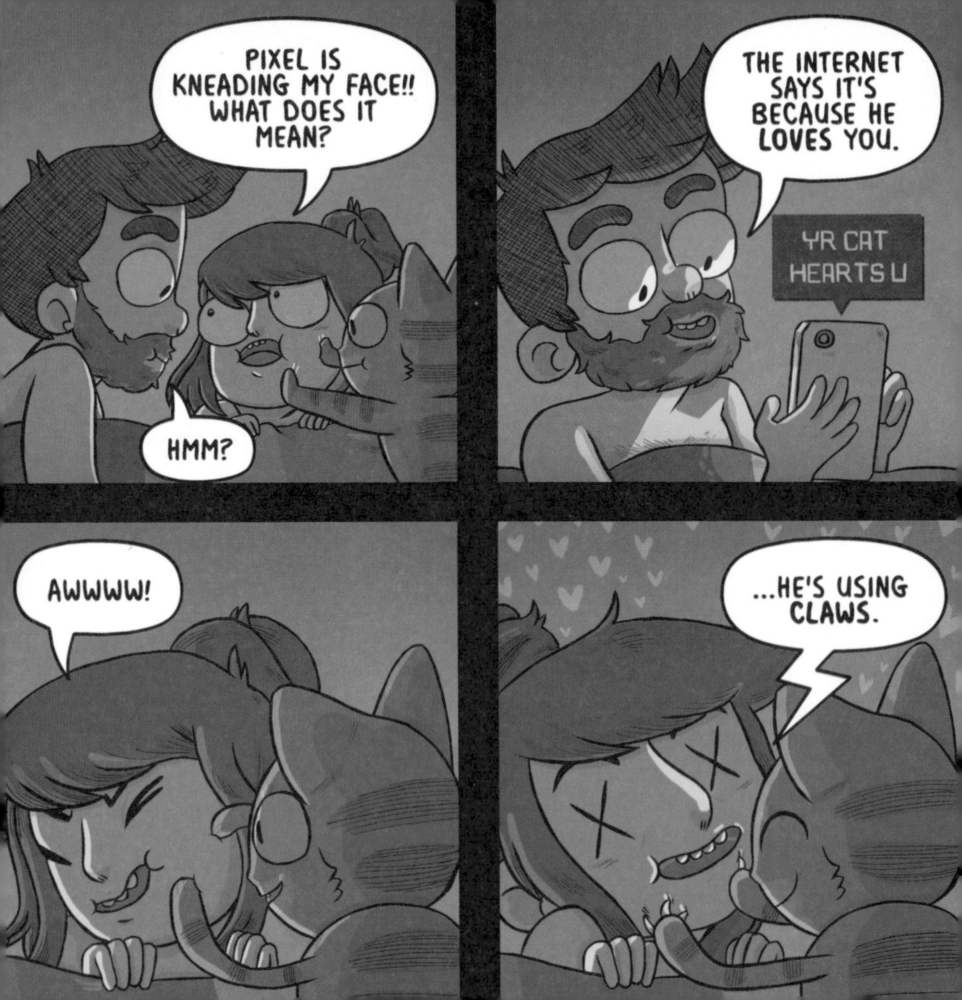
PIXEL IS KNEADING MY FACE!! WHAT DOES IT MEAN?
HMM?
THE INTERNET SAYS IT'S BECAUSE HE LOVES YOU.
YR CAT HEARTS U
AWWWW!
...HE'S USING CLAWS.

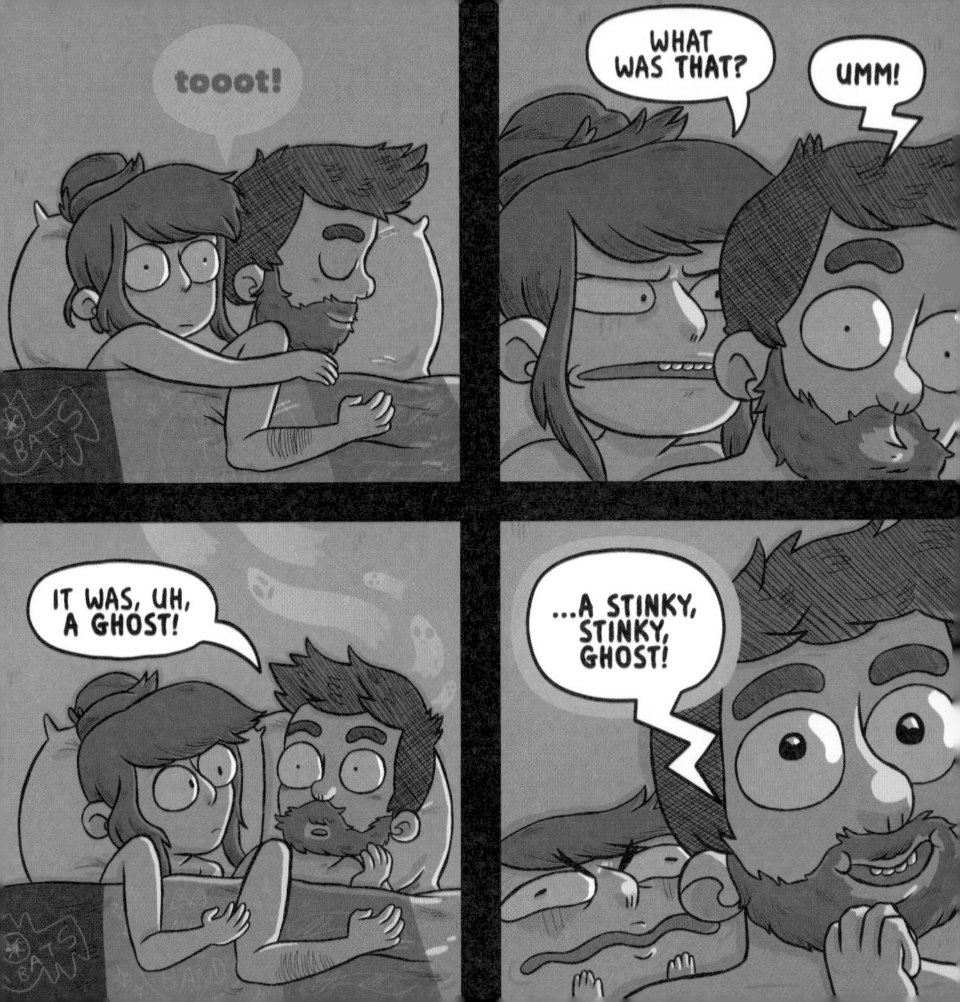
tooot!
WHAT WAS THAT?
UMM!
IT WAS, UH, A GHOST!
...A STINKY, STINKY, GHOST!

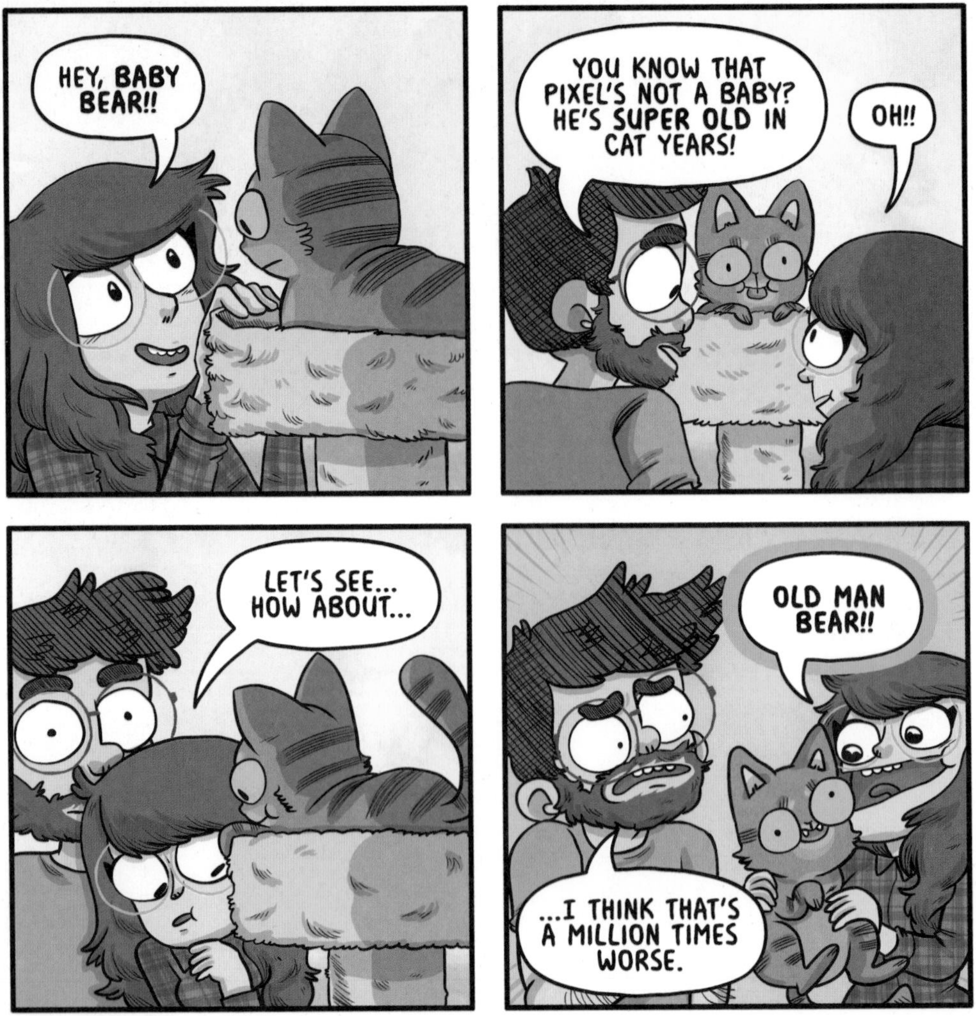
HEY, BABY BEAR!!
YOU KNOW THAT PIXEL'S NOT A BABY? HE'S SUPER OLD IN CAT YEARS!
OH!!
LET'S SEE... HOW ABOUT...
OLD MAN BEAR!!
...I THINK THAT'S A MILLION TIMES WORSE.

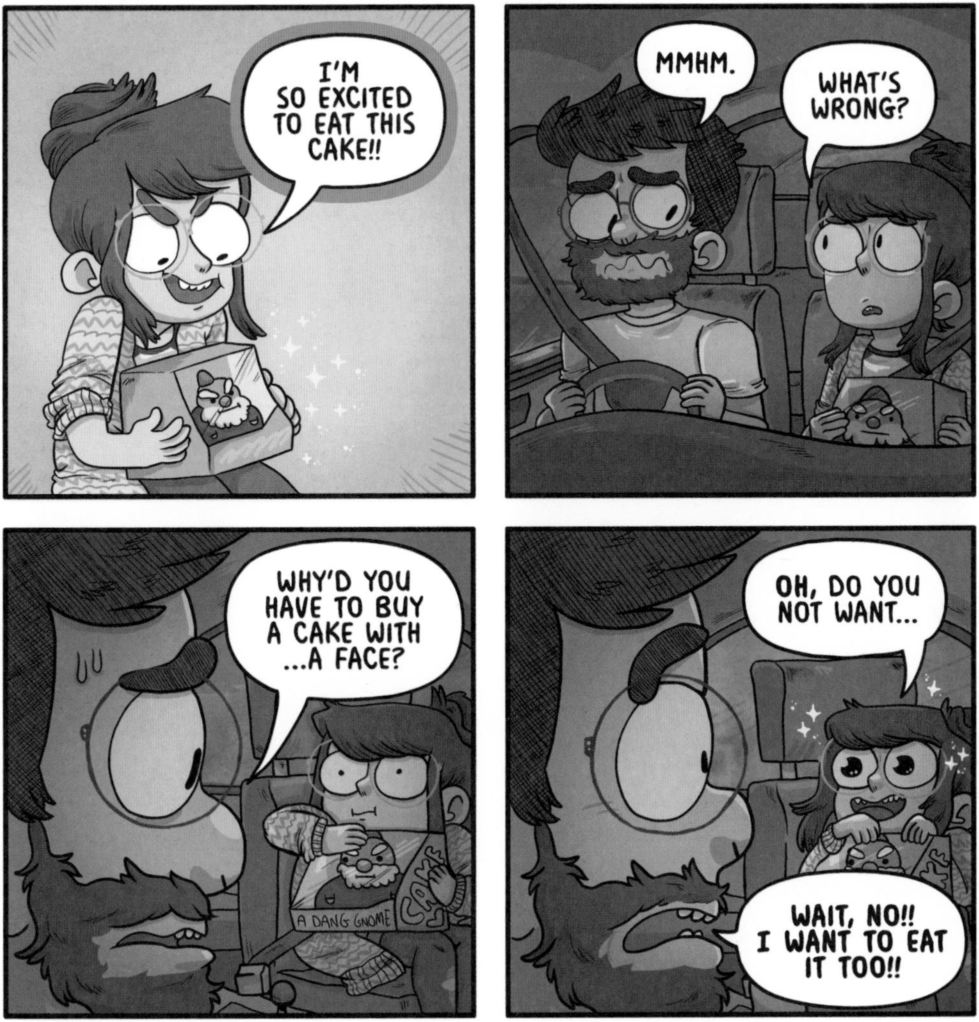
I'M SO EXCITED TO EAT THIS CAKE!!
MMHM.
WHAT'S WRONG?
WHY'D YOU HAVE TO BUY A CAKE WITH ...A FACE?
A DANG GNOME
CAKE
OH, DO YOU NOT WANT...
WAIT, NO!! I WANT TO EAT IT TOO!!

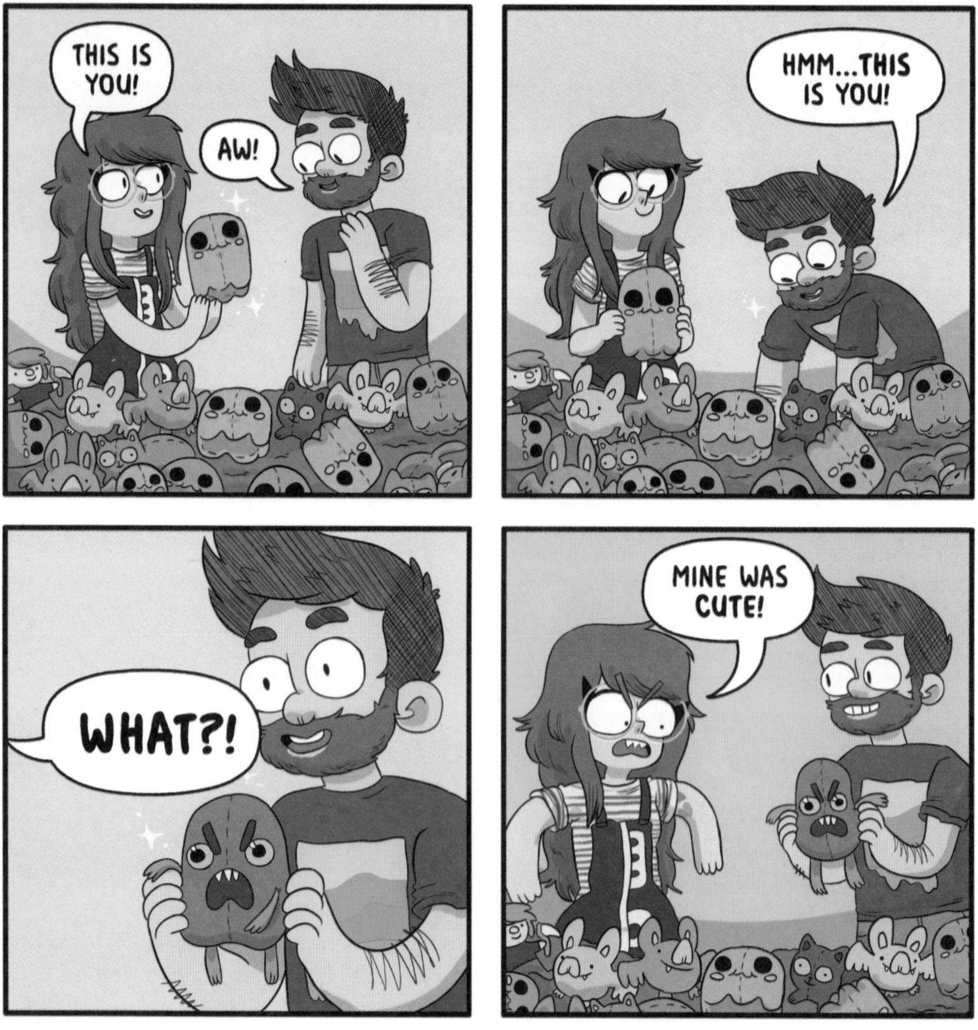
THIS IS YOU!
AW!
HMM...THIS IS YOU!
WHAT?!
MINE WAS CUTE!

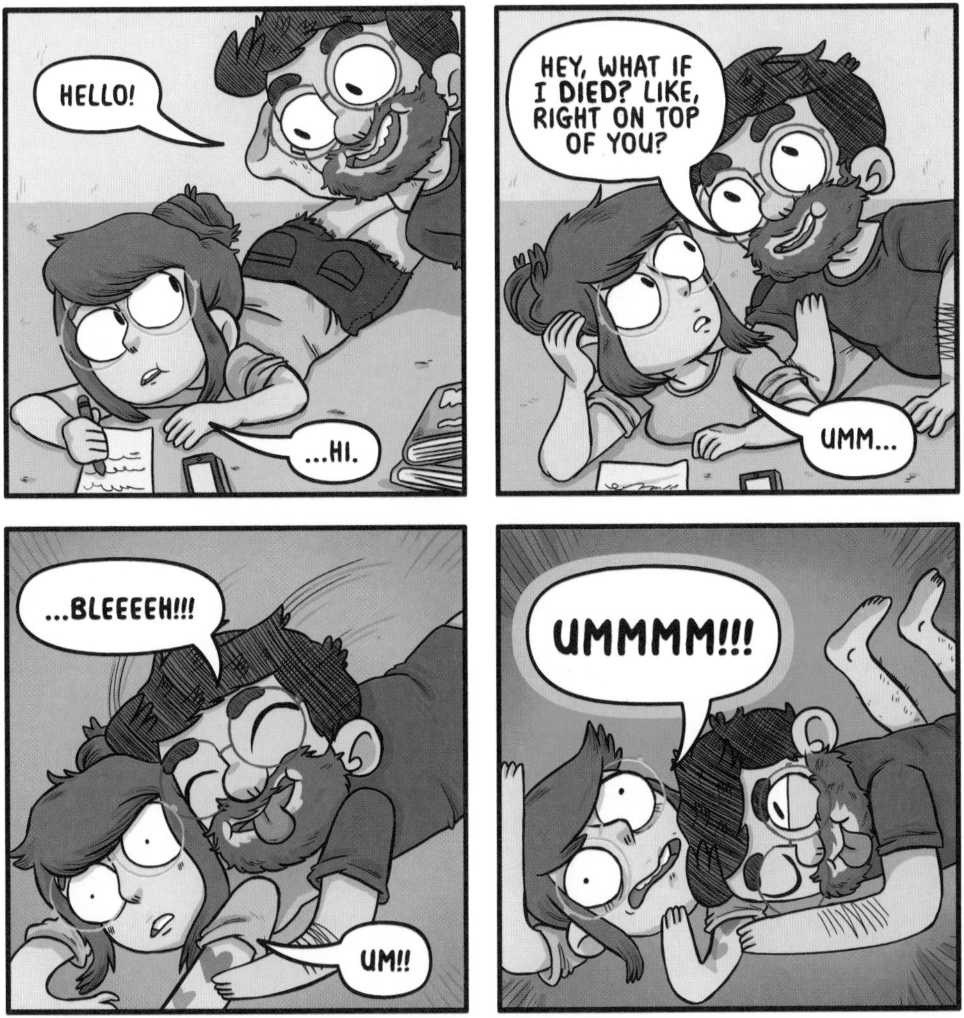
HELLO!
...HI.
HEY, WHAT IF I DIED? LIKE, RIGHT ON TOP OF YOU?
UMM...
...BLEEEEH!!!
UM!!
UMMMM!!!

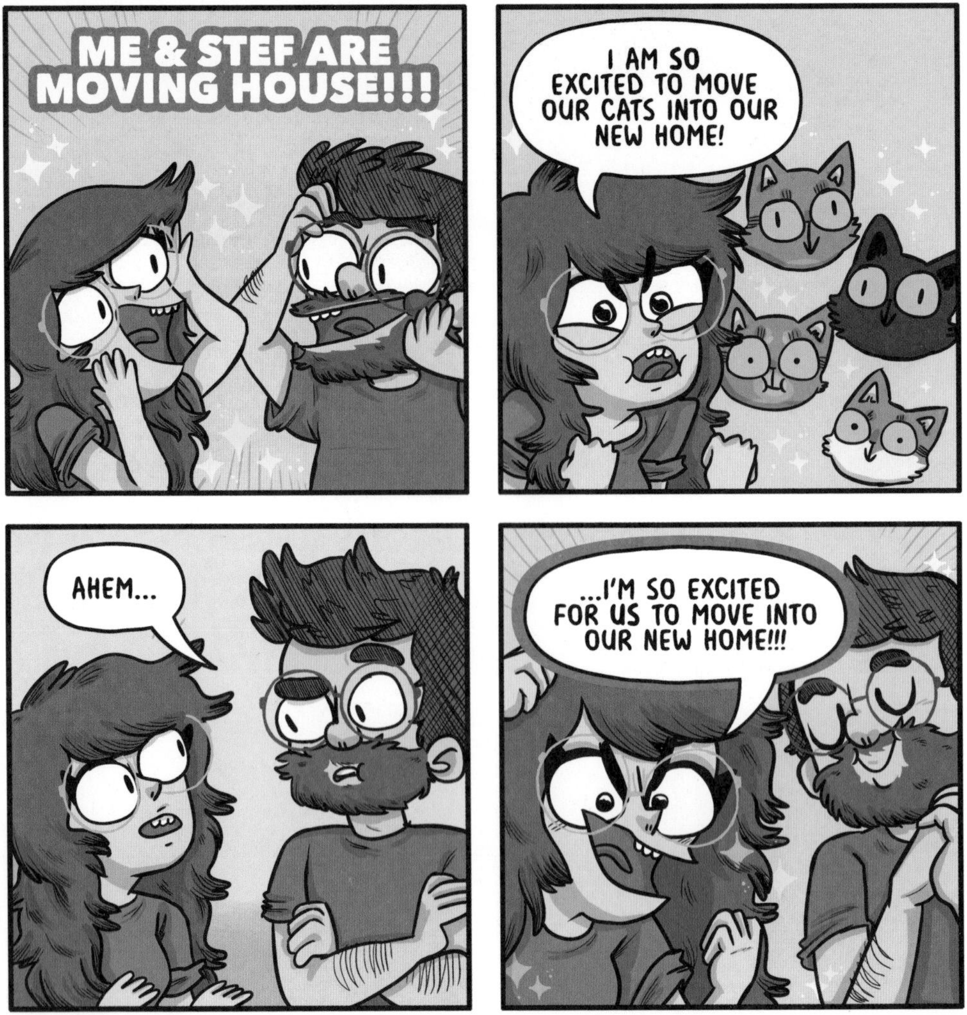
ME & STEF ARE MOVING HOUSE!!!
I AM SO EXCITED TO MOVE OUR CATS INTO OUR NEW HOME!
AHEM...
...I'M SO EXCITED FOR US TO MOVE INTO OUR NEW HOME!!!

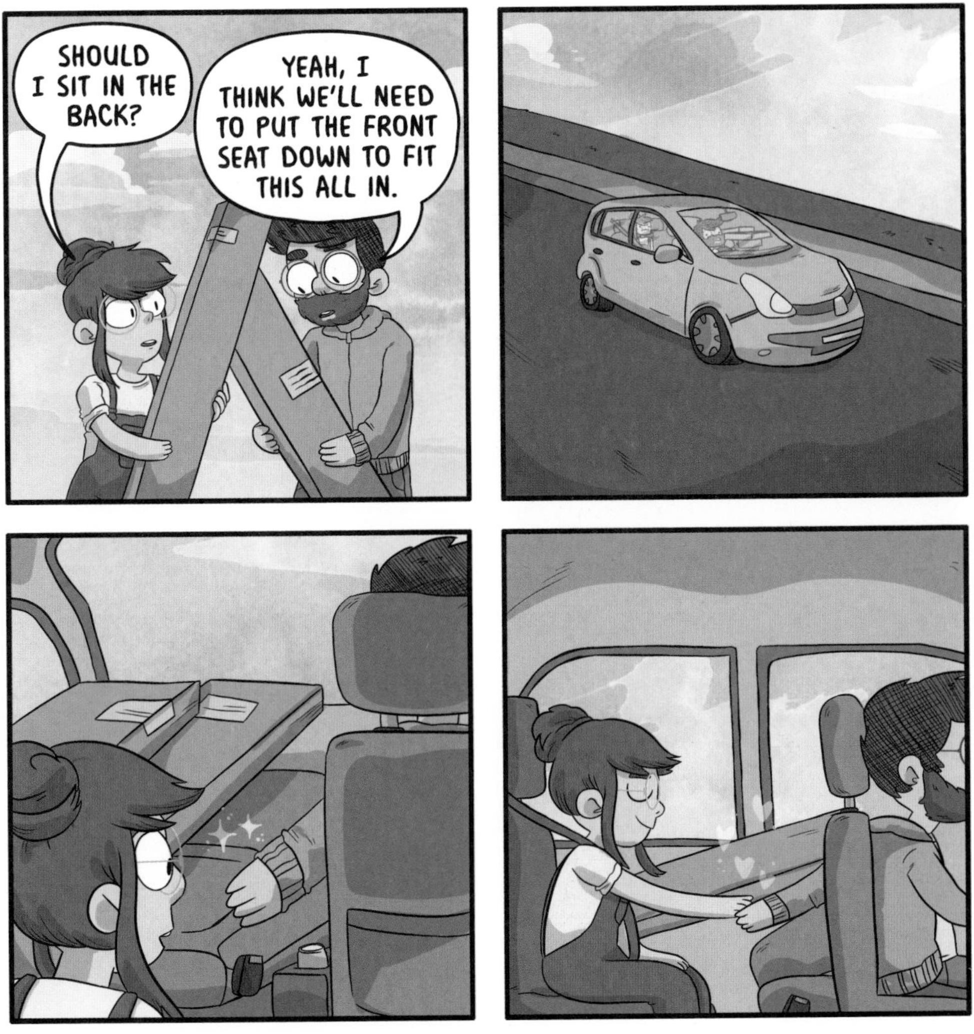
SHOULD I SIT IN THE BACK?
YEAH, I THINK WE'LL NEED TO PUT THE FRONT SEAT DOWN TO FIT THIS ALL IN.

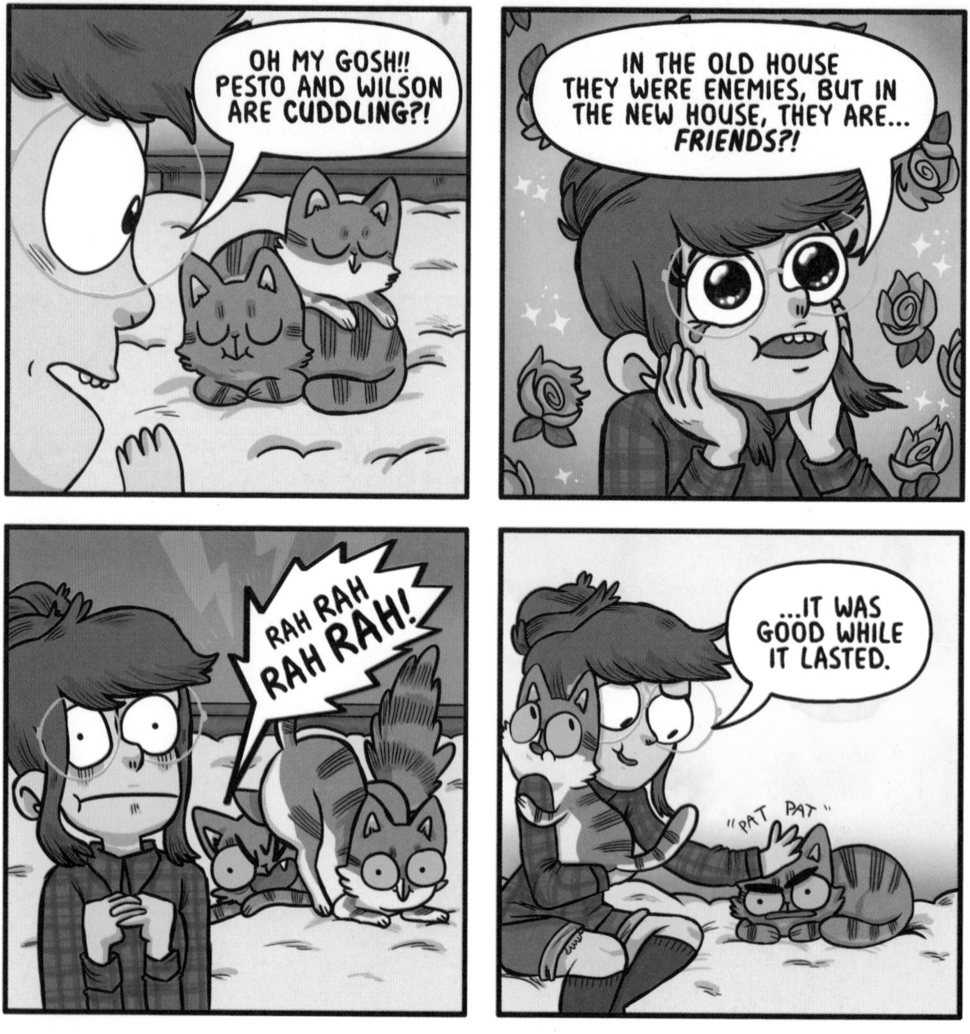
OH MY GOSH!! PESTO AND WILSON ARE CUDDLING?!
IN THE OLD HOUSE THEY WERE ENEMIES, BUT IN THE NEW HOUSE, THEY ARE... *FRIENDS?!*
RAH RAH RAH RAH!
...IT WAS GOOD WHILE IT LASTED.
"PAT PAT"

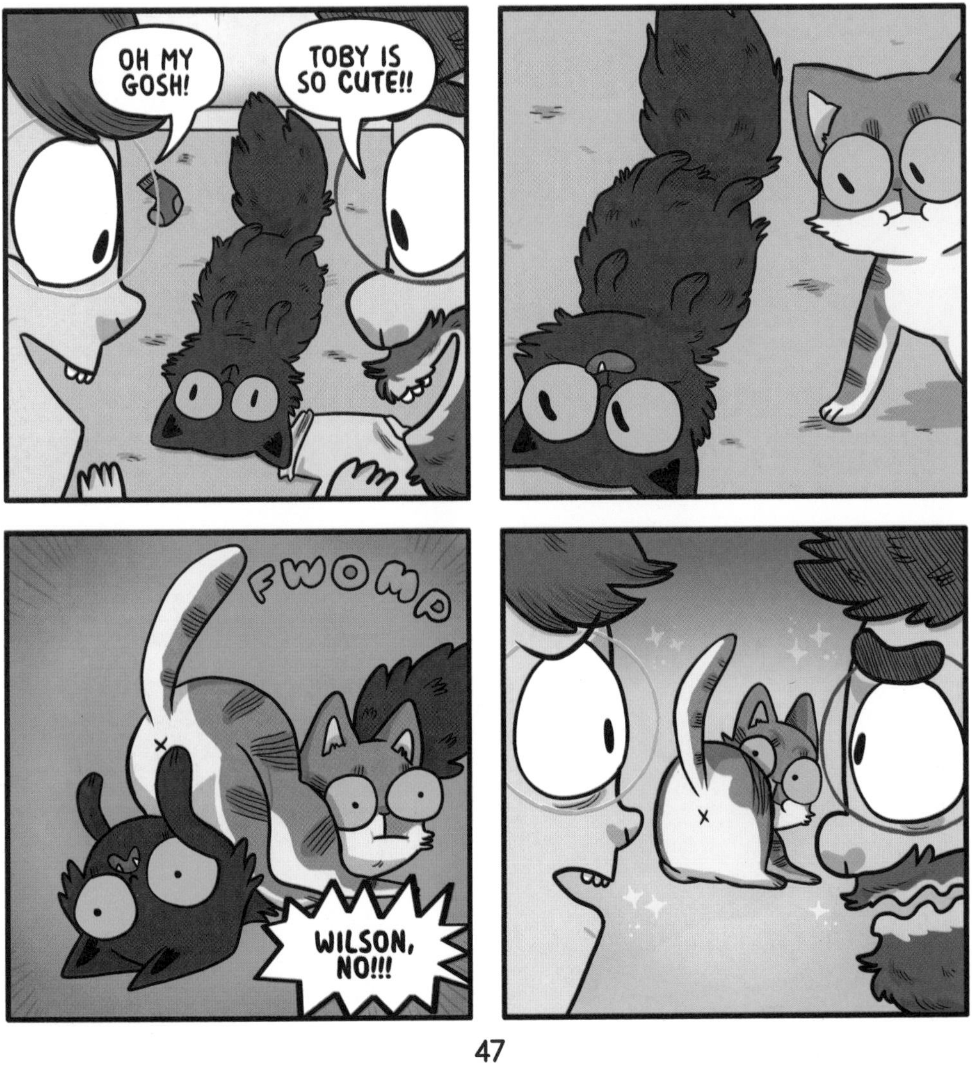
OH MY GOSH!
TOBY IS SO CUTE!!
FWOMP
WILSON, NO!!!

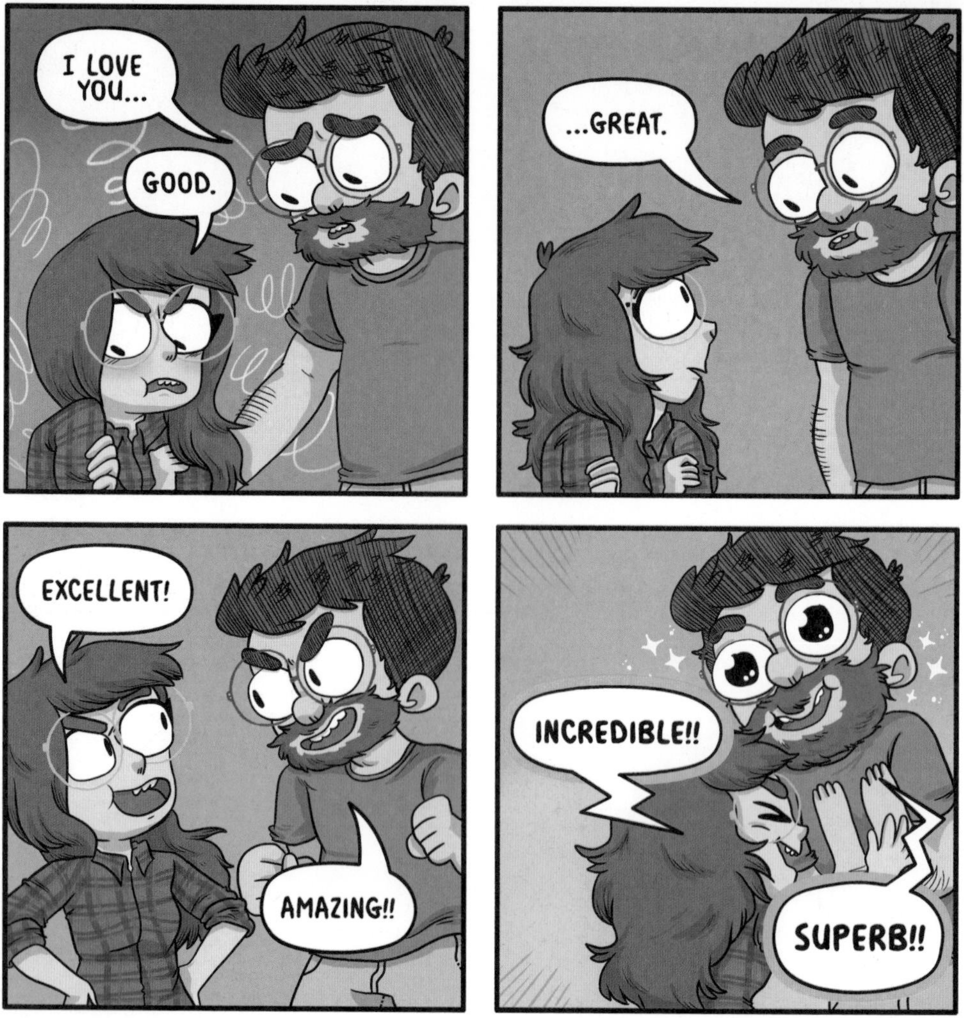
I LOVE YOU...
GOOD.
...GREAT.
EXCELLENT!
AMAZING!!
INCREDIBLE!!
SUPERB!!

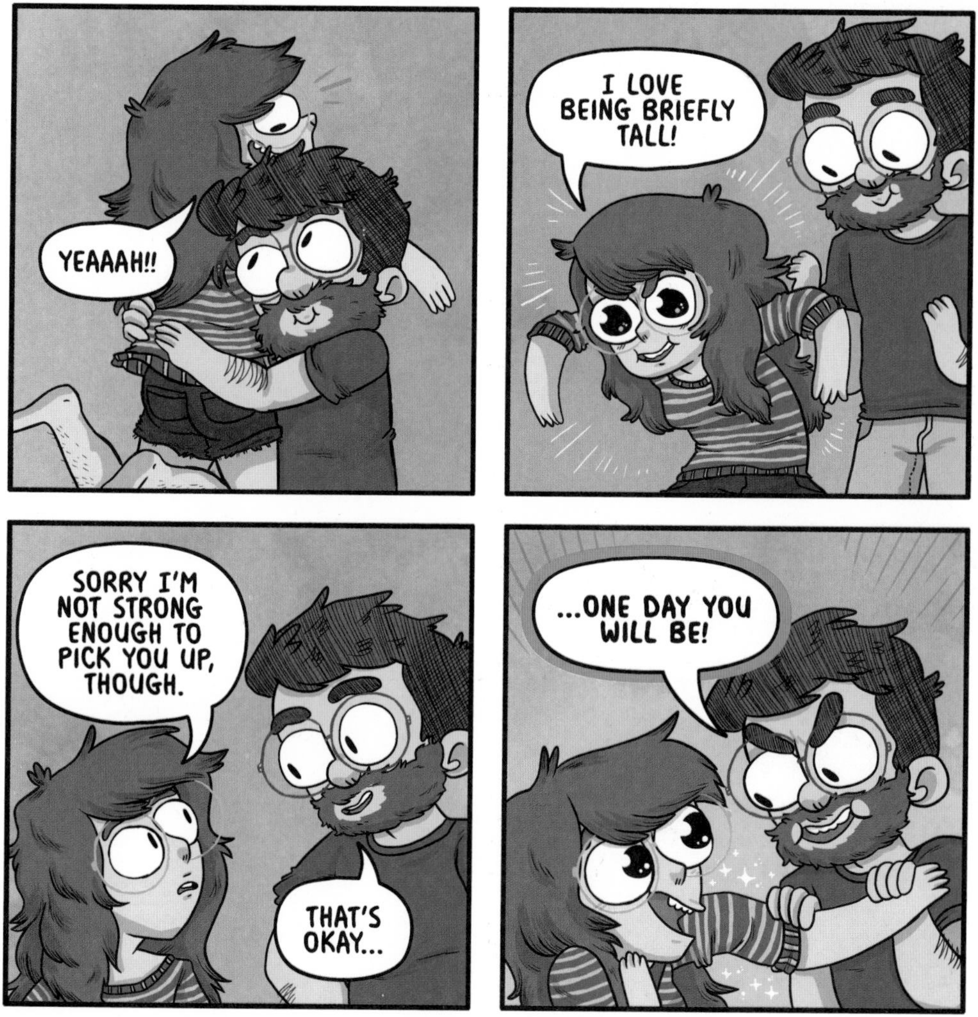
YEAAAH!!
I LOVE BEING BRIEFLY TALL!
SORRY I'M NOT STRONG ENOUGH TO PICK YOU UP, THOUGH.
THAT'S OKAY...
...ONE DAY YOU WILL BE!

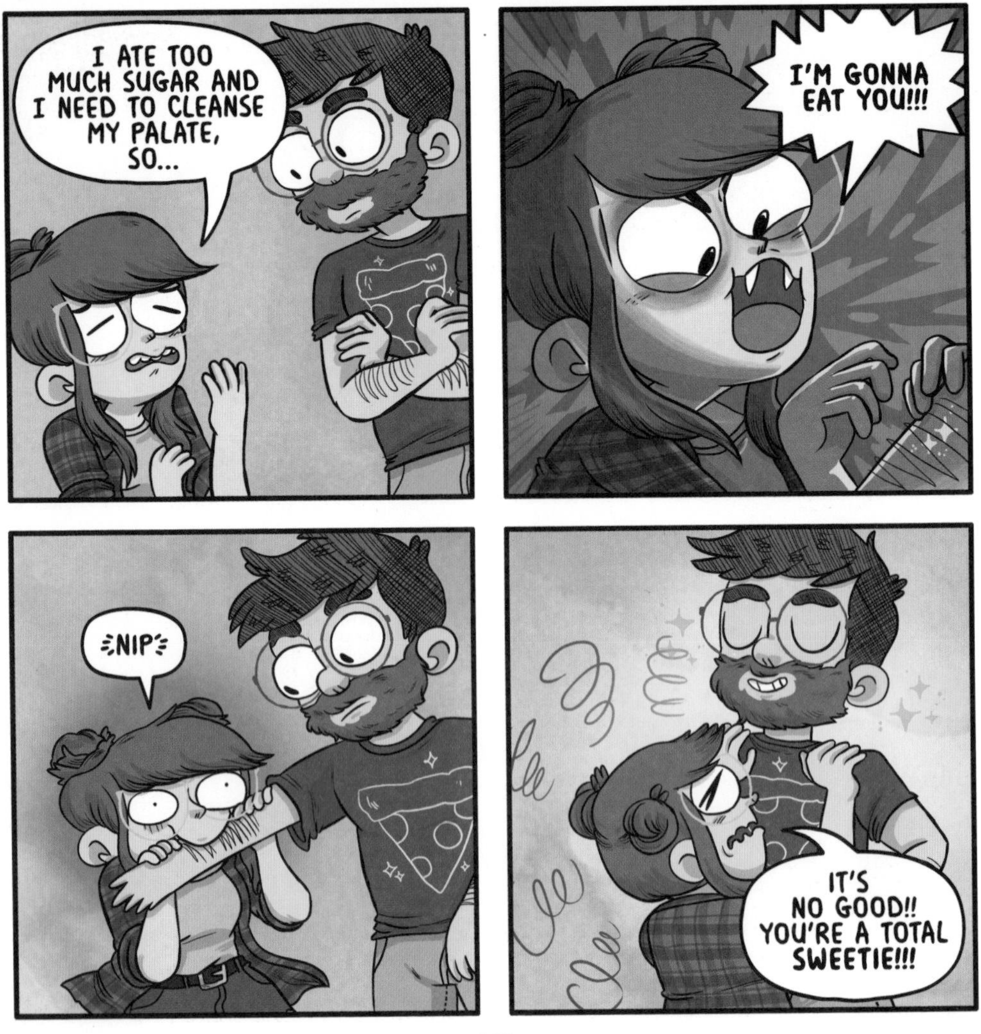
I ATE TOO MUCH SUGAR AND I NEED TO CLEANSE MY PALATE, SO...
I'M GONNA EAT YOU!!!
NIP
IT'S NO GOOD!! YOU'RE A TOTAL SWEETIE!!!

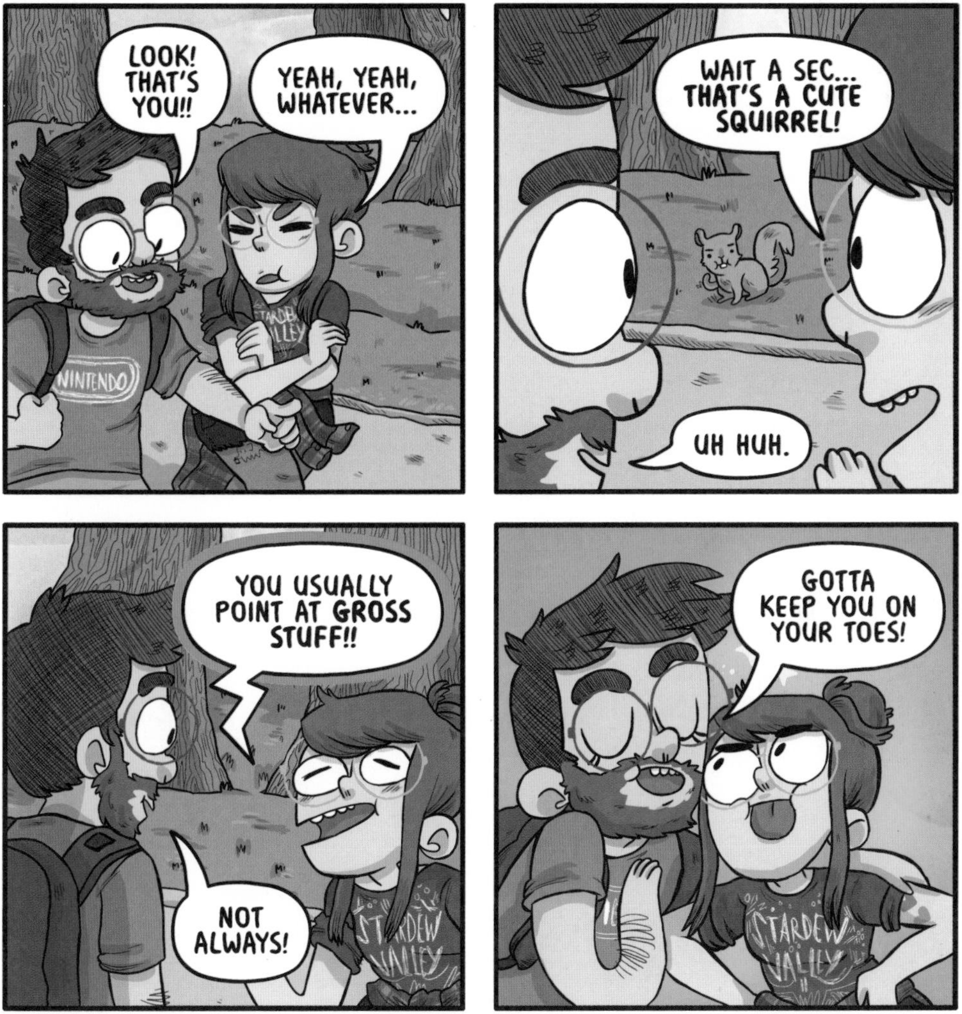
LOOK! THAT'S YOU!!
YEAH, YEAH, WHATEVER...
NINTENDO
WAIT A SEC... THAT'S A CUTE SQUIRREL!
UH HUH.
YOU USUALLY POINT AT GROSS STUFF!!
NOT ALWAYS!
STARDEW VALLEY
GOTTA KEEP YOU ON YOUR TOES!
STARDEW VALLEY

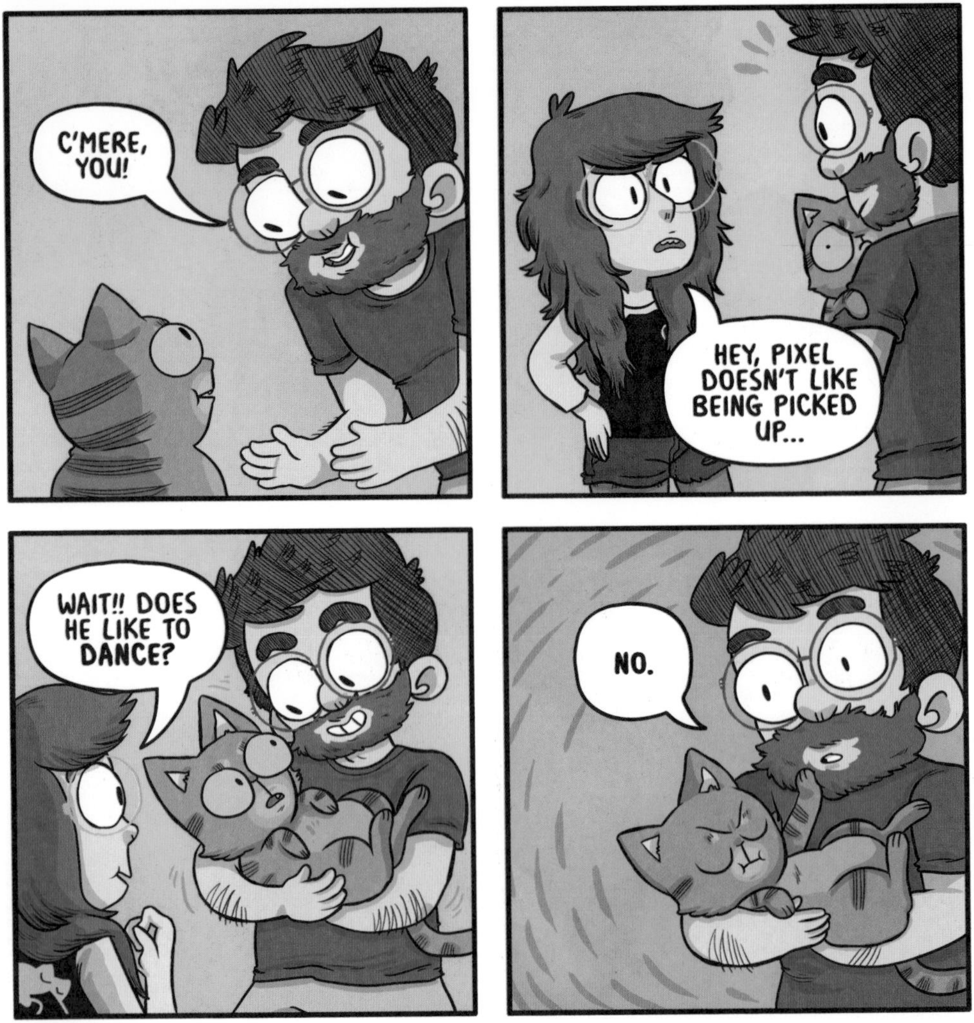
C'MERE, YOU!
HEY, PIXEL DOESN'T LIKE BEING PICKED UP...
WAIT!! DOES HE LIKE TO DANCE?
NO.

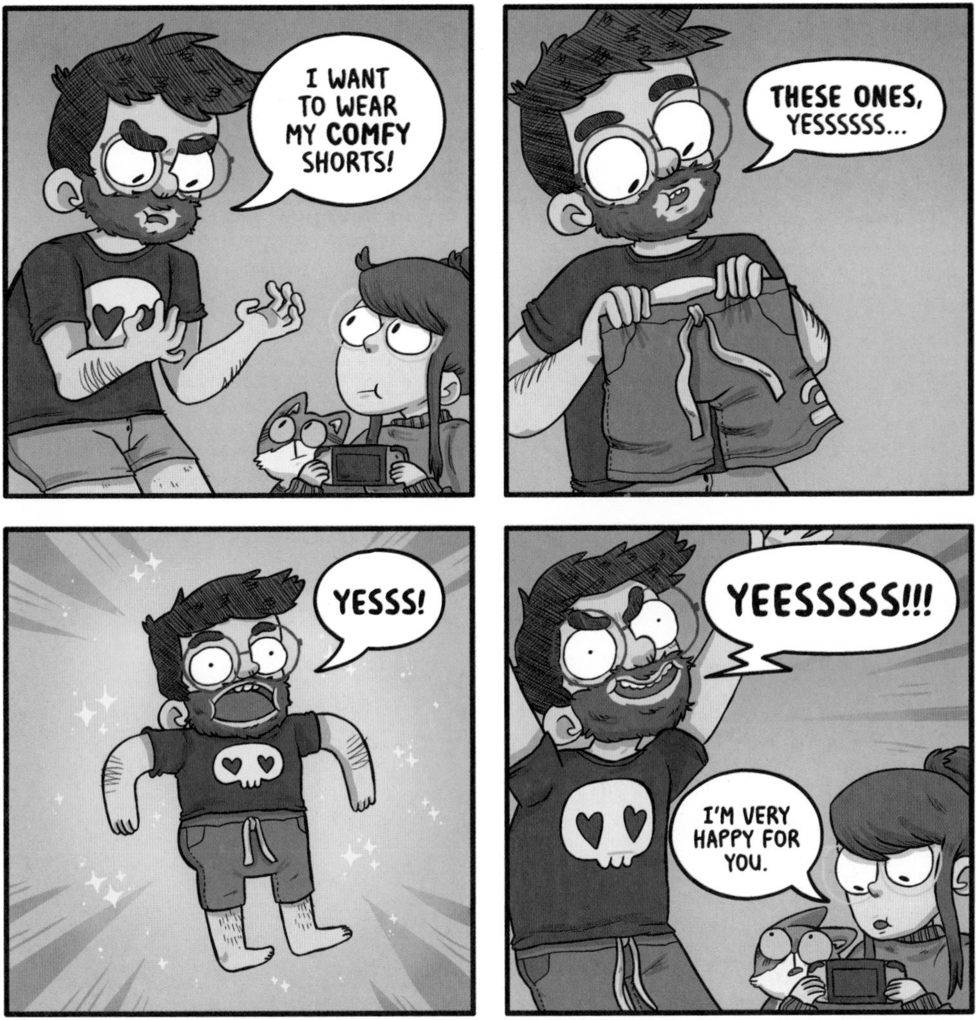
I WANT TO WEAR MY COMFY SHORTS!
THESE ONES, YESSSSSS...
YESSS!
YEESSSSSS!!!
I'M VERY HAPPY FOR YOU.

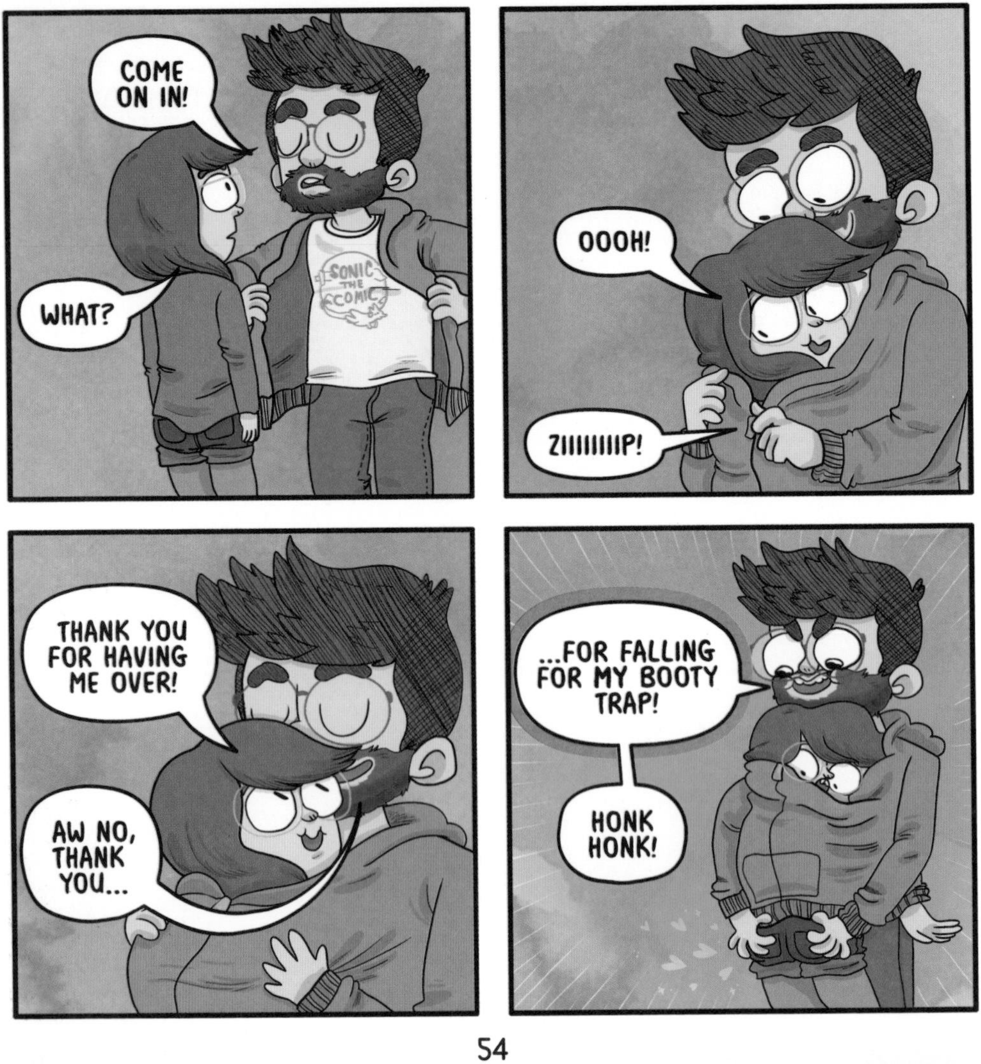
COME ON IN!
WHAT?
SONIC THE COMIC
OOOH!
ZIIIIIIIIP!
THANK YOU FOR HAVING ME OVER!
AW NO, THANK YOU...
...FOR FALLING FOR MY BOOTY TRAP!
HONK HONK!

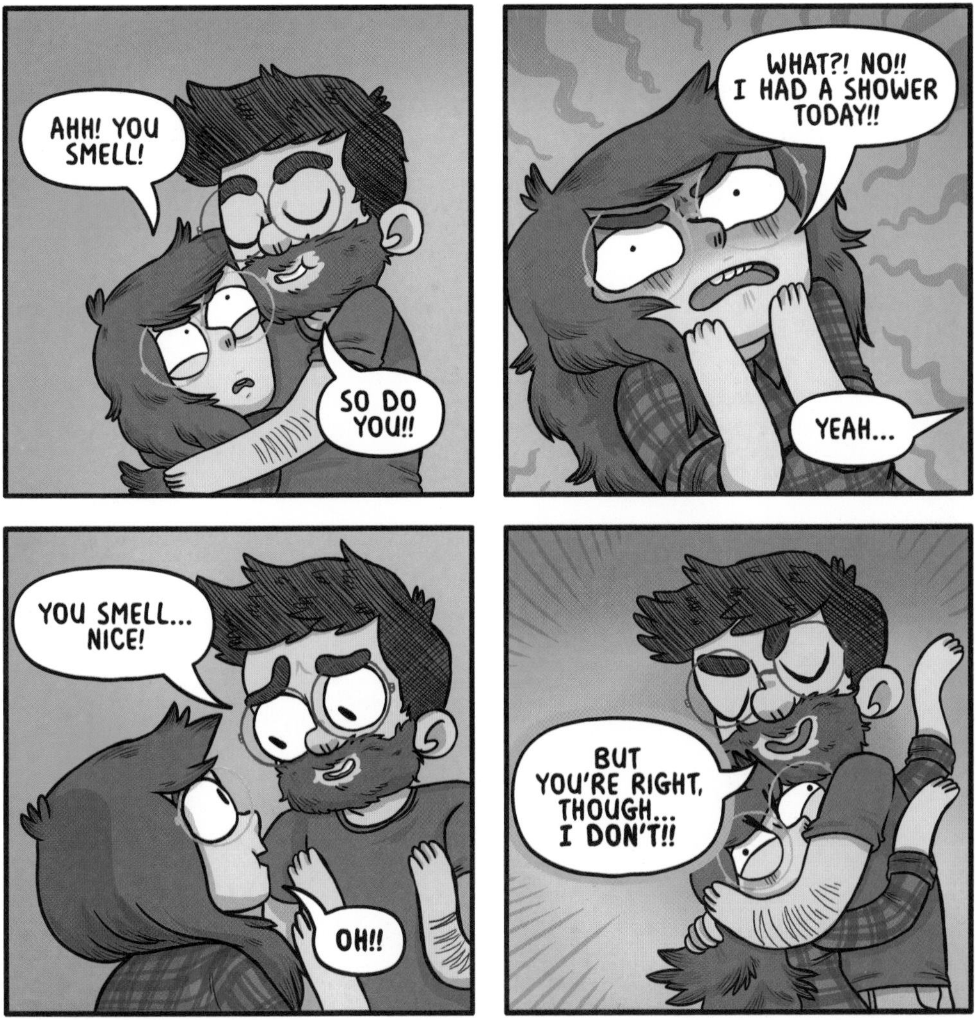
AHH! YOU SMELL!
SO DO YOU!!
WHAT?! NO!! I HAD A SHOWER TODAY!!
YEAH...
YOU SMELL... NICE!
OH!!
BUT YOU'RE RIGHT, THOUGH... I DON'T!!

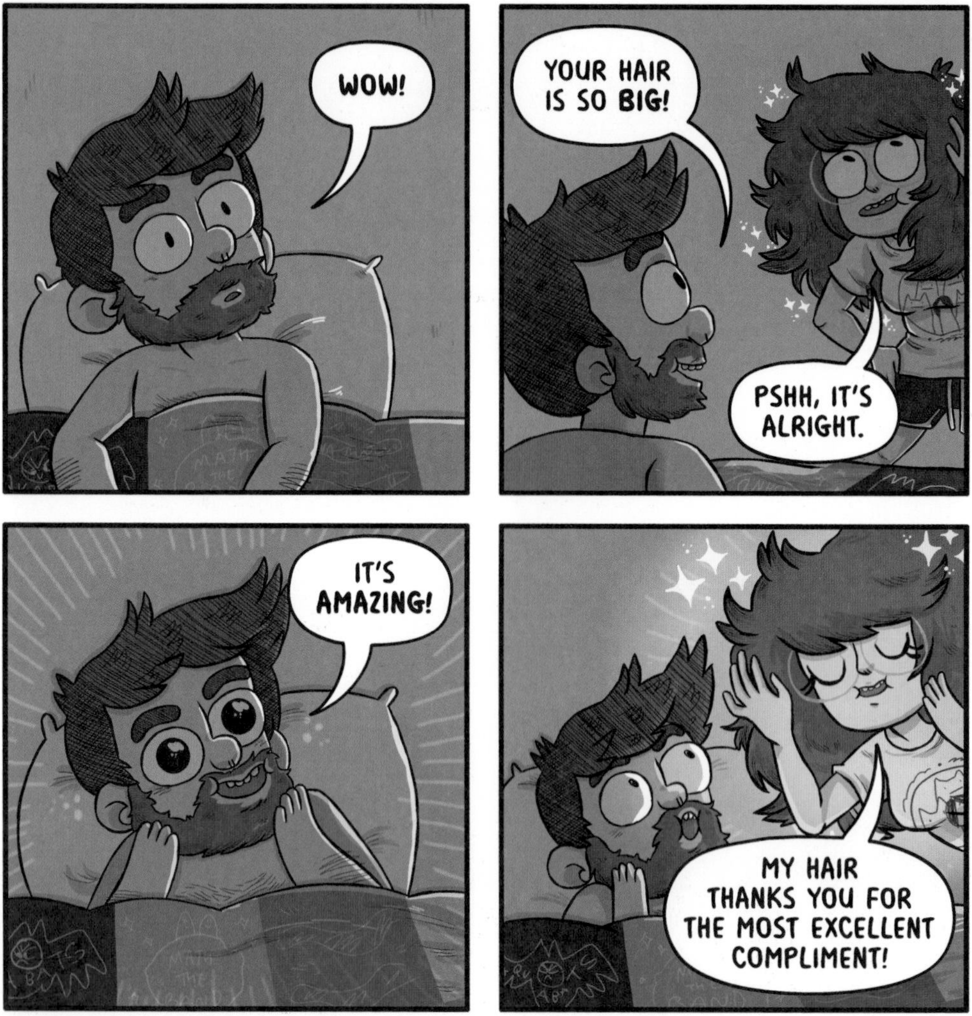
WOW!
YOUR HAIR IS SO BIG!
PSHH, IT'S ALRIGHT.
IT'S AMAZING!
MY HAIR THANKS YOU FOR THE MOST EXCELLENT COMPLIMENT!

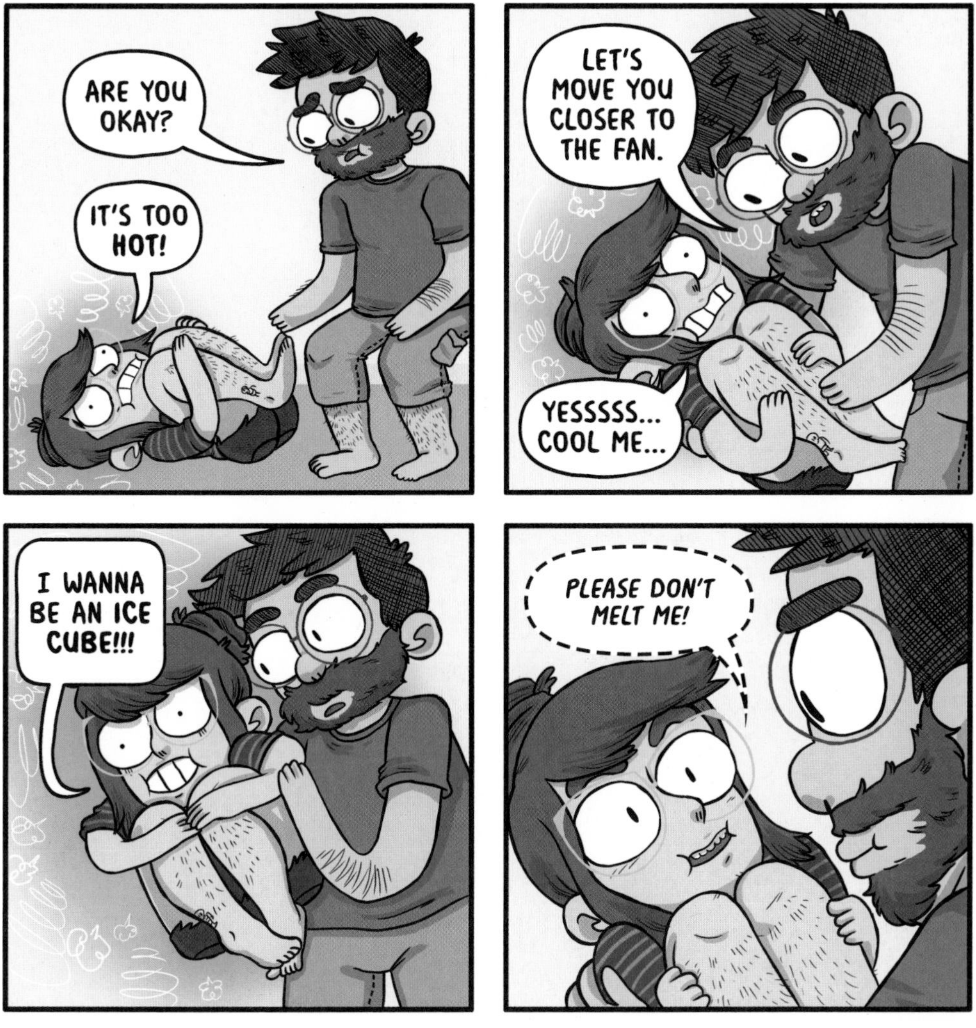
ARE YOU OKAY?
IT'S TOO HOT!
LET'S MOVE YOU CLOSER TO THE FAN.
YESSSSS... COOL ME...
I WANNA BE AN ICE CUBE!!!
PLEASE DON'T MELT ME!

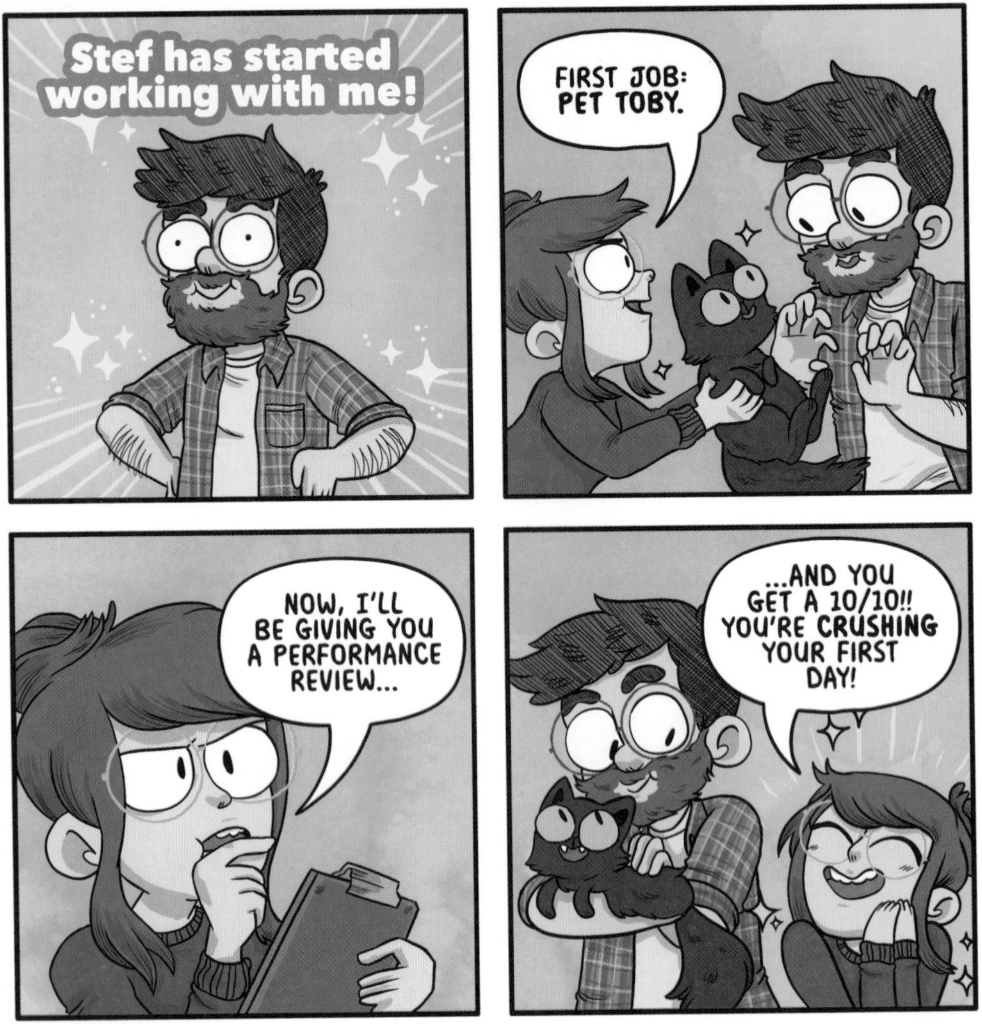
Stef has started working with me!
FIRST JOB: PET TOBY.
NOW, I'LL BE GIVING YOU A PERFORMANCE REVIEW...
...AND YOU GET A 10/10!! YOU'RE CRUSHING YOUR FIRST DAY!

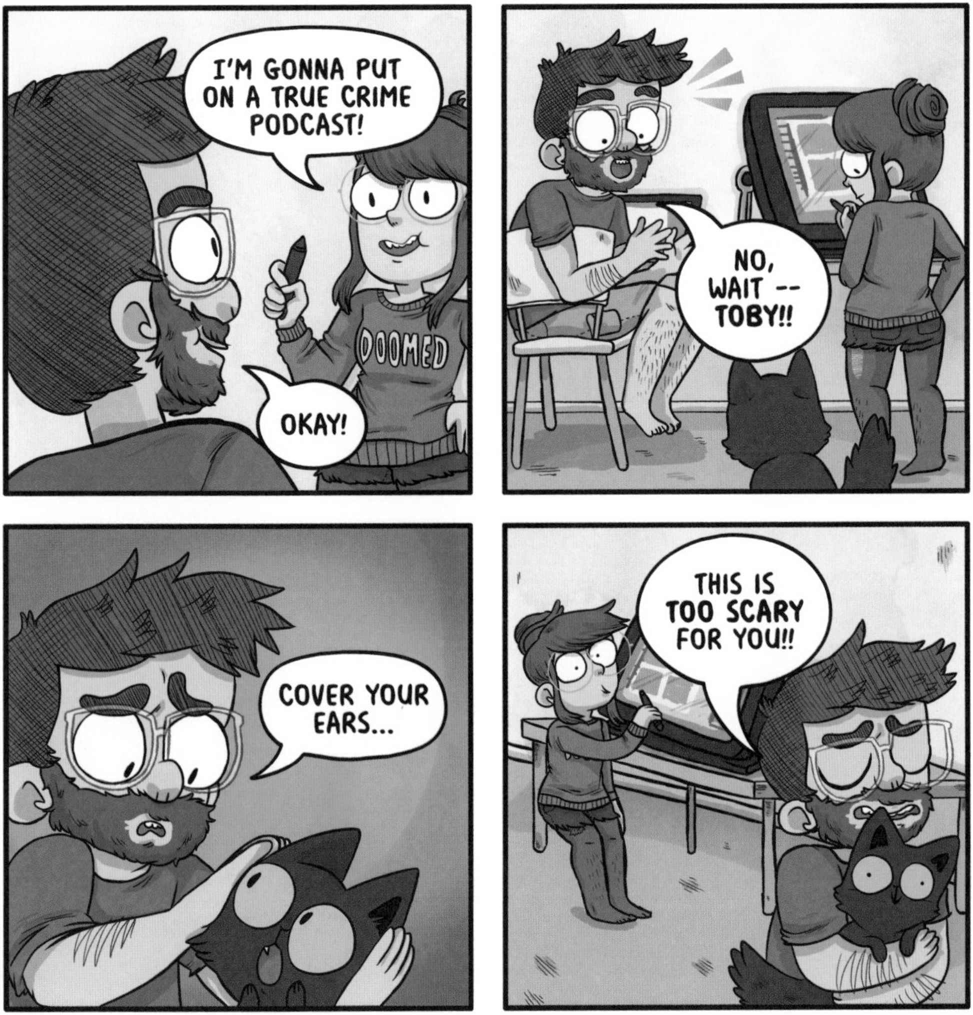
I'M GONNA PUT ON A TRUE CRIME PODCAST!
DOOMED
OKAY!
NO, WAIT -- TOBY!!
COVER YOUR EARS...
THIS IS TOO SCARY FOR YOU!!

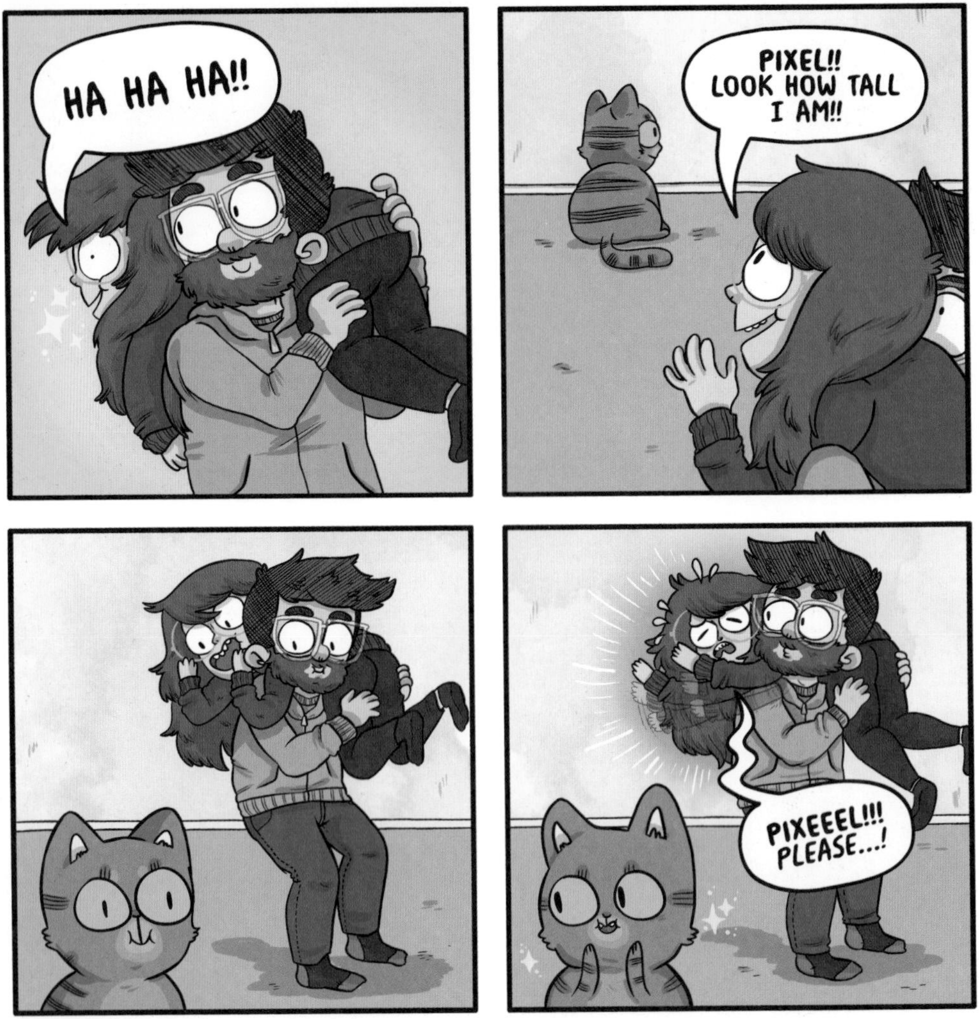
HA HA HA!!
PIXEL!! LOOK HOW TALL I AM!!
PIXEEEL!!! PLEASE...!

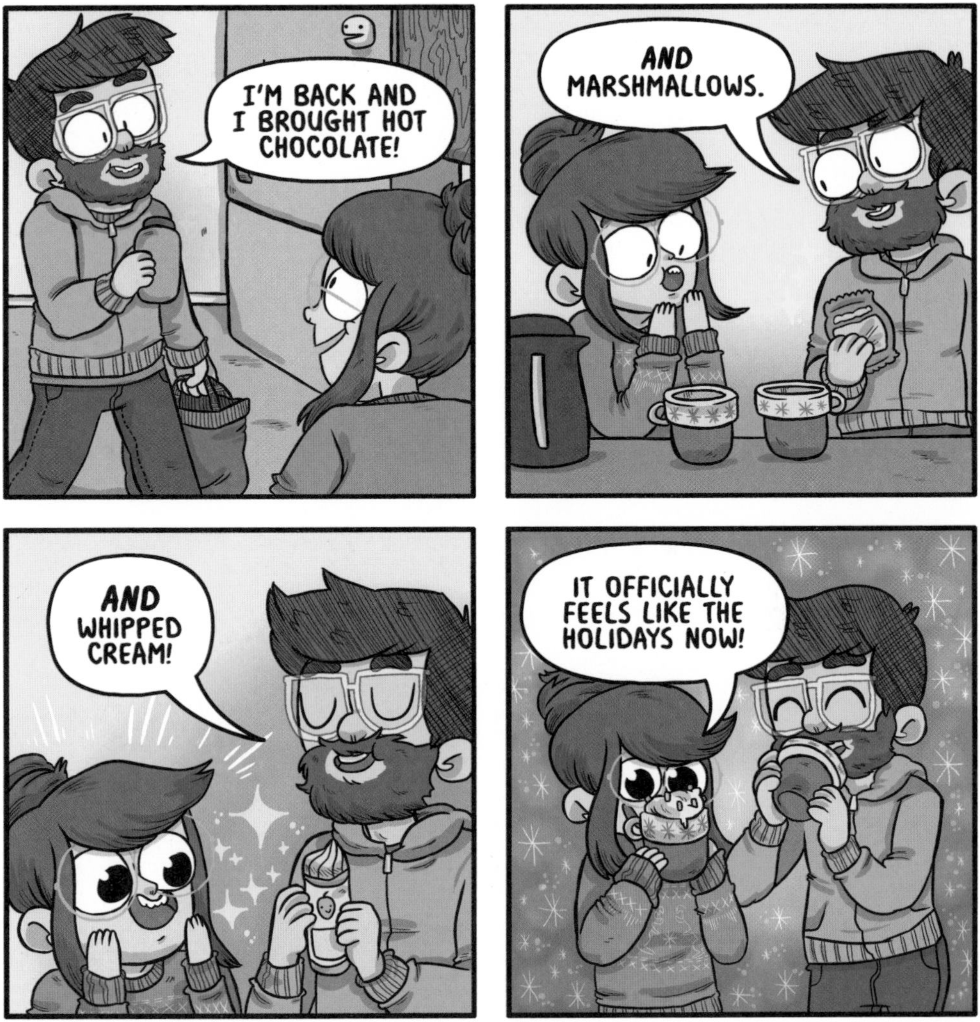
I'M BACK AND I BROUGHT HOT CHOCOLATE!
AND MARSHMALLOWS.
AND WHIPPED CREAM!
IT OFFICIALLY FEELS LIKE THE HOLIDAYS NOW!

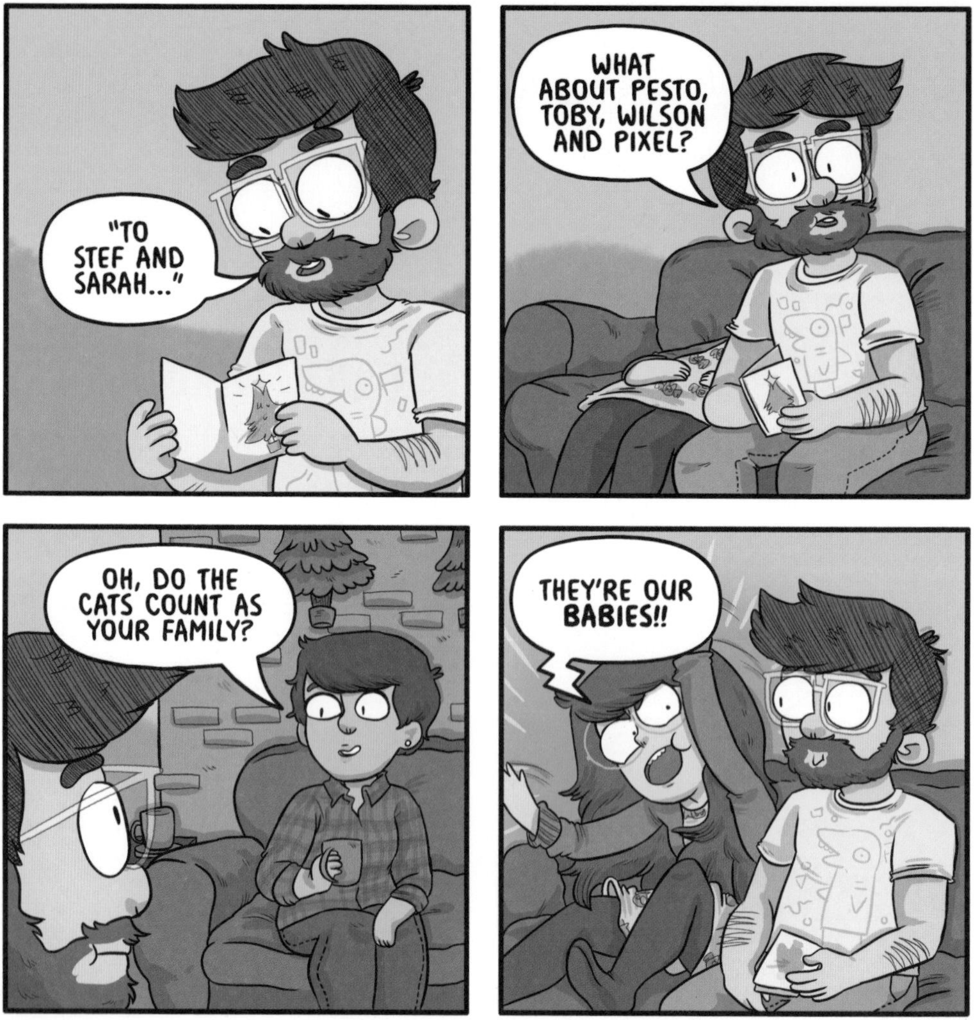
"TO STEF AND SARAH..."
WHAT ABOUT PESTO, TOBY, WILSON AND PIXEL?
OH, DO THE CATS COUNT AS YOUR FAMILY?
THEY'RE OUR **BABIES!!**

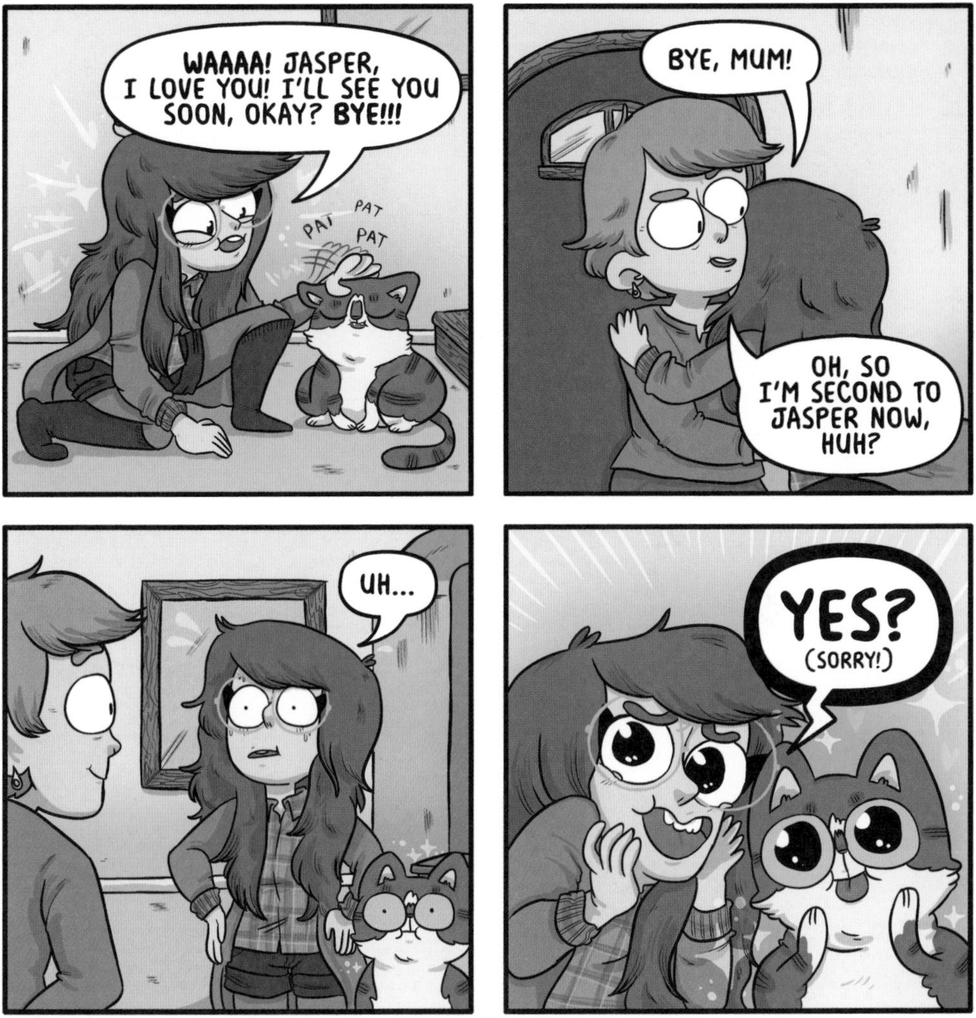
WAAAA! JASPER, I LOVE YOU! I'LL SEE YOU SOON, OKAY? **BYE!!!**
PAT PAT PAT
BYE, MUM!
OH, SO I'M SECOND TO JASPER NOW, HUH?
UH...
YES?
(SORRY!)

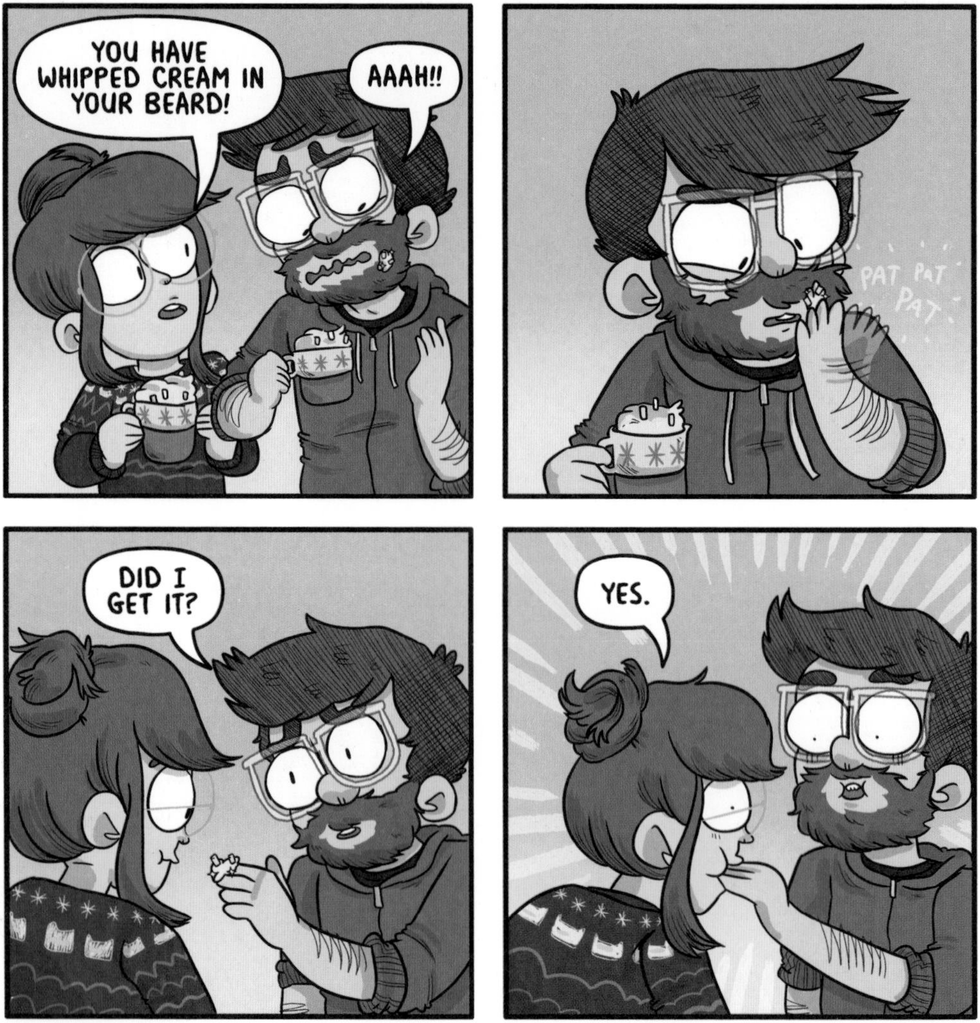
YOU HAVE WHIPPED CREAM IN YOUR BEARD!
AAAH!!
PAT PAT PAT
DID I GET IT?
YES.

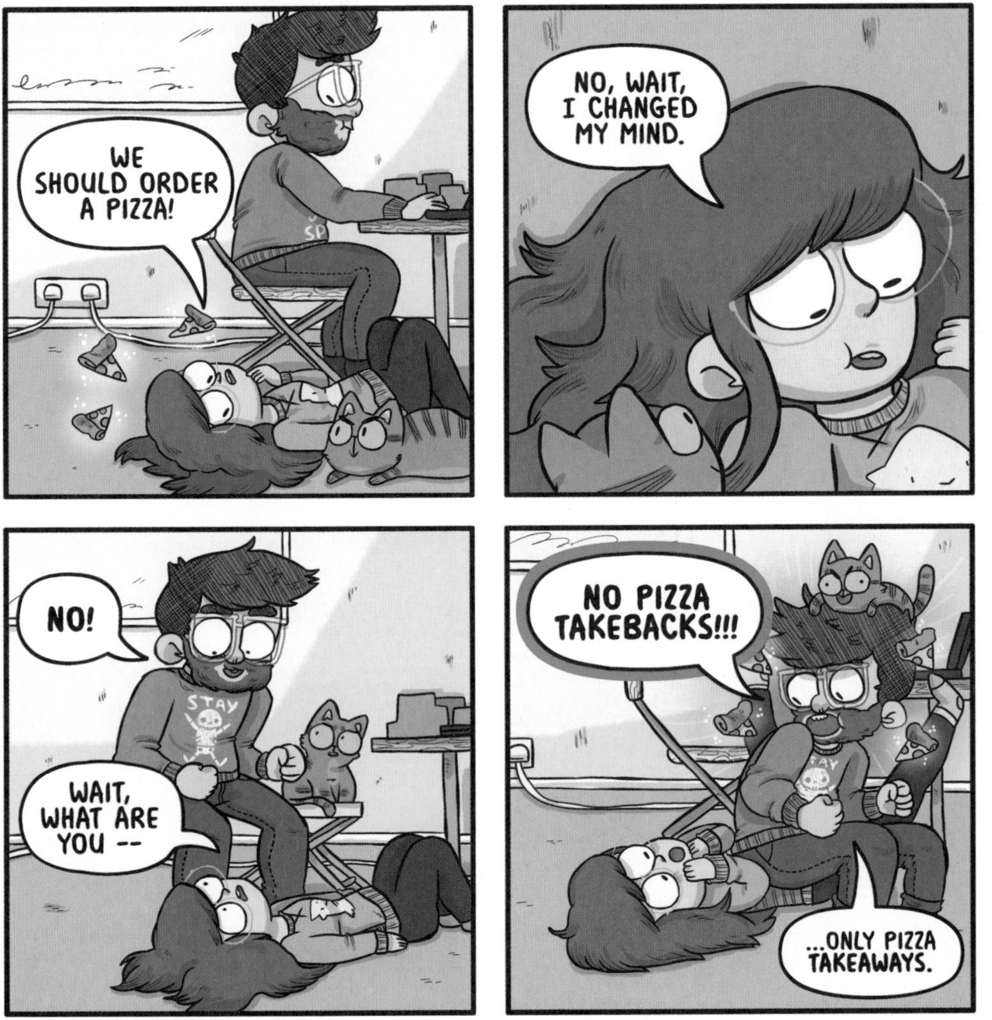
WE SHOULD ORDER A PIZZA!
NO, WAIT, I CHANGED MY MIND.
NO!
WAIT, WHAT ARE YOU --
NO PIZZA TAKEBACKS!!!
...ONLY PIZZA TAKEAWAYS.

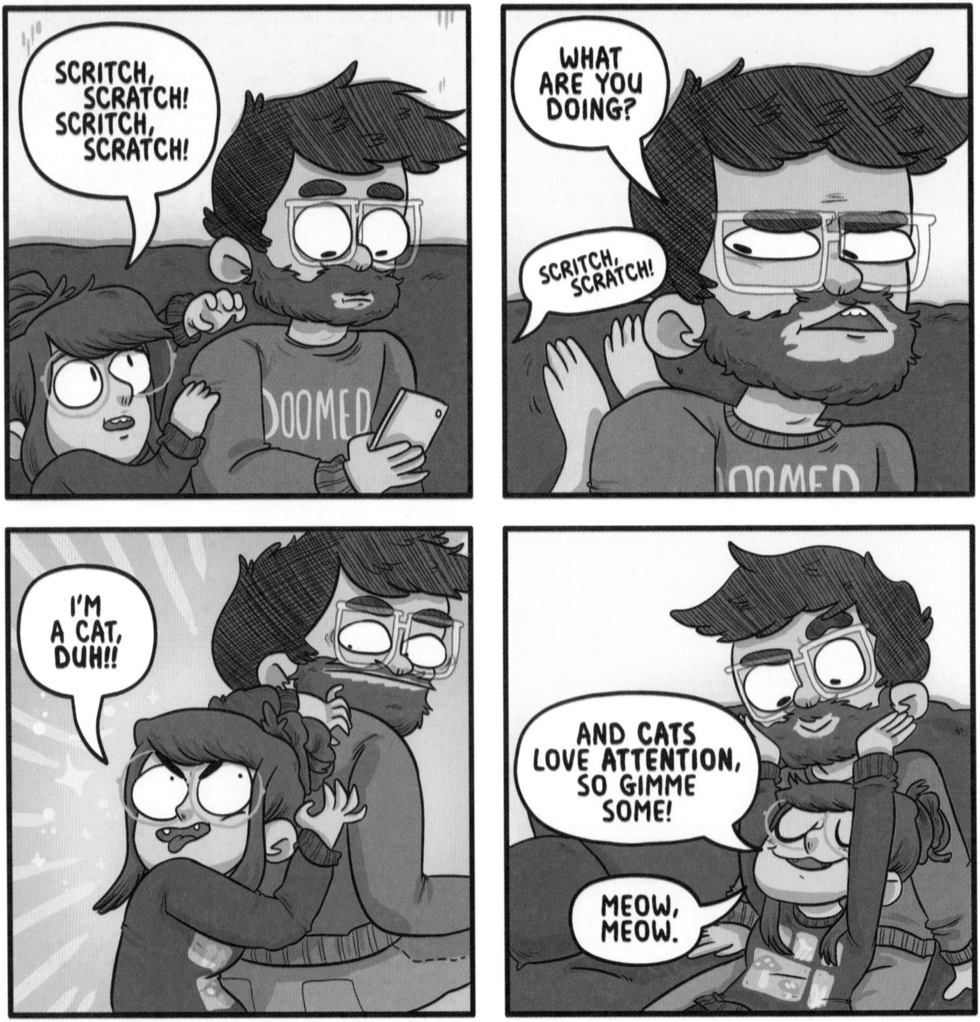
SCRITCH, SCRATCH! SCRITCH, SCRATCH!
DOOMED
WHAT ARE YOU DOING?
SCRITCH, SCRATCH!
DOOMED
I'M A CAT, DUH!!
AND CATS LOVE ATTENTION, SO GIMME SOME!
MEOW, MEOW.

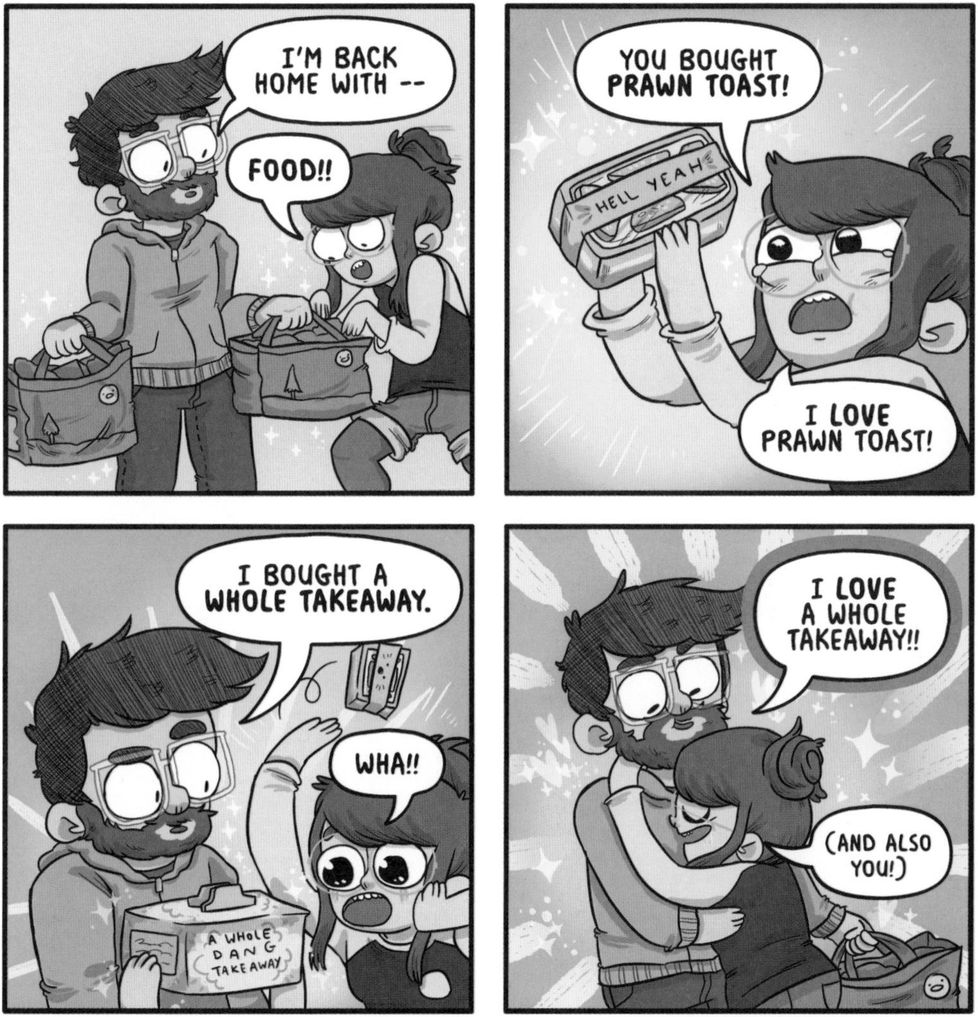
I'M BACK HOME WITH --
FOOD!!
YOU BOUGHT PRAWN TOAST!
HELL YEAH
I LOVE PRAWN TOAST!
I BOUGHT A WHOLE TAKEAWAY.
WHA!!
A WHOLE DANG TAKEAWAY
I LOVE A WHOLE TAKEAWAY!!
(AND ALSO YOU!)

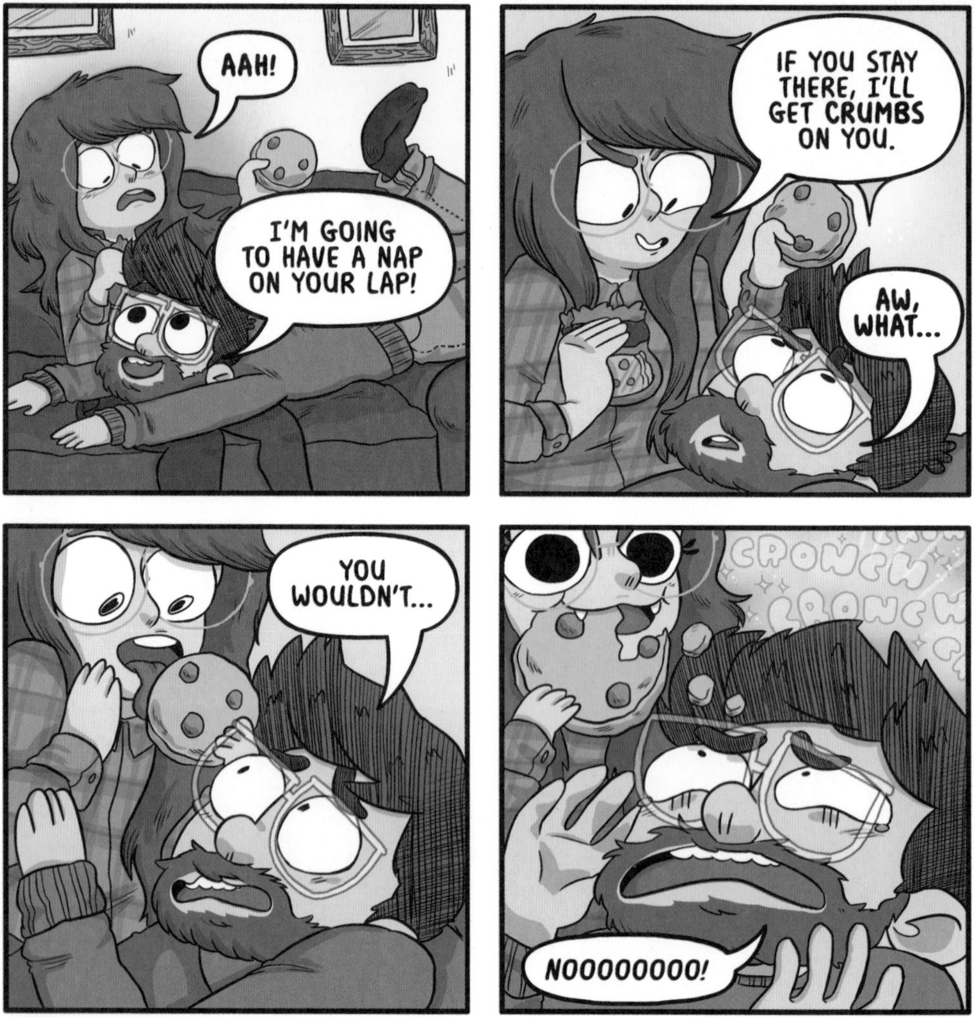
AAH!
I'M GOING TO HAVE A NAP ON YOUR LAP!
IF YOU STAY THERE, I'LL GET CRUMBS ON YOU.
AW, WHAT...
YOU WOULDN'T...
CRONCH
CRONCH
NOOOOOOOO!

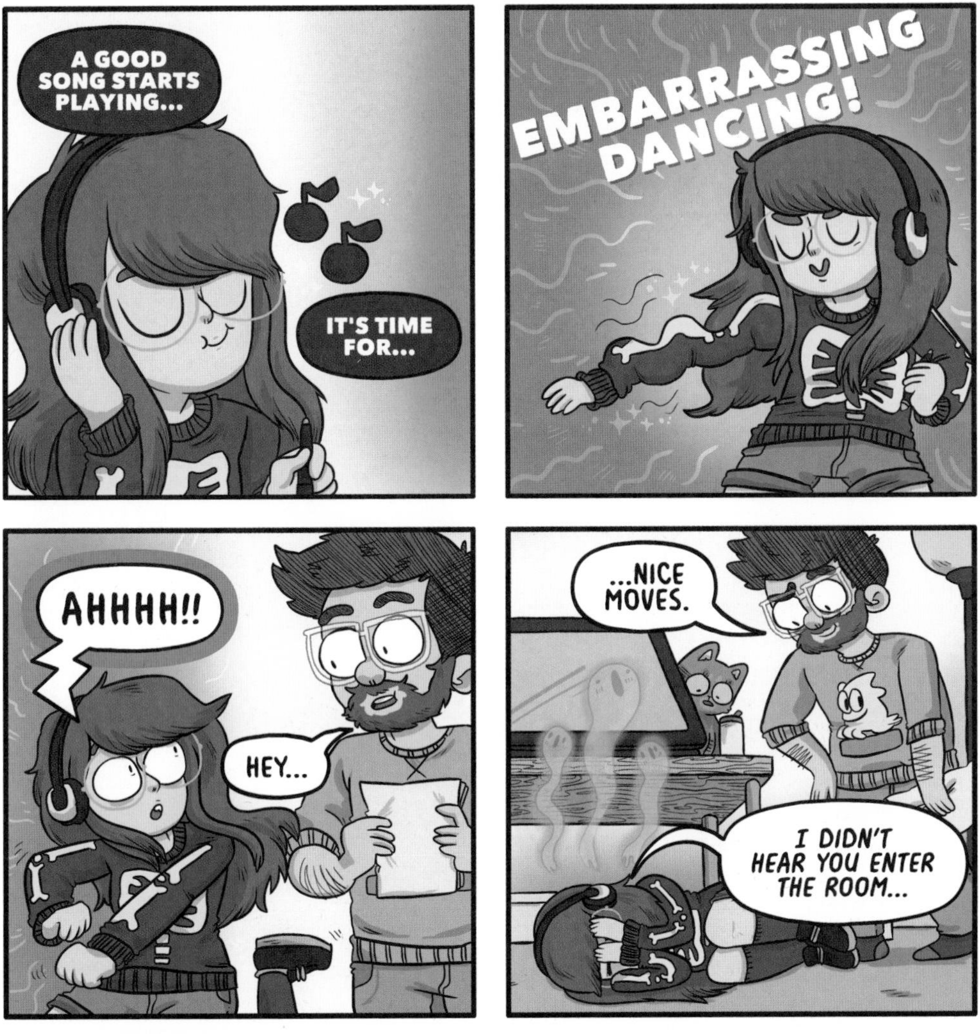
A GOOD SONG STARTS PLAYING...
IT'S TIME FOR...
EMBARRASSING DANCING!
AHHHH!!
HEY...
...NICE MOVES.
I DIDN'T HEAR YOU ENTER THE ROOM...

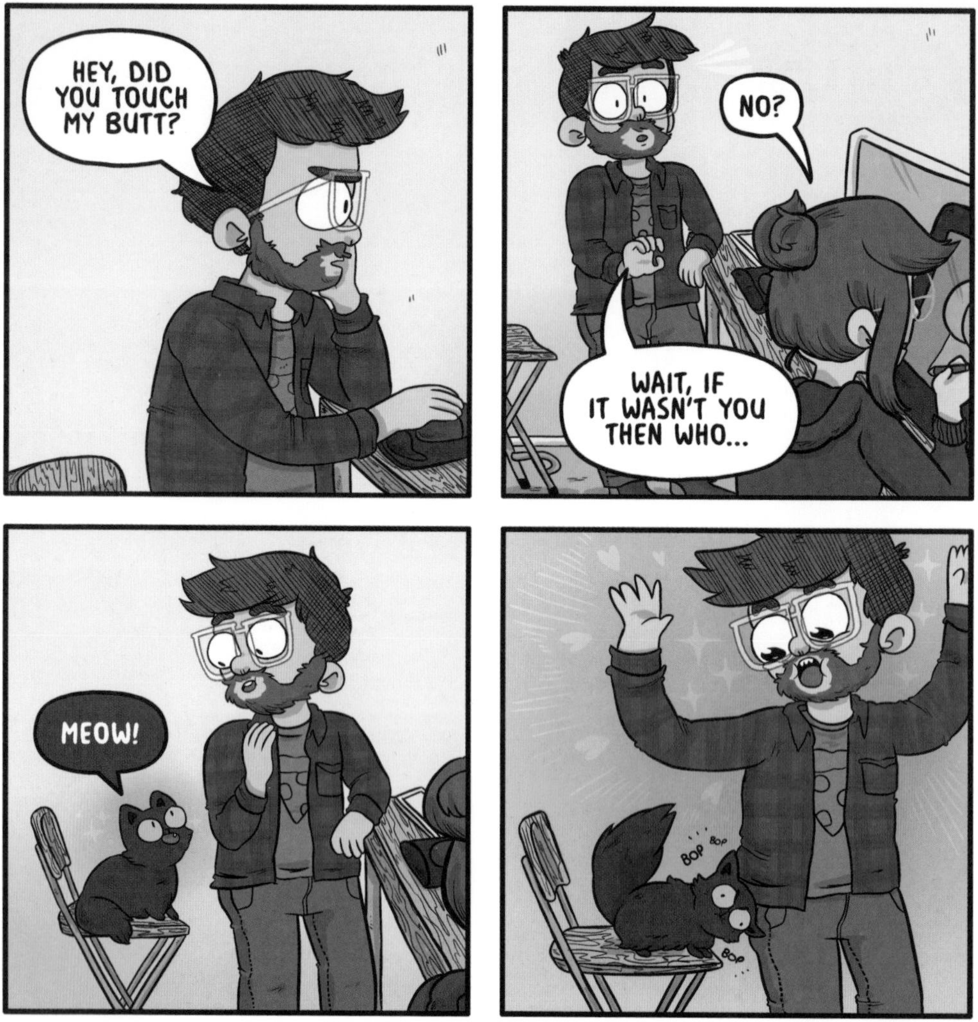
HEY, DID YOU TOUCH MY BUTT?
NO?
WAIT, IF IT WASN'T YOU THEN WHO...
MEOW!
BOP BOP
BOP BOP

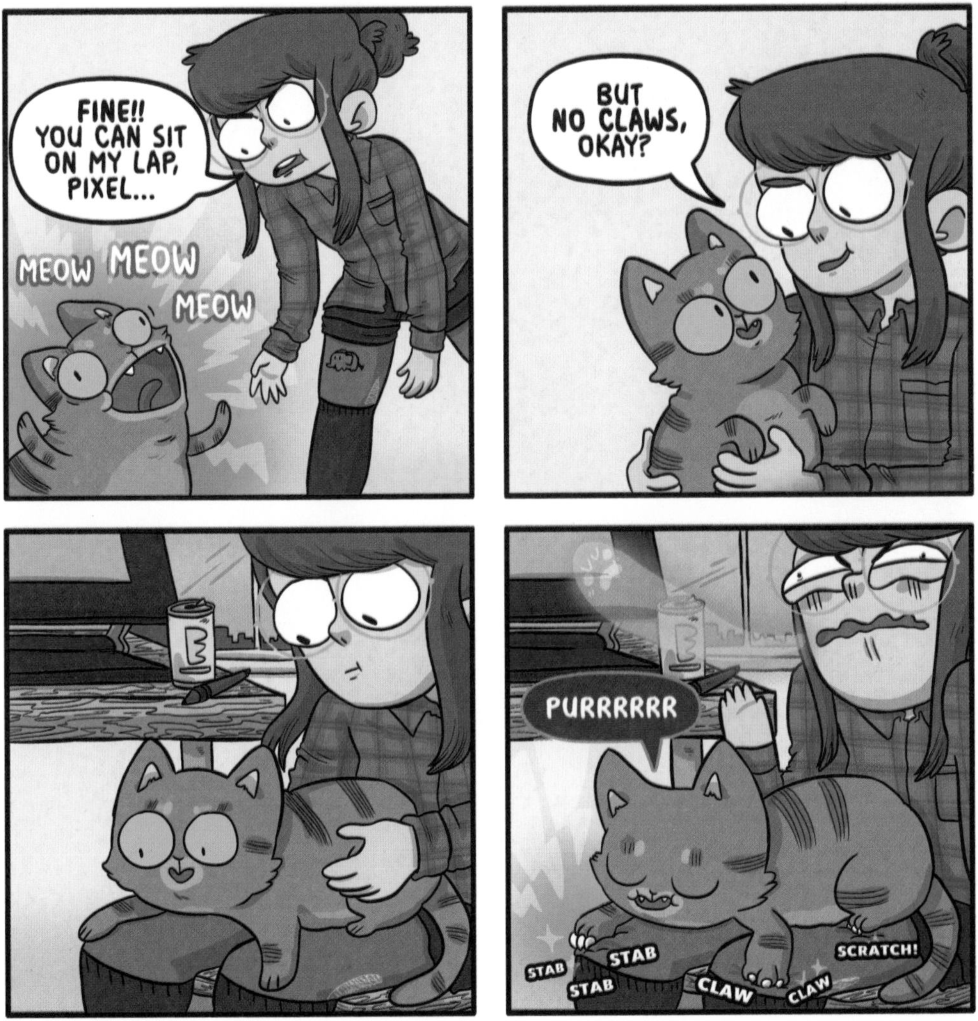
FINE!! YOU CAN SIT ON MY LAP, PIXEL...
MEOW MEOW
MEOW
BUT NO CLAWS, OKAY?
PURRRRRR
STAB
STAB
STAB
CLAW
CLAW
SCRATCH!

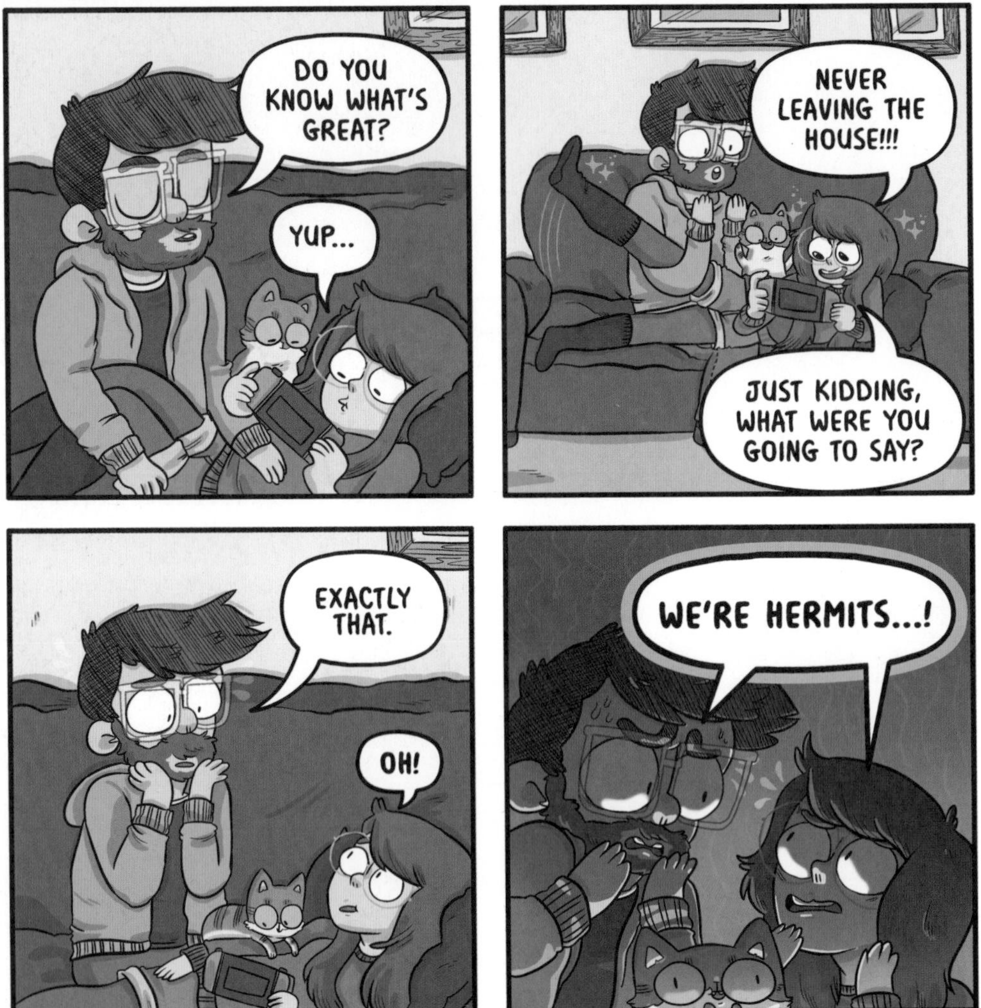
DO YOU KNOW WHAT'S GREAT?
YUP...
NEVER LEAVING THE HOUSE!!!
JUST KIDDING, WHAT WERE YOU GOING TO SAY?
EXACTLY THAT.
OH!
WE'RE HERMITS...!

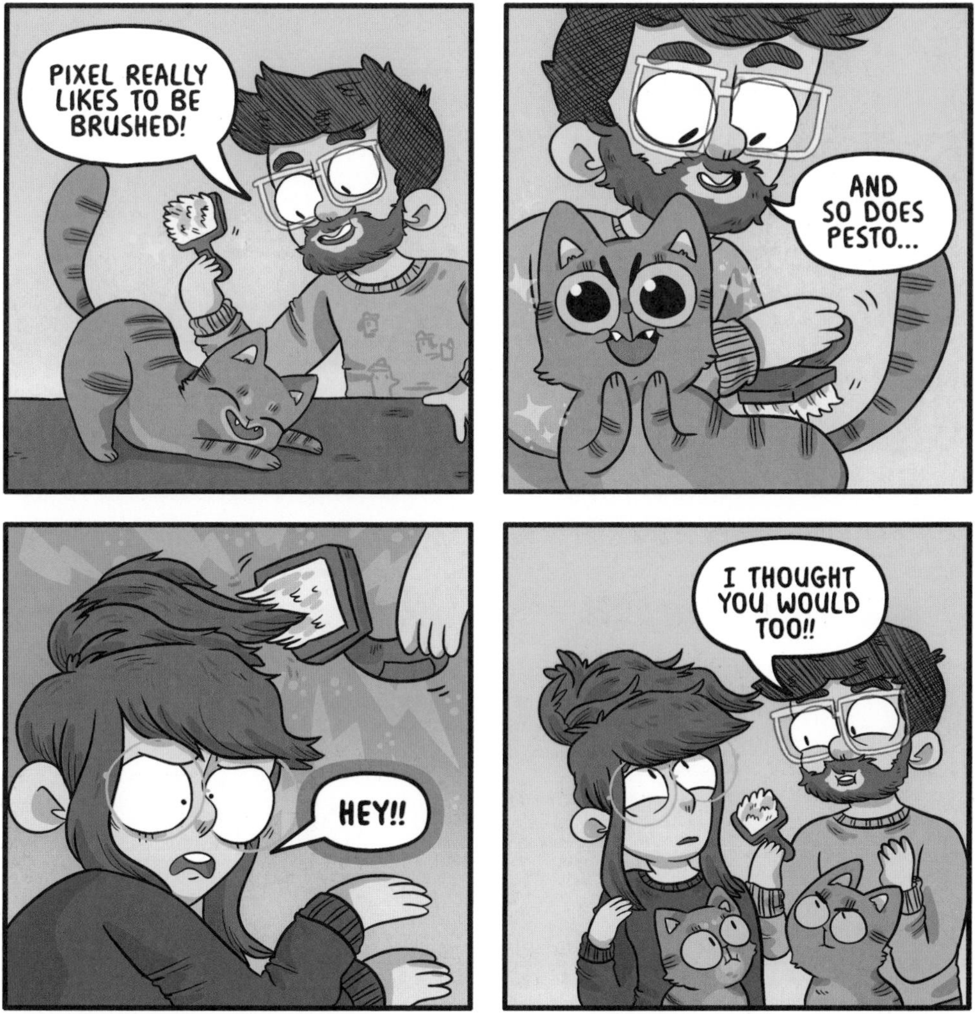
PIXEL REALLY LIKES TO BE BRUSHED!
AND SO DOES PESTO...
HEY!!
I THOUGHT YOU WOULD TOO!!

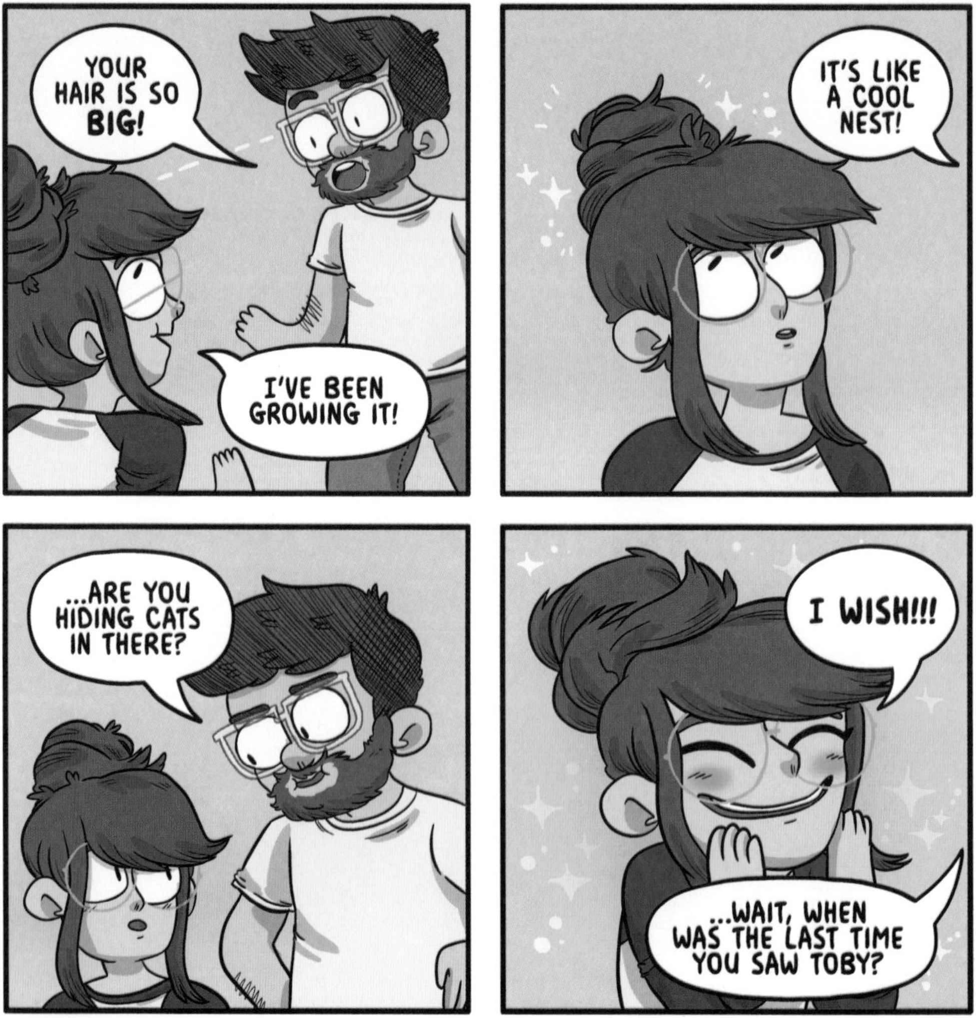
YOUR HAIR IS SO BIG!
I'VE BEEN GROWING IT!
IT'S LIKE A COOL NEST!
...ARE YOU HIDING CATS IN THERE?
I WISH!!!
...WAIT, WHEN WAS THE LAST TIME YOU SAW TOBY?

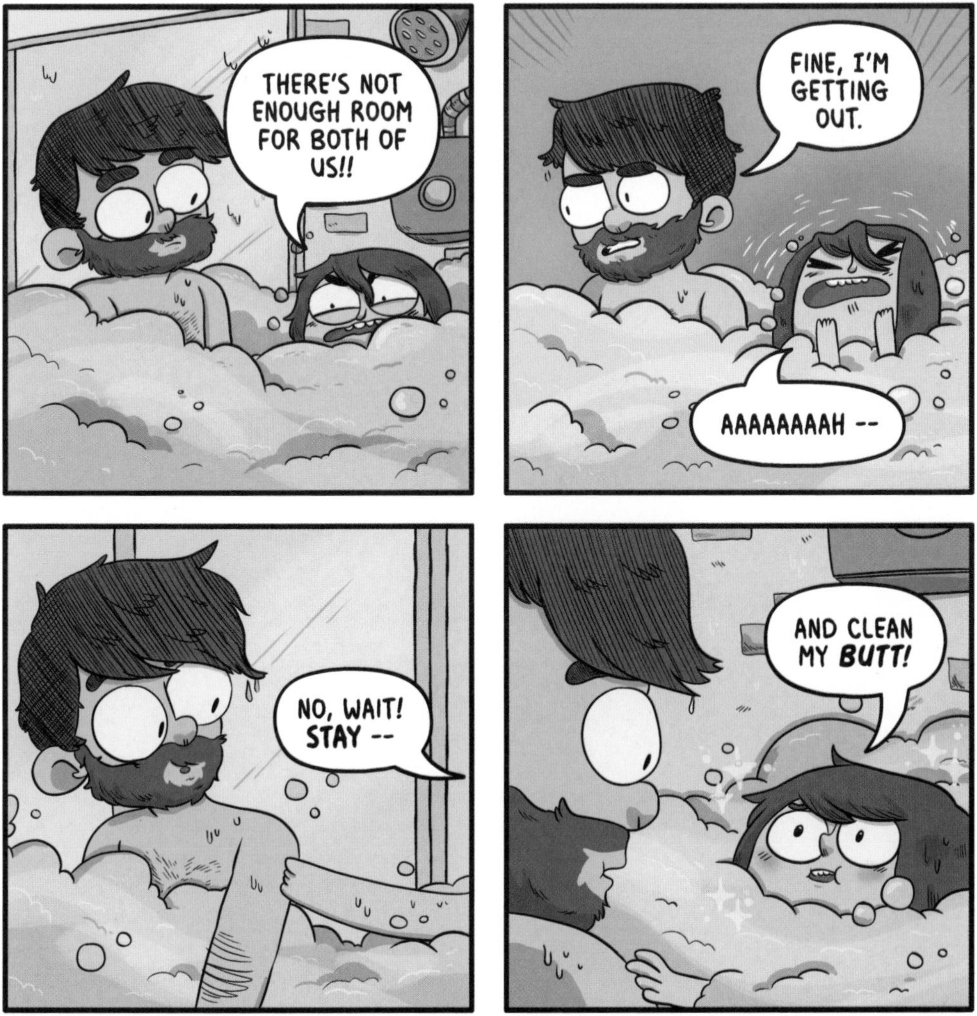
THERE'S NOT ENOUGH ROOM FOR BOTH OF US!!
FINE, I'M GETTING OUT.
AAAAAAAAH --
NO, WAIT! STAY --
AND CLEAN MY **BUTT!**

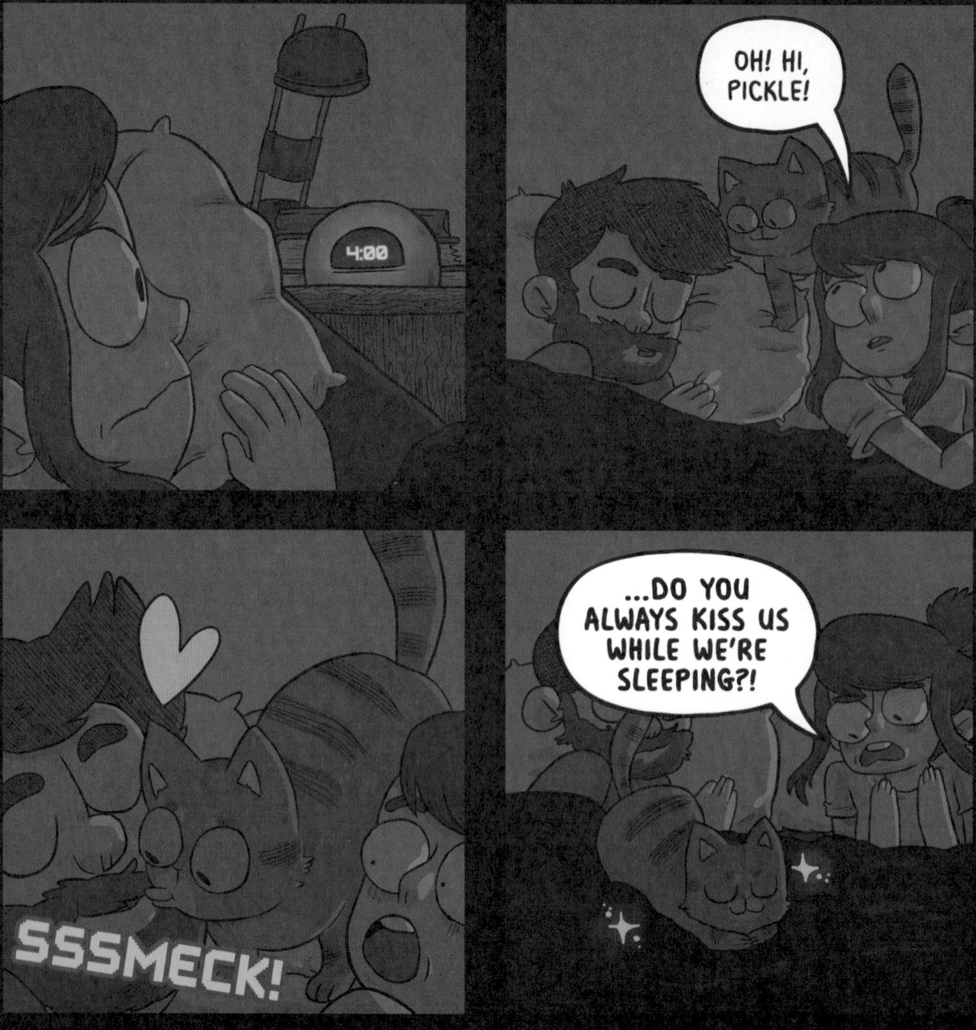
4:00
OH! HI, PICKLE!
SSSMECK!
...DO YOU ALWAYS KISS US WHILE WE'RE SLEEPING?!

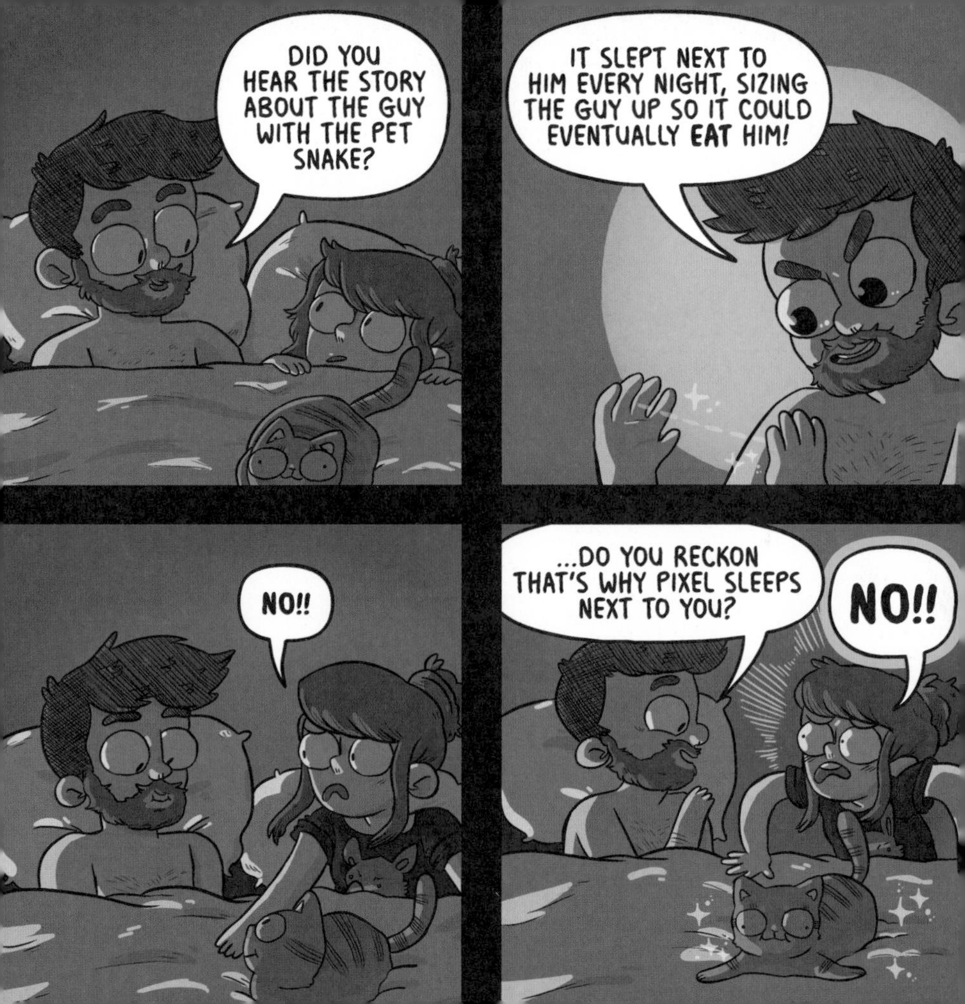
DID YOU HEAR THE STORY ABOUT THE GUY WITH THE PET SNAKE?
IT SLEPT NEXT TO HIM EVERY NIGHT, SIZING THE GUY UP SO IT COULD EVENTUALLY **EAT** HIM!
NO!!
...DO YOU RECKON THAT'S WHY PIXEL SLEEPS NEXT TO YOU?
NO!!

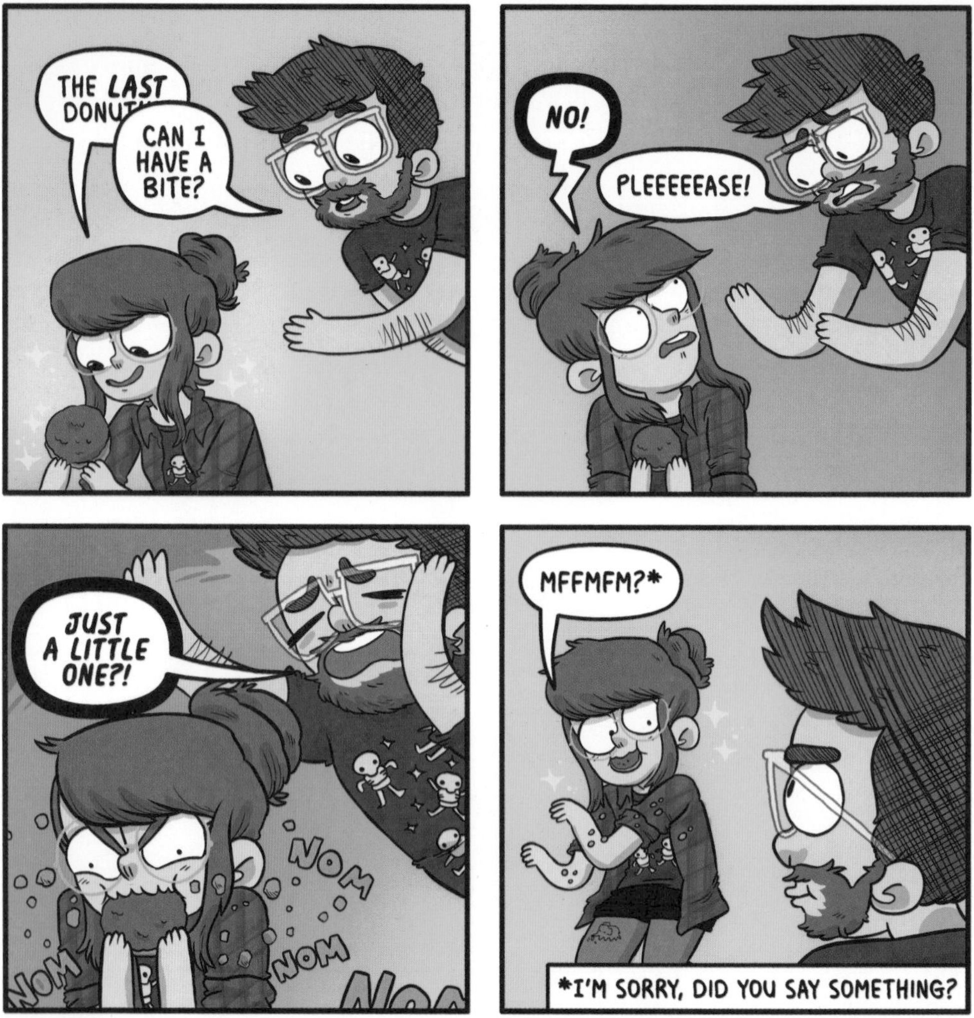
THE LAST DONUT
CAN I HAVE A BITE?
NO!
PLEEEEEEASE!
JUST A LITTLE ONE?!
NOM
NOM
NOM
MFFMFM?*
*I'M SORRY, DID YOU SAY SOMETHING?

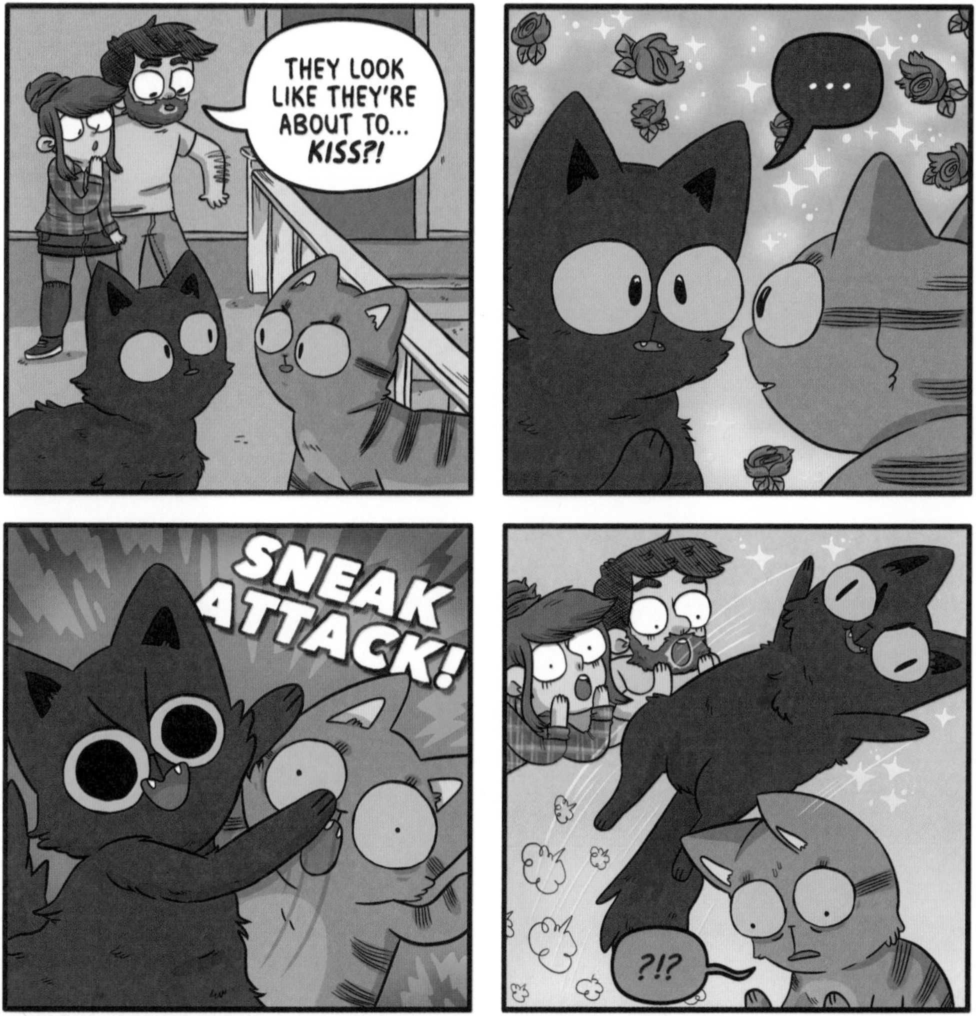
THEY LOOK LIKE THEY'RE ABOUT TO... KISS?!
...
SNEAK ATTACK!
?!?

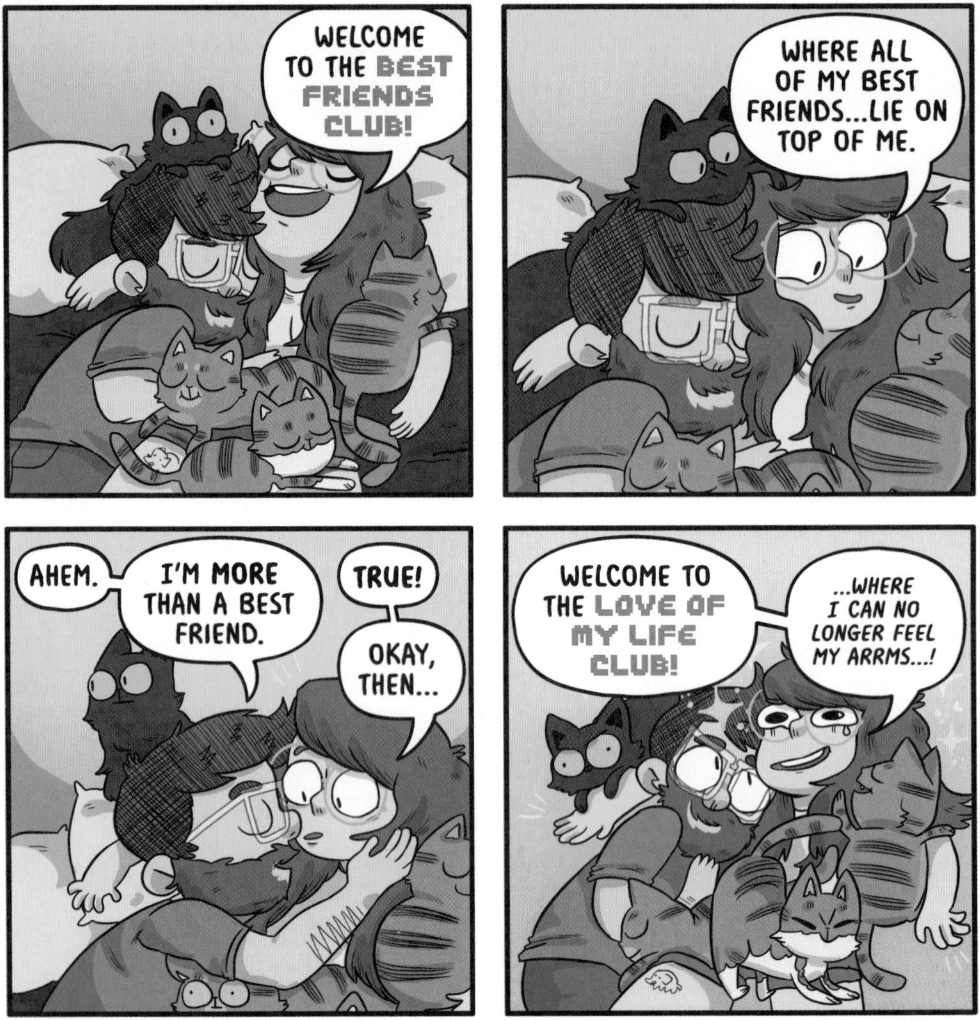
WELCOME TO THE BEST FRIENDS CLUB!
WHERE ALL OF MY BEST FRIENDS...LIE ON TOP OF ME.
AHEM.
I'M MORE THAN A BEST FRIEND.
TRUE!
OKAY, THEN...
WELCOME TO THE LOVE OF MY LIFE CLUB!
...WHERE I CAN NO LONGER FEEL MY ARRMS...!

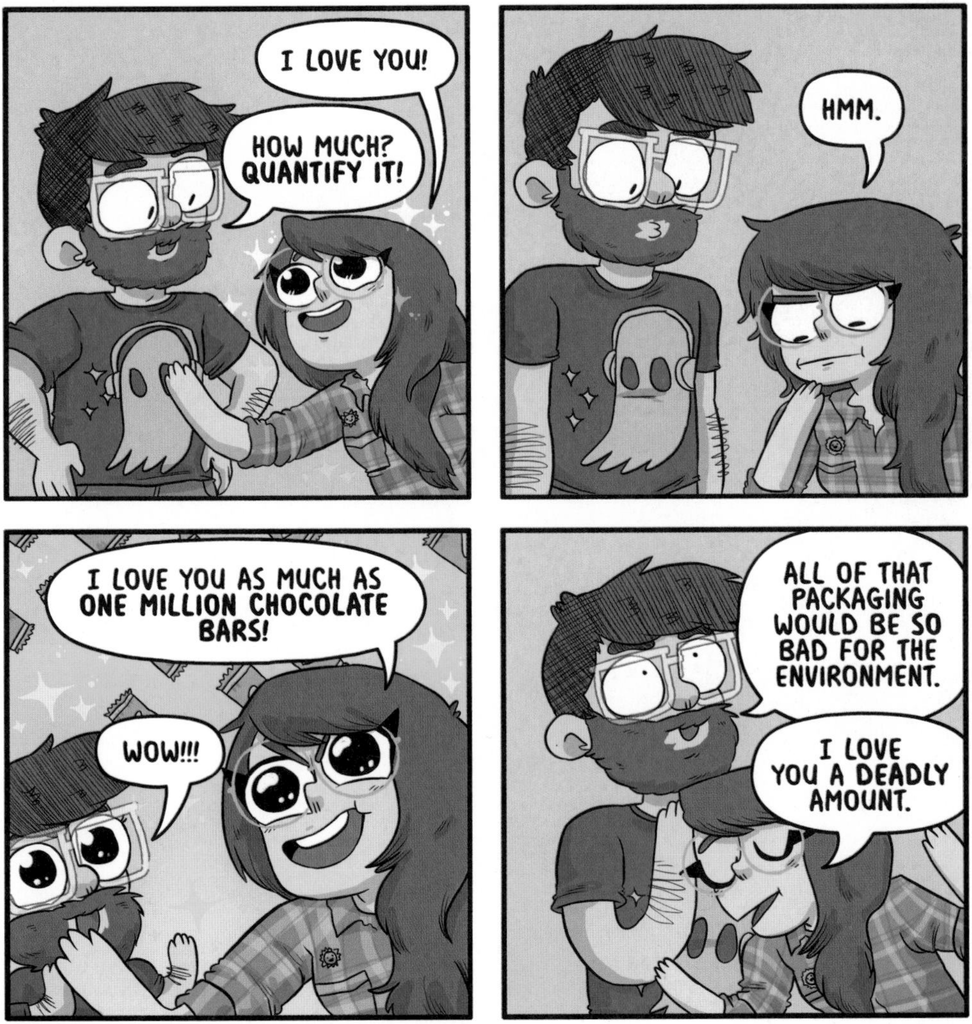
I LOVE YOU!
HOW MUCH? QUANTIFY IT!
HMM.
I LOVE YOU AS MUCH AS ONE MILLION CHOCOLATE BARS!
WOW!!!
ALL OF THAT PACKAGING WOULD BE SO BAD FOR THE ENVIRONMENT.
I LOVE YOU A DEADLY AMOUNT.

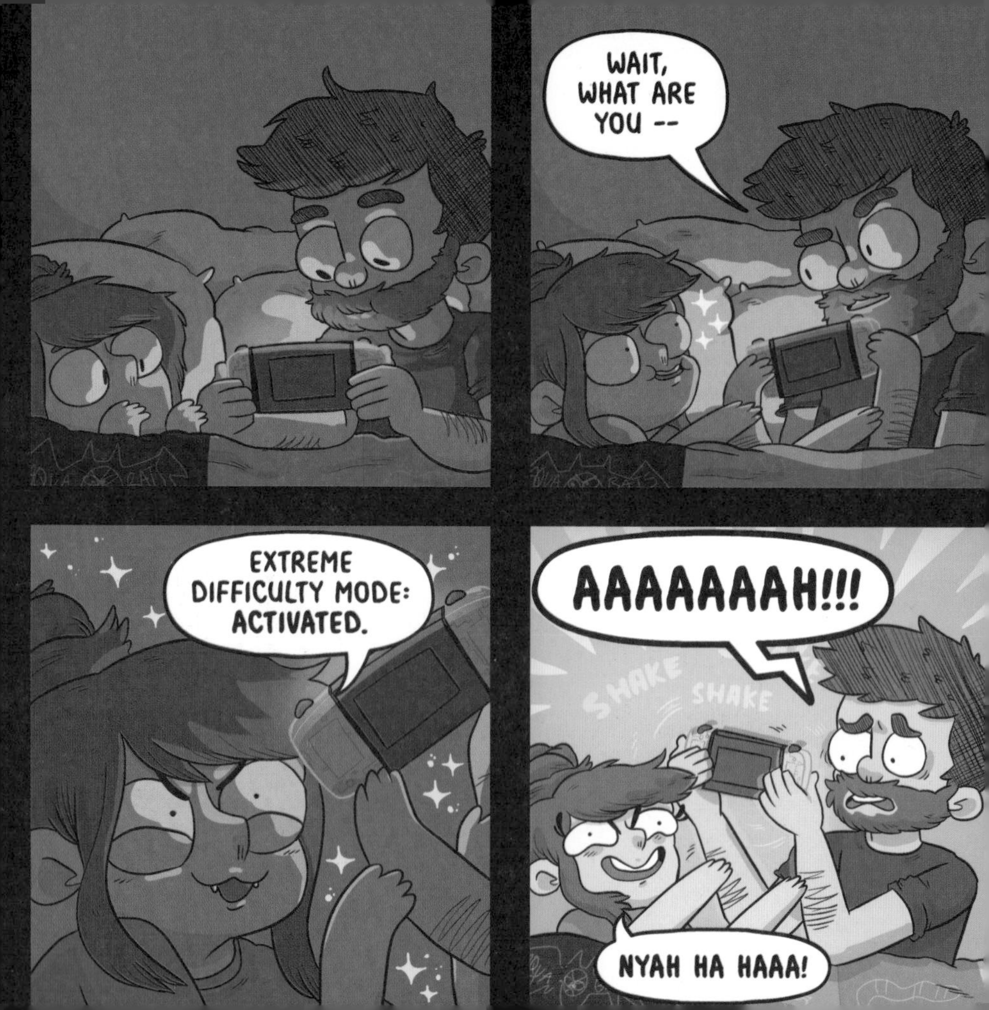
WAIT, WHAT ARE YOU --
EXTREME DIFFICULTY MODE: ACTIVATED.
AAAAAAAH!!!
SHAKE
SHAKE
NYAH HA HAAA!

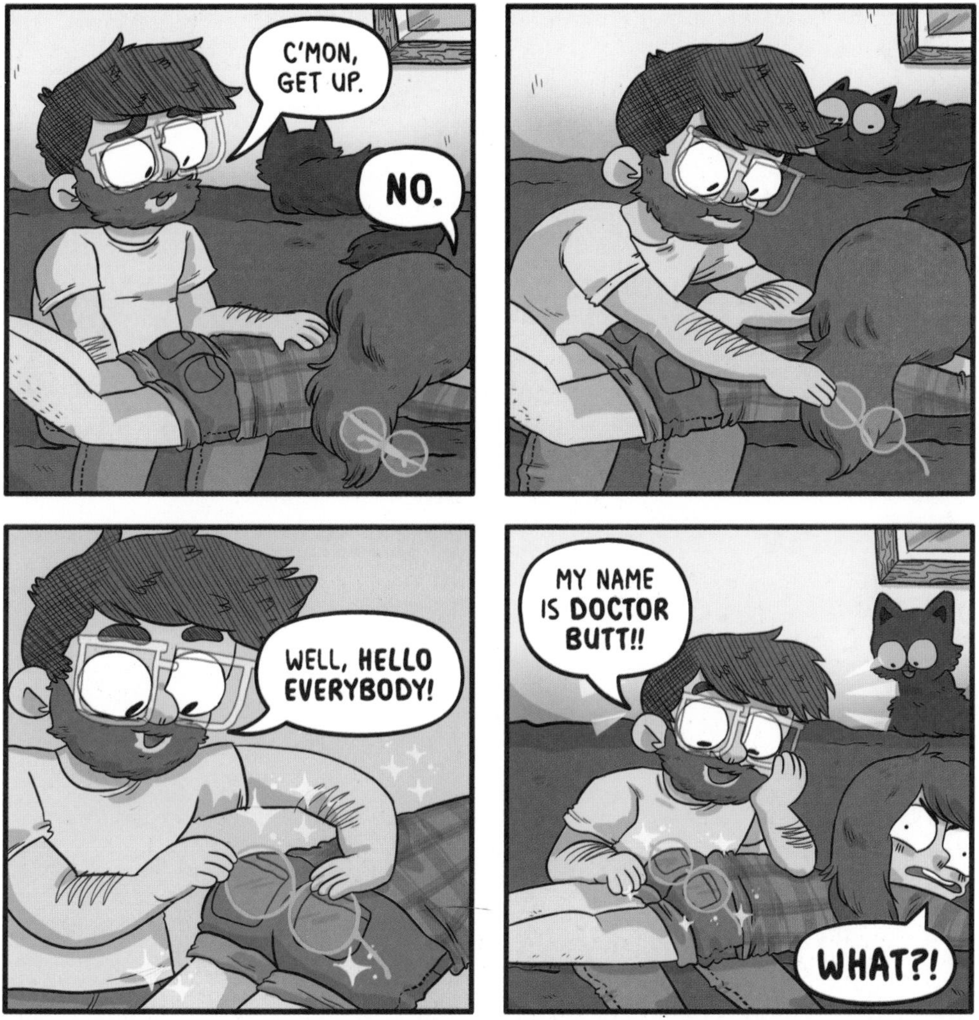
C'MON, GET UP.
NO.
WELL, HELLO EVERYBODY!
MY NAME IS DOCTOR BUTT!!
WHAT?!

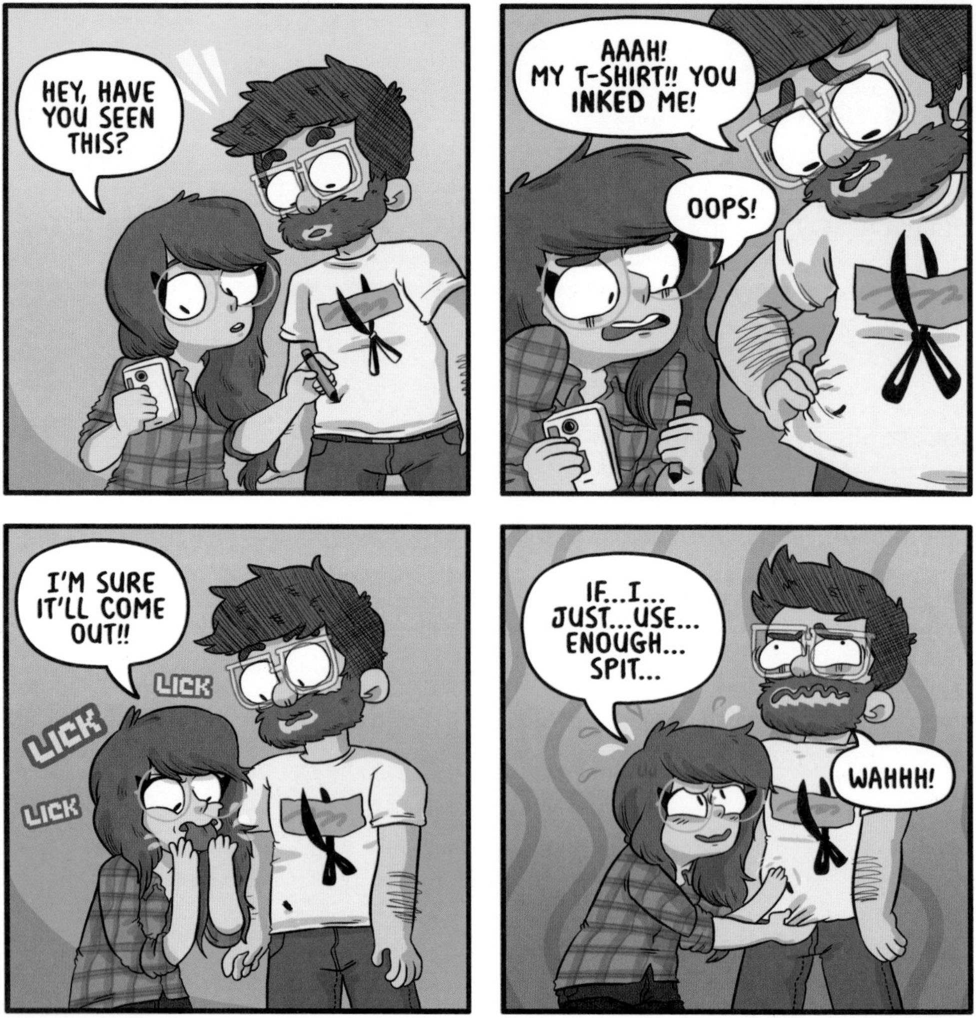
HEY, HAVE YOU SEEN THIS?
AAAH! MY T-SHIRT!! YOU INKED ME!
OOPS!
I'M SURE IT'LL COME OUT!!
LICK
LICK
LICK
IF...I... JUST...USE... ENOUGH... SPIT...
WAHHH!

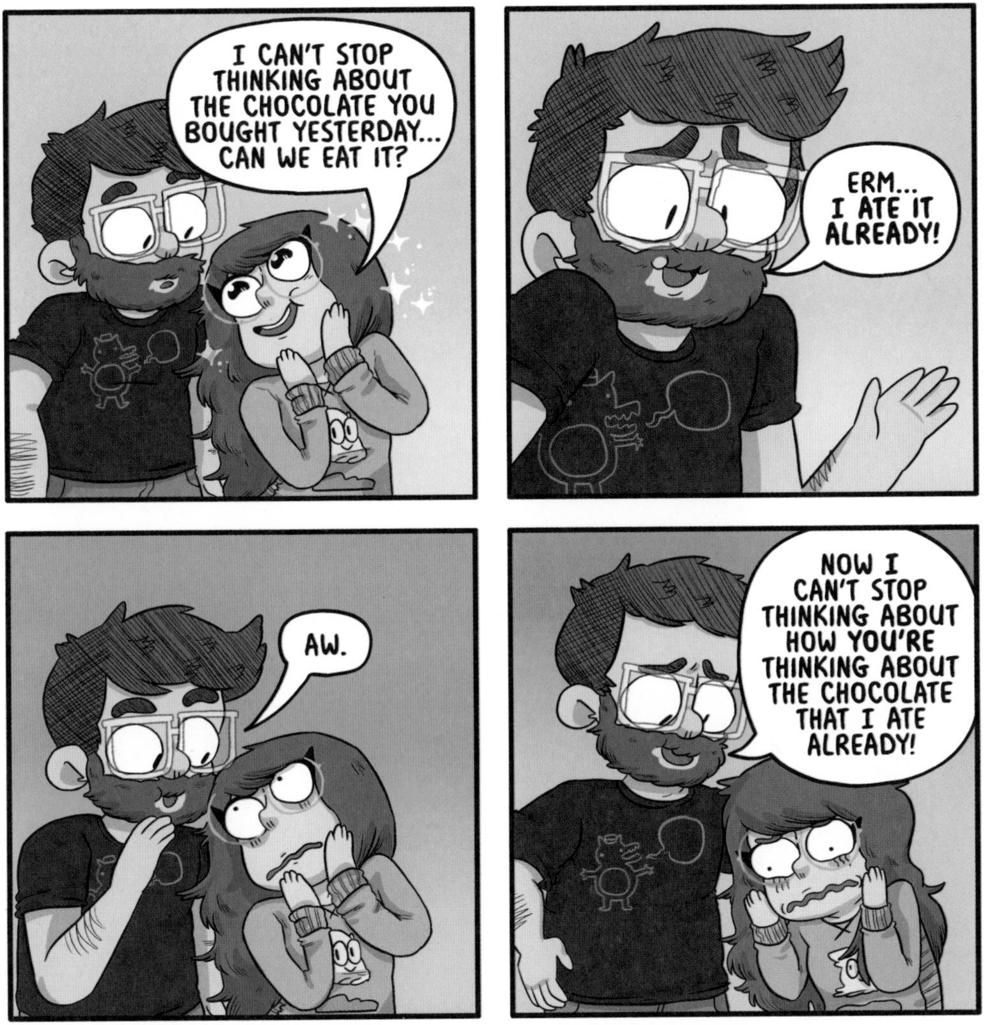
I CAN'T STOP THINKING ABOUT THE CHOCOLATE YOU BOUGHT YESTERDAY... CAN WE EAT IT?
ERM... I ATE IT ALREADY!
AW.
NOW I CAN'T STOP THINKING ABOUT HOW YOU'RE THINKING ABOUT THE CHOCOLATE THAT I ATE ALREADY!

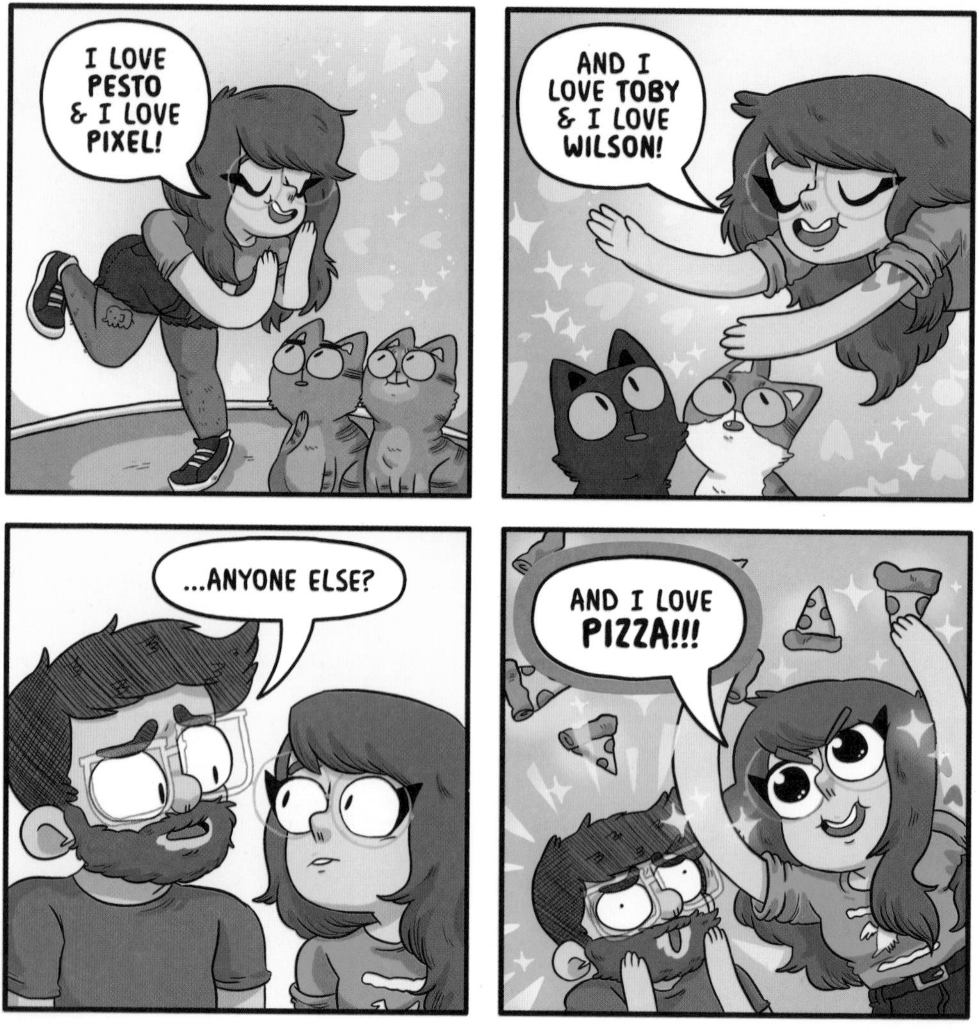
I LOVE PESTO & I LOVE PIXEL!
AND I LOVE TOBY & I LOVE WILSON!
...ANYONE ELSE?
AND I LOVE PIZZA!!!

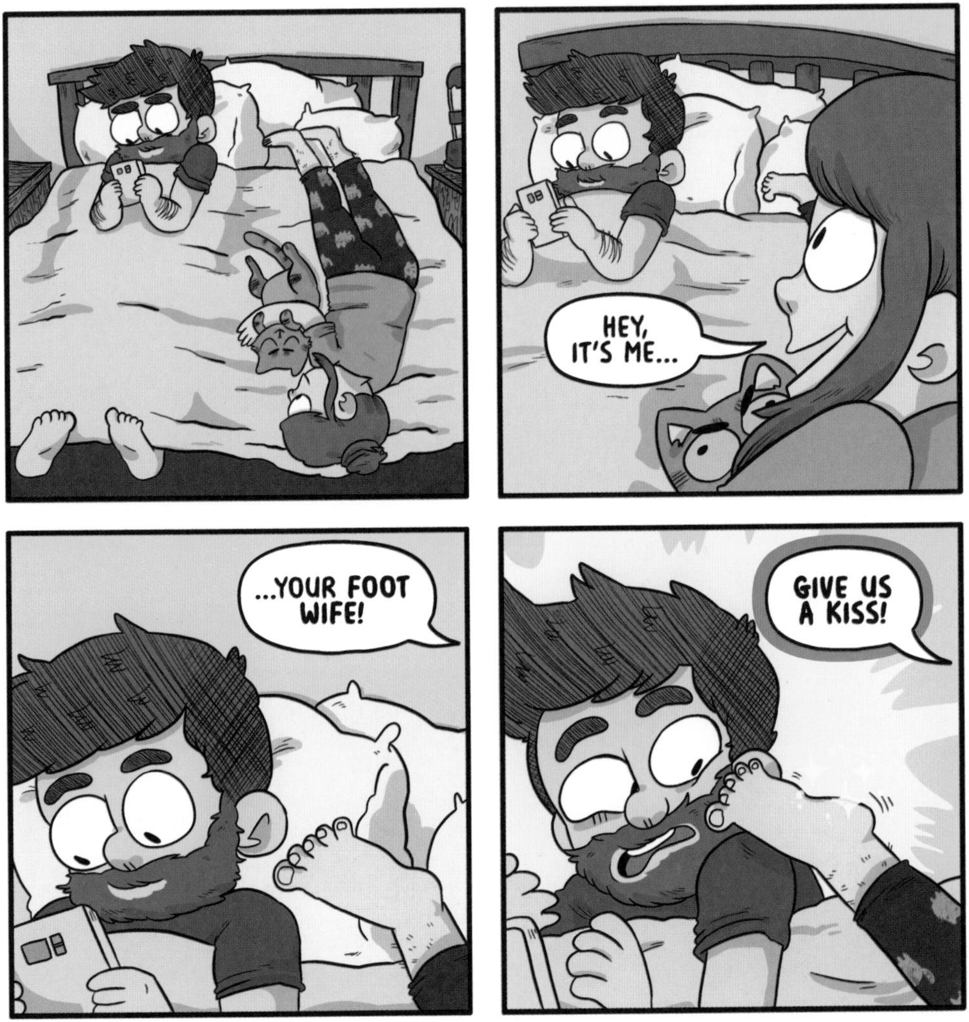
HEY, IT'S ME...
...YOUR FOOT WIFE!
GIVE US A KISS!

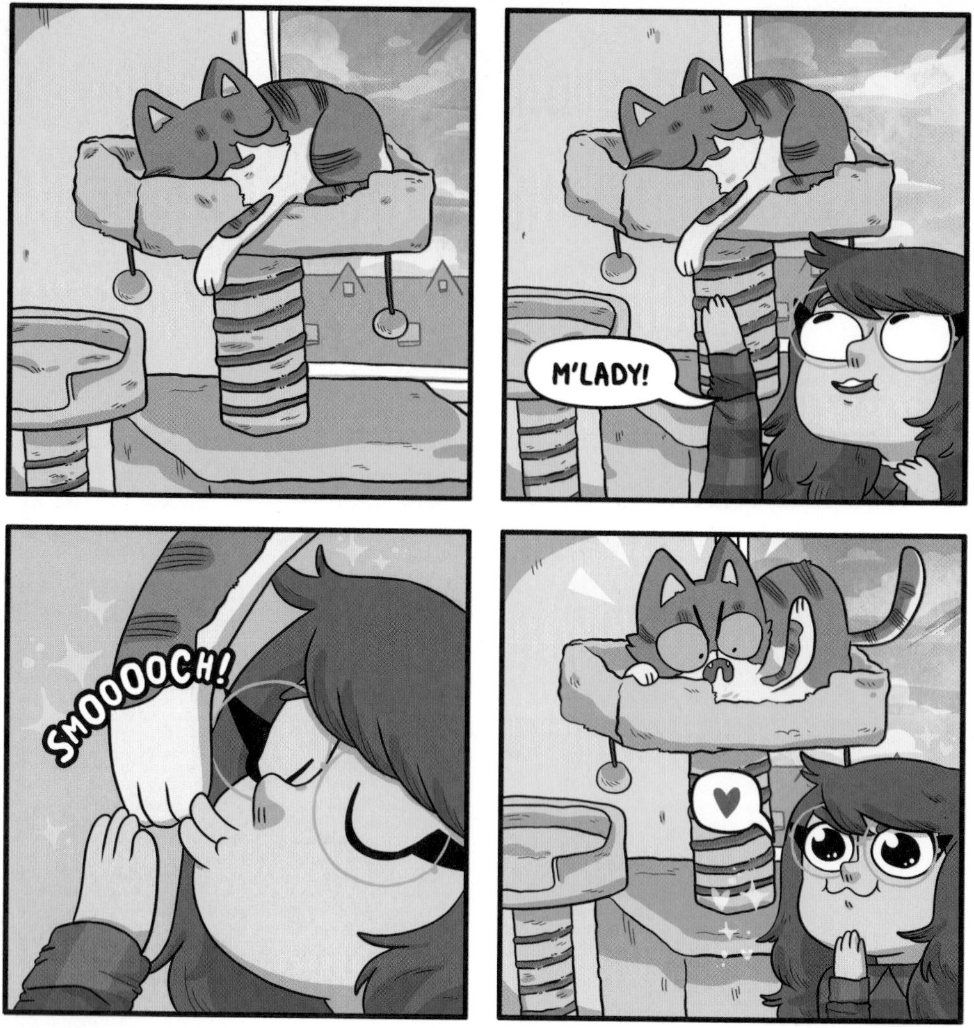
M'LADY!
SMOOOOCH!

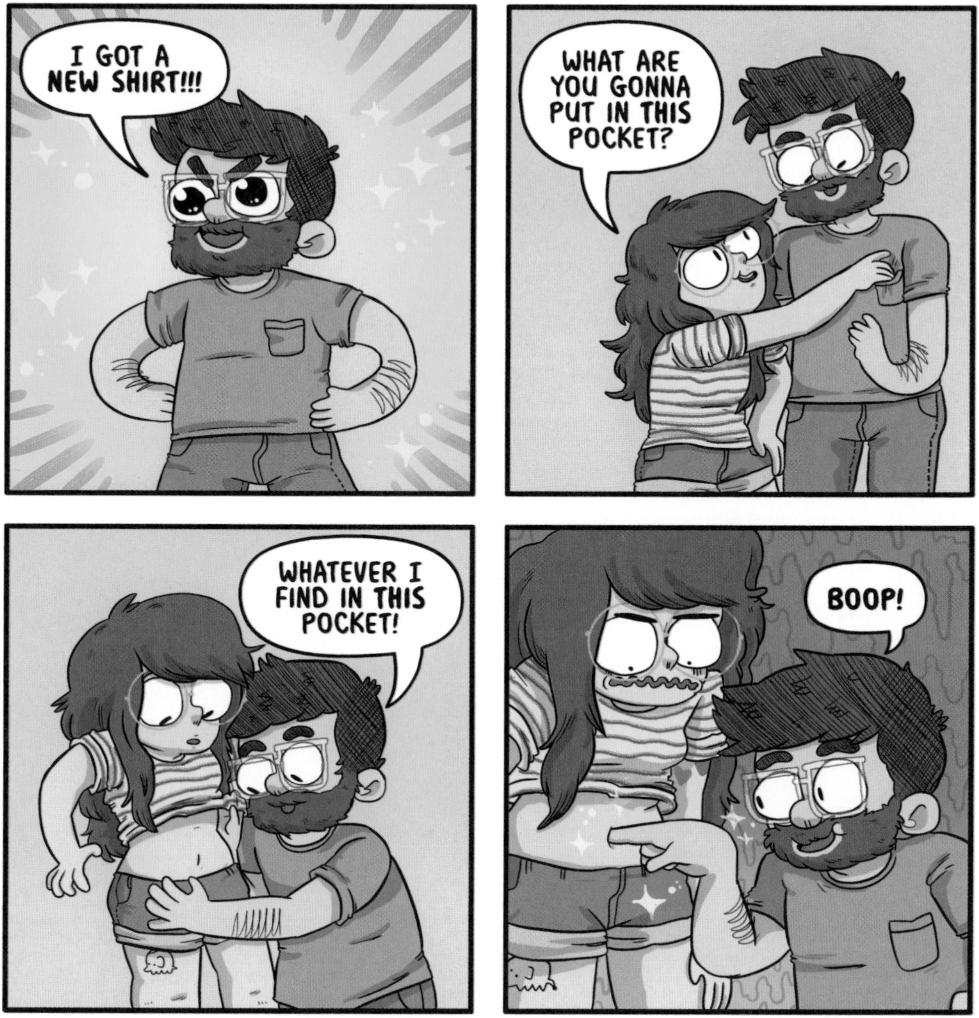
I GOT A NEW SHIRT!!!
WHAT ARE YOU GONNA PUT IN THIS POCKET?
WHATEVER I FIND IN THIS POCKET!
BOOP!

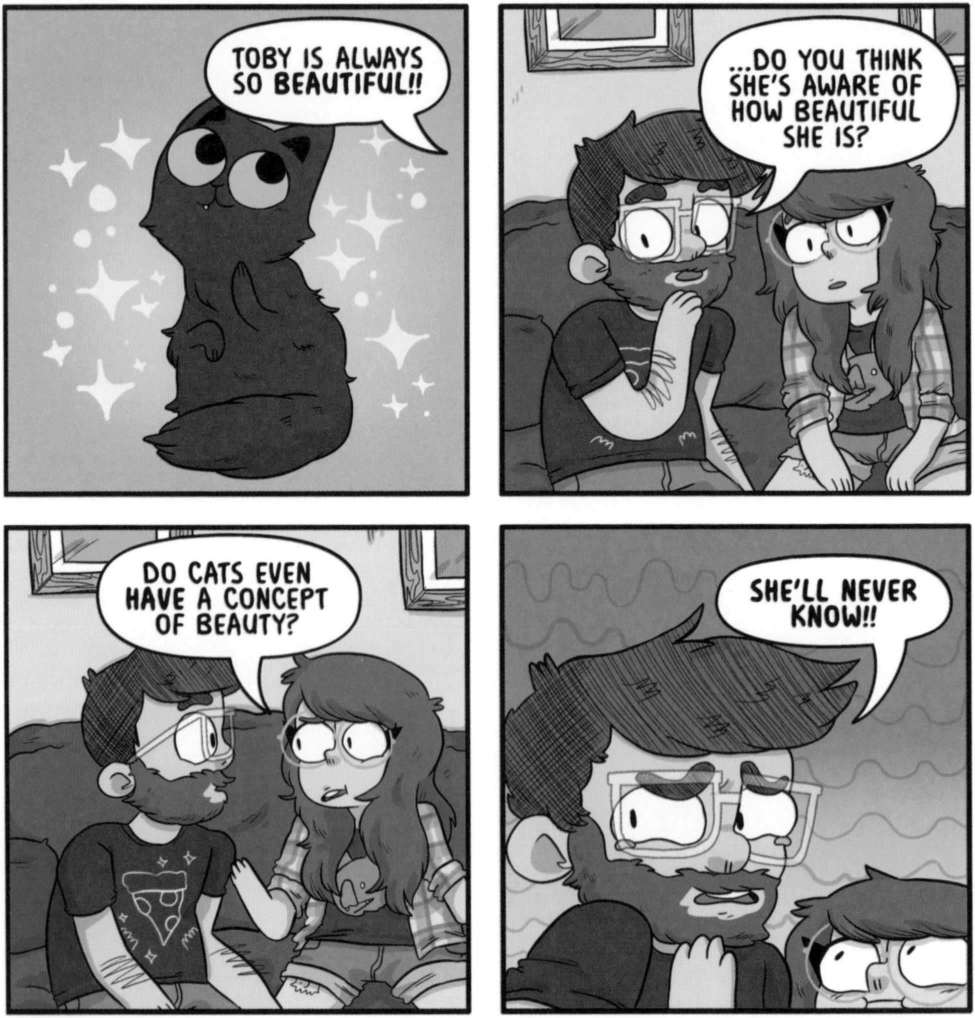
TOBY IS ALWAYS SO BEAUTIFUL!!
...DO YOU THINK SHE'S AWARE OF HOW BEAUTIFUL SHE IS?
DO CATS EVEN HAVE A CONCEPT OF BEAUTY?
SHE'LL NEVER KNOW!!

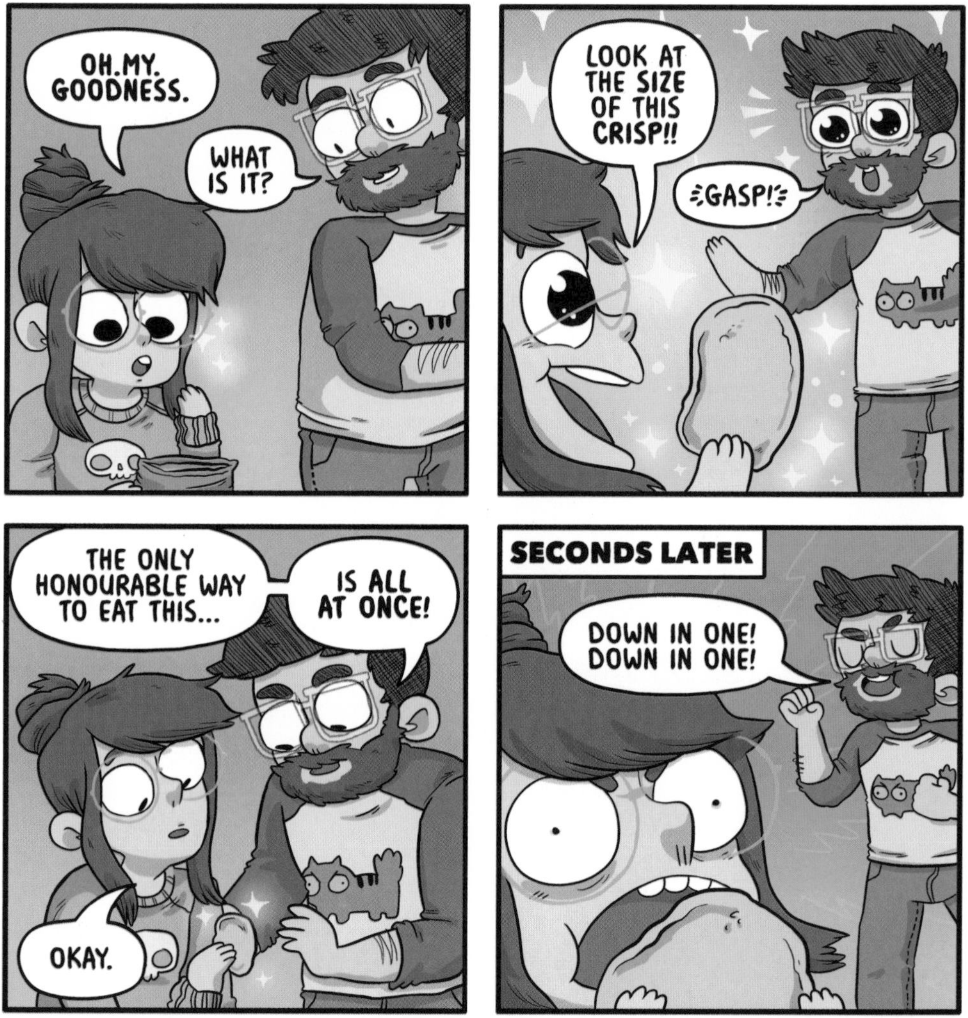
OH. MY. GOODNESS.
WHAT IS IT?
LOOK AT THE SIZE OF THIS CRISP!!
GASP!
THE ONLY HONOURABLE WAY TO EAT THIS...
IS ALL AT ONCE!
OKAY.
SECONDS LATER
DOWN IN ONE! DOWN IN ONE!

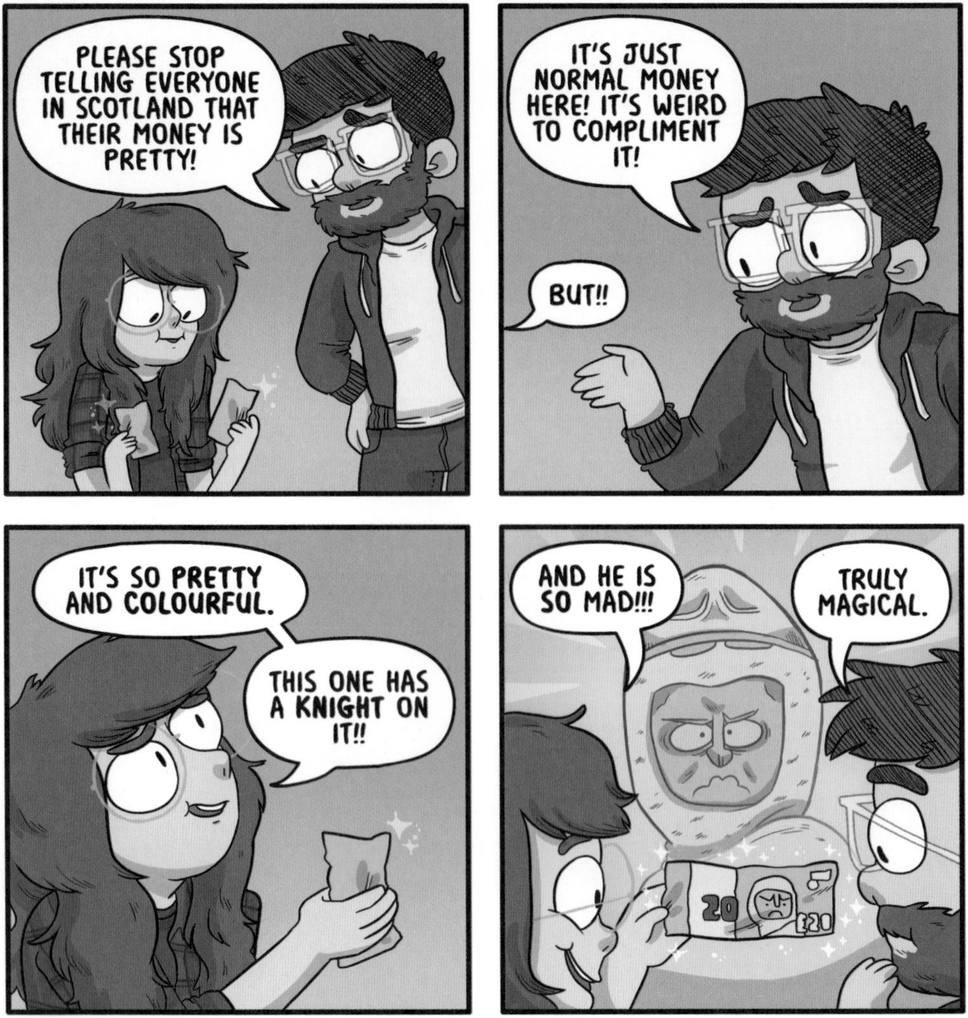
PLEASE STOP TELLING EVERYONE IN SCOTLAND THAT THEIR MONEY IS PRETTY!
IT'S JUST NORMAL MONEY HERE! IT'S WEIRD TO COMPLIMENT IT!
BUT!!
IT'S SO PRETTY AND COLOURFUL.
THIS ONE HAS A KNIGHT ON IT!!
AND HE IS SO MAD!!!
TRULY MAGICAL.
20
£20

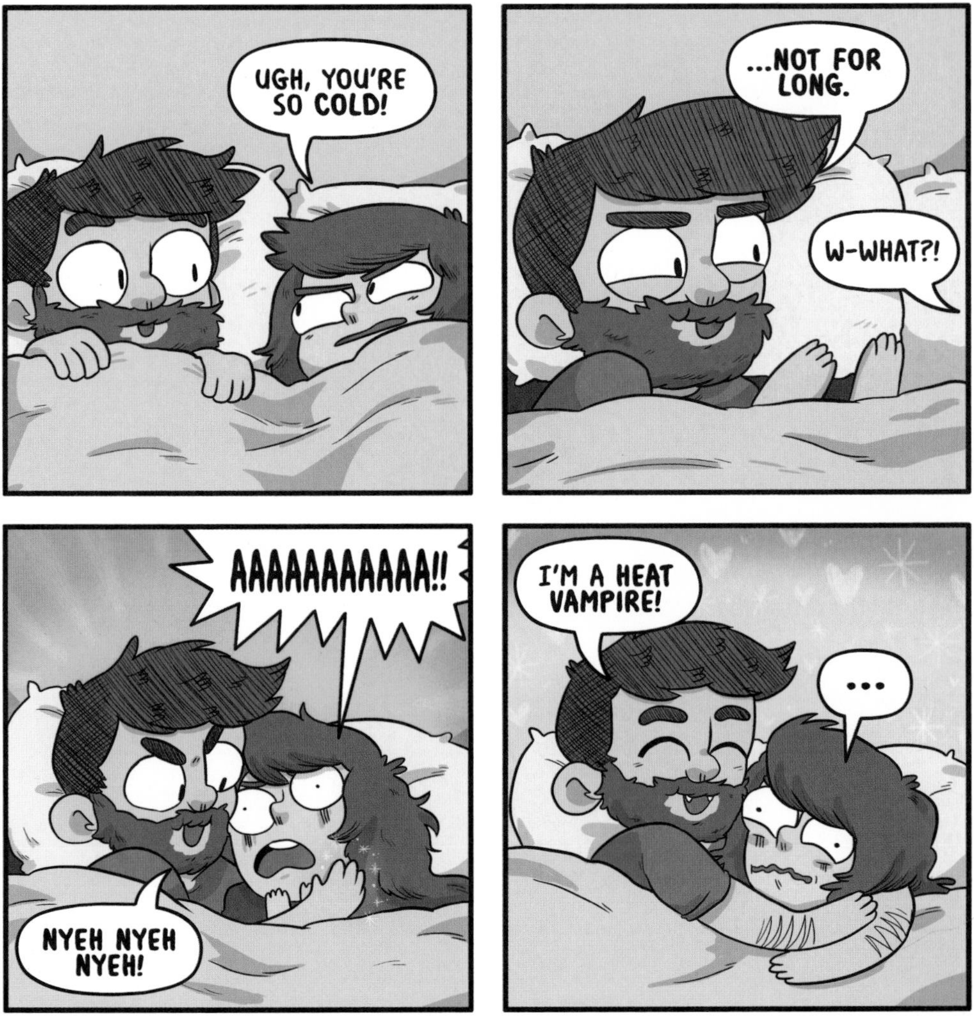
UGH, YOU'RE SO COLD!
...NOT FOR LONG.
W-WHAT?!
AAAAAAAAAAA!!
NYEH NYEH NYEH!
I'M A HEAT VAMPIRE!
...

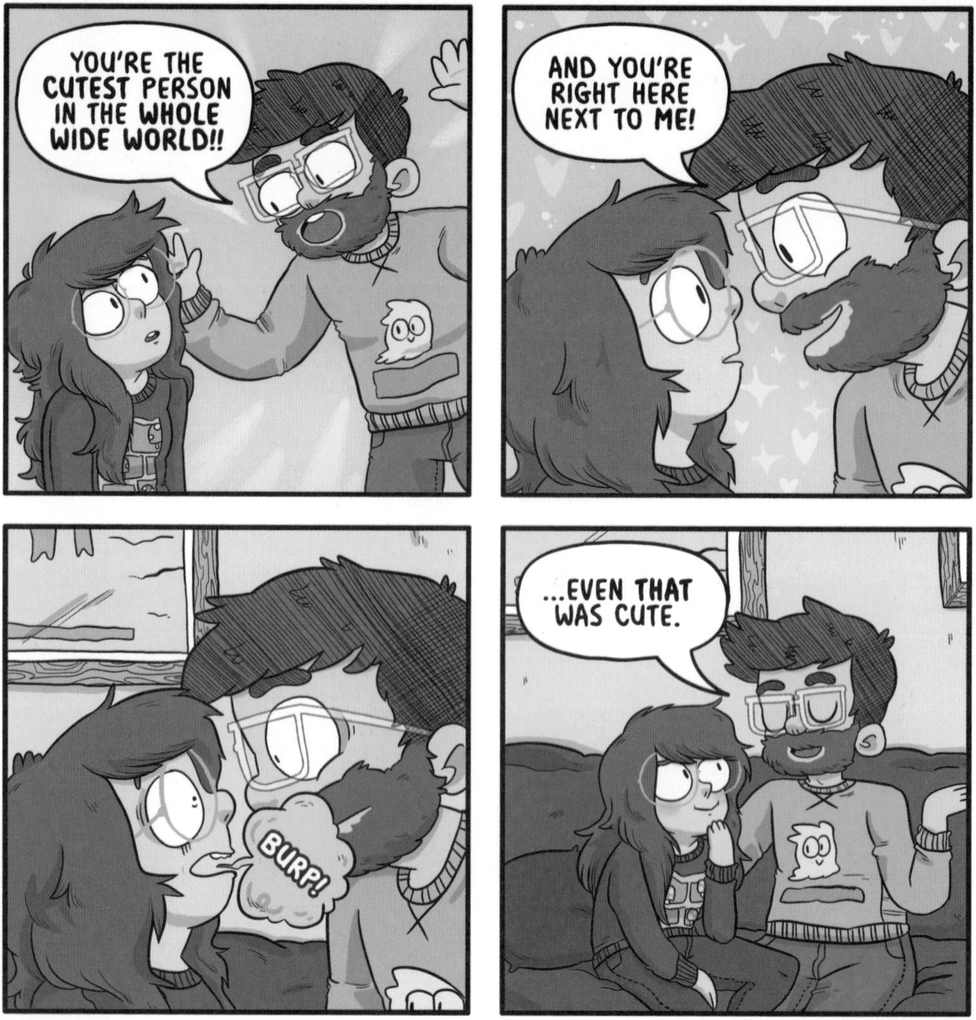
YOU'RE THE CUTEST PERSON IN THE WHOLE WIDE WORLD!!
AND YOU'RE RIGHT HERE NEXT TO ME!
BURP!
...EVEN THAT WAS CUTE.

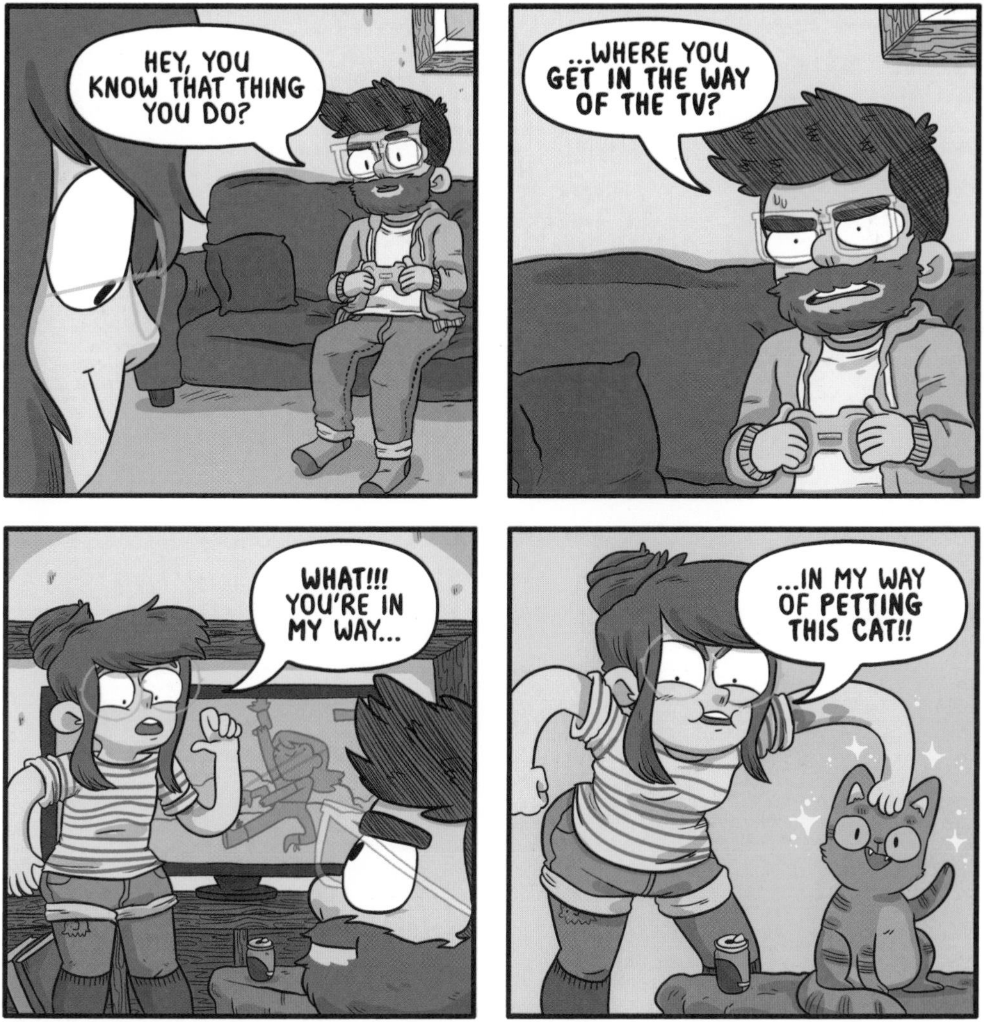
HEY, YOU KNOW THAT THING YOU DO?
...WHERE YOU GET IN THE WAY OF THE TV?
WHAT!!! YOU'RE IN MY WAY...
...IN MY WAY OF PETTING THIS CAT!!

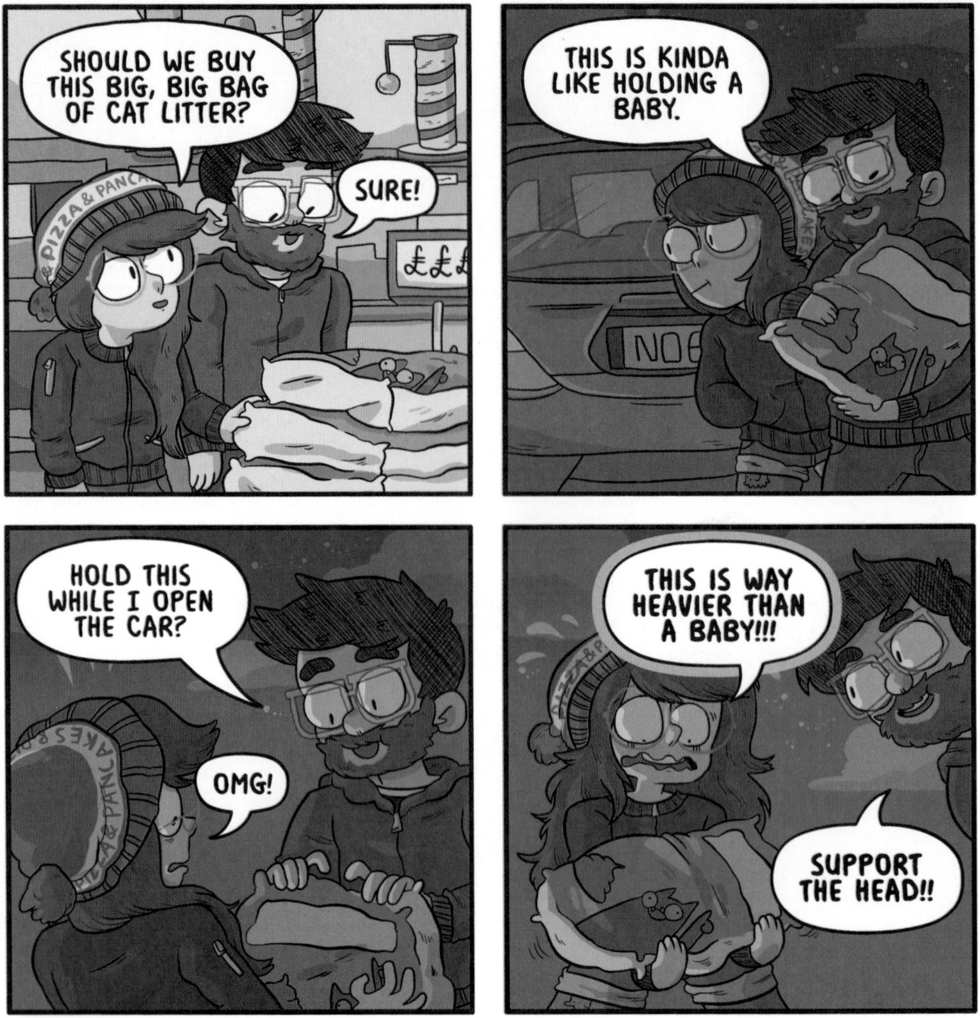
SHOULD WE BUY THIS BIG, BIG BAG OF CAT LITTER?
SURE!
THIS IS KINDA LIKE HOLDING A BABY.
HOLD THIS WHILE I OPEN THE CAR?
OMG!
THIS IS WAY HEAVIER THAN A BABY!!!
SUPPORT THE HEAD!!

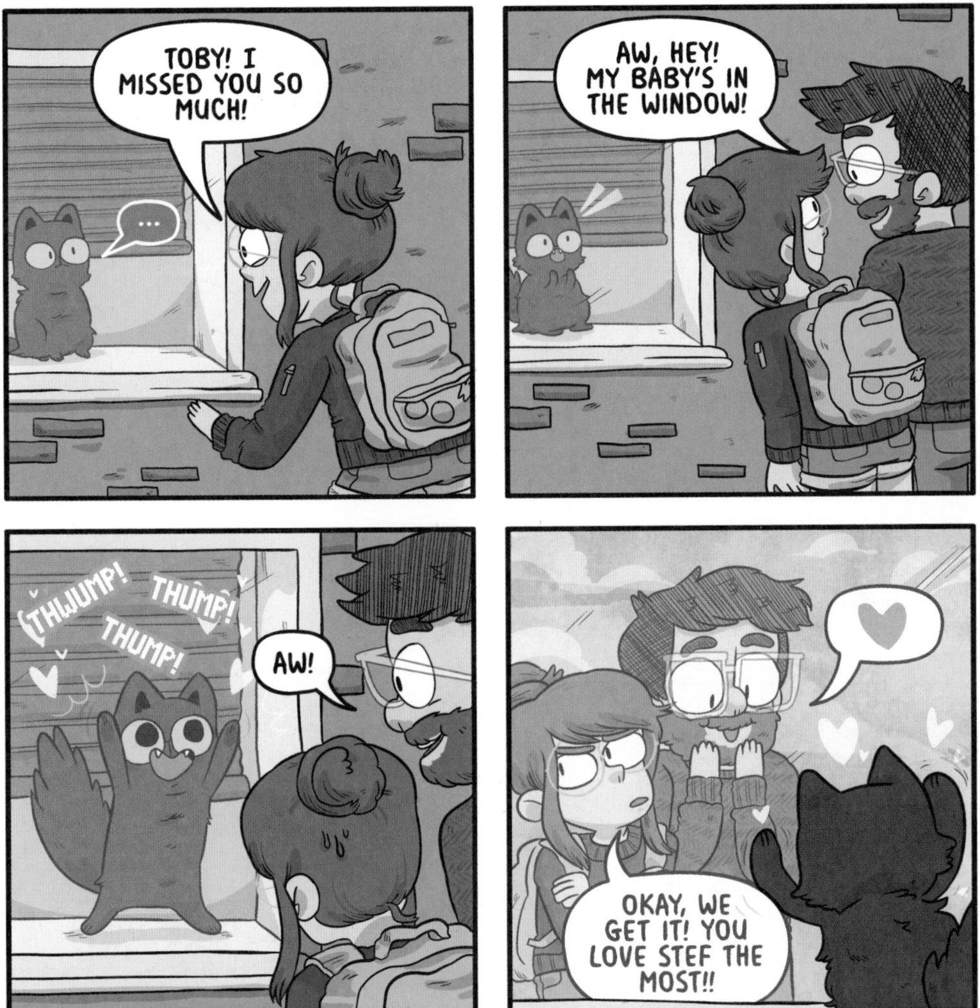
TOBY! I MISSED YOU SO MUCH!
...
AW, HEY! MY BABY'S IN THE WINDOW!
THWUMP!
THUMP!
THUMP!
AW!
OKAY, WE GET IT! YOU LOVE STEF THE MOST!!

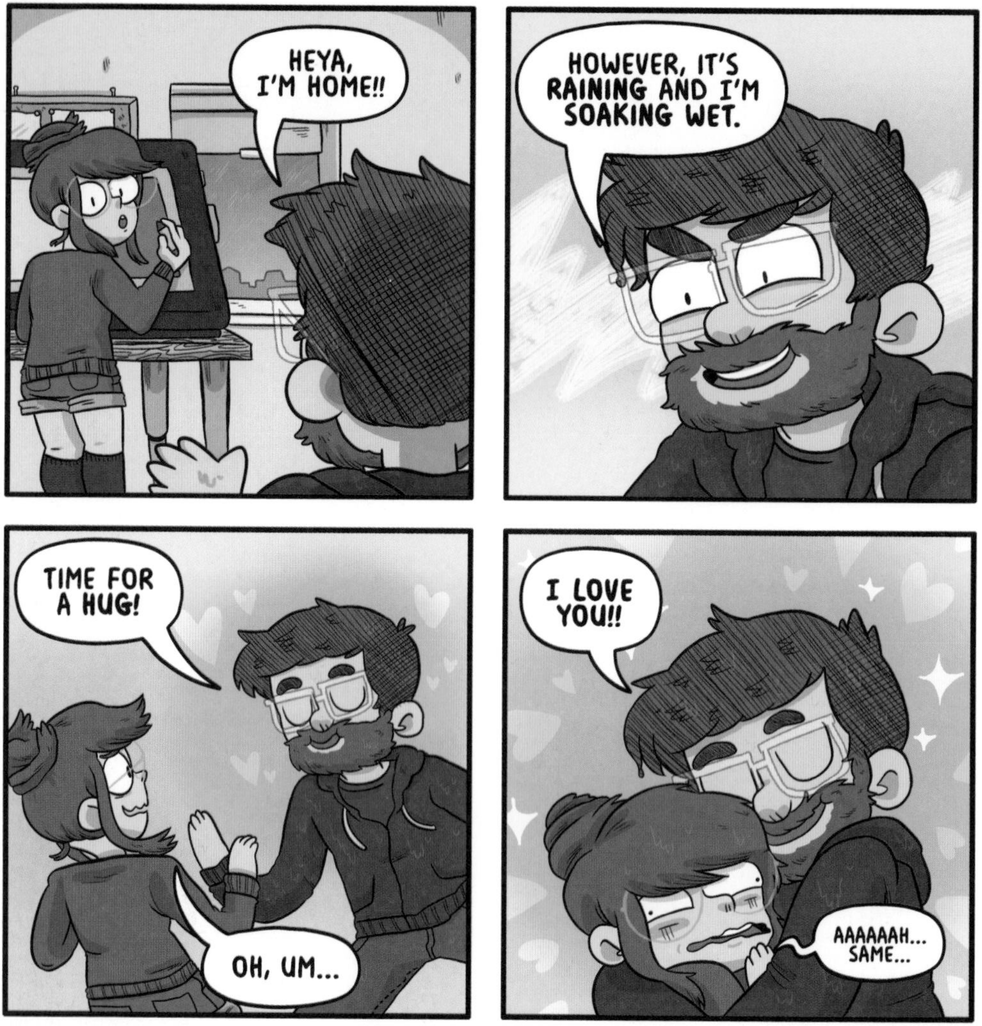
HEYA, I'M HOME!!
HOWEVER, IT'S RAINING AND I'M SOAKING WET.
TIME FOR A HUG!
OH, UM...
I LOVE YOU!!
AAAAAAH... SAME...

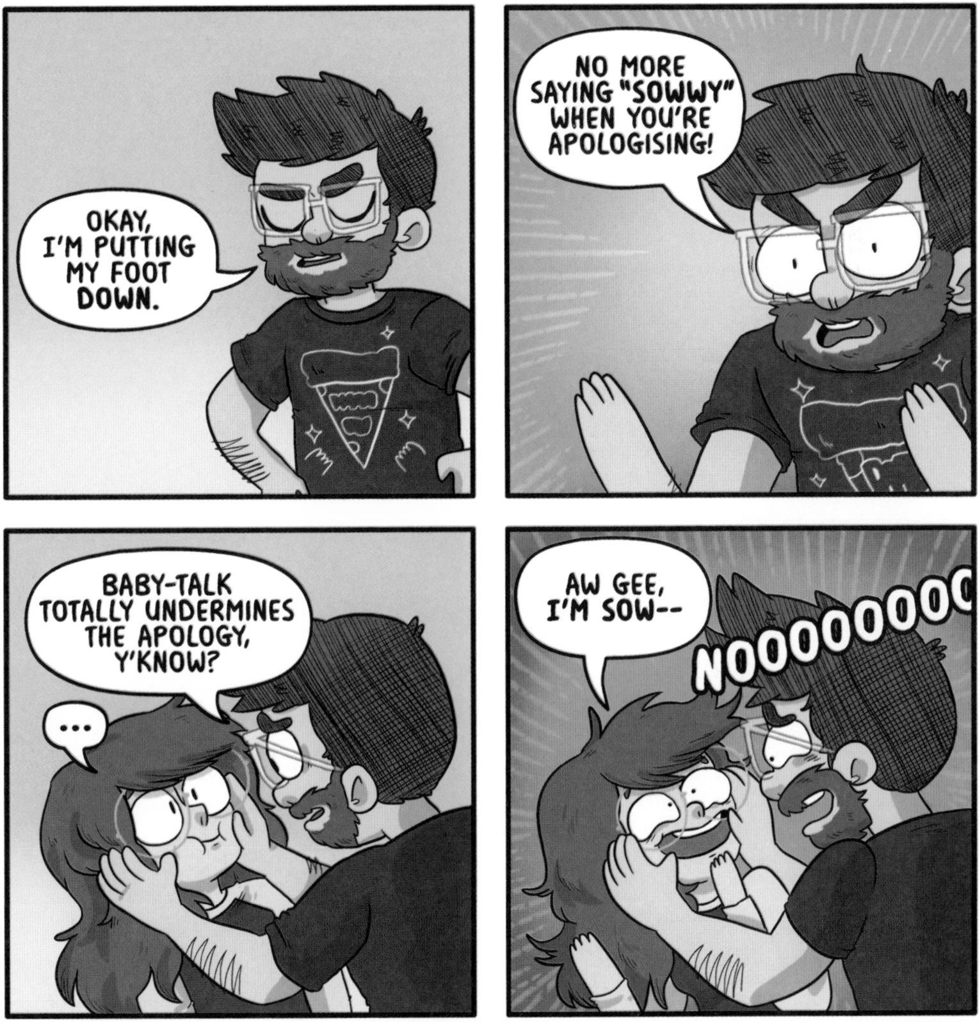
OKAY, I'M PUTTING MY FOOT DOWN.
NO MORE SAYING "SOWWY" WHEN YOU'RE APOLOGISING!
BABY-TALK TOTALLY UNDERMINES THE APOLOGY, Y'KNOW?
...
AW GEE, I'M SOW--
NOOOOOOOOO

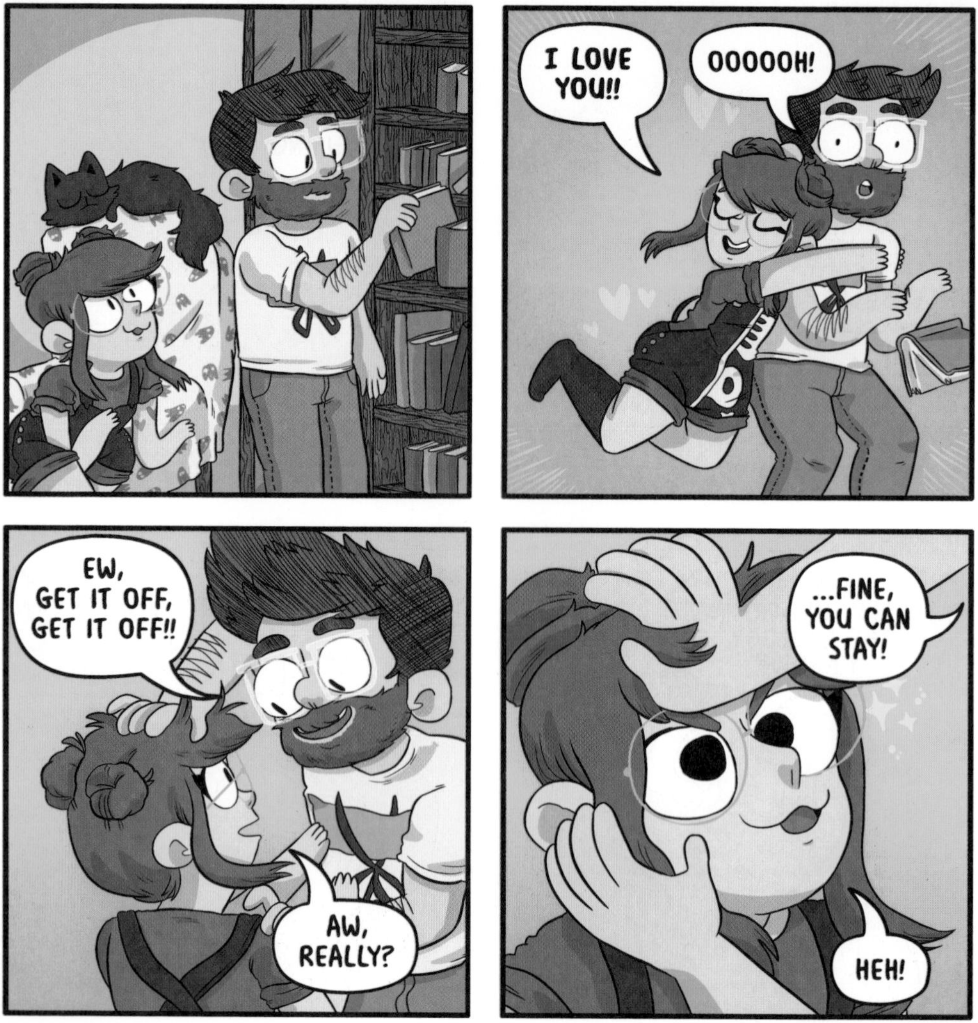
I LOVE YOU!!
OOOOOH!
EW, GET IT OFF, GET IT OFF!!
AW, REALLY?
...FINE, YOU CAN STAY!
HEH!

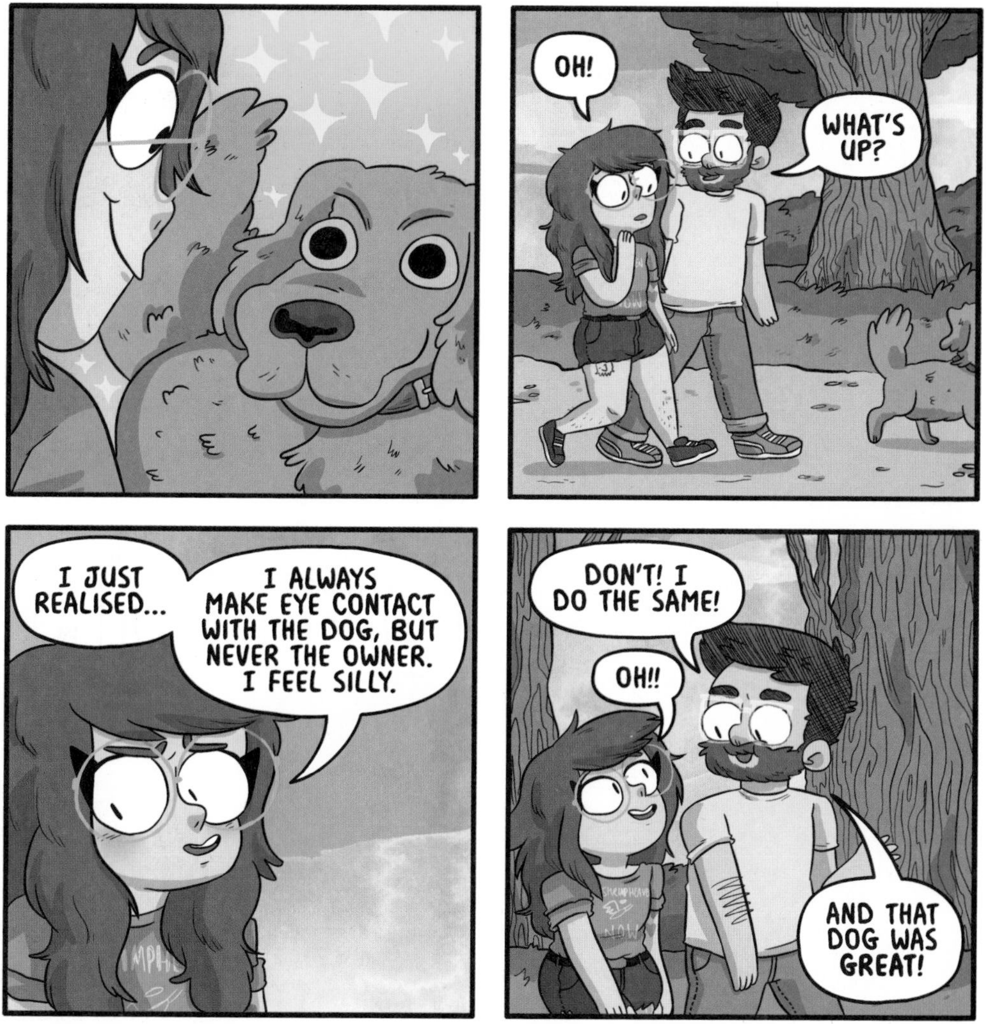
OH!
WHAT'S UP?
I JUST REALISED...
I ALWAYS MAKE EYE CONTACT WITH THE DOG, BUT NEVER THE OWNER. I FEEL SILLY.
DON'T! I DO THE SAME!
OH!!
AND THAT DOG WAS GREAT!

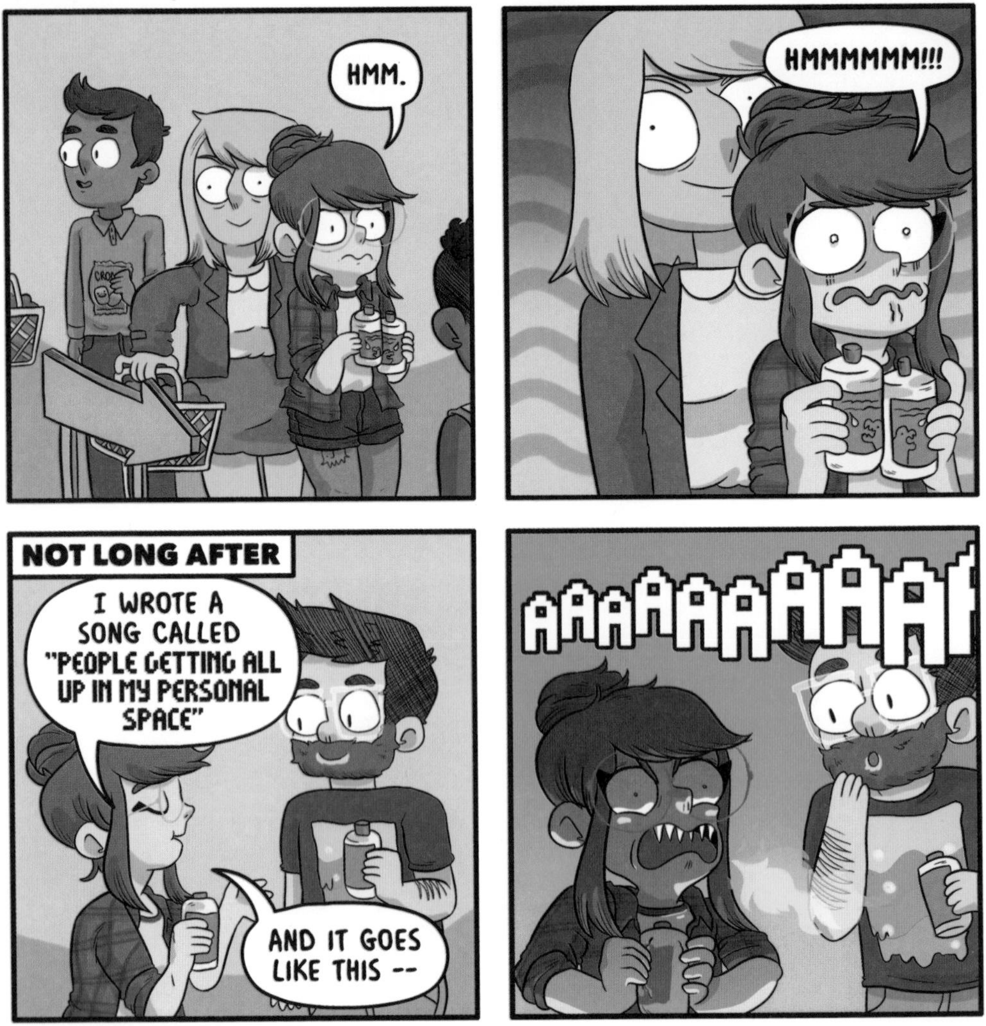
HMM.
HMMMMMM!!!
NOT LONG AFTER
I WROTE A SONG CALLED "PEOPLE GETTING ALL UP IN MY PERSONAL SPACE"
AND IT GOES LIKE THIS --
AAAAAAAAAA

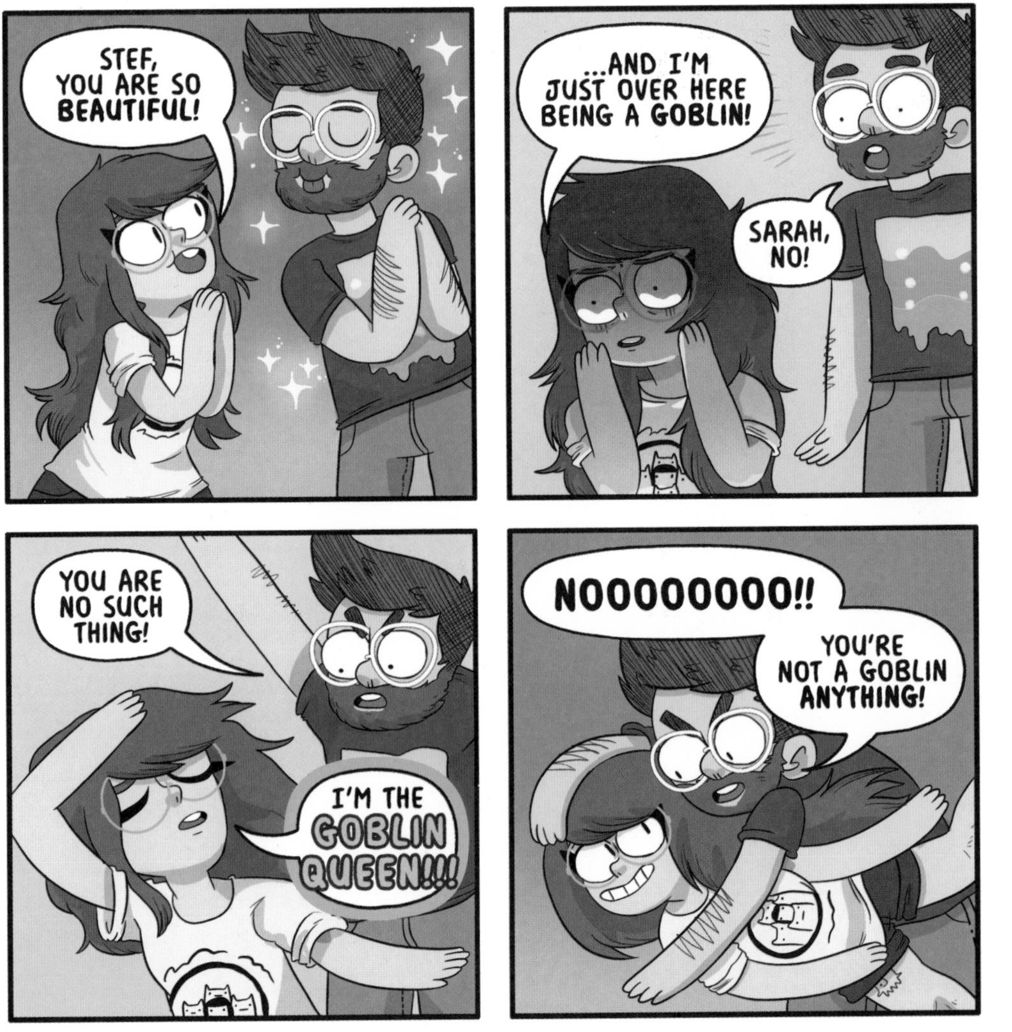
STEF, YOU ARE SO BEAUTIFUL!
...AND I'M JUST OVER HERE BEING A GOBLIN!
SARAH, NO!
YOU ARE NO SUCH THING!
I'M THE GOBLIN QUEEN!!!
NOOOOOOOO!!
YOU'RE NOT A GOBLIN ANYTHING!

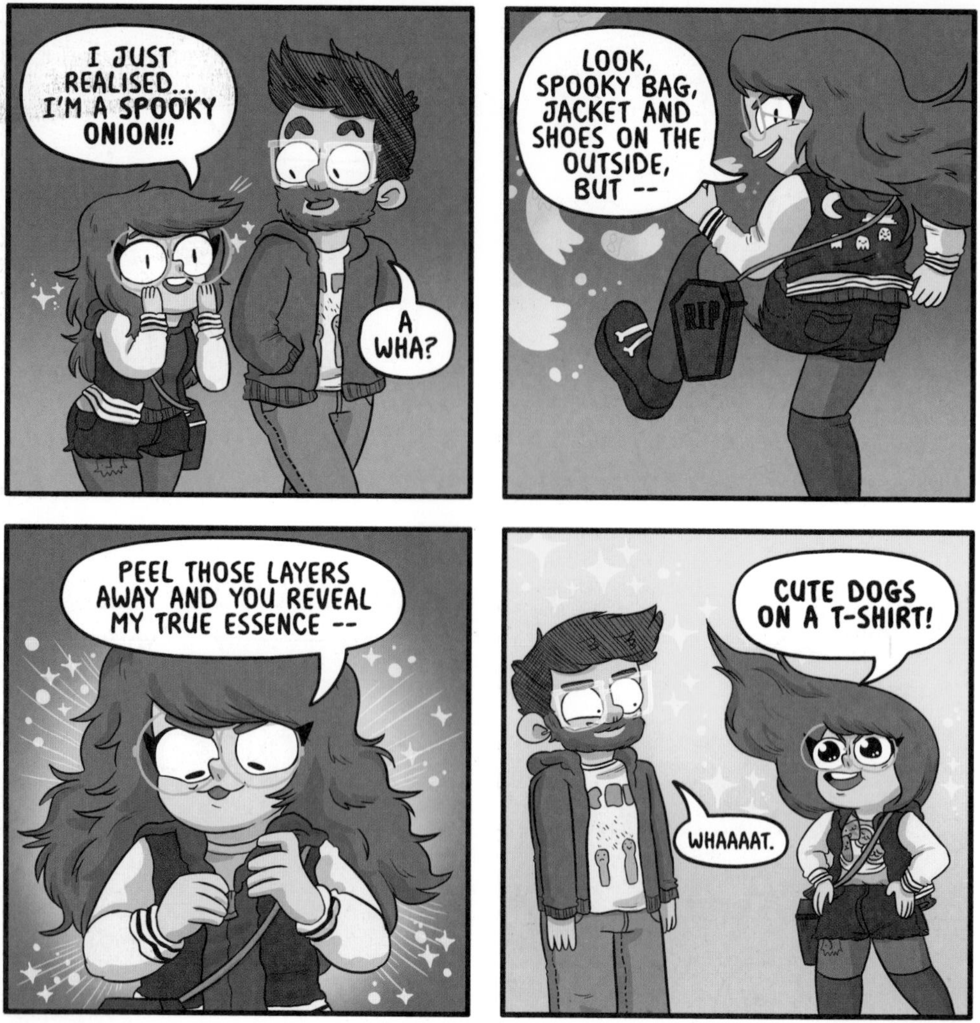
I JUST REALISED... I'M A SPOOKY ONION!!
A WHA?
LOOK, SPOOKY BAG, JACKET AND SHOES ON THE OUTSIDE, BUT --
RIP
PEEL THOSE LAYERS AWAY AND YOU REVEAL MY TRUE ESSENCE --
CUTE DOGS ON A T-SHIRT!
WHAAAAT.

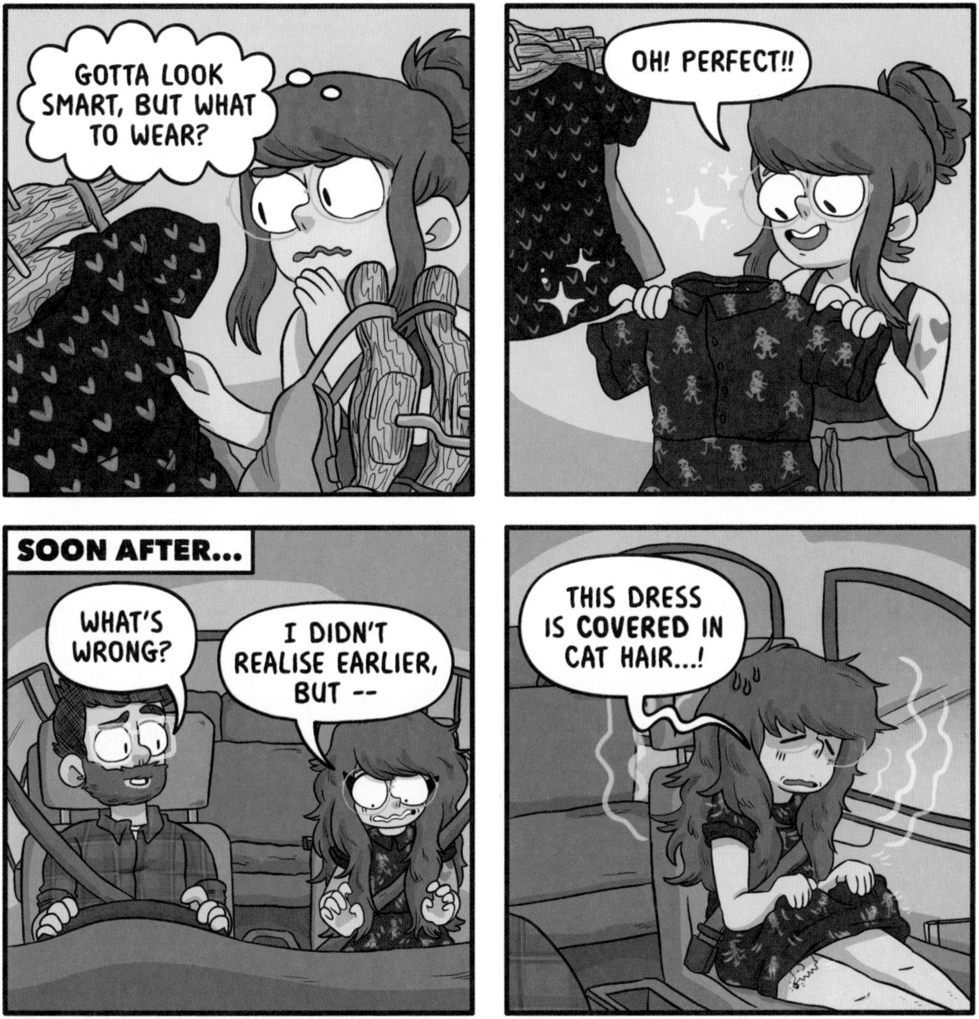
GOTTA LOOK SMART, BUT WHAT TO WEAR?
OH! PERFECT!!
SOON AFTER...
WHAT'S WRONG?
I DIDN'T REALISE EARLIER, BUT --
THIS DRESS IS COVERED IN CAT HAIR...!

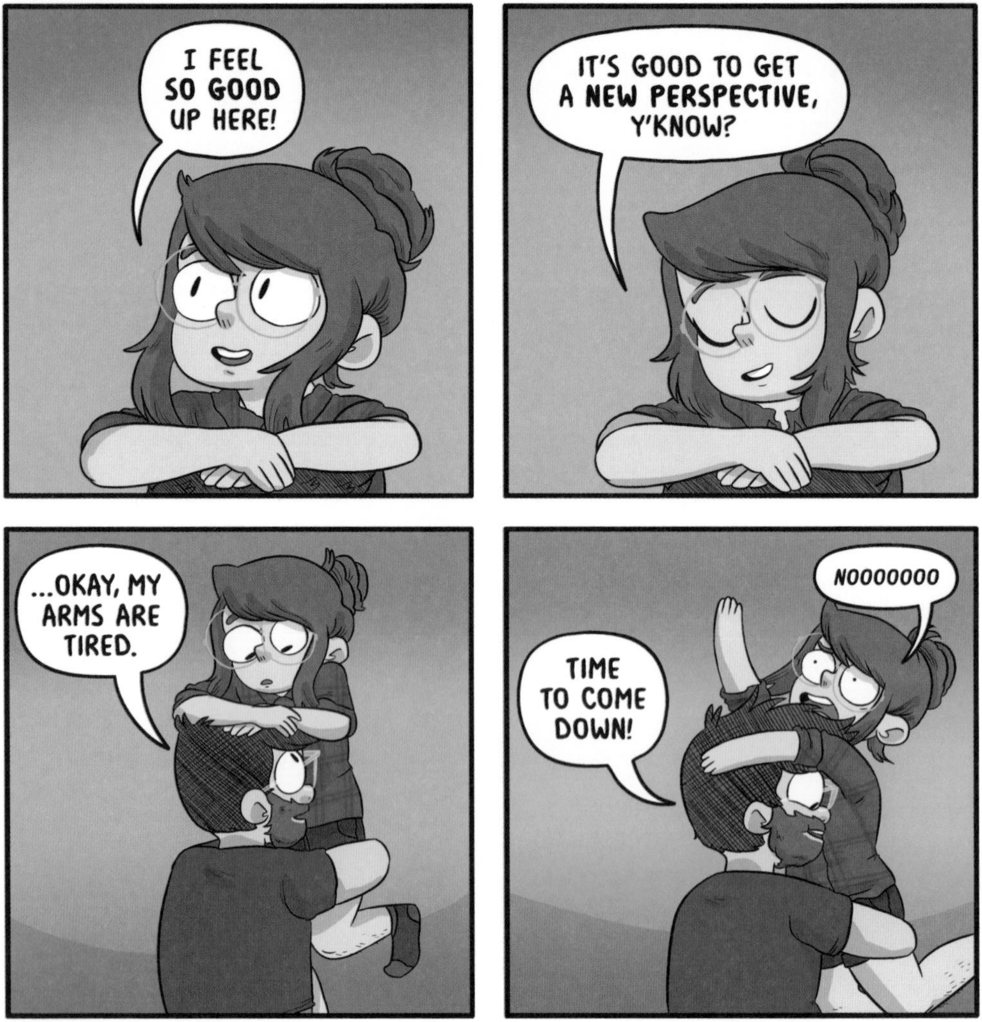
I FEEL SO GOOD UP HERE!
IT'S GOOD TO GET A NEW PERSPECTIVE, Y'KNOW?
...OKAY, MY ARMS ARE TIRED.
NOOOOOOO
TIME TO COME DOWN!

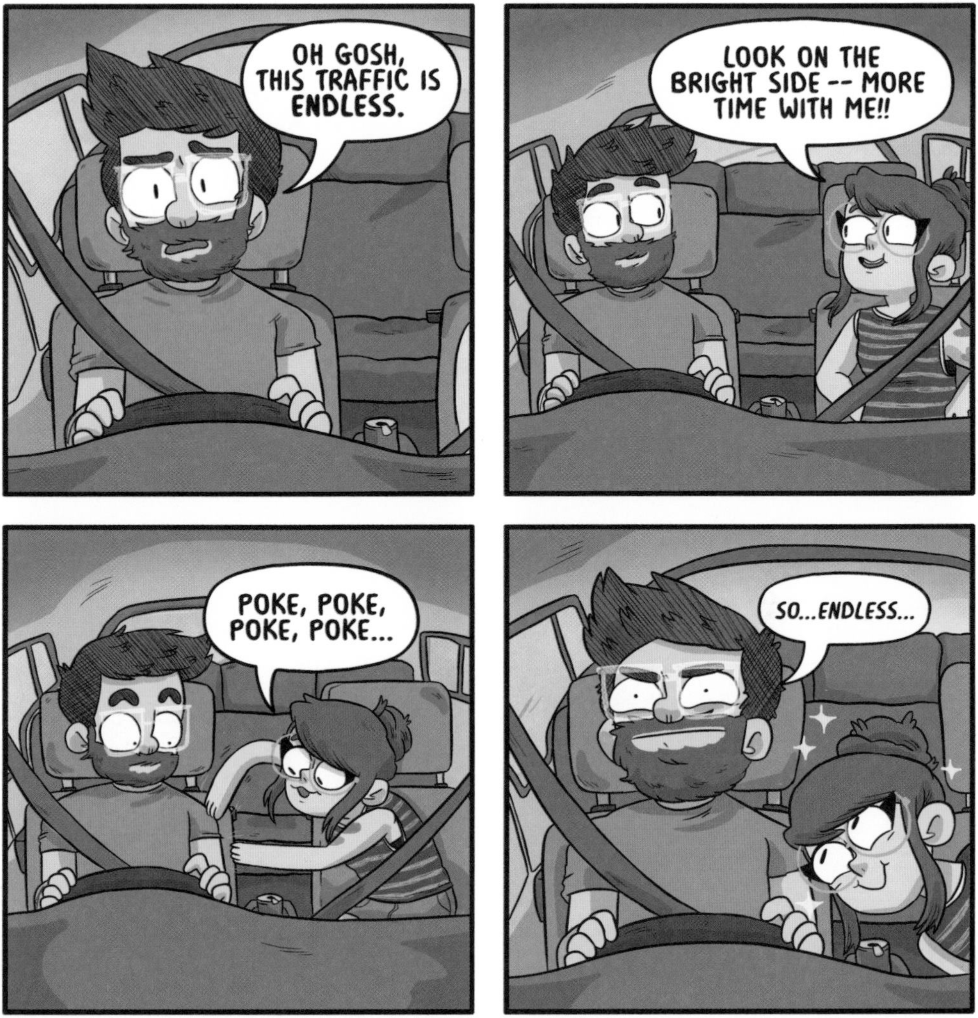
OH GOSH, THIS TRAFFIC IS ENDLESS.
LOOK ON THE BRIGHT SIDE -- MORE TIME WITH ME!!
POKE, POKE, POKE, POKE...
SO...ENDLESS...

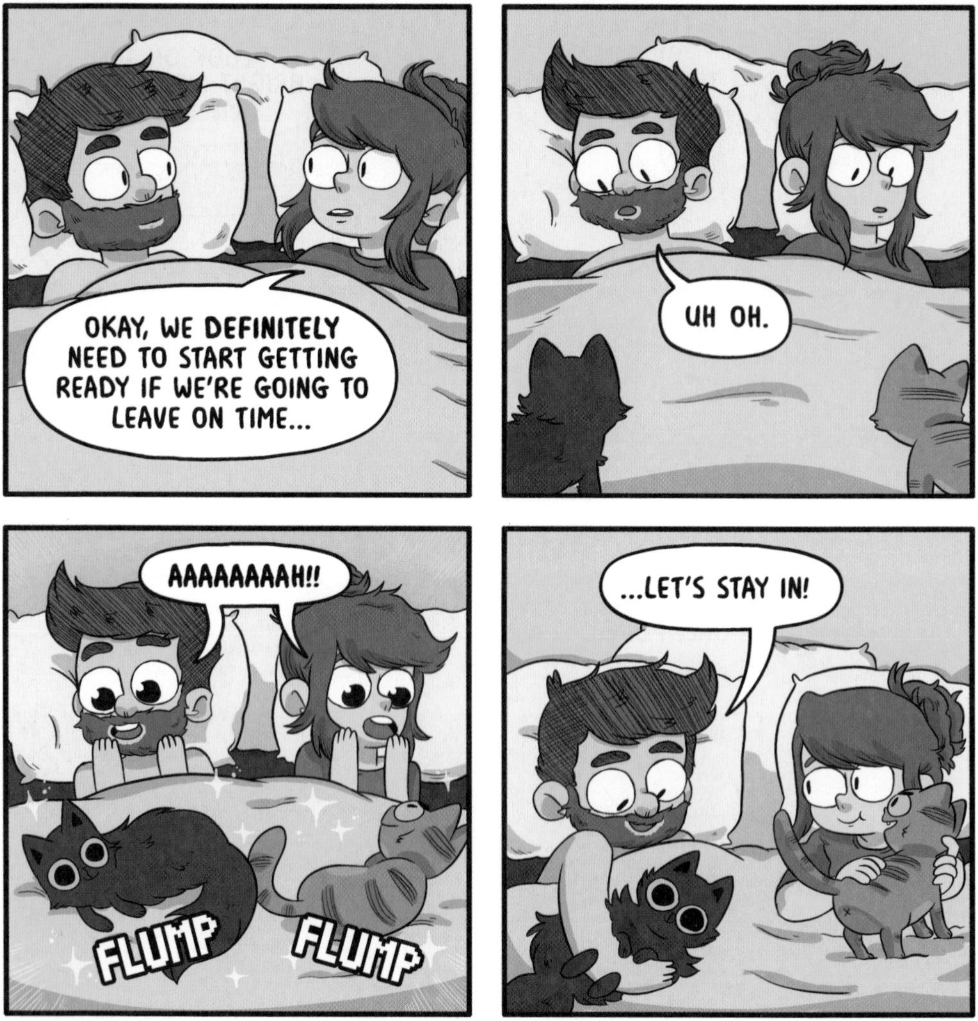
OKAY, WE DEFINITELY NEED TO START GETTING READY IF WE'RE GOING TO LEAVE ON TIME...
UH OH.
AAAAAAAAH!!
FLUMP
FLUMP
...LET'S STAY IN!

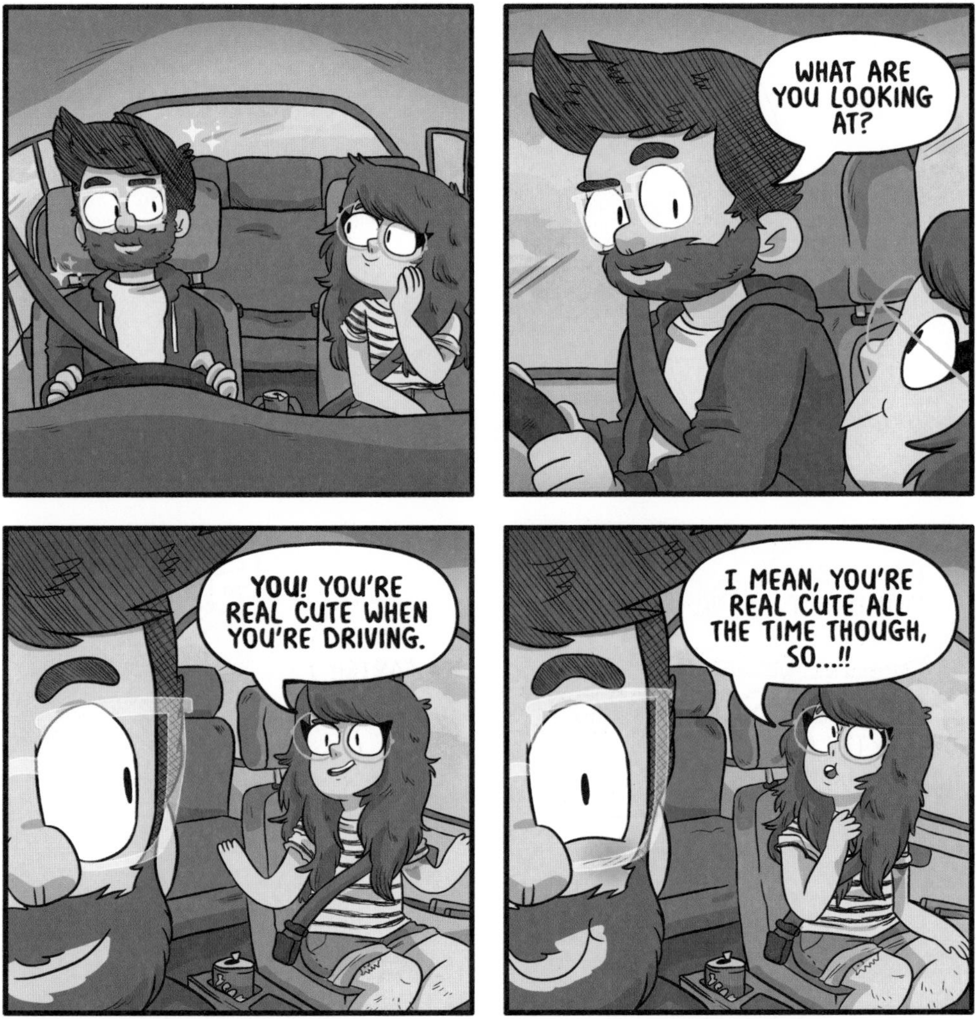
WHAT ARE YOU LOOKING AT?
YOU! YOU'RE REAL CUTE WHEN YOU'RE DRIVING.
I MEAN, YOU'RE REAL CUTE ALL THE TIME THOUGH, SO...!!

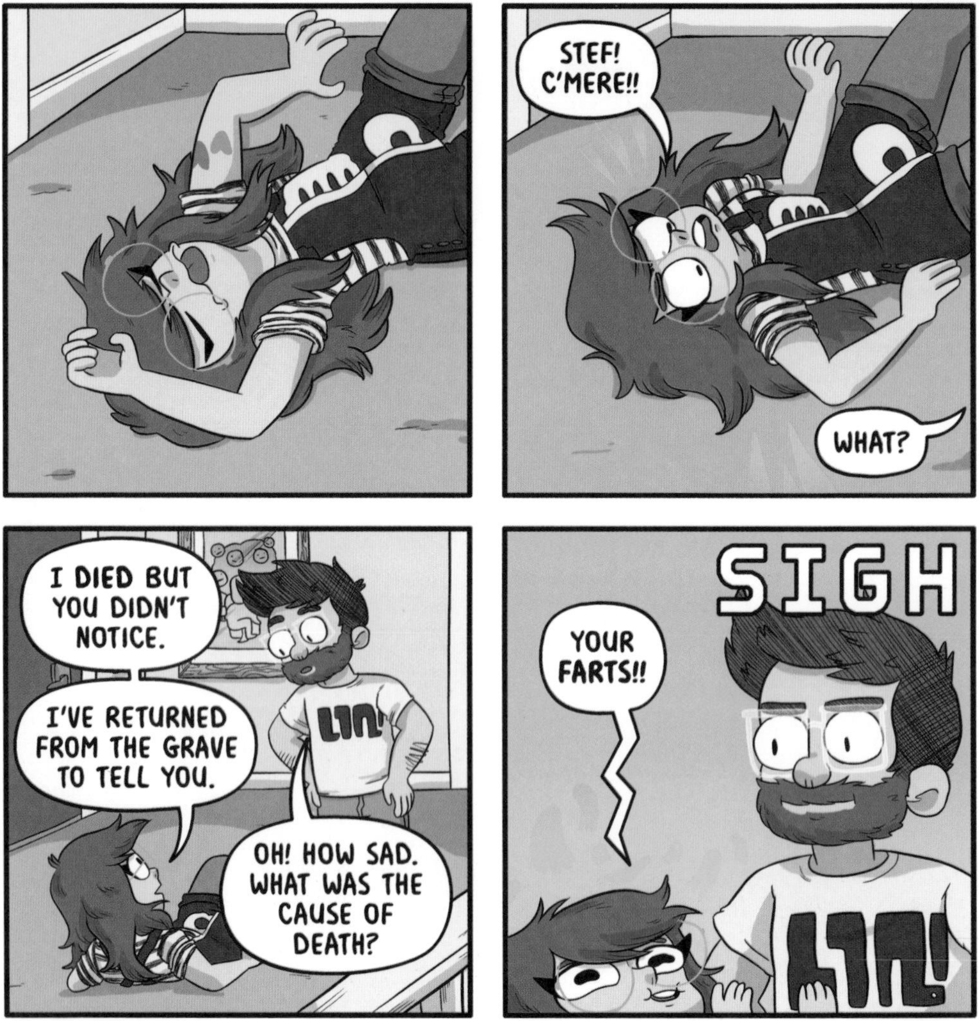
STEF!
C'MERE!!
WHAT?
I DIED BUT YOU DIDN'T NOTICE.
I'VE RETURNED FROM THE GRAVE TO TELL YOU.
OH! HOW SAD. WHAT WAS THE CAUSE OF DEATH?
SIGH
YOUR FARTS!!

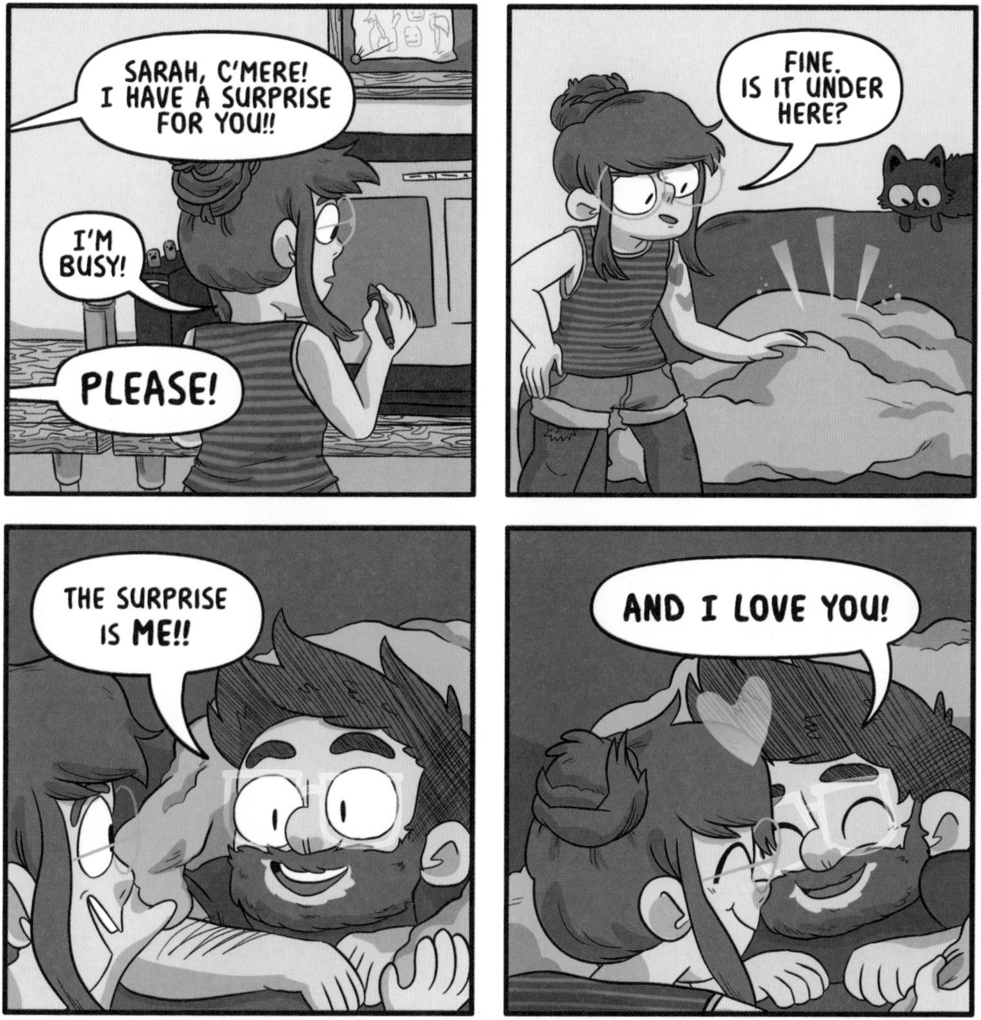
SARAH, C'MERE! I HAVE A SURPRISE FOR YOU!!
I'M BUSY!
PLEASE!
FINE. IS IT UNDER HERE?
THE SURPRISE IS **ME!!**
AND I LOVE YOU!

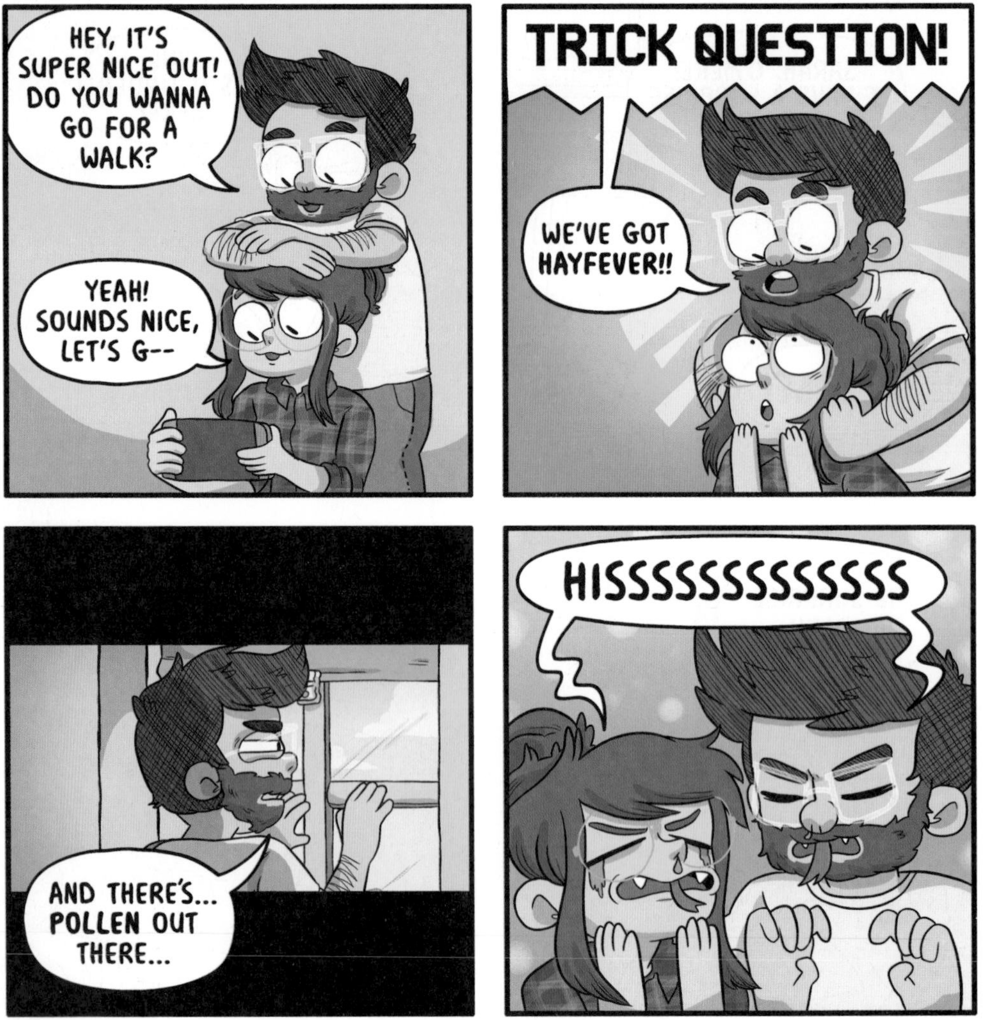
HEY, IT'S SUPER NICE OUT! DO YOU WANNA GO FOR A WALK?
YEAH! SOUNDS NICE, LET'S G--
TRICK QUESTION!
WE'VE GOT HAYFEVER!!
AND THERE'S... POLLEN OUT THERE...
HISSSSSSSSSSSSSS

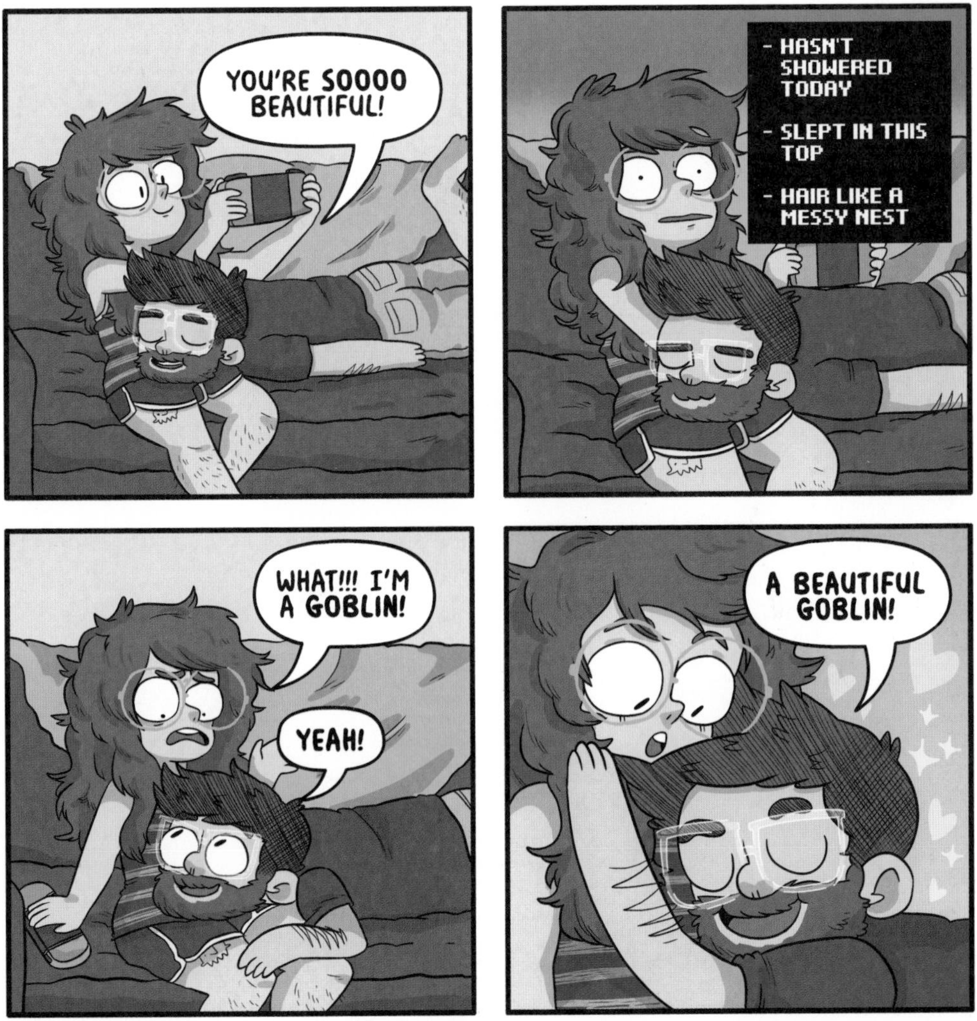
YOU'RE SOOOO BEAUTIFUL!
- HASN'T SHOWERED TODAY
- SLEPT IN THIS TOP
- HAIR LIKE A MESSY NEST
WHAT!!! I'M A GOBLIN!
YEAH!
A BEAUTIFUL GOBLIN!

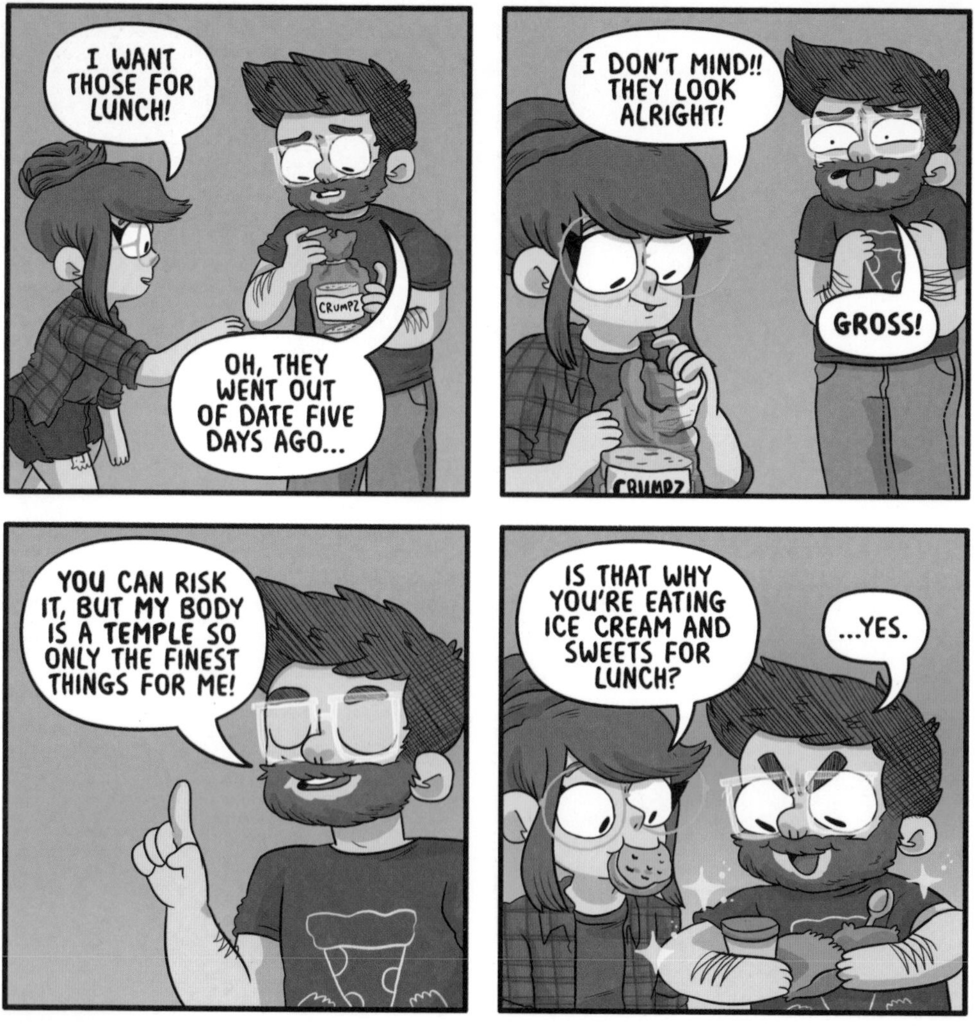
I WANT THOSE FOR LUNCH!
CRUMPZ
OH, THEY WENT OUT OF DATE FIVE DAYS AGO...
I DON'T MIND!! THEY LOOK ALRIGHT!
GROSS!
YOU CAN RISK IT, BUT MY BODY IS A TEMPLE SO ONLY THE FINEST THINGS FOR ME!
IS THAT WHY YOU'RE EATING ICE CREAM AND SWEETS FOR LUNCH?
...YES.

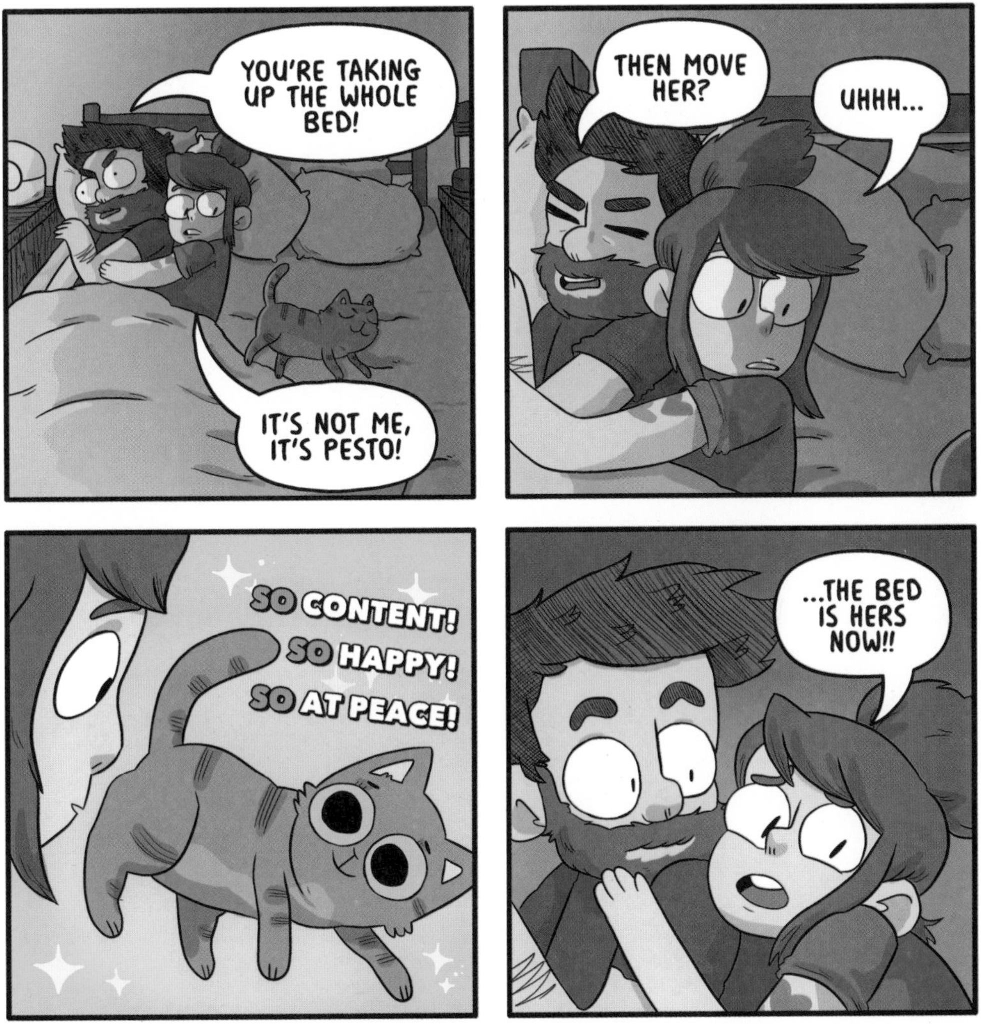
YOU'RE TAKING UP THE WHOLE BED!
IT'S NOT ME, IT'S PESTO!
THEN MOVE HER?
UHHH...
SO CONTENT!
SO HAPPY!
SO AT PEACE!
...THE BED IS HERS NOW!!

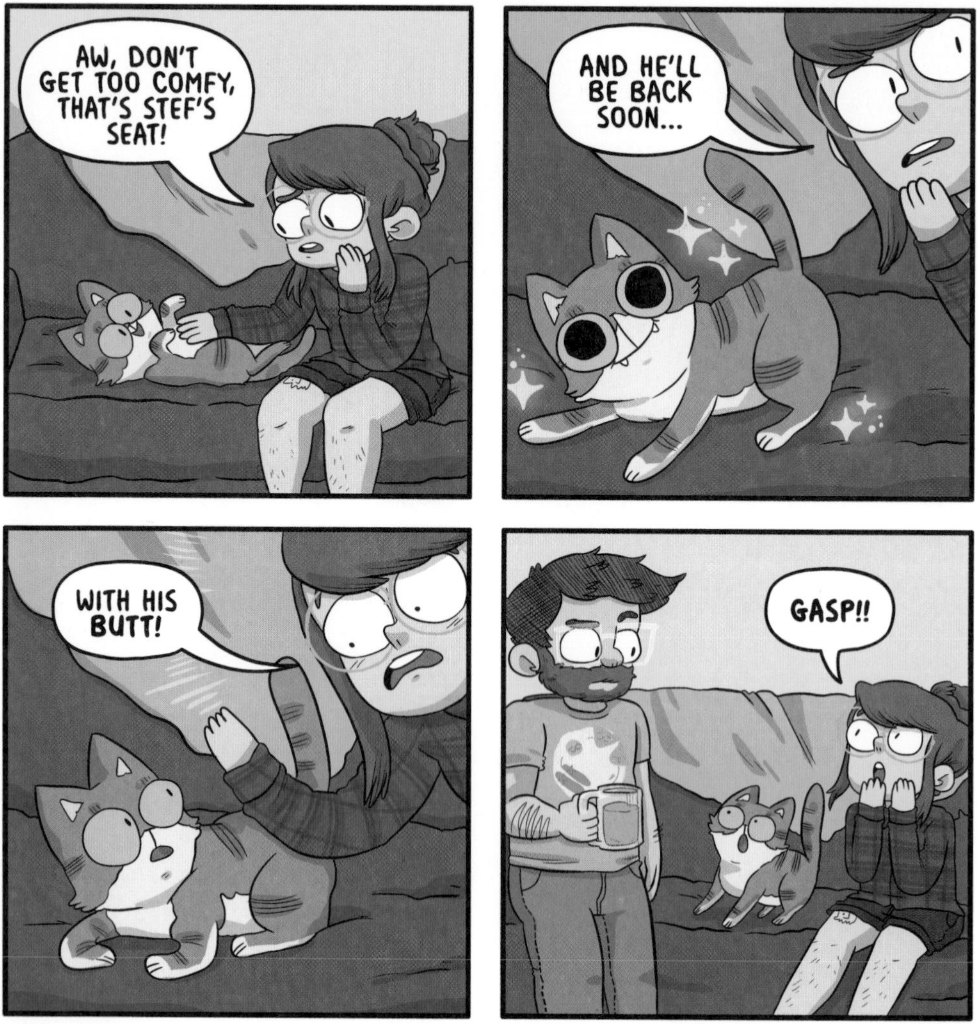
AW, DON'T GET TOO COMFY, THAT'S STEF'S SEAT!
AND HE'LL BE BACK SOON...
WITH HIS BUTT!
GASP!!

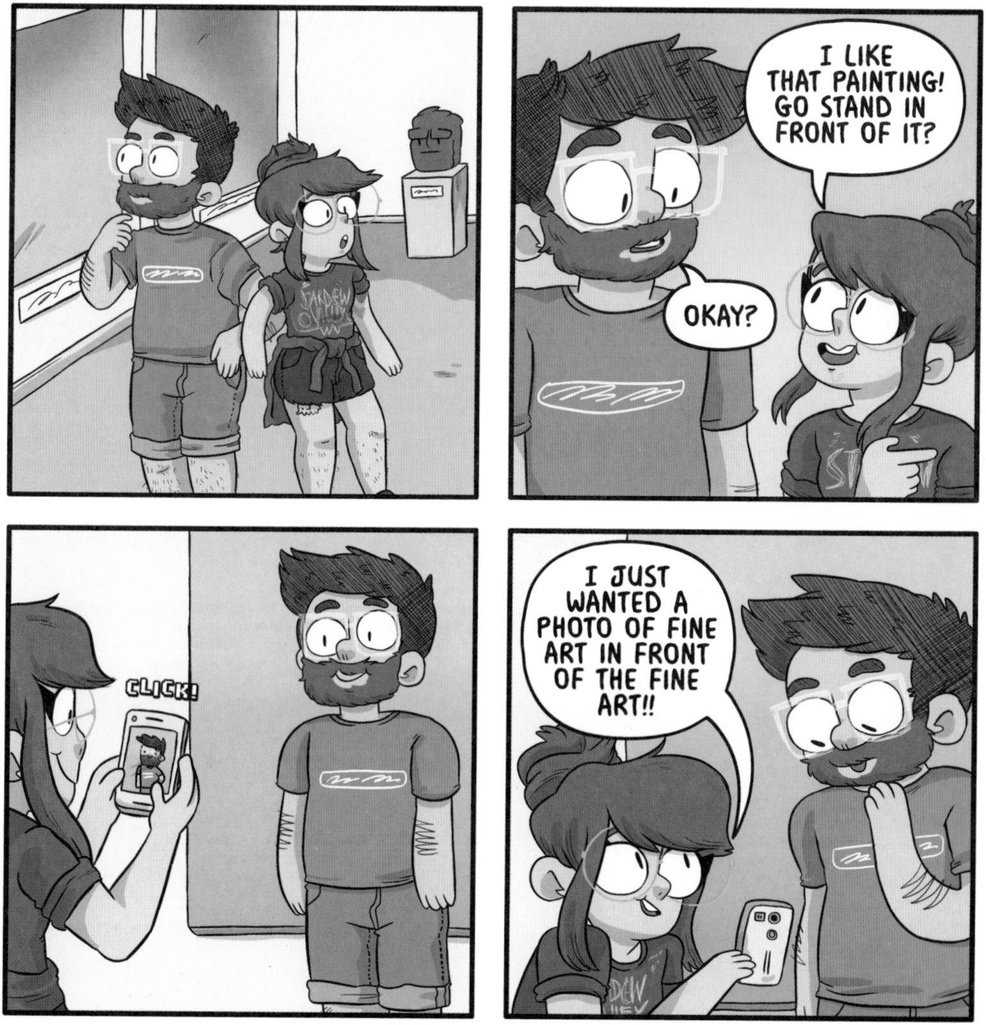
I LIKE THAT PAINTING! GO STAND IN FRONT OF IT?
OKAY?
CLICK!
I JUST WANTED A PHOTO OF FINE ART IN FRONT OF THE FINE ART!!

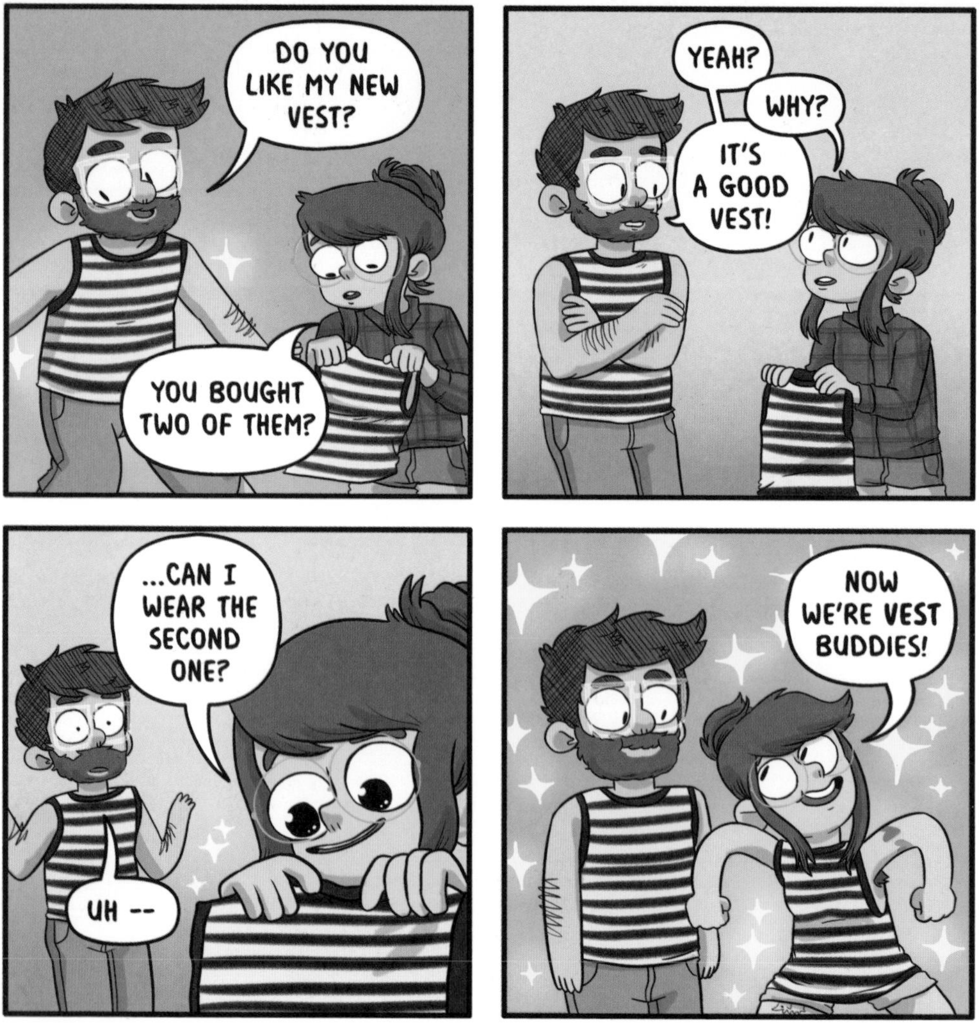
DO YOU LIKE MY NEW VEST?
YOU BOUGHT TWO OF THEM?
YEAH?
IT'S A GOOD VEST!
WHY?
...CAN I WEAR THE SECOND ONE?
UH --
NOW WE'RE VEST BUDDIES!

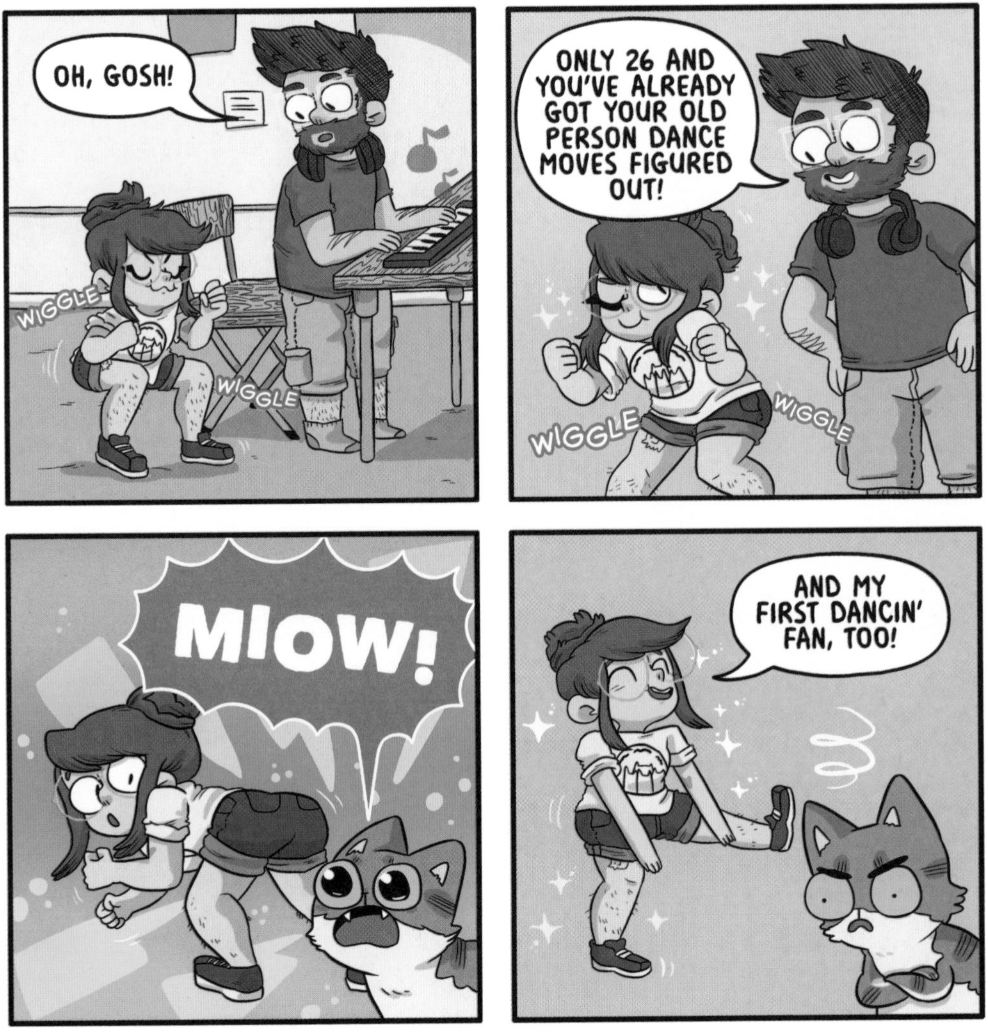
OH, GOSH!
WIGGLE
WIGGLE
ONLY 26 AND YOU'VE ALREADY GOT YOUR OLD PERSON DANCE MOVES FIGURED OUT!
WIGGLE
WIGGLE
MIOW!
AND MY FIRST DANCIN' FAN, TOO!

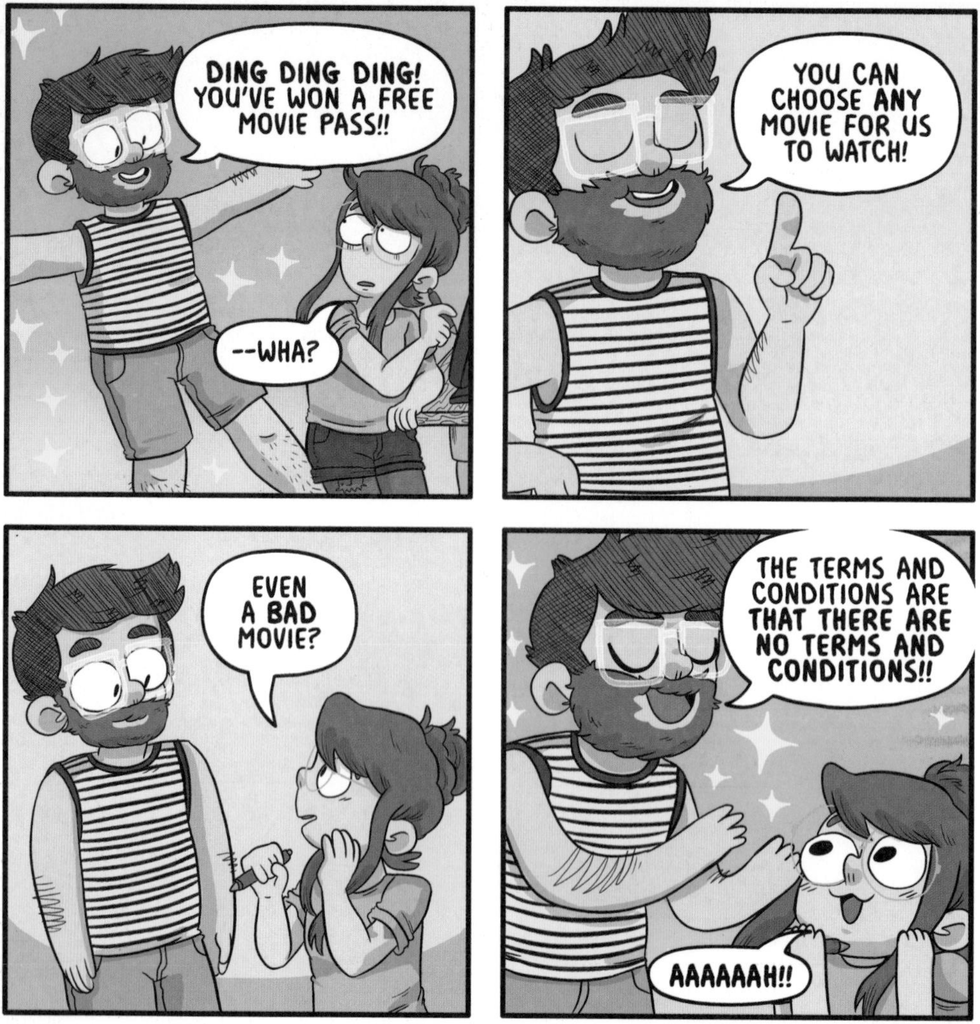
DING DING DING! YOU'VE WON A FREE MOVIE PASS!!
--WHA?
YOU CAN CHOOSE ANY MOVIE FOR US TO WATCH!
EVEN A BAD MOVIE?
THE TERMS AND CONDITIONS ARE THAT THERE ARE NO TERMS AND CONDITIONS!!
AAAAAAH!!

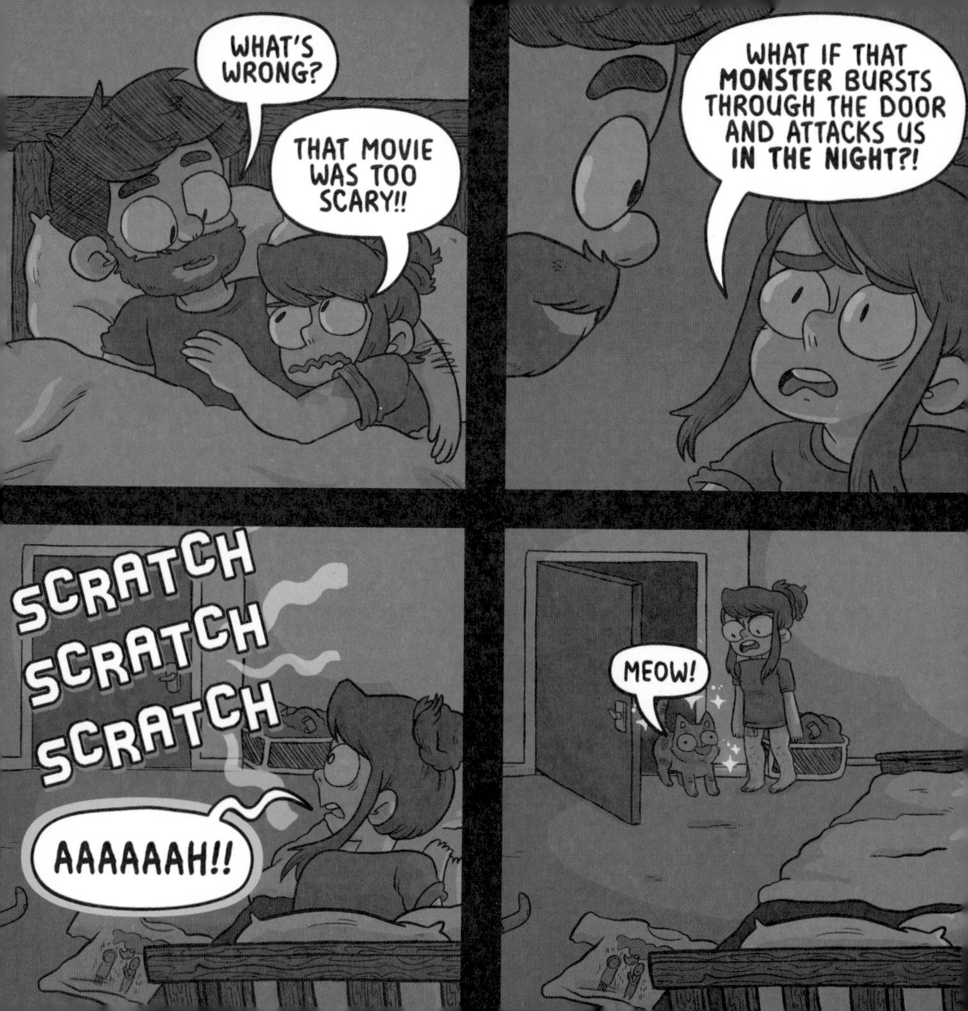
WHAT'S WRONG?
THAT MOVIE WAS TOO SCARY!!
WHAT IF THAT MONSTER BURSTS THROUGH THE DOOR AND ATTACKS US IN THE NIGHT?!
SCRATCH SCRATCH SCRATCH
AAAAAAH!!
MEOW!

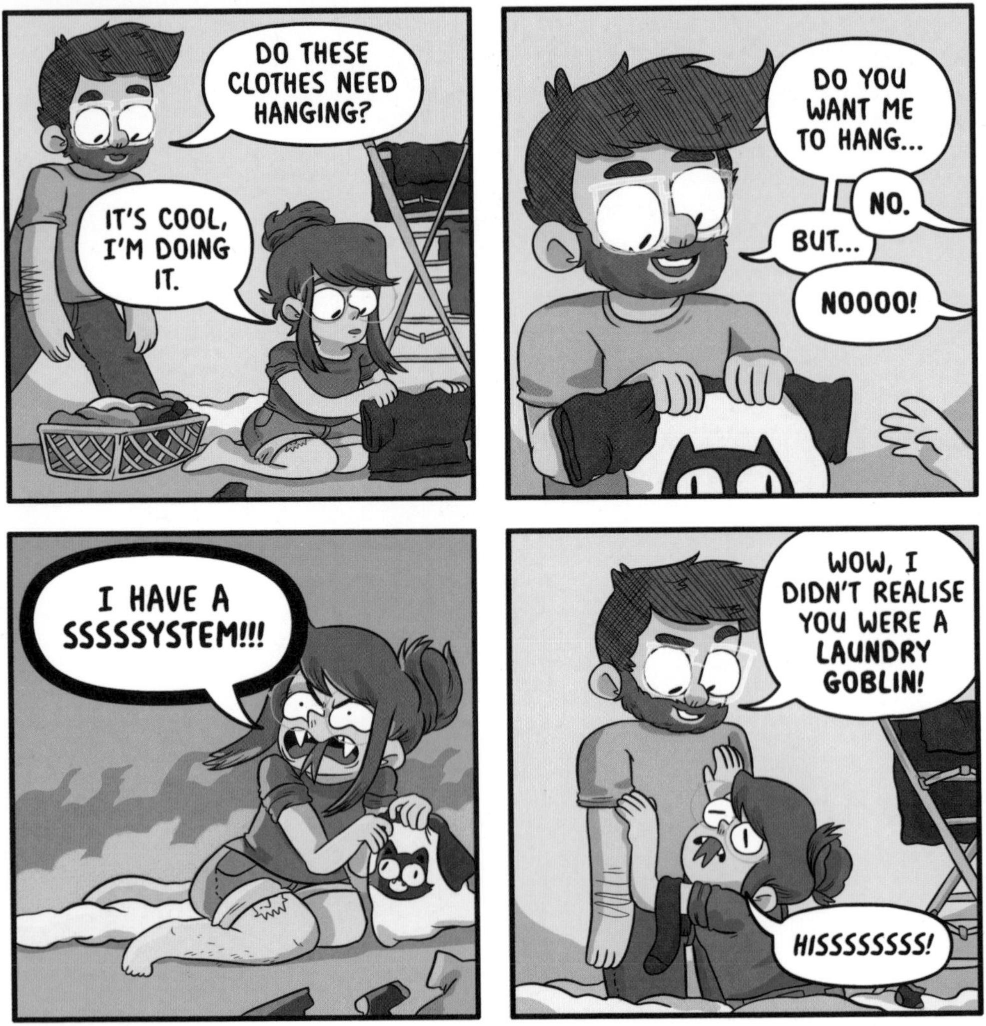
DO THESE CLOTHES NEED HANGING?
IT'S COOL, I'M DOING IT.
DO YOU WANT ME TO HANG...
NO.
BUT...
NOOOO!
I HAVE A SSSSSYSTEM!!!
WOW, I DIDN'T REALISE YOU WERE A LAUNDRY GOBLIN!
HISSSSSSSS!

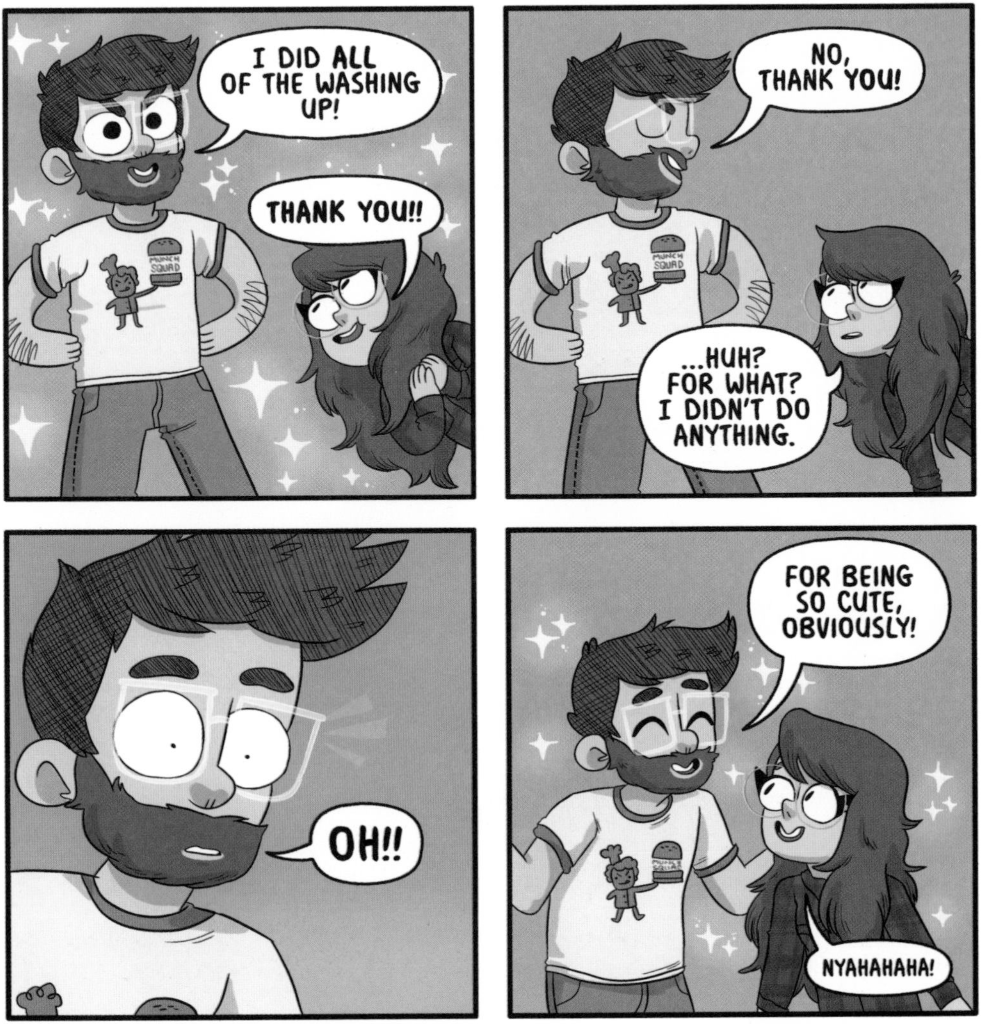
I DID ALL OF THE WASHING UP!
THANK YOU!!
MUNCH SQUAD
NO, THANK YOU!
...HUH? FOR WHAT? I DIDN'T DO ANYTHING.
OH!!
FOR BEING SO CUTE, OBVIOUSLY!
NYAHAHAHA!

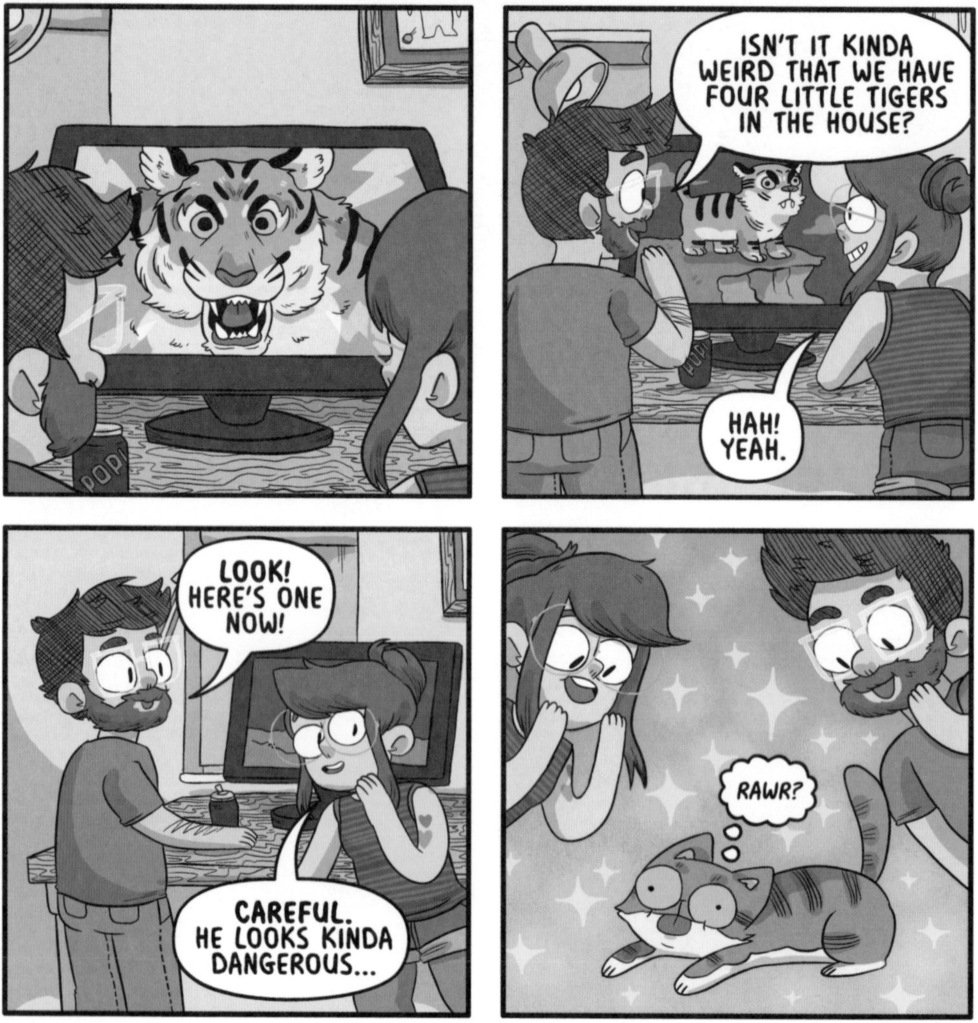
POP!
ISN'T IT KINDA WEIRD THAT WE HAVE FOUR LITTLE TIGERS IN THE HOUSE?
HAH! YEAH.
LOOK! HERE'S ONE NOW!
CAREFUL. HE LOOKS KINDA DANGEROUS...
RAWR?

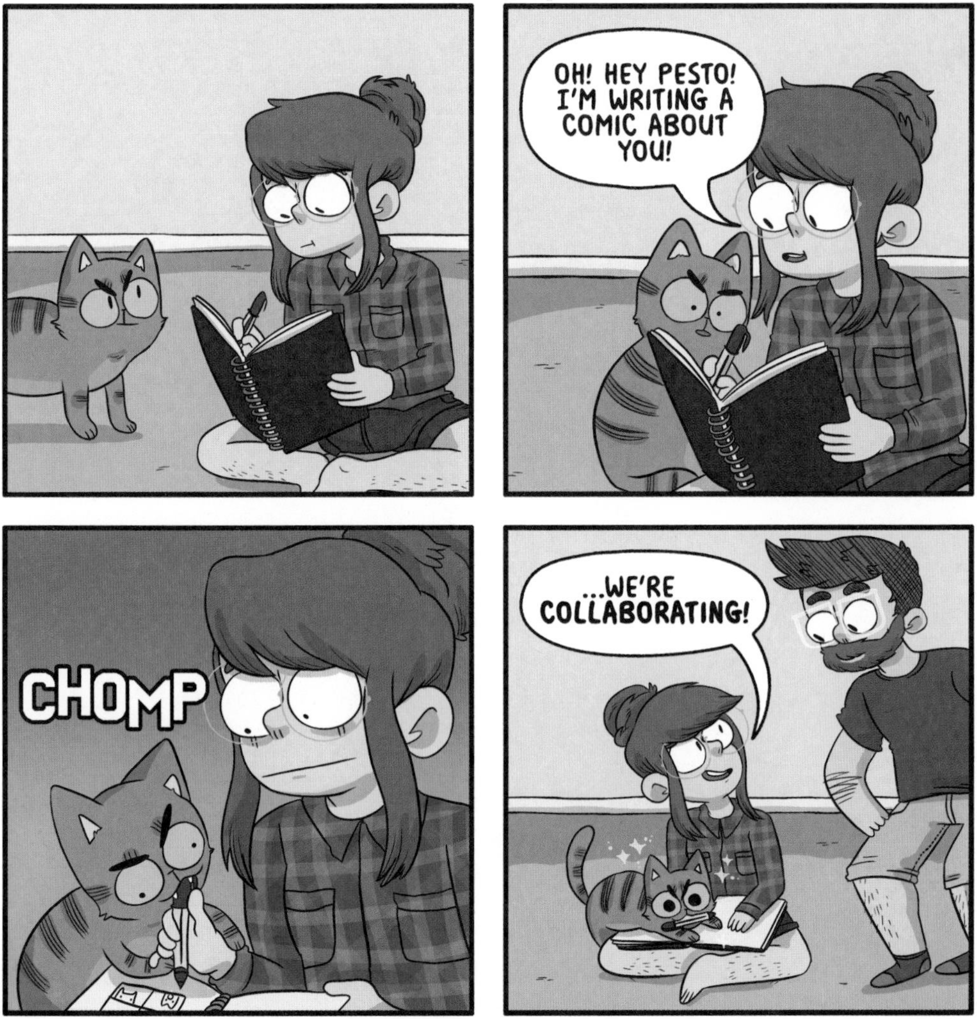
OH! HEY PESTO! I'M WRITING A COMIC ABOUT YOU!
CHOMP
...WE'RE COLLABORATING!

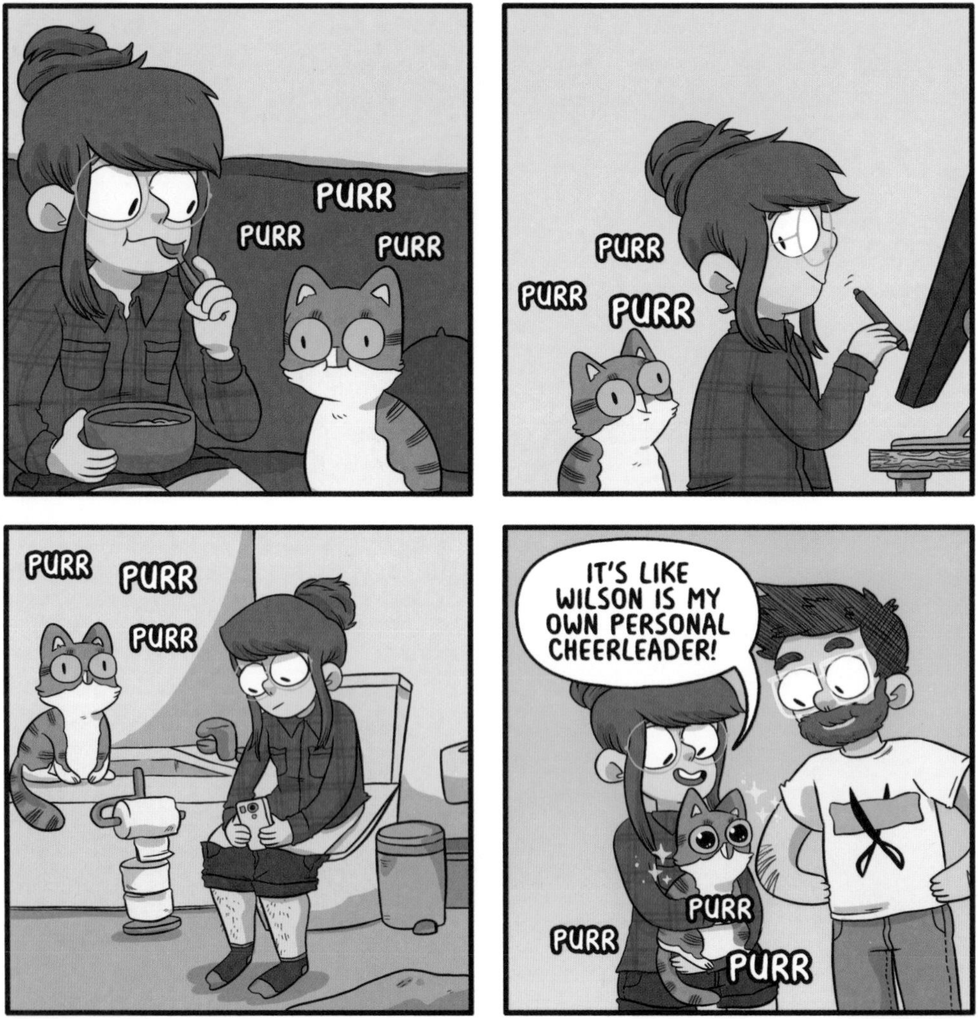
PURR
PURR
PURR
PURR
PURR
PURR
PURR
PURR
PURR
IT'S LIKE WILSON IS MY OWN PERSONAL CHEERLEADER!
PURR
PURR
PURR

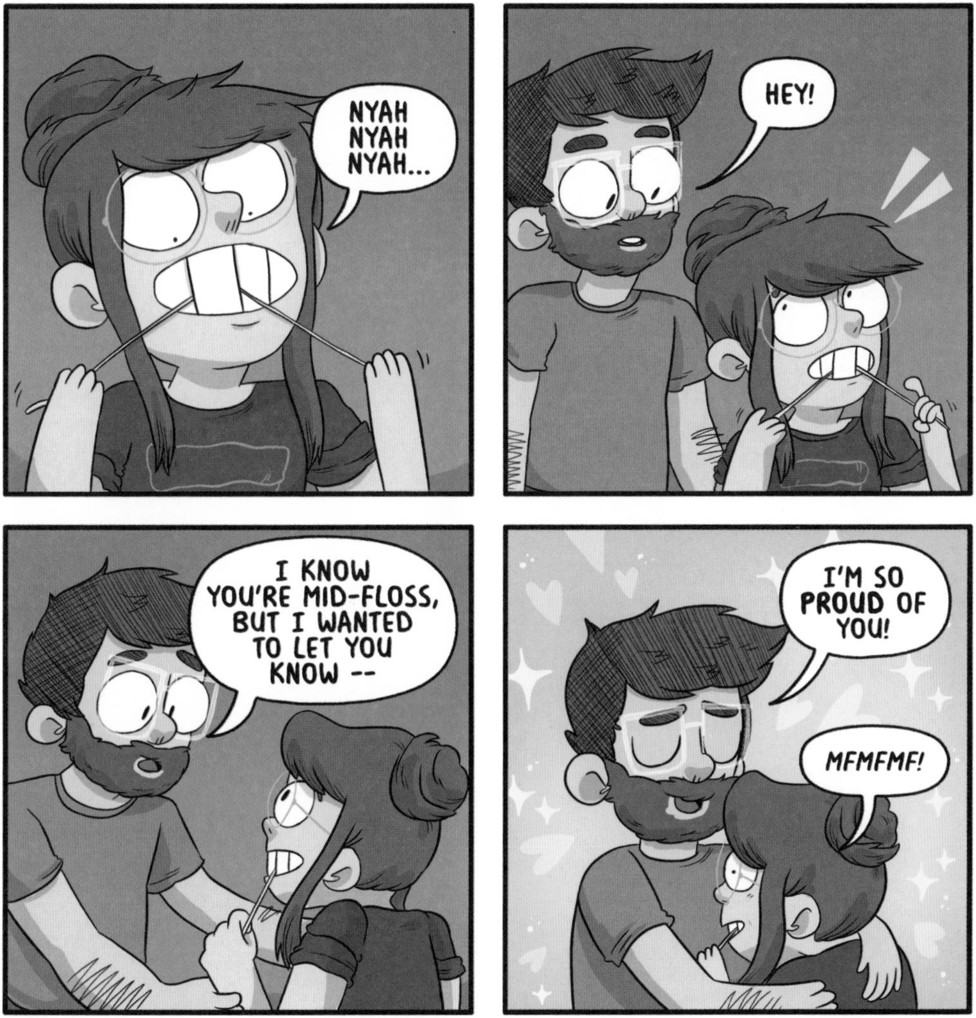
NYAH NYAH NYAH...
HEY!
I KNOW YOU'RE MID-FLOSS, BUT I WANTED TO LET YOU KNOW --
I'M SO PROUD OF YOU!
MFMFMF!

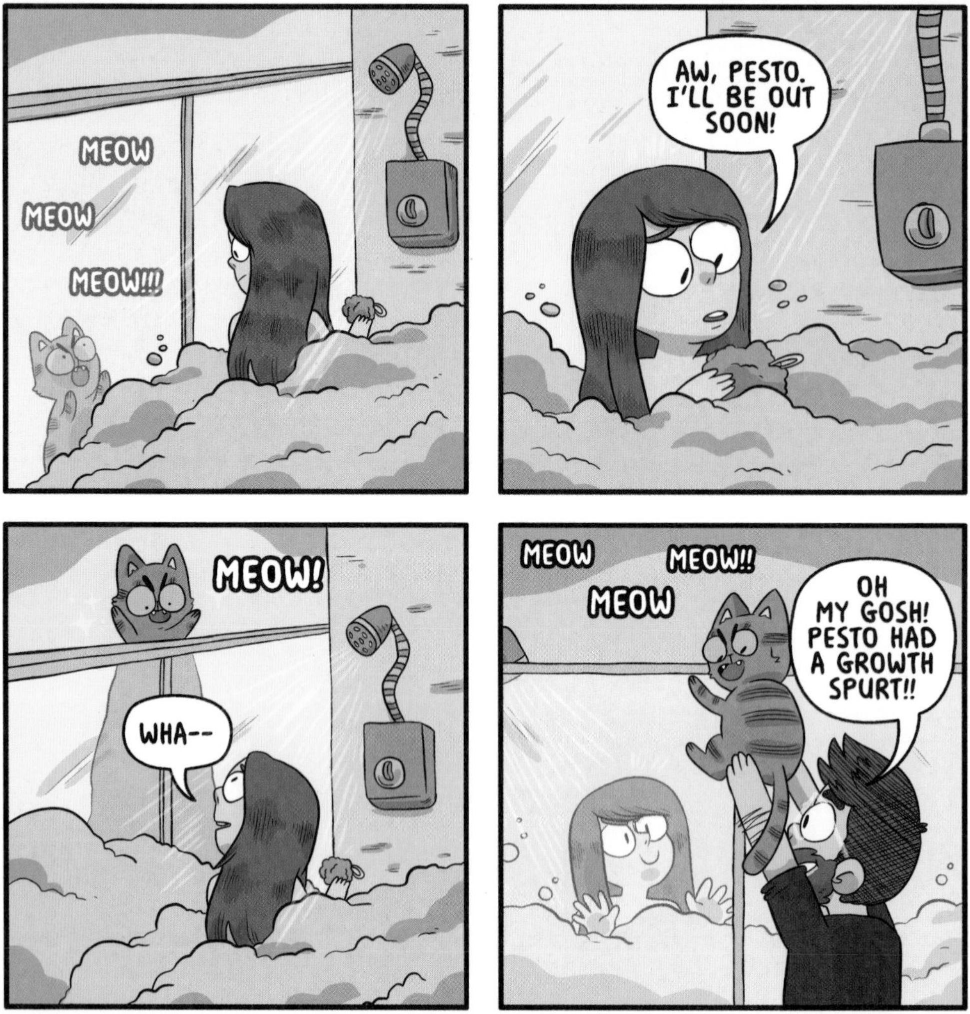
MEOW
MEOW
MEOW!!!
AW, PESTO. I'LL BE OUT SOON!
MEOW!
WHA--
MEOW
MEOW!!
MEOW
OH MY GOSH! PESTO HAD A GROWTH SPURT!!

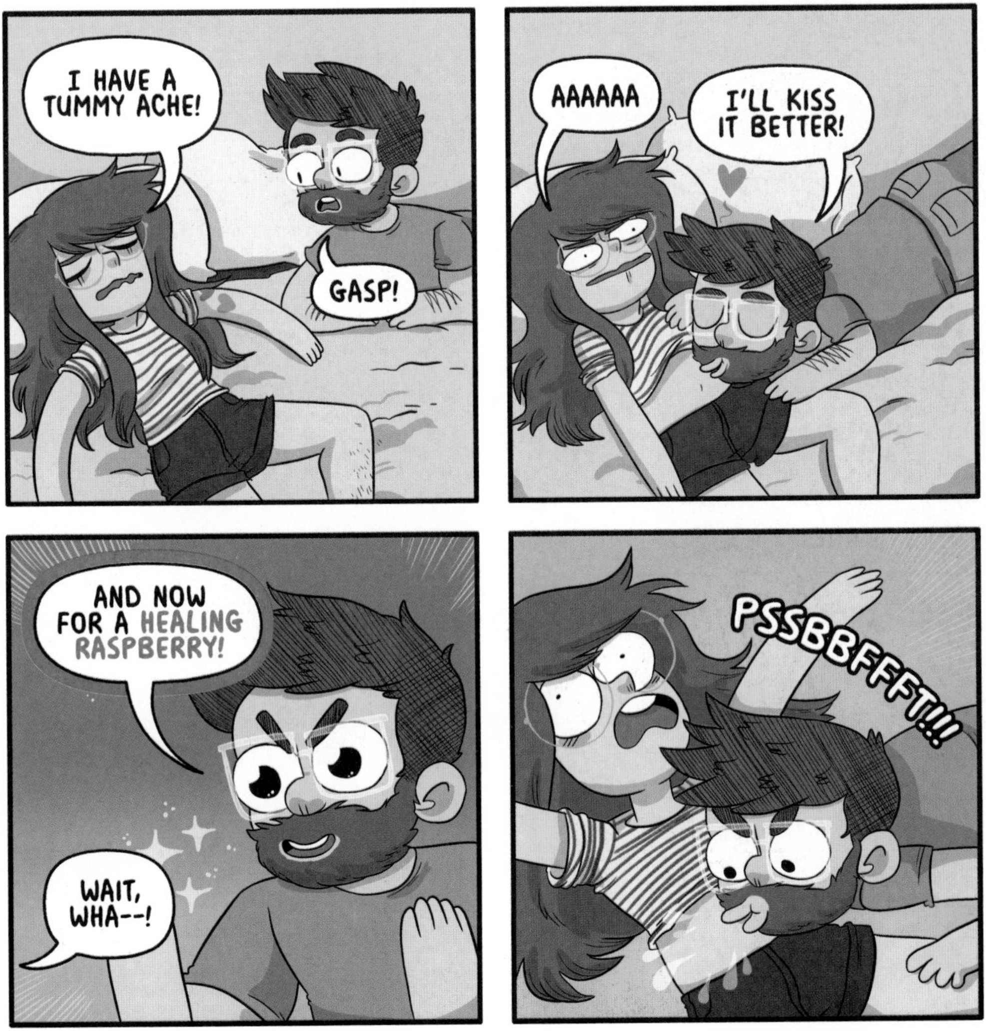
I HAVE A TUMMY ACHE!
GASP!
AAAAAA
I'LL KISS IT BETTER!
AND NOW FOR A HEALING RASPBERRY!
WAIT, WHA--!
PSSBBFFFT!!!

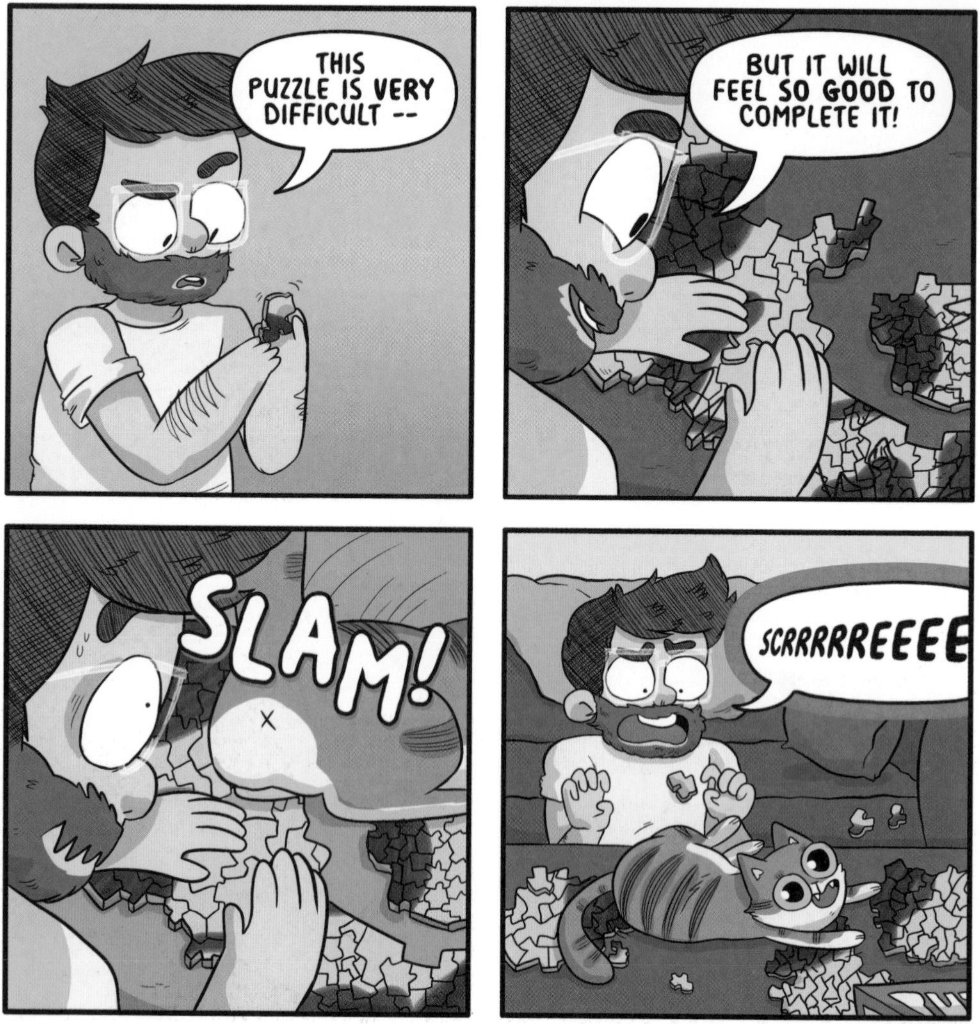
THIS PUZZLE IS VERY DIFFICULT --
BUT IT WILL FEEL SO GOOD TO COMPLETE IT!
SLAM!
SCRRRRREEEE

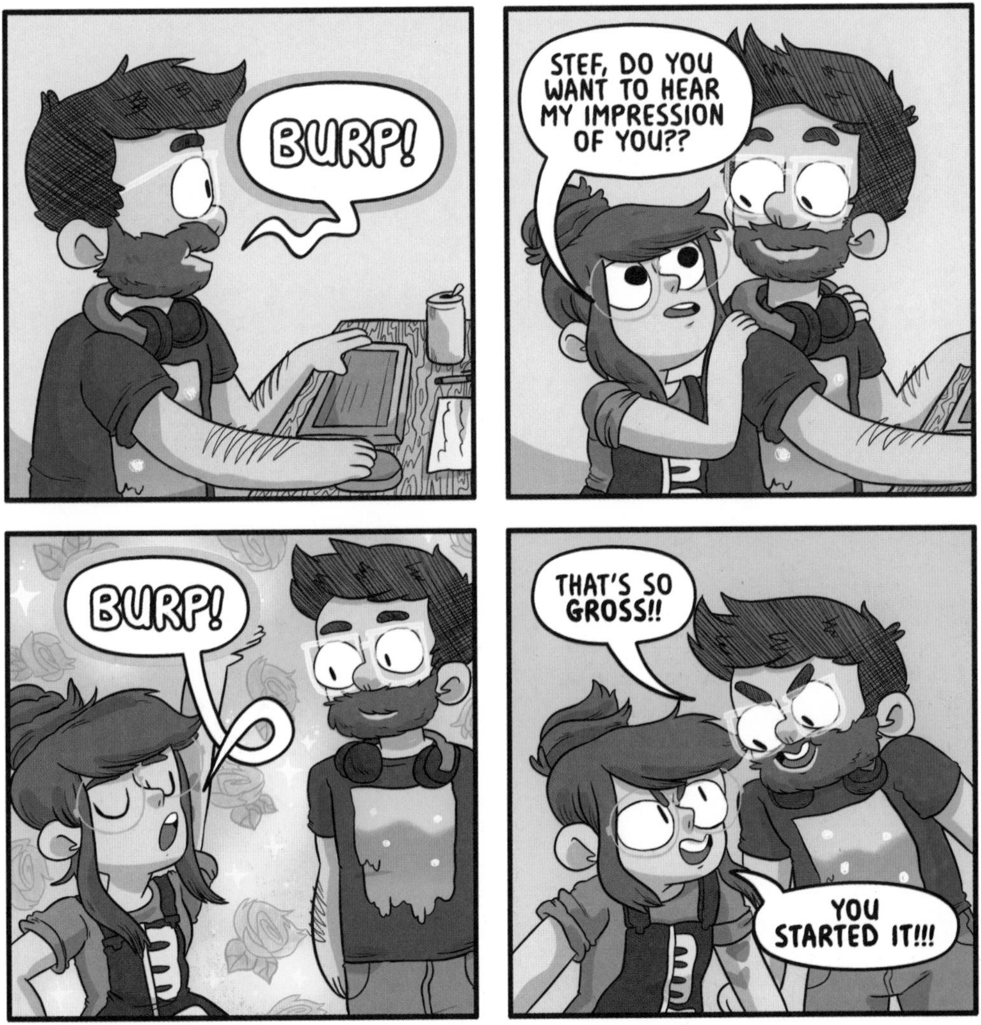
BURP!
STEF, DO YOU WANT TO HEAR MY IMPRESSION OF YOU??
BURP!
THAT'S SO GROSS!!
YOU STARTED IT!!!

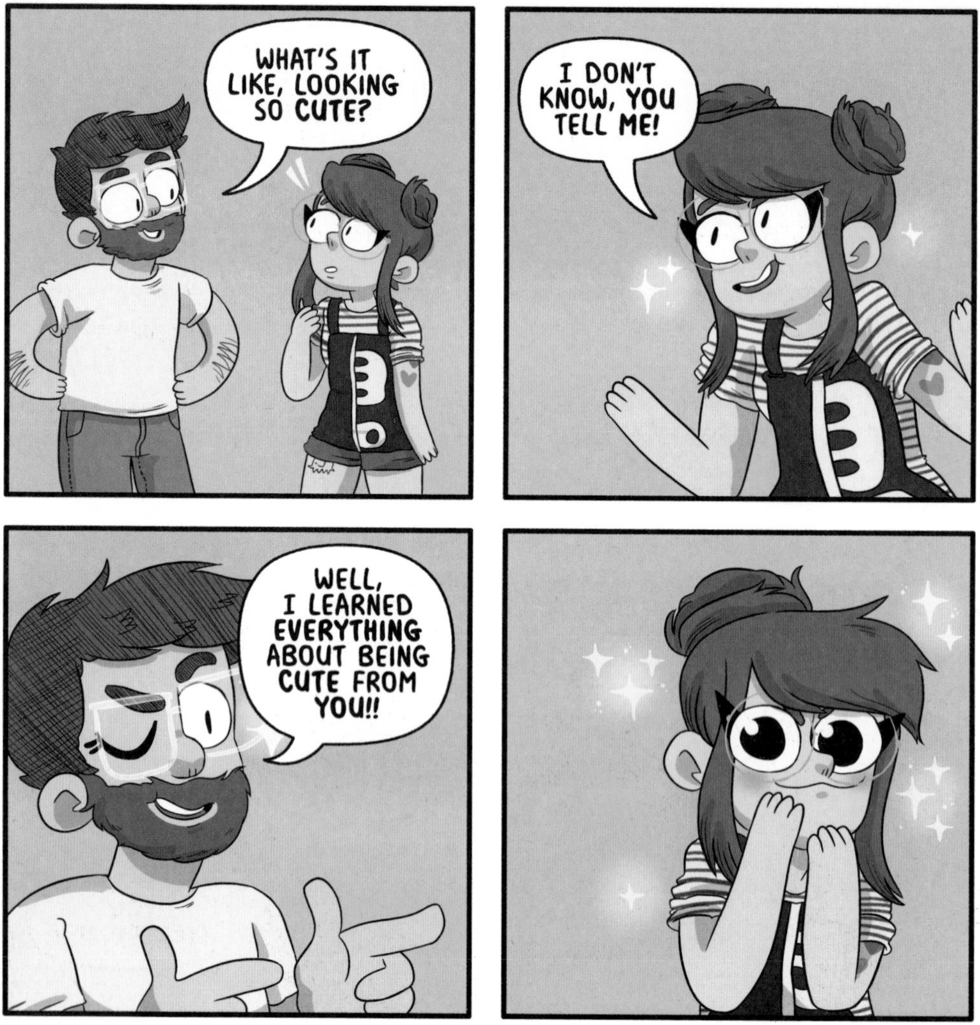
WHAT'S IT LIKE, LOOKING SO CUTE?
I DON'T KNOW, YOU TELL ME!
WELL, I LEARNED EVERYTHING ABOUT BEING CUTE FROM YOU!!

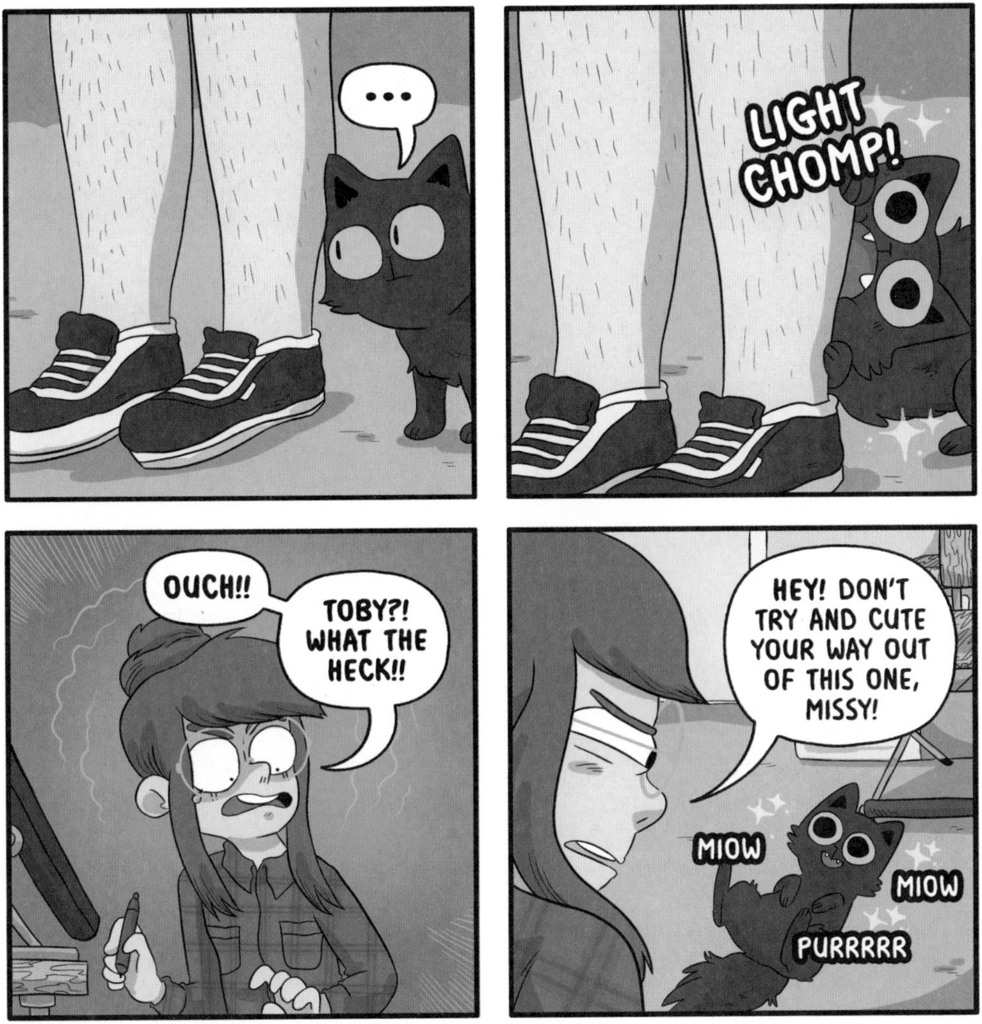
...
LIGHT CHOMP!
OUCH!!
TOBY?! WHAT THE HECK!!
HEY! DON'T TRY AND CUTE YOUR WAY OUT OF THIS ONE, MISSY!
MIOW
MIOW
PURRRRR

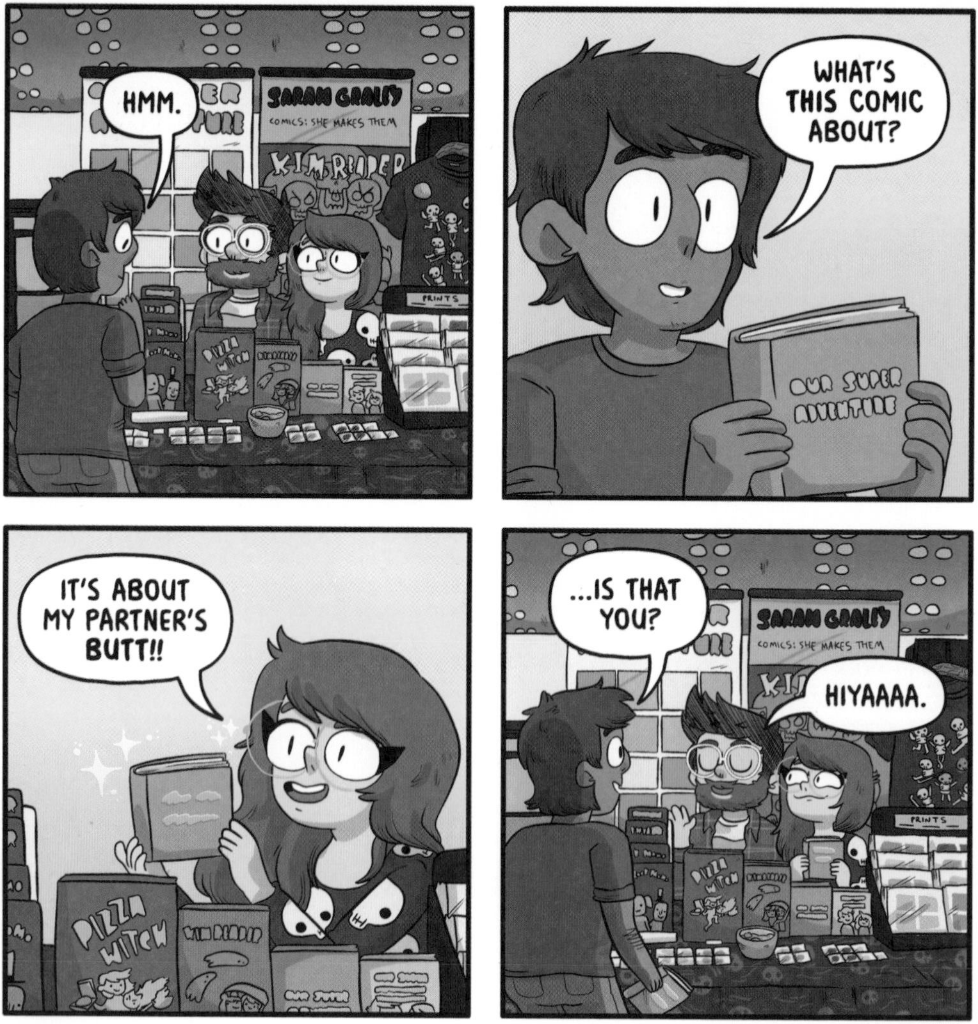
HMM.
SARAH GRALEY
COMICS: SHE MAKES THEM
PRINTS
PIZZA WITCH
WHAT'S THIS COMIC ABOUT?
OUR SUPER ADVENTURE
IT'S ABOUT MY PARTNER'S BUTT!!
PIZZA WITCH
...IS THAT YOU?
SARAH GRALEY
COMICS: SHE MAKES THEM
HIYAAAA.
PRINTS

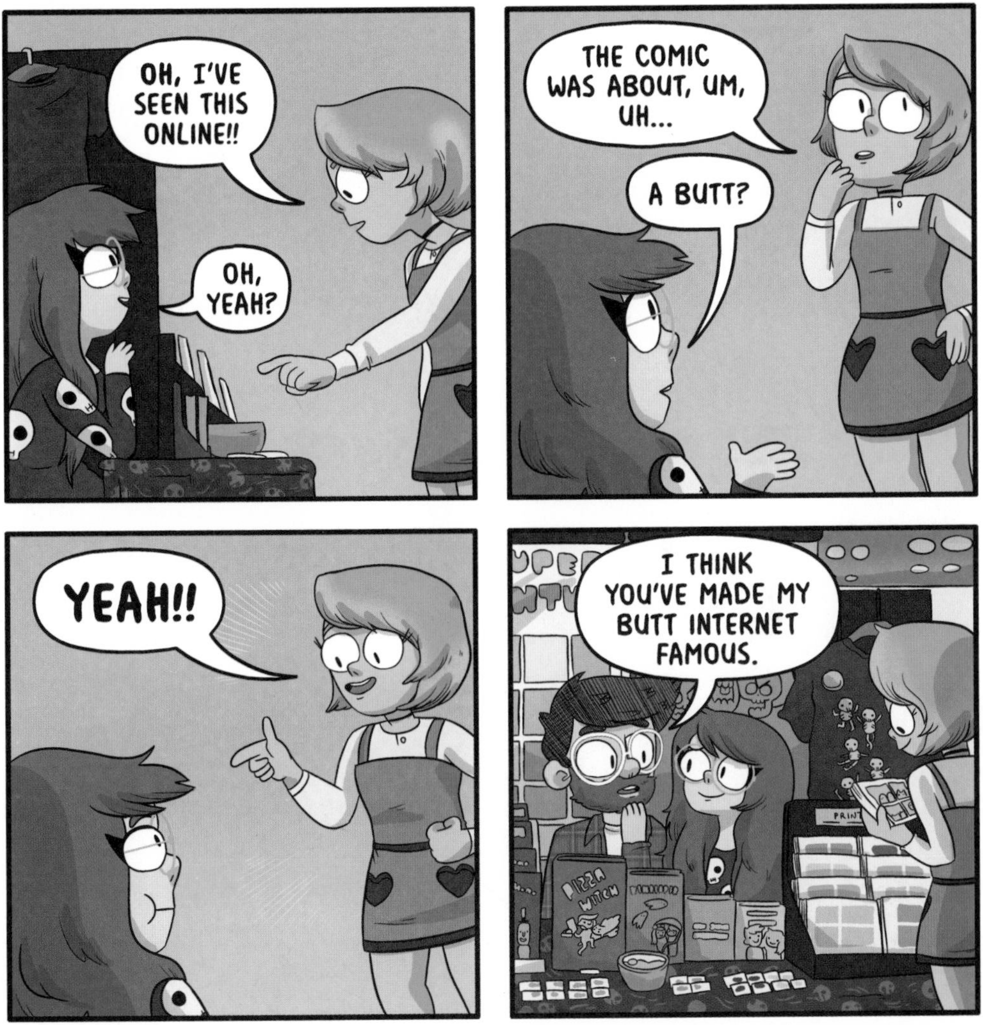
OH, I'VE SEEN THIS ONLINE!!
OH, YEAH?
THE COMIC WAS ABOUT, UM, UH...
A BUTT?
YEAH!!
I THINK YOU'VE MADE MY BUTT INTERNET FAMOUS.
PIZZA WITCH
PRINT

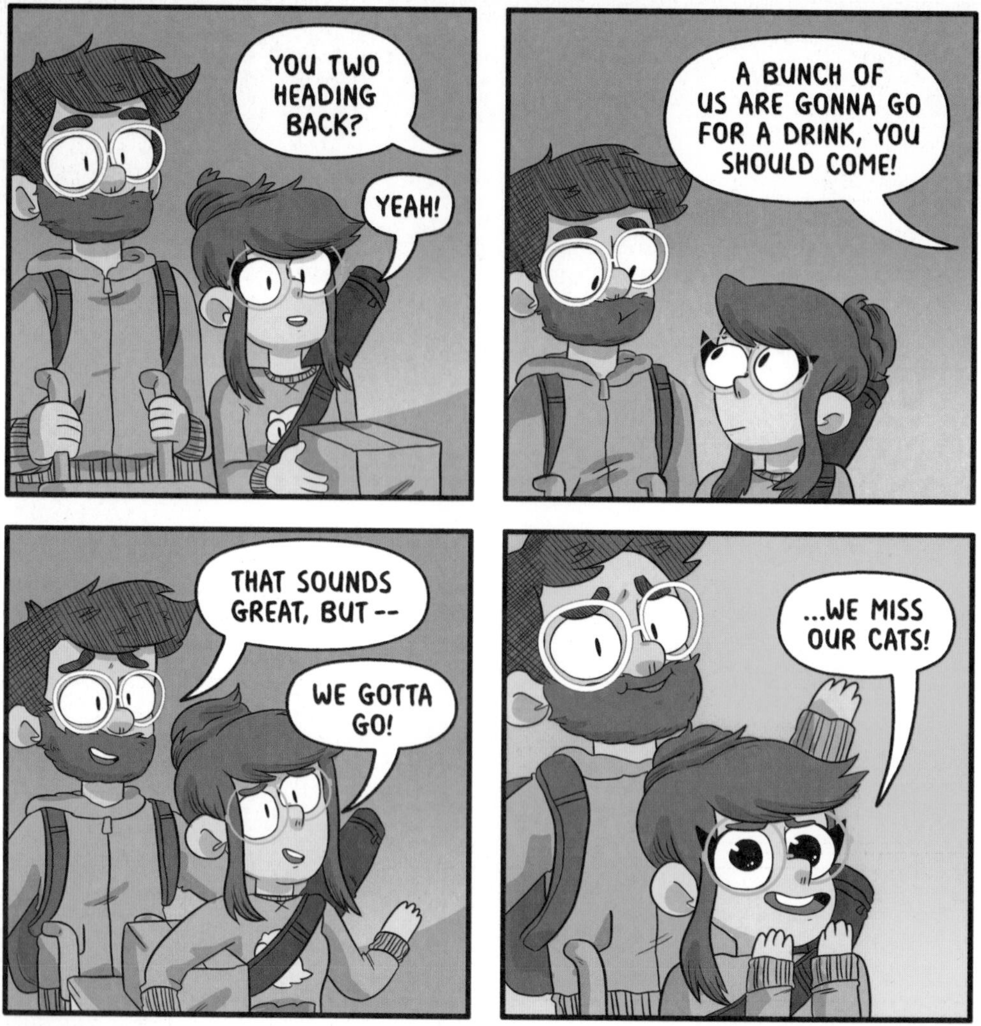
YOU TWO HEADING BACK?
YEAH!
A BUNCH OF US ARE GONNA GO FOR A DRINK, YOU SHOULD COME!
THAT SOUNDS GREAT, BUT --
WE GOTTA GO!
...WE MISS OUR CATS!

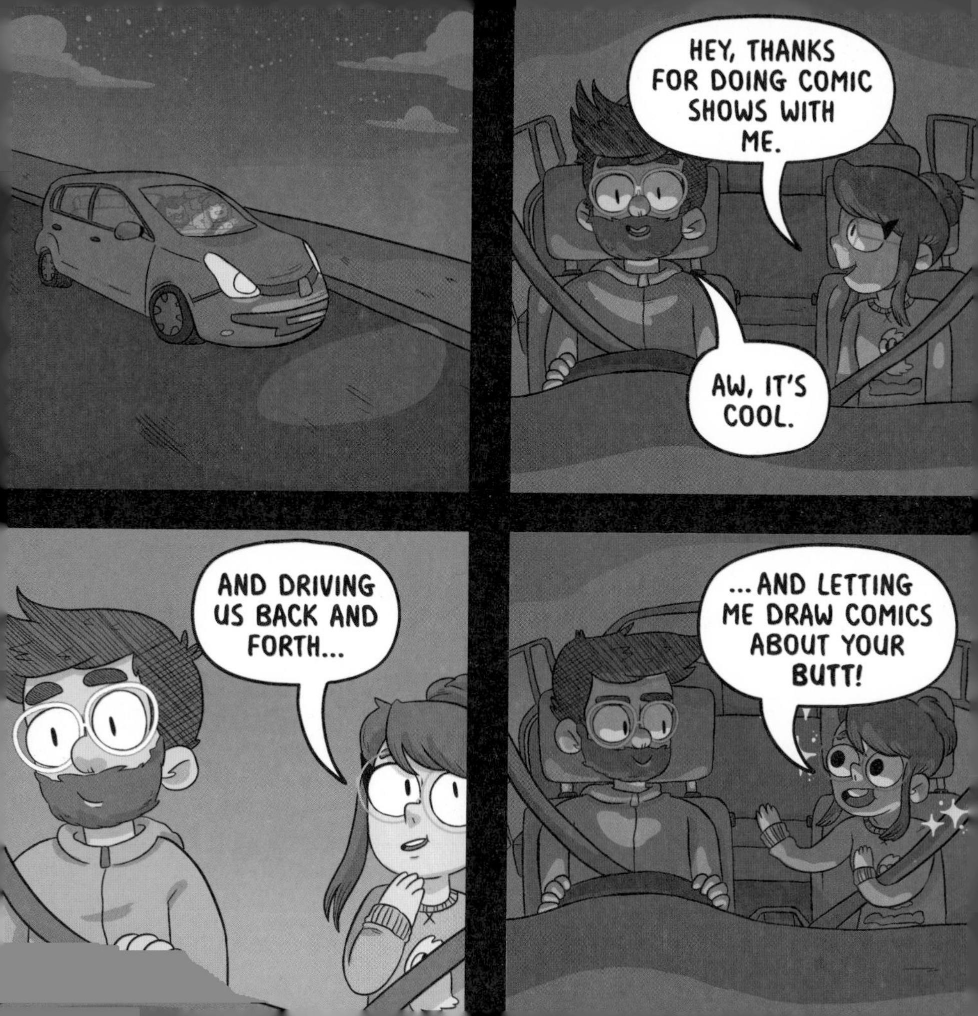
HEY, THANKS FOR DOING COMIC SHOWS WITH ME.
AW, IT'S COOL.
AND DRIVING US BACK AND FORTH...
...AND LETTING ME DRAW COMICS ABOUT YOUR BUTT!

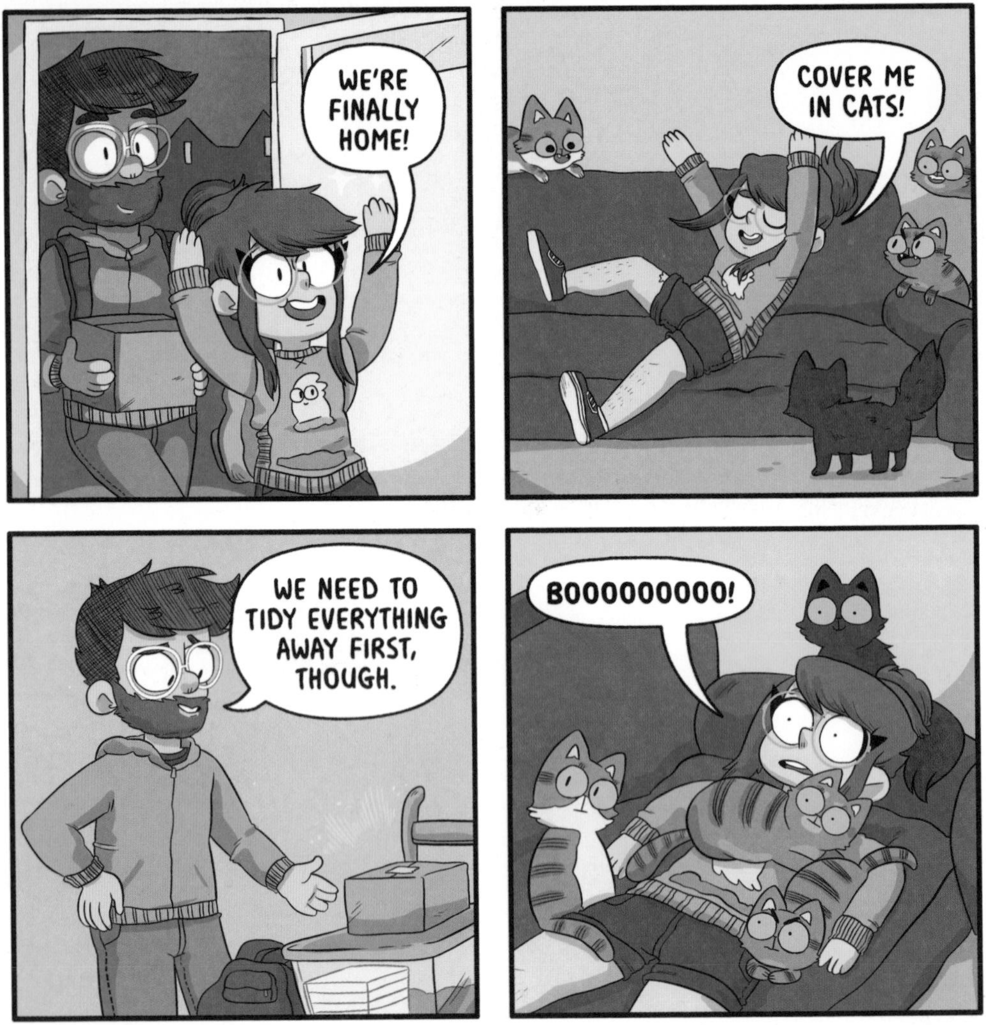
WE'RE FINALLY HOME!
COVER ME IN CATS!
WE NEED TO TIDY EVERYTHING AWAY FIRST, THOUGH.
BOOOOOOOOO!

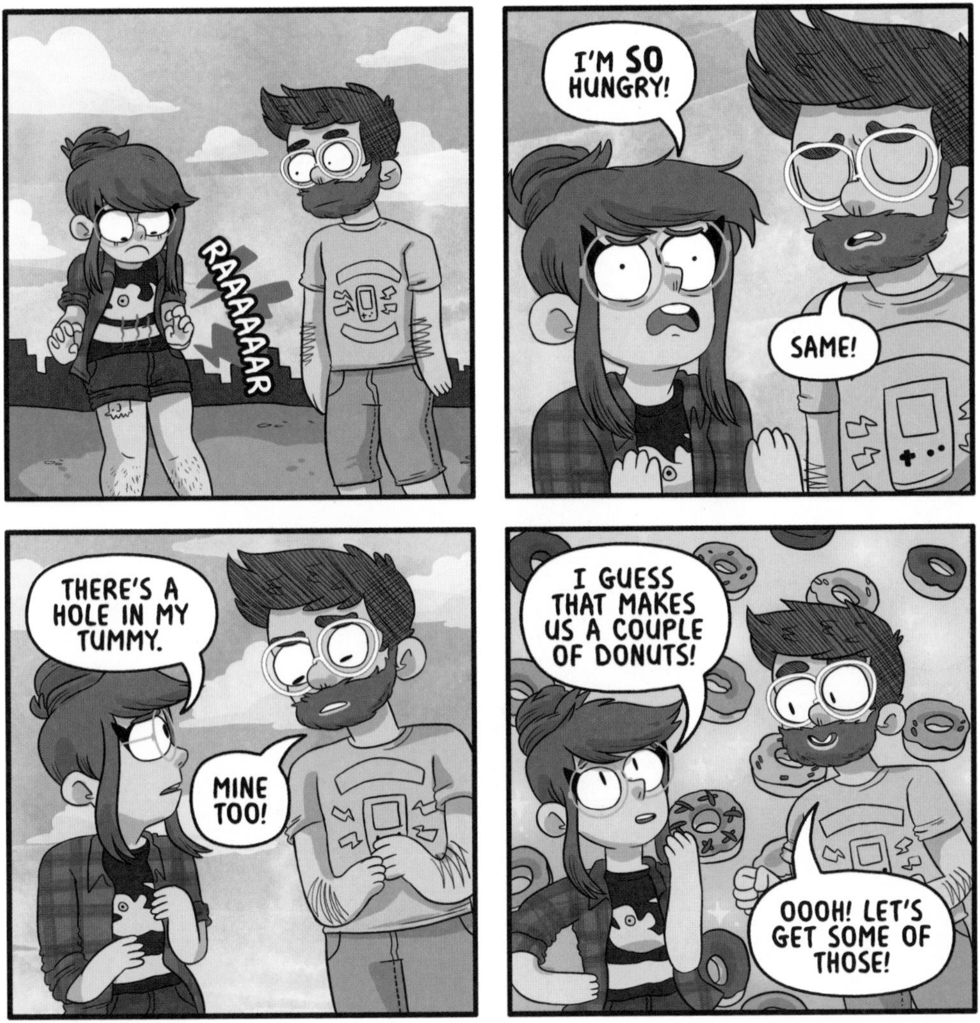
RAAAAAAR
I'M SO HUNGRY!
SAME!
THERE'S A HOLE IN MY TUMMY.
MINE TOO!
I GUESS THAT MAKES US A COUPLE OF DONUTS!
OOOH! LET'S GET SOME OF THOSE!

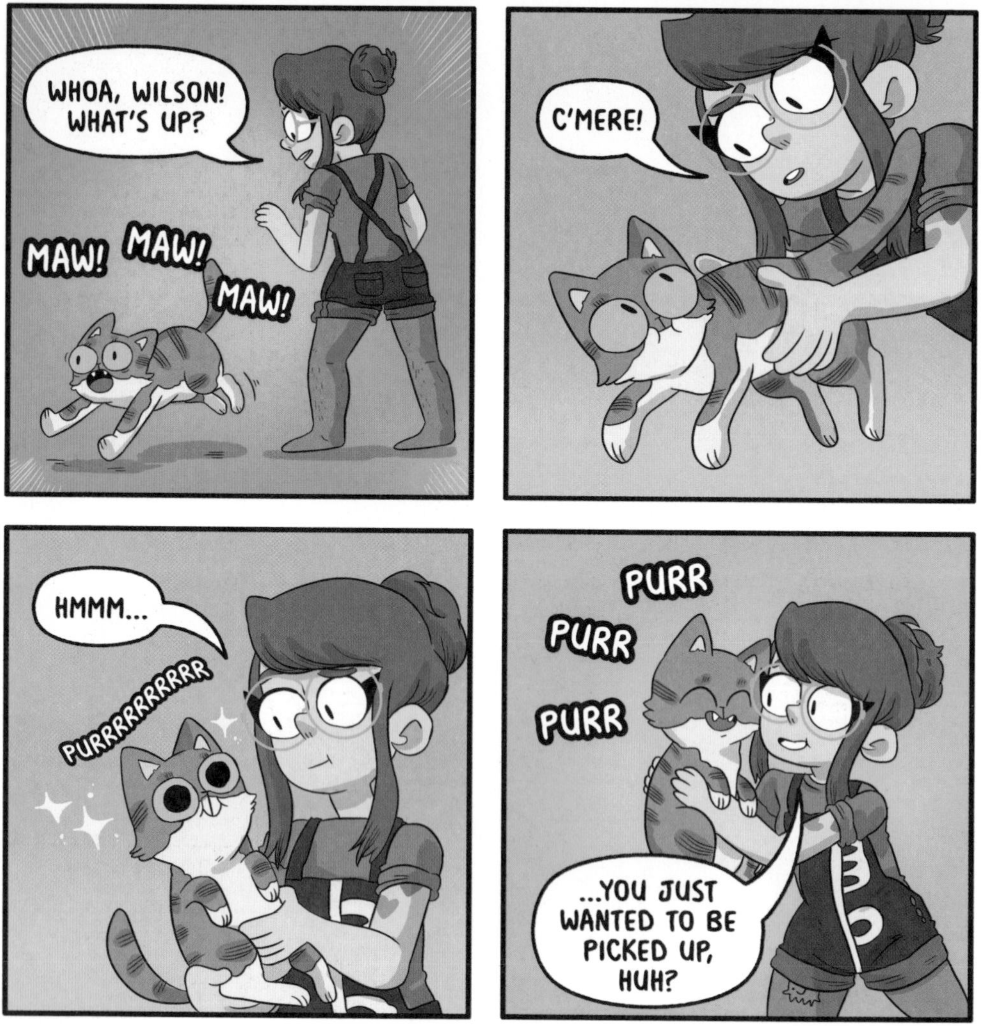
WHOA, WILSON! WHAT'S UP?
MAW! MAW!
MAW!
C'MERE!
HMMM...
PURRRRRRRRRR
PURR
PURR
PURR
...YOU JUST WANTED TO BE PICKED UP, HUH?

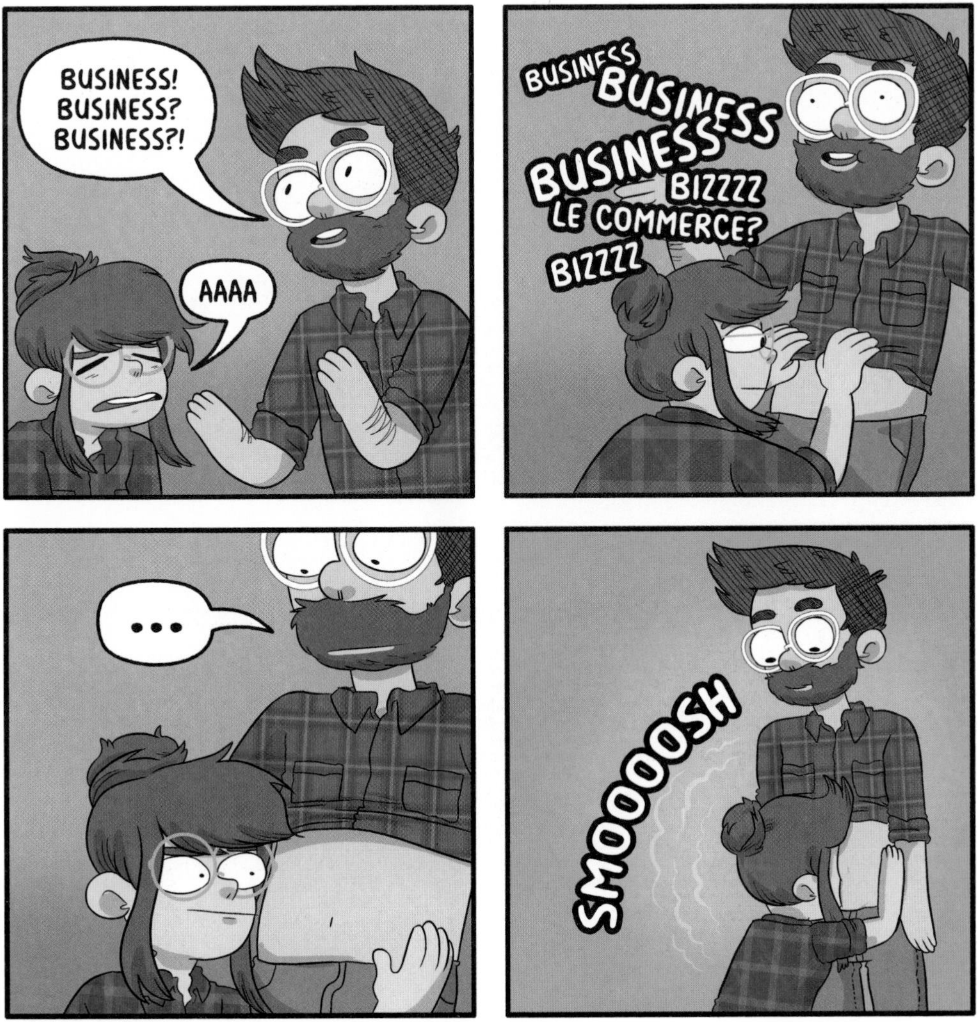
BUSINESS!
BUSINESS?
BUSINESS?!
AAAA
BUSINESS
BUSINESS
BUSINESS
BIZZZZ
LE COMMERCE?
BIZZZZ
...
SMOOOOSH

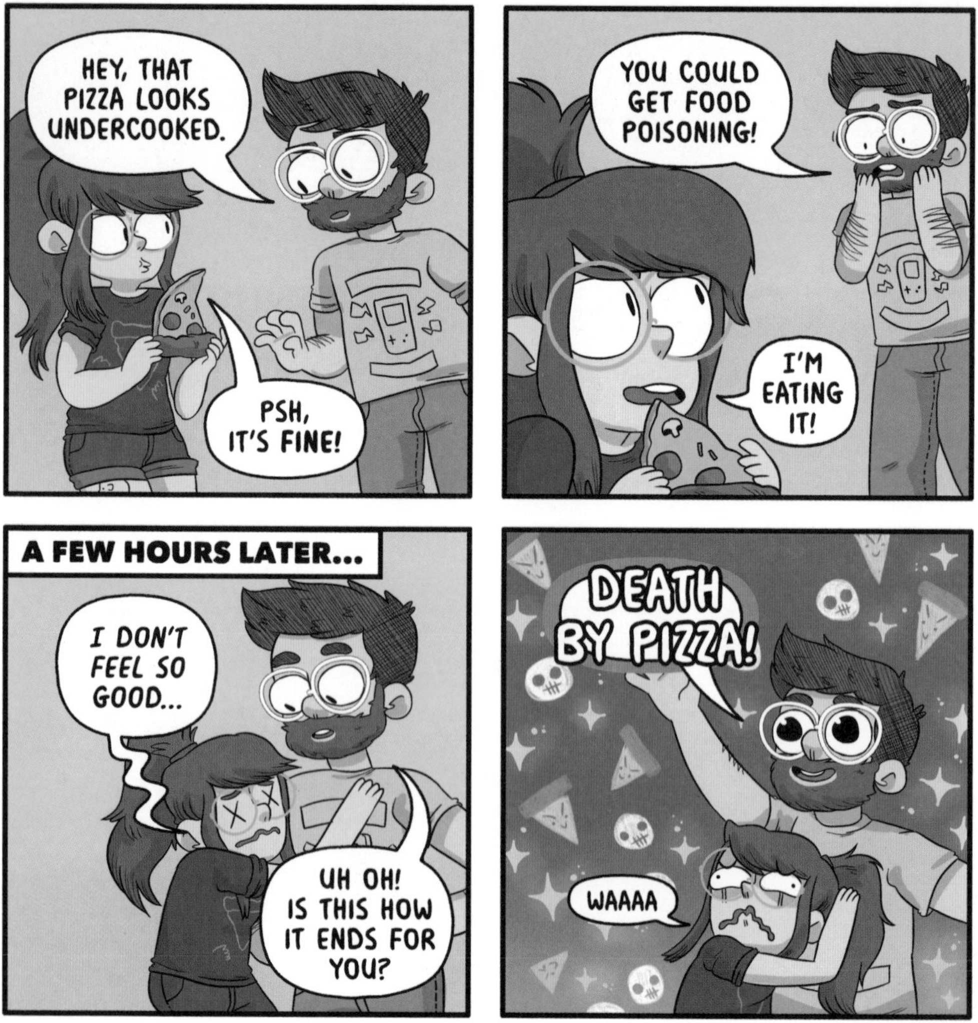
HEY, THAT PIZZA LOOKS UNDERCOOKED.
PSH, IT'S FINE!
YOU COULD GET FOOD POISONING!
I'M EATING IT!
A FEW HOURS LATER...
I DON'T FEEL SO GOOD...
UH OH! IS THIS HOW IT ENDS FOR YOU?
DEATH BY PIZZA!
WAAAA

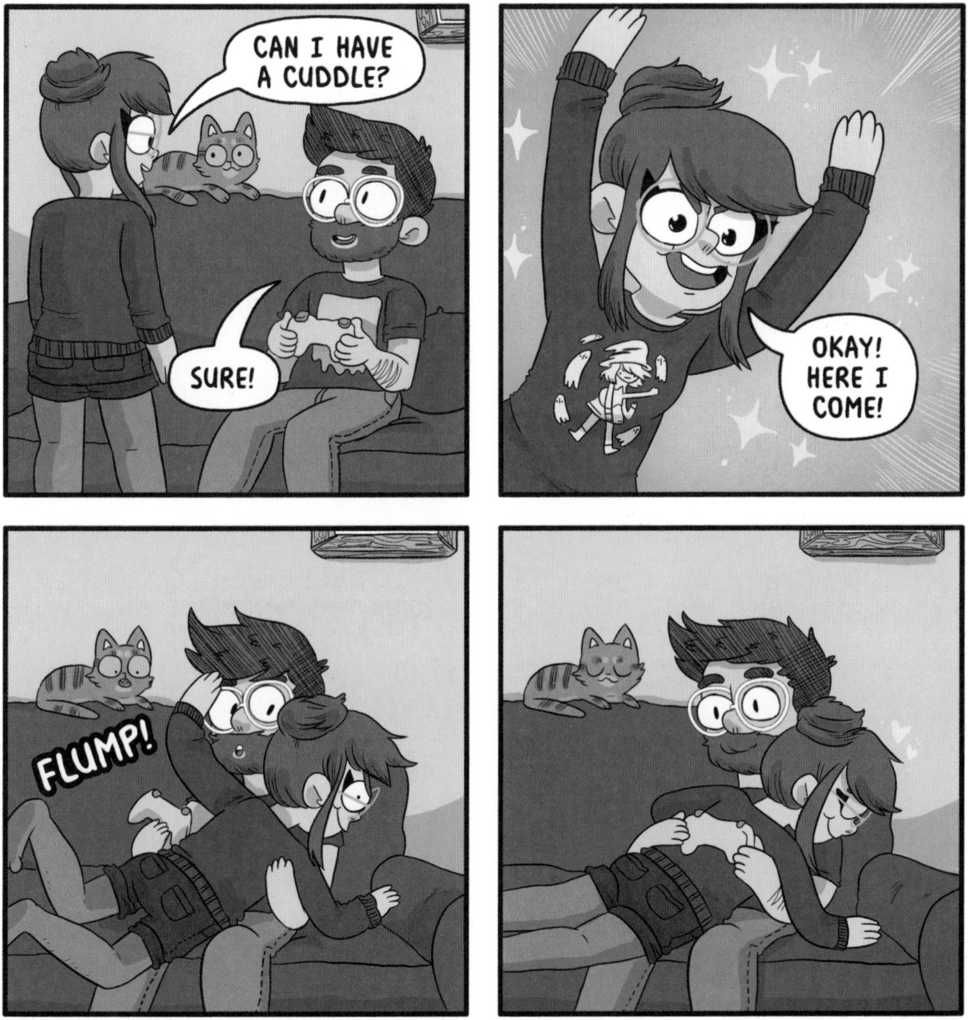
CAN I HAVE A CUDDLE?
SURE!
OKAY! HERE I COME!
FLUMP!

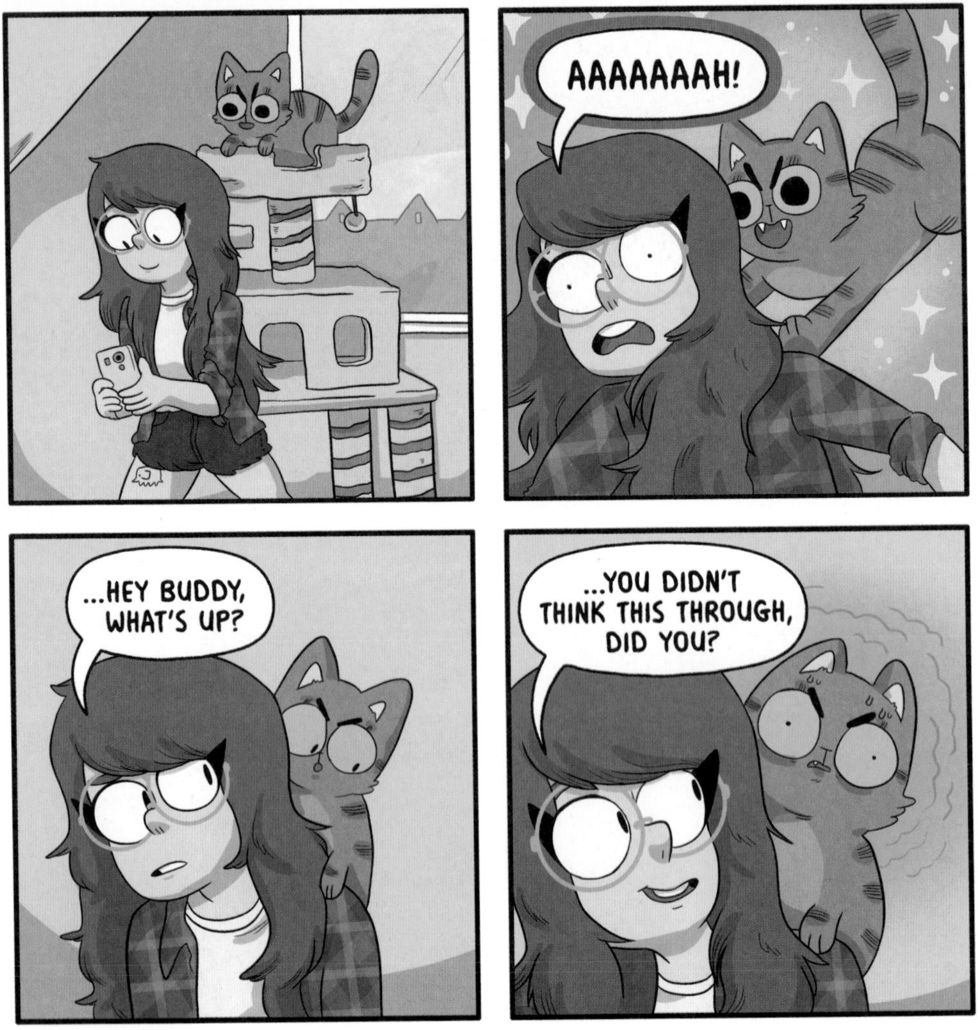
AAAAAAAH!
...HEY BUDDY, WHAT'S UP?
...YOU DIDN'T THINK THIS THROUGH, DID YOU?

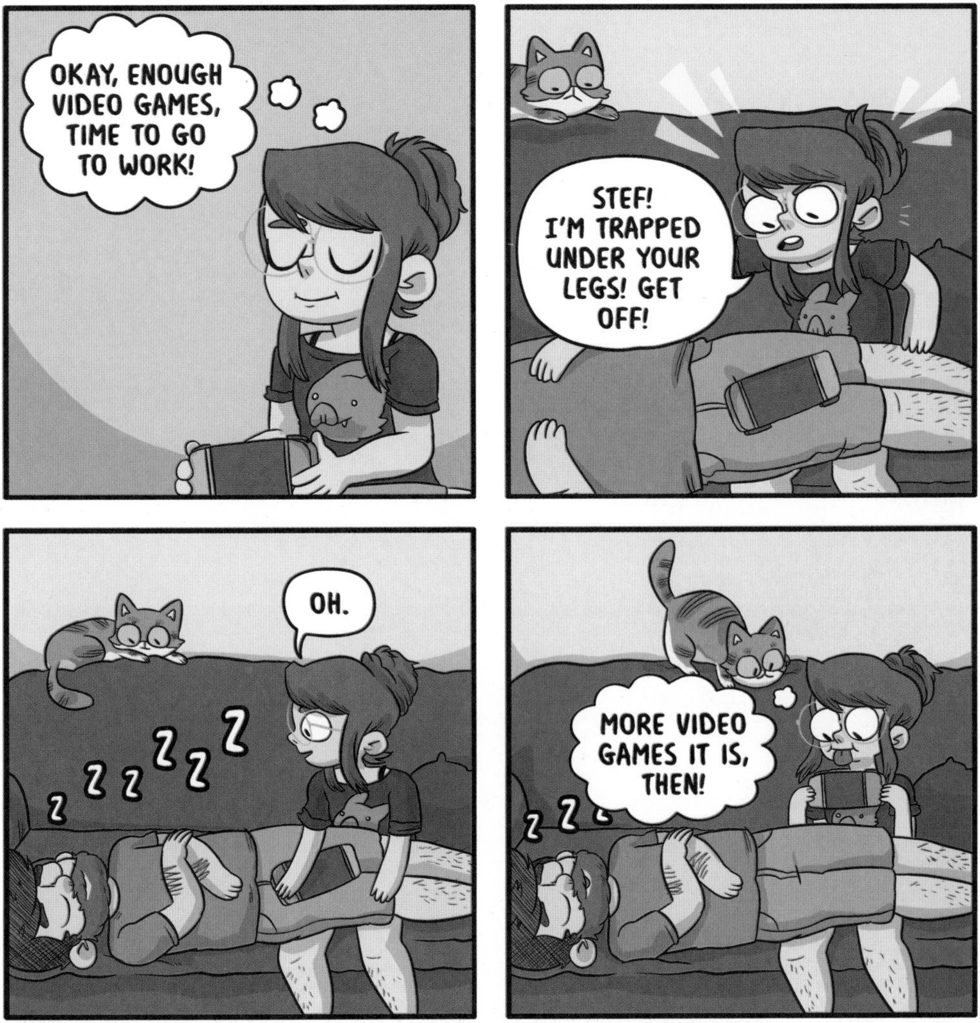
OKAY, ENOUGH VIDEO GAMES, TIME TO GO TO WORK!
STEF! I'M TRAPPED UNDER YOUR LEGS! GET OFF!
OH.
Z Z Z Z Z Z
MORE VIDEO GAMES IT IS, THEN!

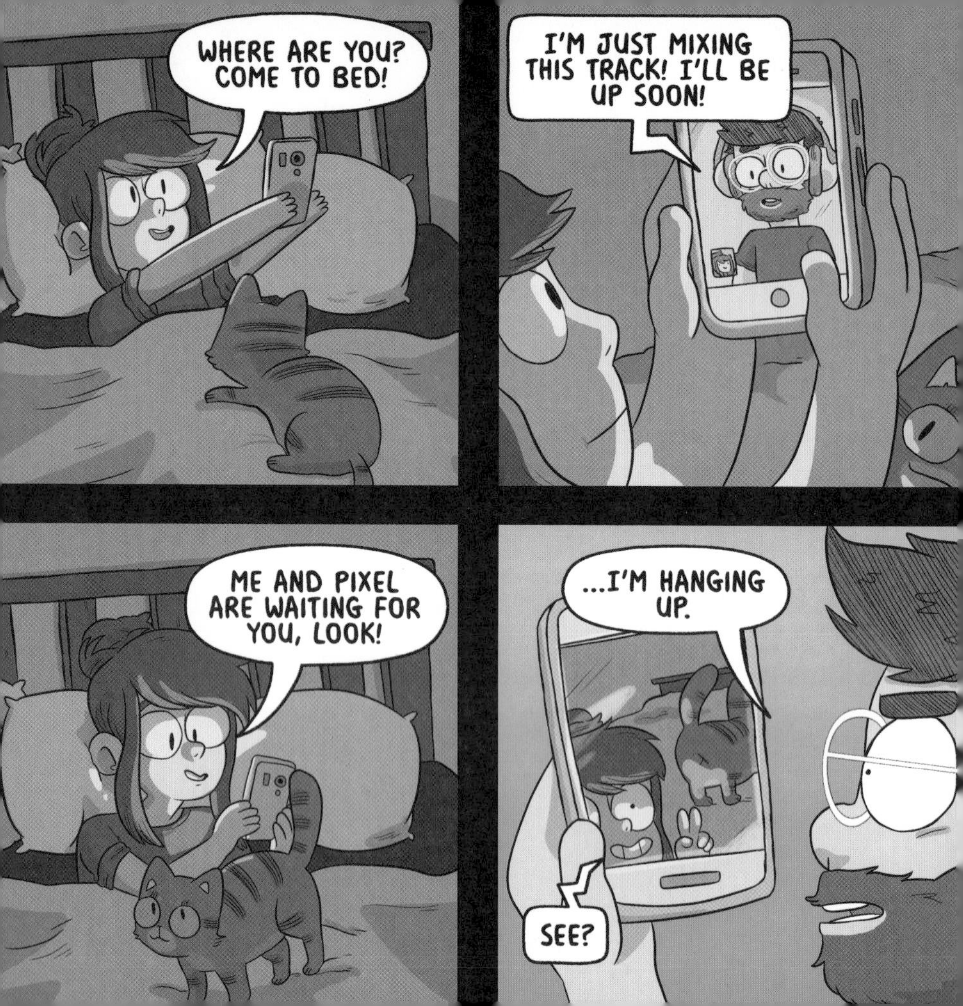
WHERE ARE YOU? COME TO BED!
I'M JUST MIXING THIS TRACK! I'LL BE UP SOON!
ME AND PIXEL ARE WAITING FOR YOU, LOOK!
SEE?
...I'M HANGING UP.

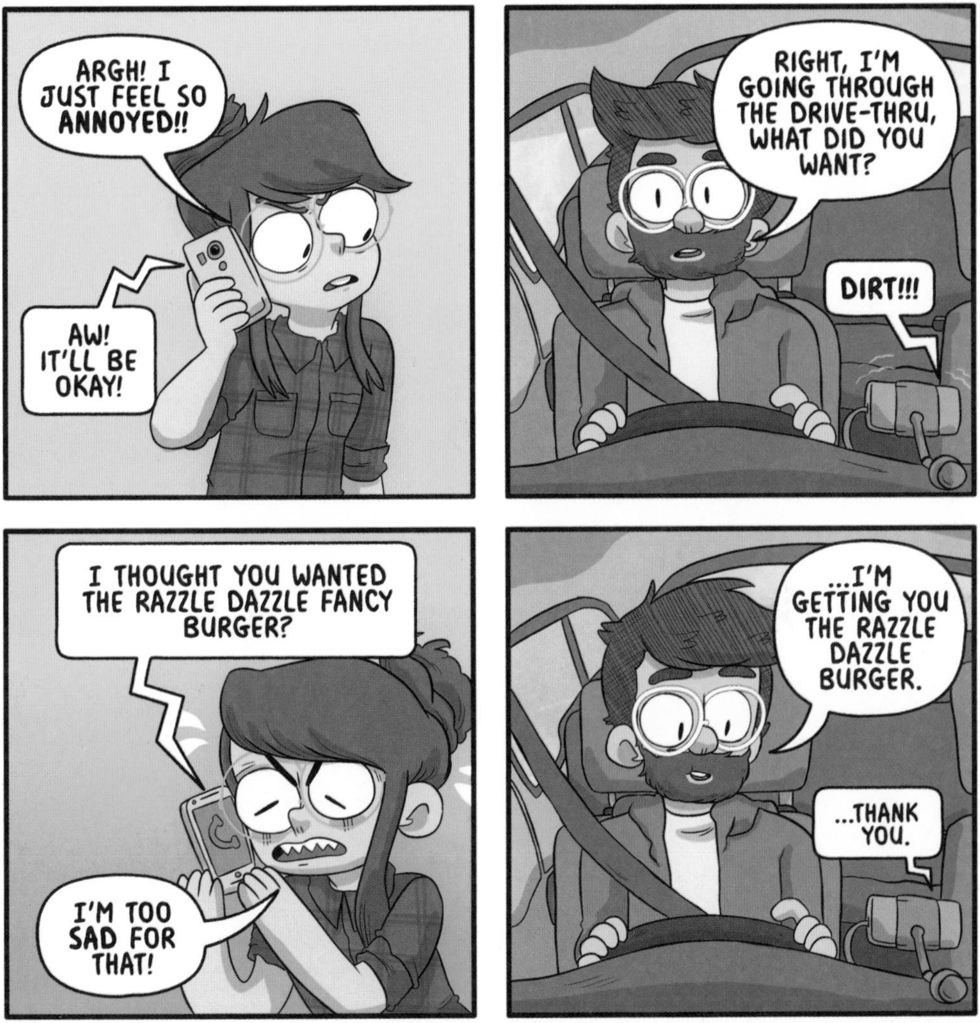
ARGH! I JUST FEEL SO ANNOYED!!
AW! IT'LL BE OKAY!
RIGHT, I'M GOING THROUGH THE DRIVE-THRU, WHAT DID YOU WANT?
DIRT!!!
I THOUGHT YOU WANTED THE RAZZLE DAZZLE FANCY BURGER?
I'M TOO SAD FOR THAT!
...I'M GETTING YOU THE RAZZLE DAZZLE BURGER.
...THANK YOU.

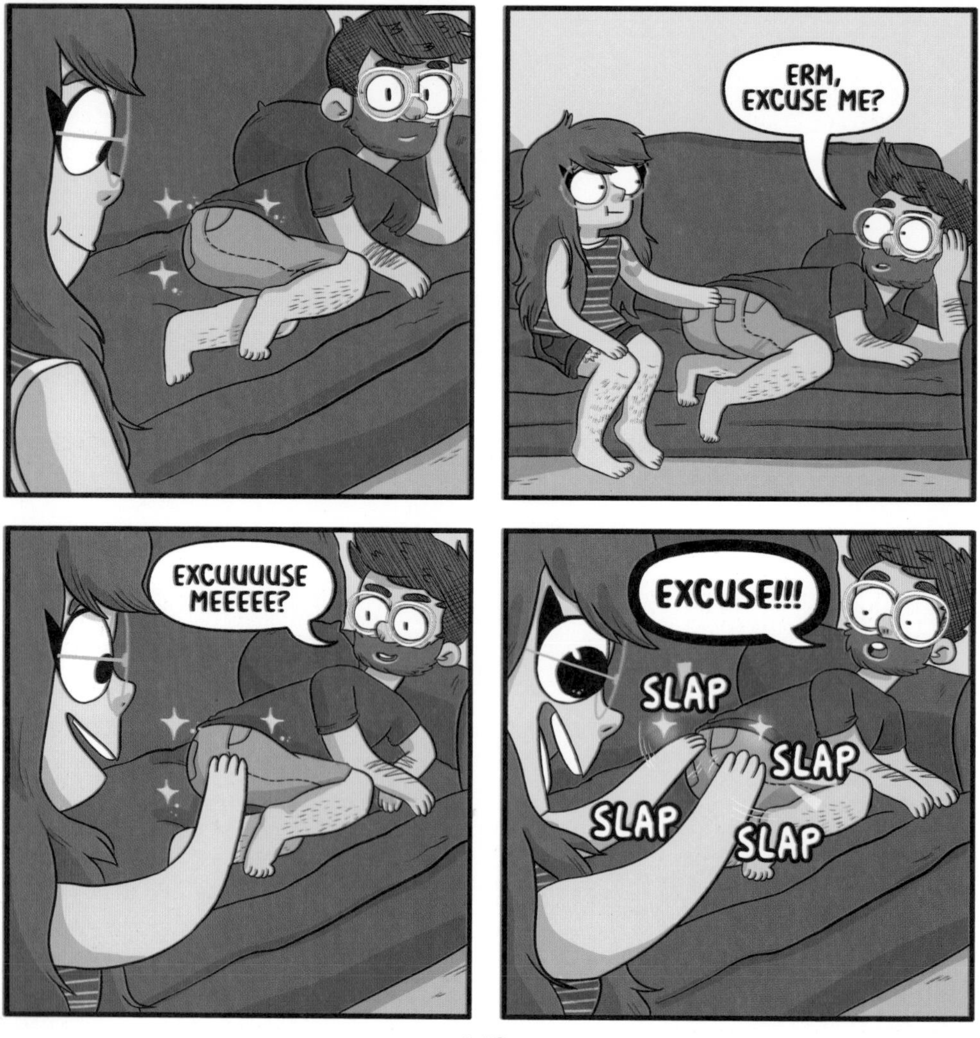
ERM, EXCUSE ME?
EXCUUUUSE MEEEEE?
EXCUSE!!!
SLAP
SLAP
SLAP
SLAP

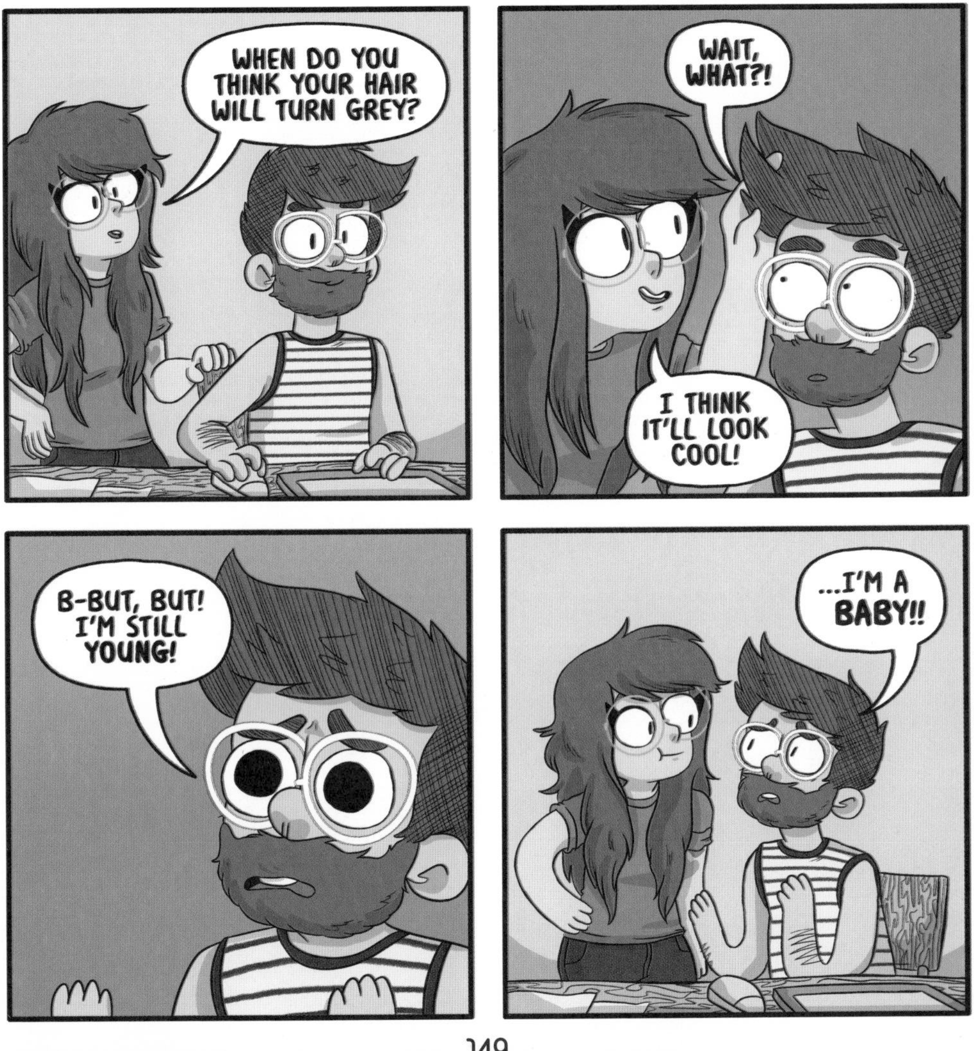
WHEN DO YOU THINK YOUR HAIR WILL TURN GREY?
WAIT, WHAT?!
I THINK IT'LL LOOK COOL!
B-BUT, BUT! I'M STILL YOUNG!
...I'M A BABY!!

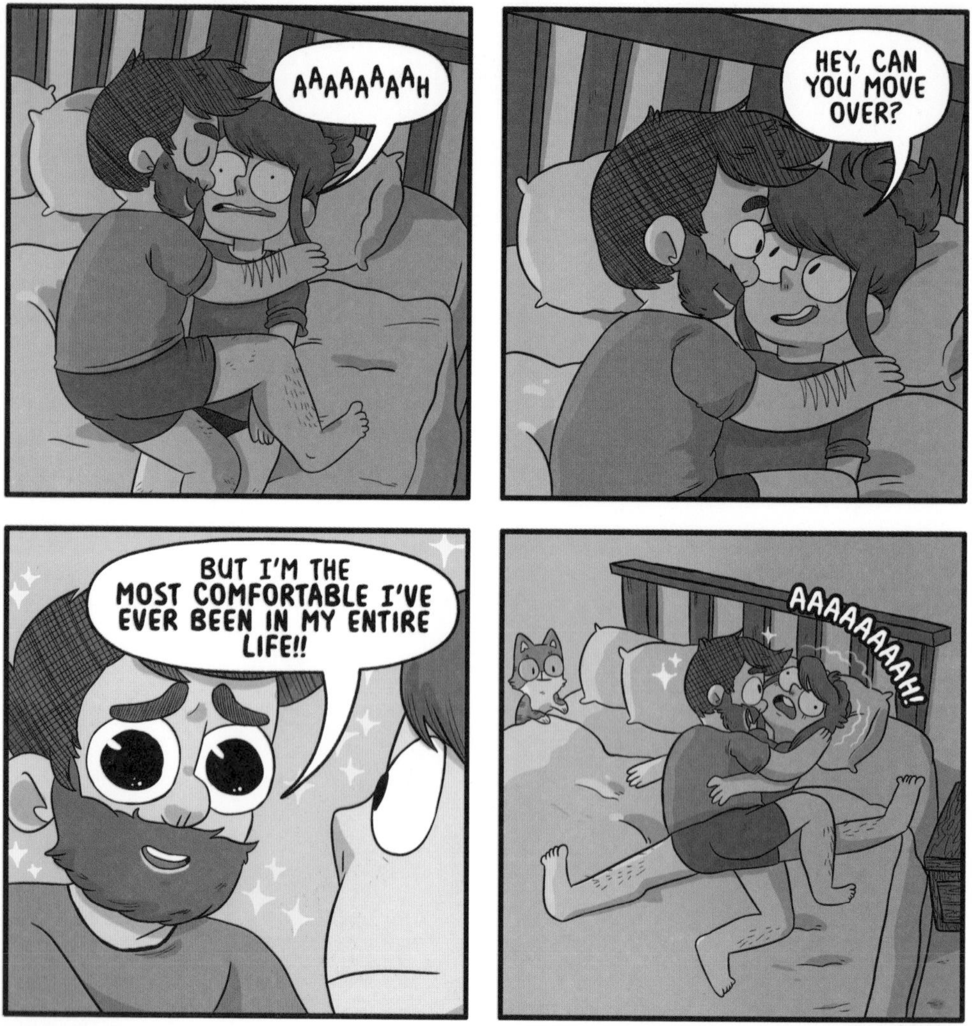
AAAAAAAAH
HEY, CAN YOU MOVE OVER?
BUT I'M THE MOST COMFORTABLE I'VE EVER BEEN IN MY ENTIRE LIFE!!
AAAAAAAAAH!

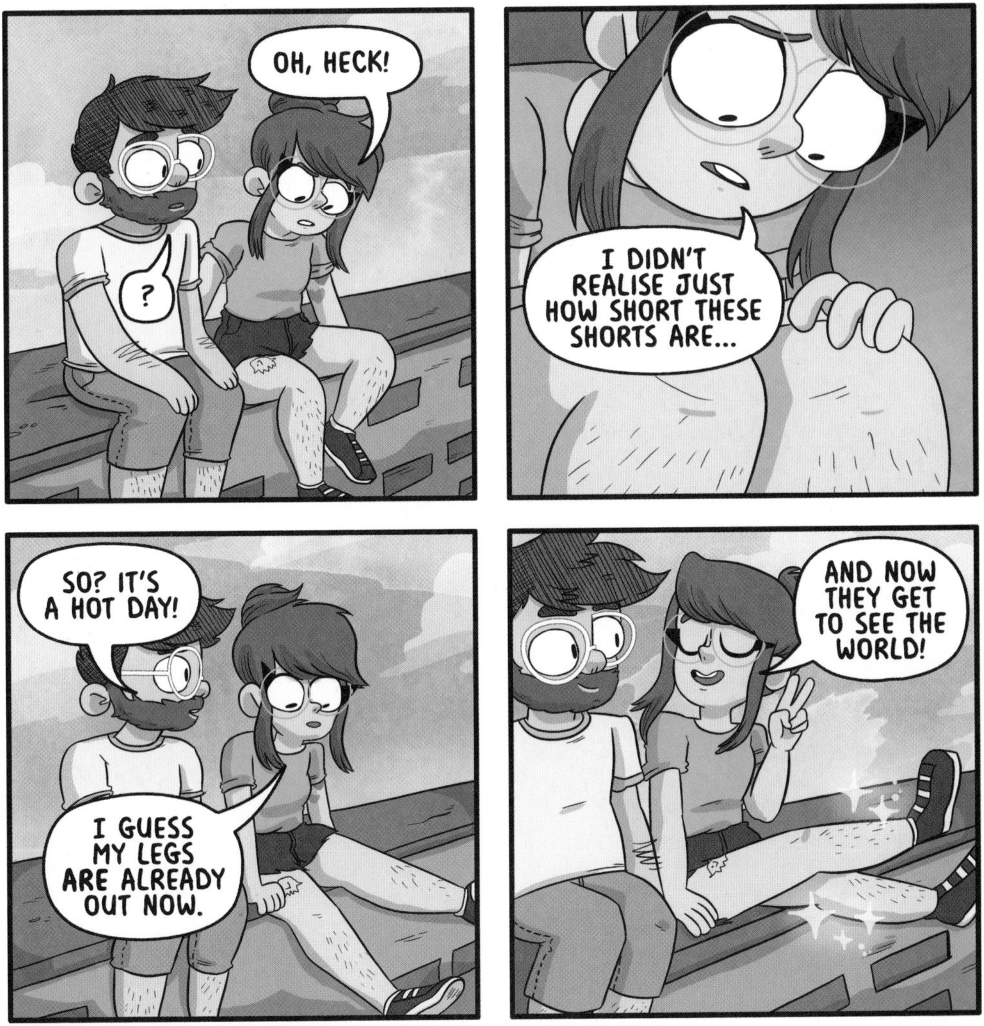
OH, HECK!
?
I DIDN'T REALISE JUST HOW SHORT THESE SHORTS ARE...
SO? IT'S A HOT DAY!
I GUESS MY LEGS ARE ALREADY OUT NOW.
AND NOW THEY GET TO SEE THE WORLD!

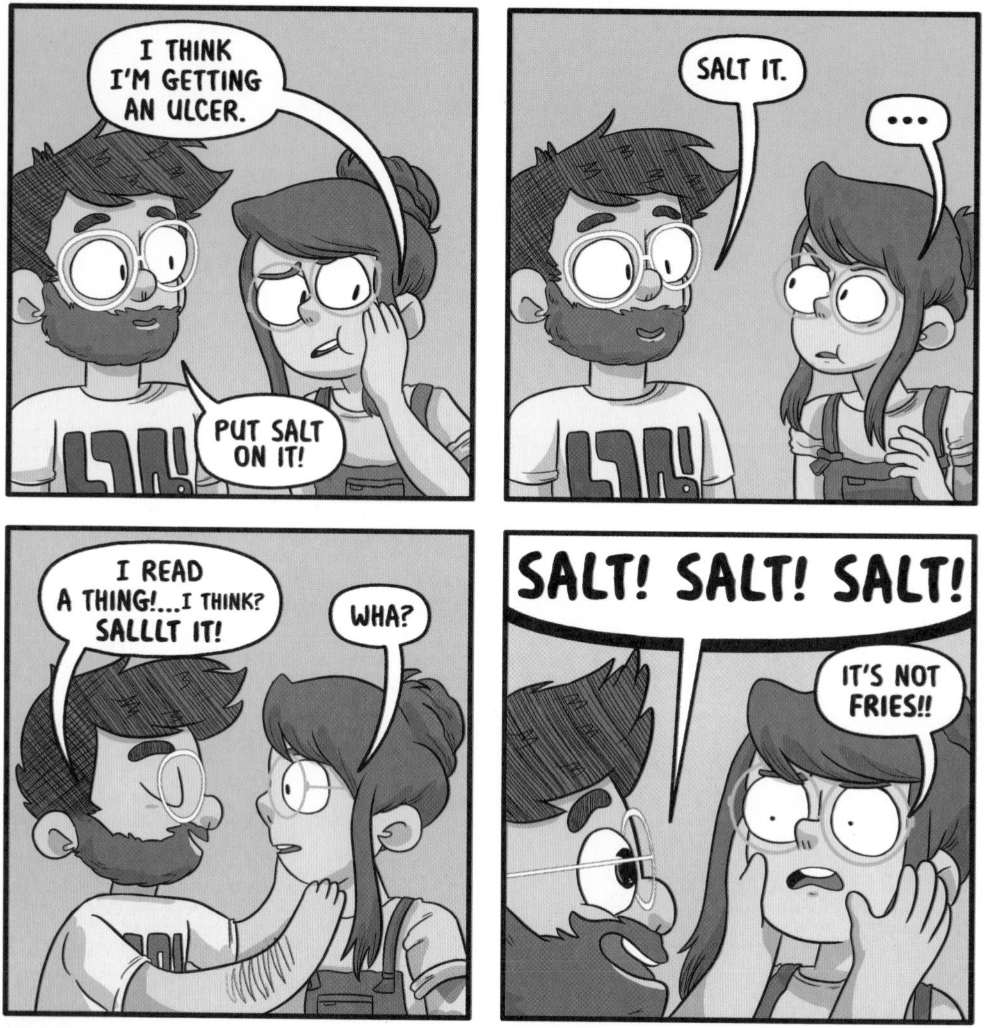
I THINK I'M GETTING AN ULCER.
PUT SALT ON IT!
SALT IT.
...
I READ A THING!...I THINK? SALLLT IT!
WHA?
SALT! SALT! SALT!
IT'S NOT FRIES!!

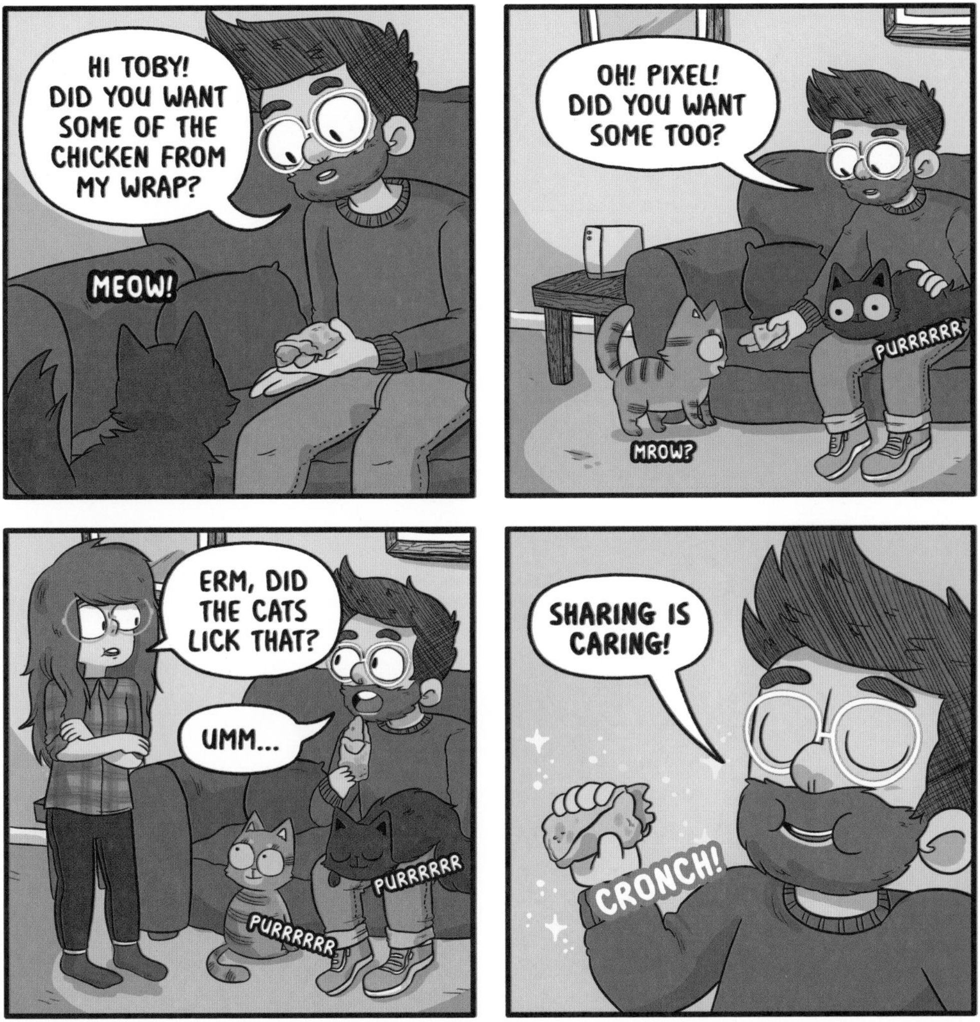
HI TOBY! DID YOU WANT SOME OF THE CHICKEN FROM MY WRAP?
MEOW!
OH! PIXEL! DID YOU WANT SOME TOO?
PURRRRRR
MROW?
ERM, DID THE CATS LICK THAT?
UMM...
PURRRRRR
PURRRRRR
SHARING IS CARING!
CRONCH!

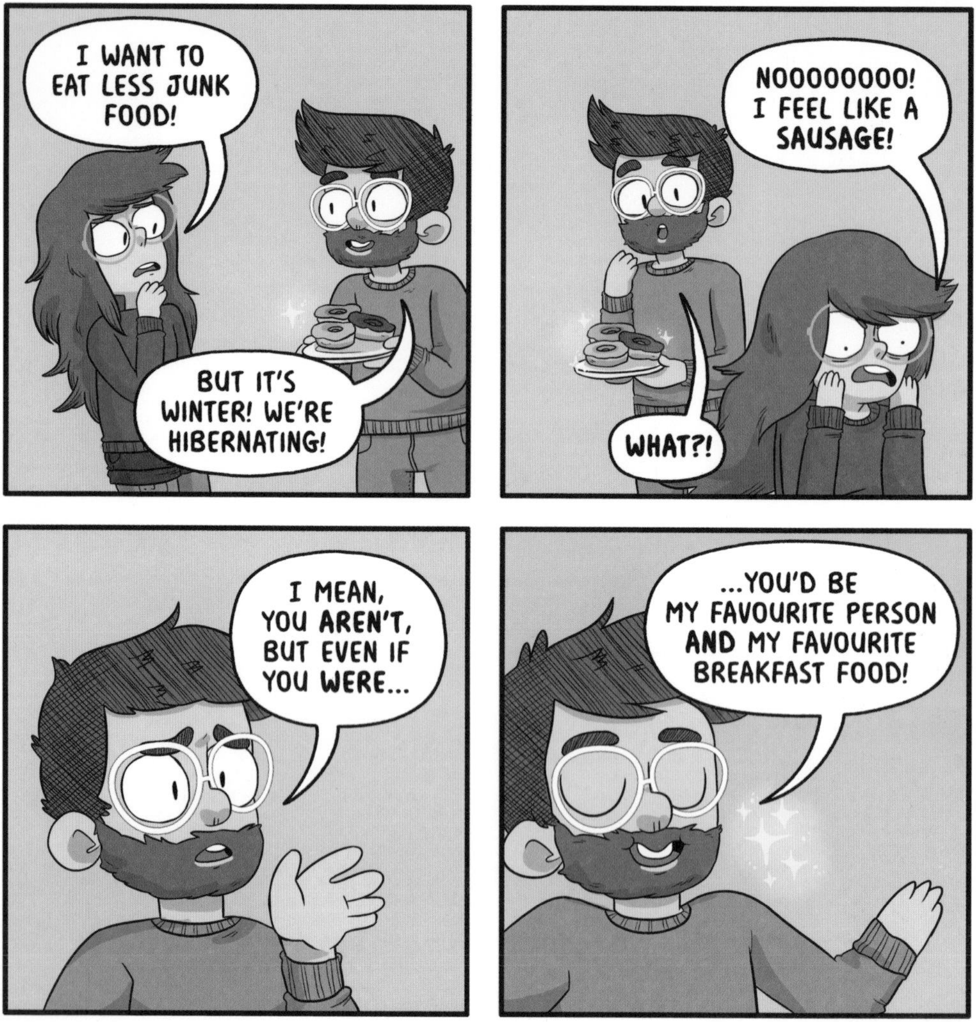
I WANT TO EAT LESS JUNK FOOD!
BUT IT'S WINTER! WE'RE HIBERNATING!
NOOOOOOOO! I FEEL LIKE A SAUSAGE!
WHAT?!
I MEAN, YOU AREN'T, BUT EVEN IF YOU WERE...
...YOU'D BE MY FAVOURITE PERSON AND MY FAVOURITE BREAKFAST FOOD!

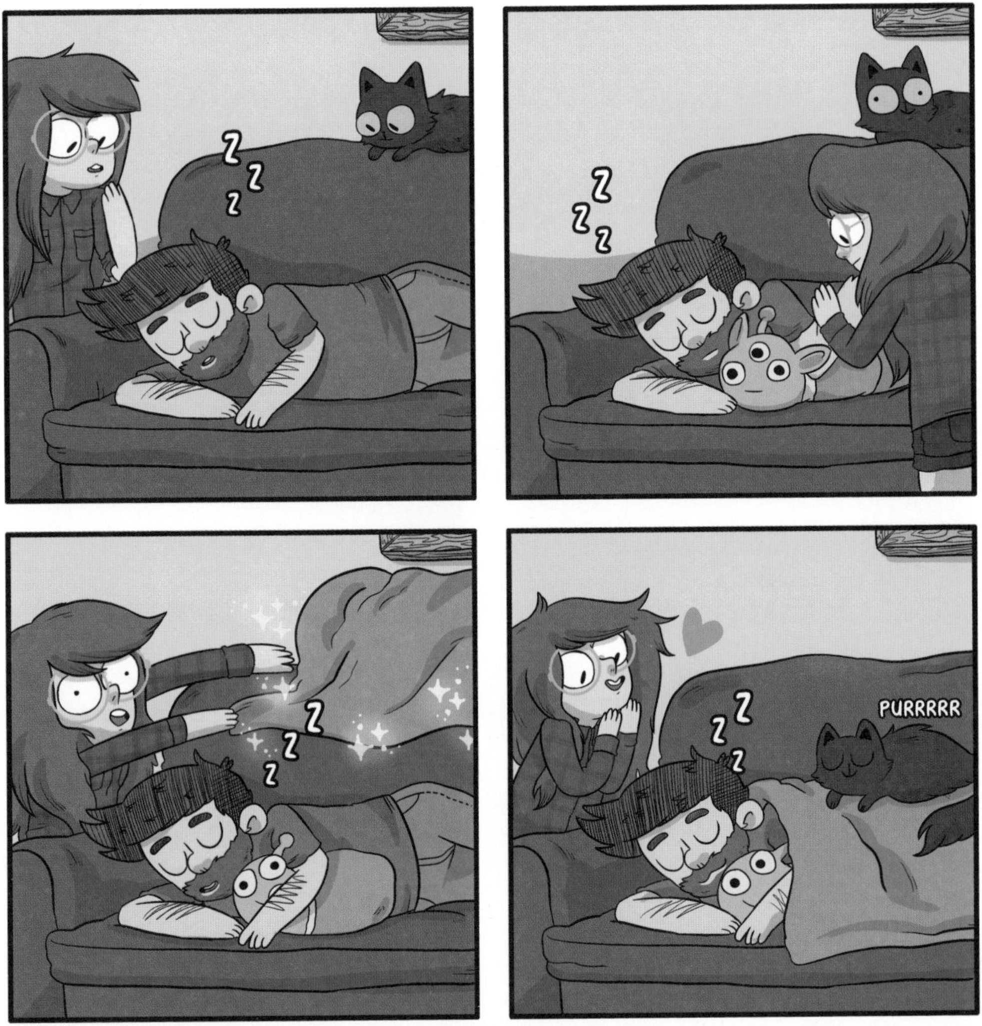
Z Z Z
Z Z Z
Z Z Z
Z Z Z
PURRRRR

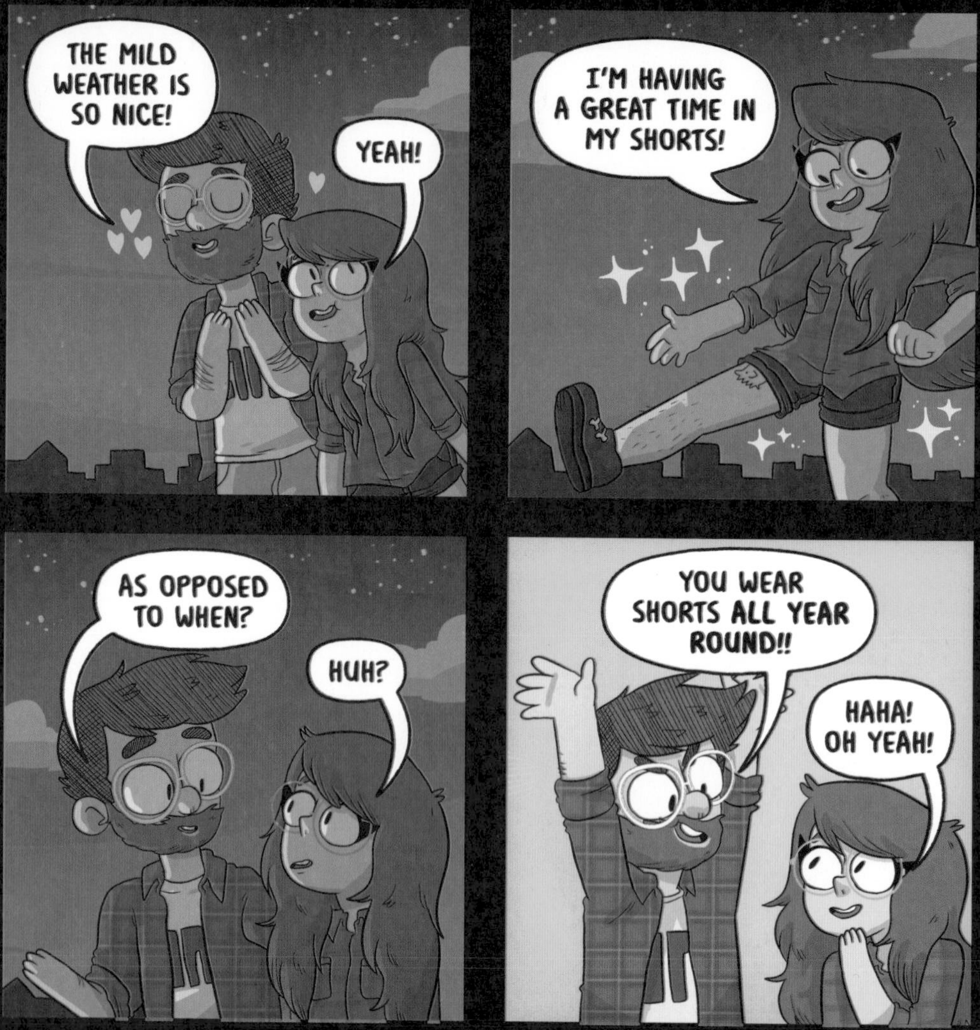
THE MILD WEATHER IS SO NICE!
YEAH!
I'M HAVING A GREAT TIME IN MY SHORTS!
AS OPPOSED TO WHEN?
HUH?
YOU WEAR SHORTS ALL YEAR ROUND!!
HAHA! OH YEAH!

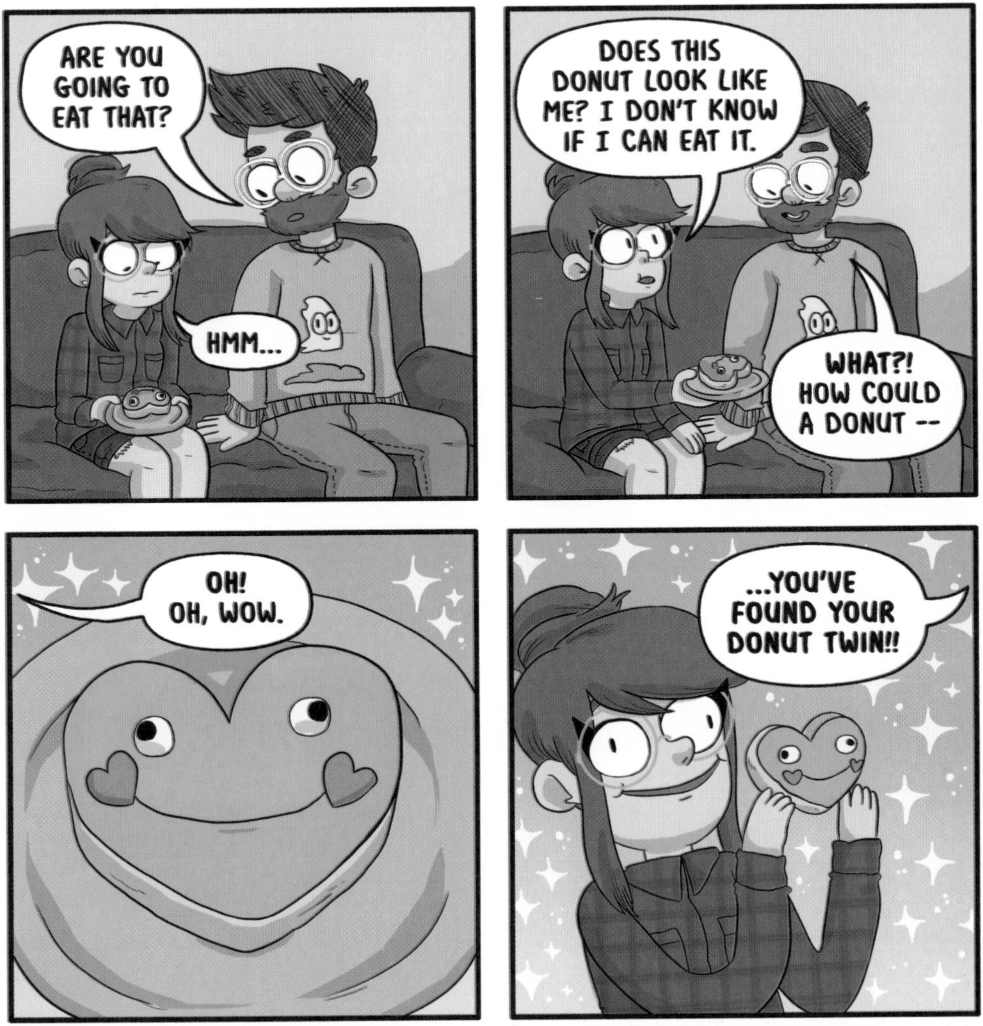
ARE YOU GOING TO EAT THAT?
HMM...
DOES THIS DONUT LOOK LIKE ME? I DON'T KNOW IF I CAN EAT IT.
WHAT?! HOW COULD A DONUT --
OH! OH, WOW.
...YOU'VE FOUND YOUR DONUT TWIN!!

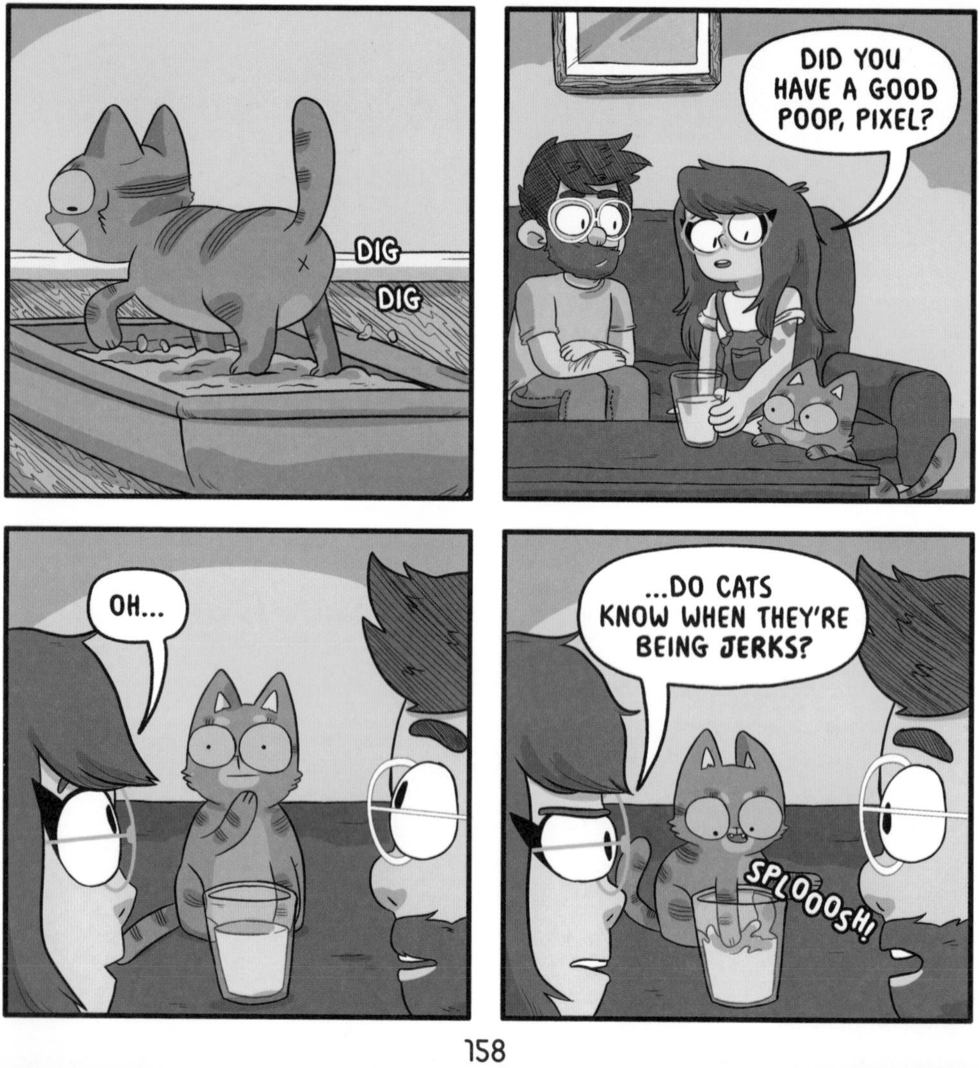
DIG
DIG
DID YOU HAVE A GOOD POOP, PIXEL?
OH...
...DO CATS KNOW WHEN THEY'RE BEING JERKS?
SPLOOOSH!

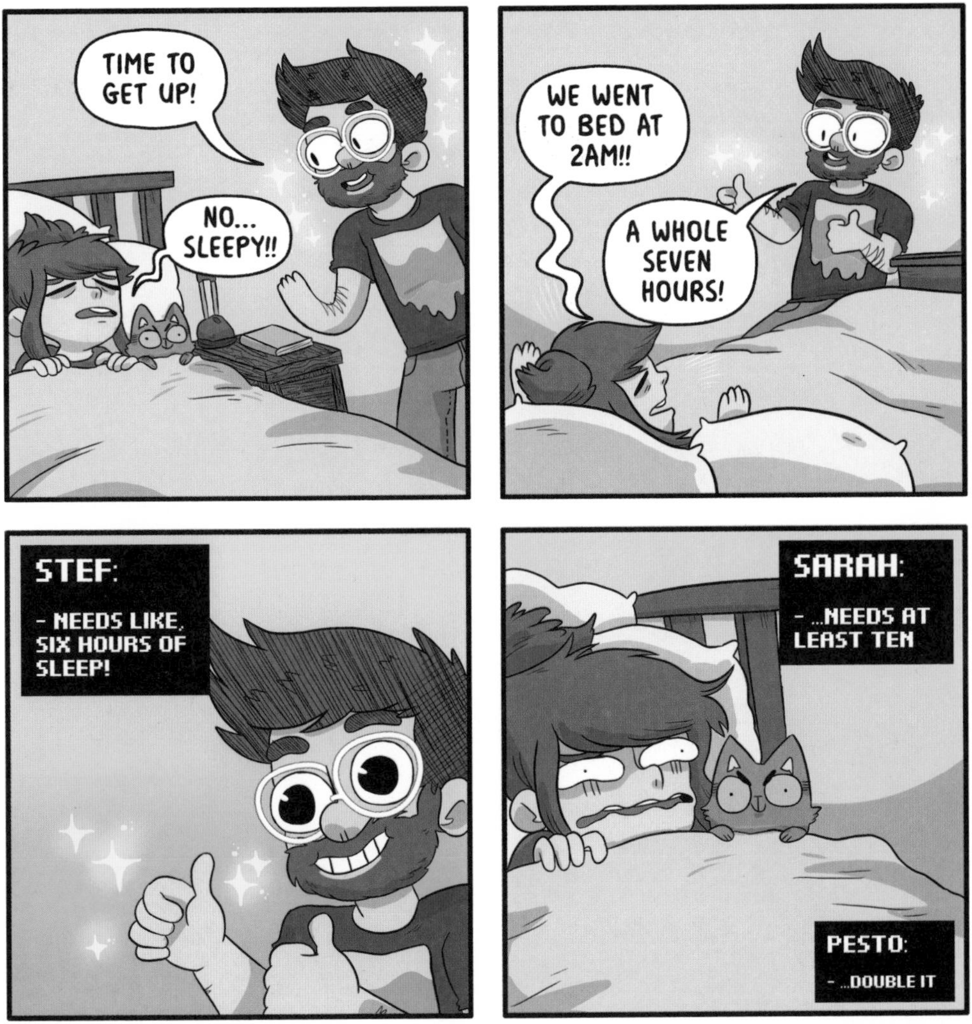
TIME TO GET UP!
NO... SLEEPY!!
WE WENT TO BED AT 2AM!!
A WHOLE SEVEN HOURS!
STEF:
- NEEDS LIKE, SIX HOURS OF SLEEP!
SARAH:
- ...NEEDS AT LEAST TEN
PESTO:
- ...DOUBLE IT

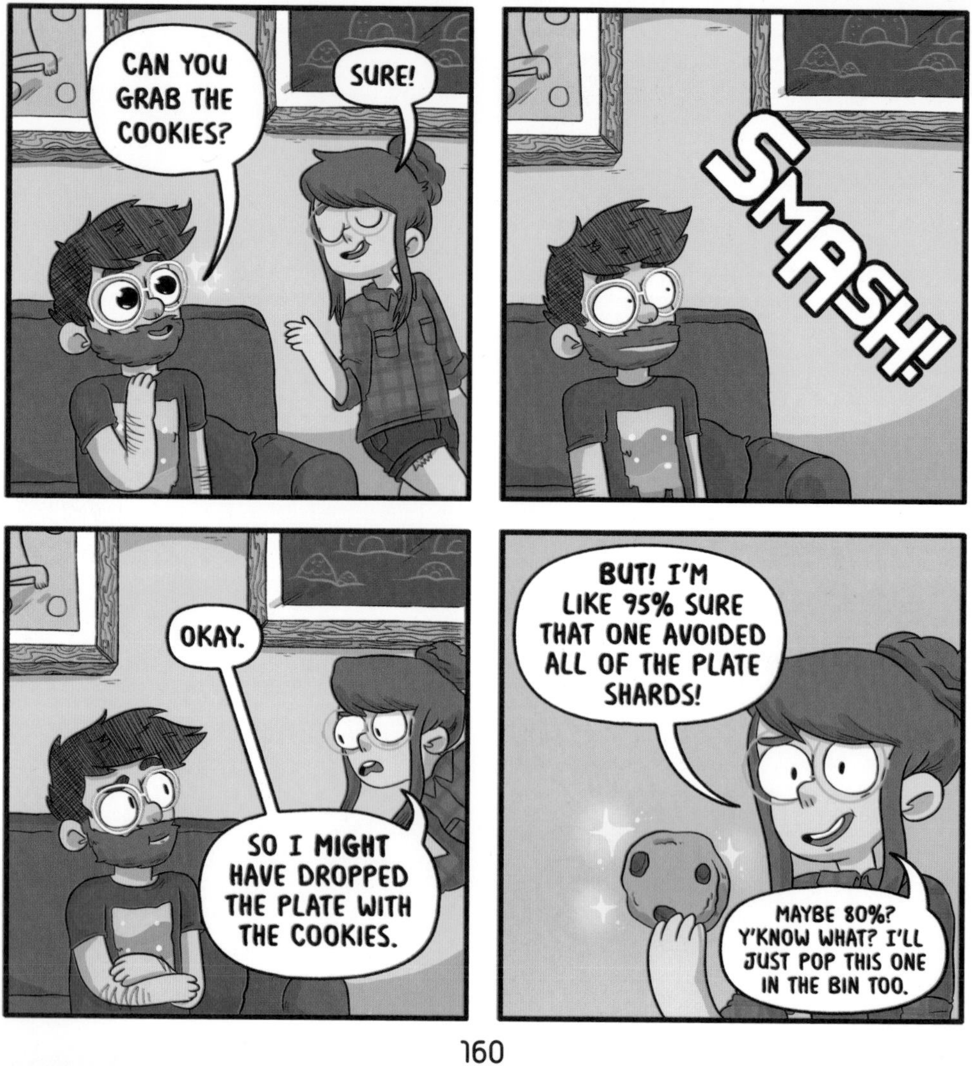
CAN YOU GRAB THE COOKIES?
SURE!
SMASH!
OKAY.
SO I MIGHT HAVE DROPPED THE PLATE WITH THE COOKIES.
BUT! I'M LIKE 95% SURE THAT ONE AVOIDED ALL OF THE PLATE SHARDS!
MAYBE 80%? Y'KNOW WHAT? I'LL JUST POP THIS ONE IN THE BIN TOO.

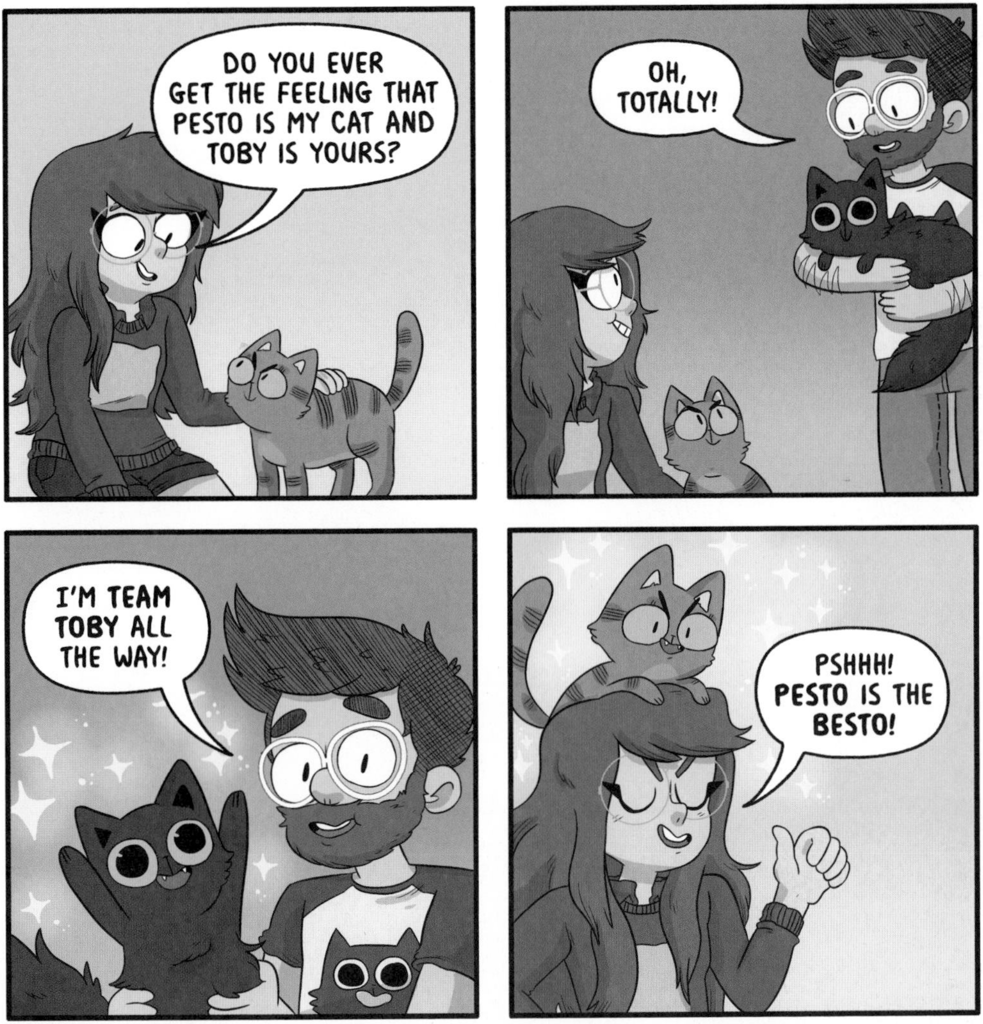
DO YOU EVER GET THE FEELING THAT PESTO IS MY CAT AND TOBY IS YOURS?
OH, TOTALLY!
I'M TEAM TOBY ALL THE WAY!
PSHHH! PESTO IS THE BESTO!

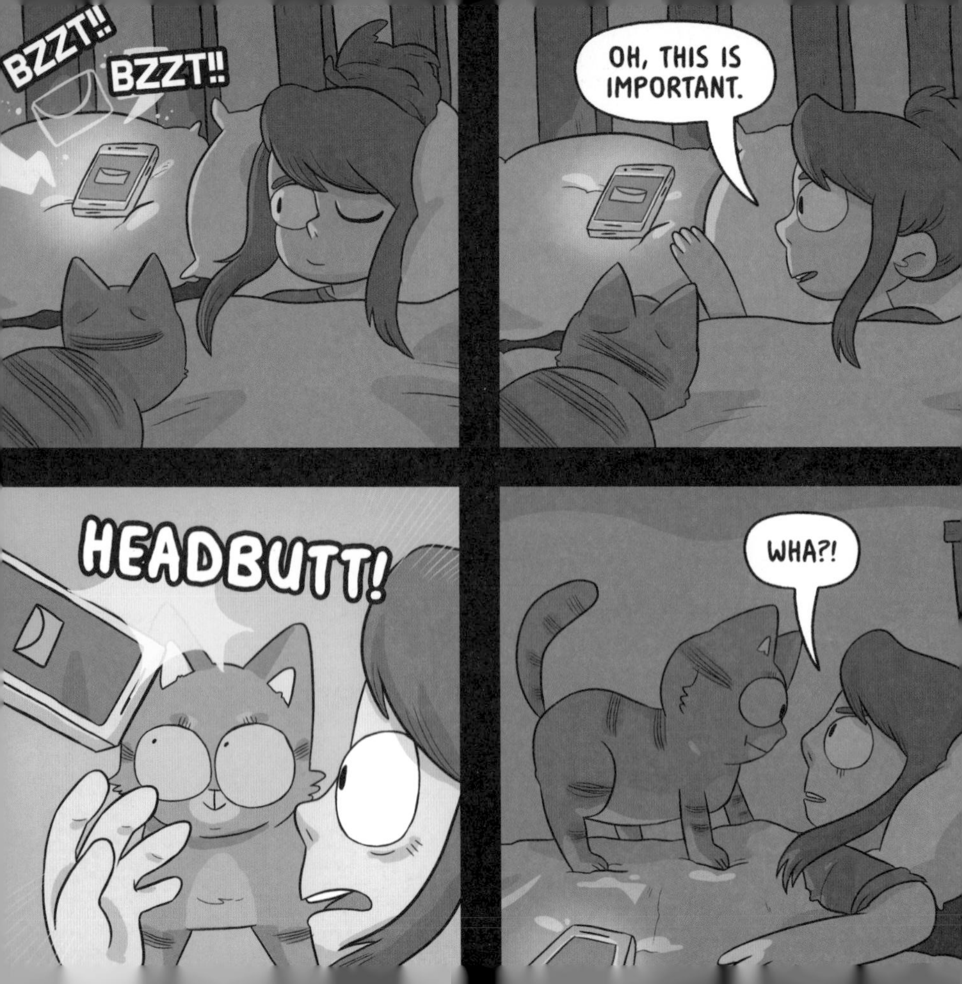
BZZT!!
BZZT!!
OH, THIS IS IMPORTANT.
HEADBUTT!
WHA?!

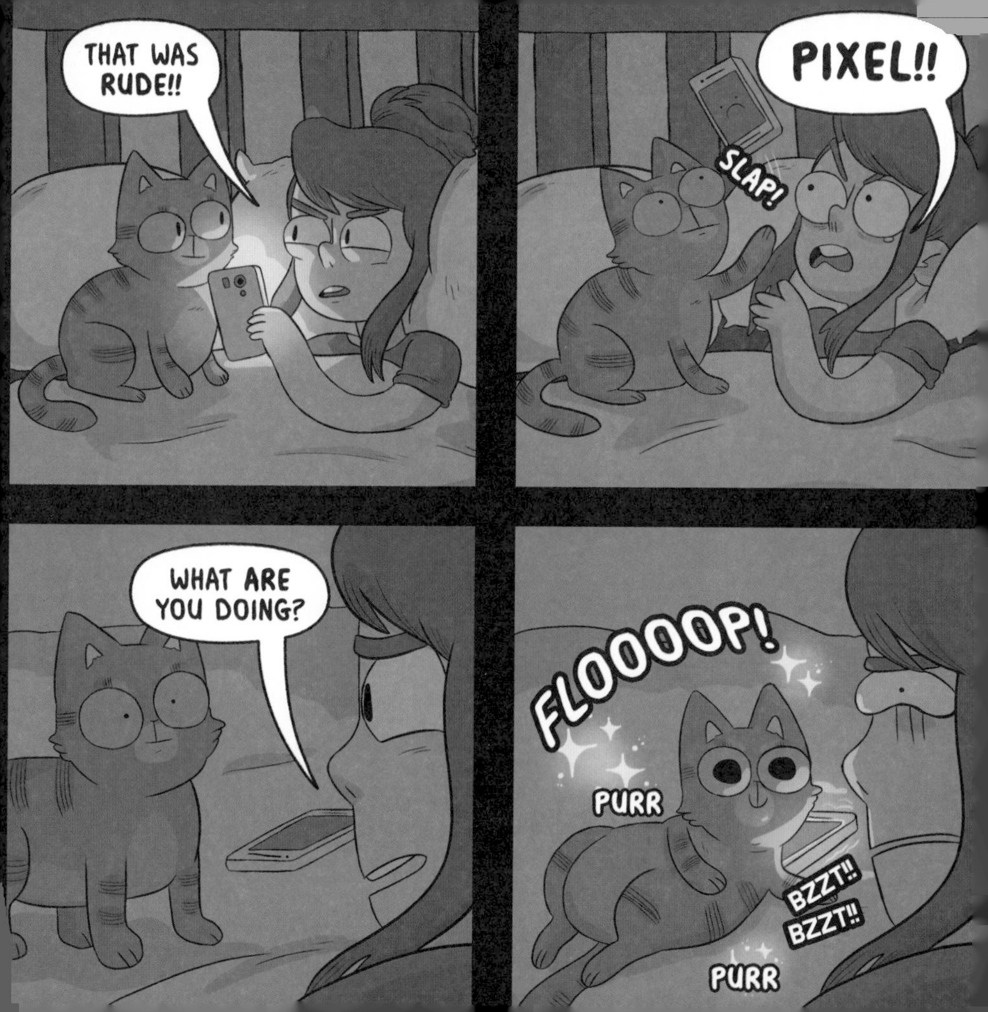
THAT WAS RUDE!!
PIXEL!!
SLAP!
WHAT ARE YOU DOING?
FLOOOOP!
PURR
BZZT!! BZZT!!
PURR

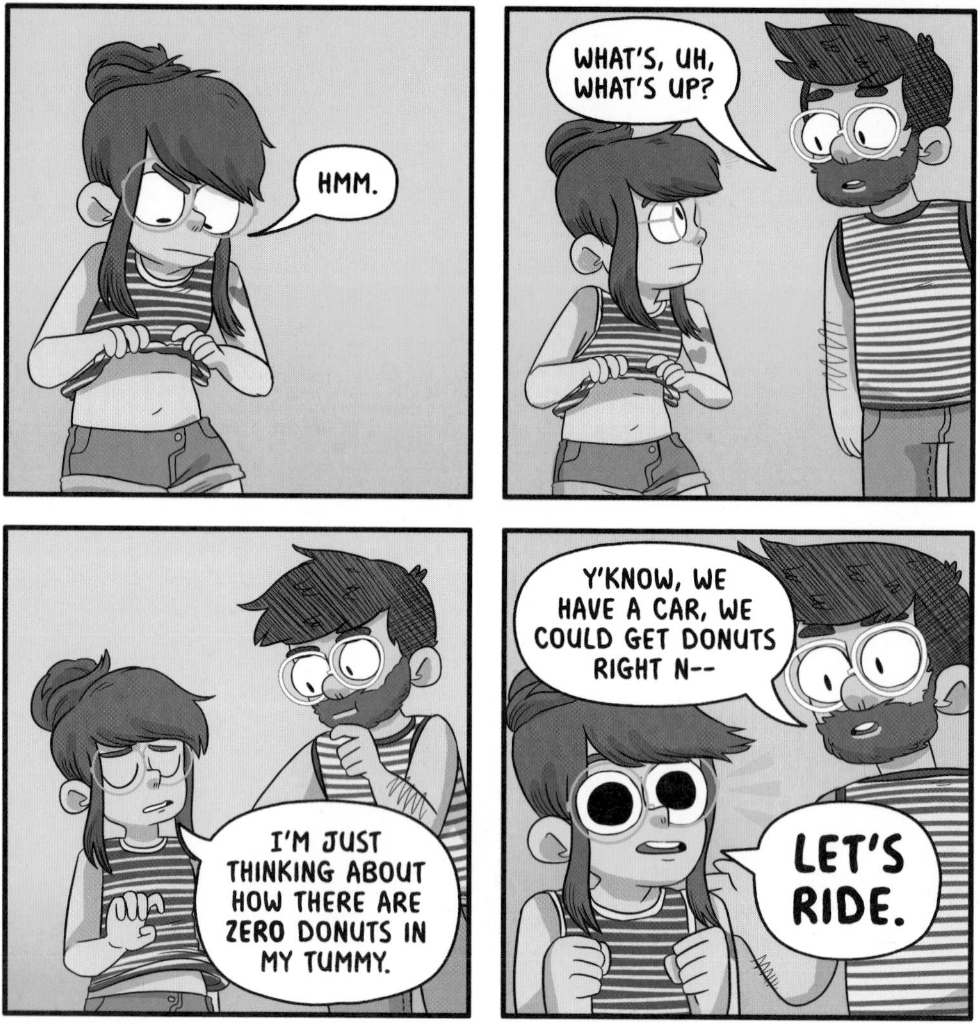
HMM.
WHAT'S, UH, WHAT'S UP?
I'M JUST THINKING ABOUT HOW THERE ARE ZERO DONUTS IN MY TUMMY.
Y'KNOW, WE HAVE A CAR, WE COULD GET DONUTS RIGHT N--
LET'S RIDE.

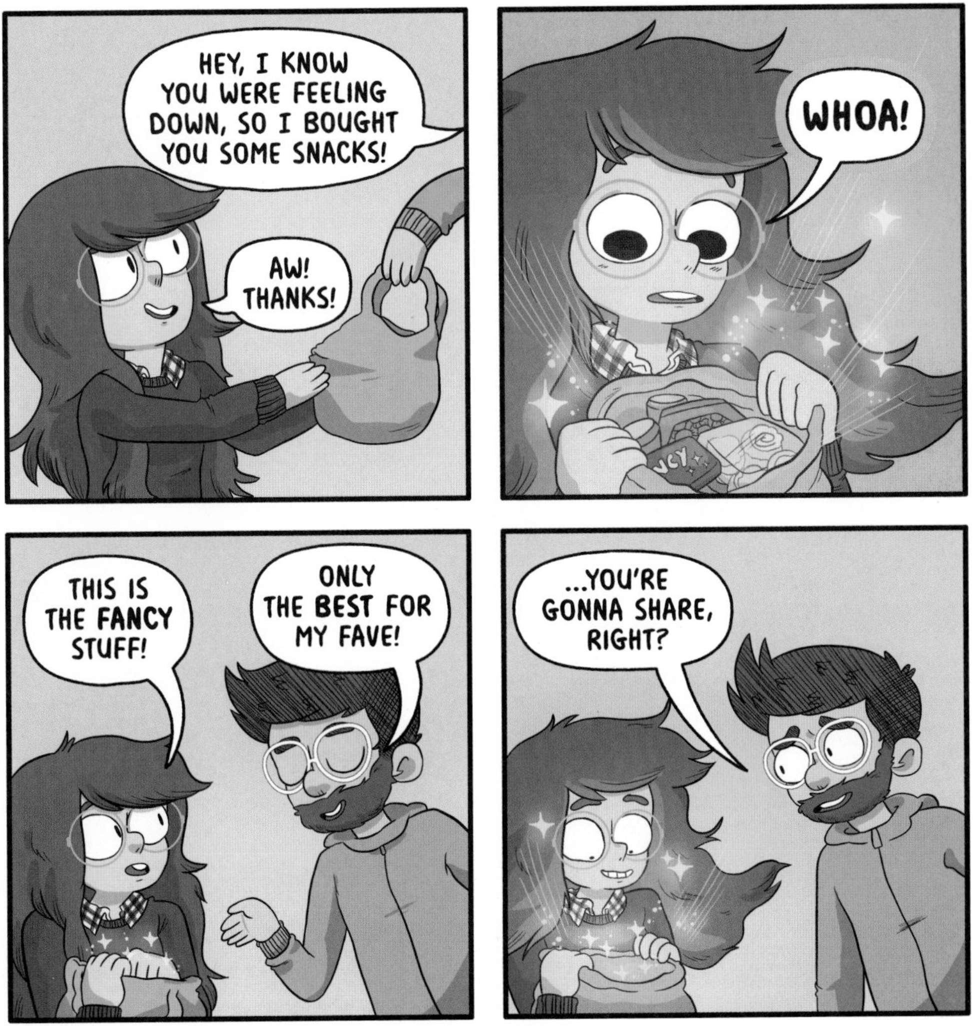
HEY, I KNOW YOU WERE FEELING DOWN, SO I BOUGHT YOU SOME SNACKS!
AW! THANKS!
WHOA!
THIS IS THE **FANCY** STUFF!
ONLY THE **BEST** FOR MY FAVE!
...YOU'RE GONNA SHARE, RIGHT?

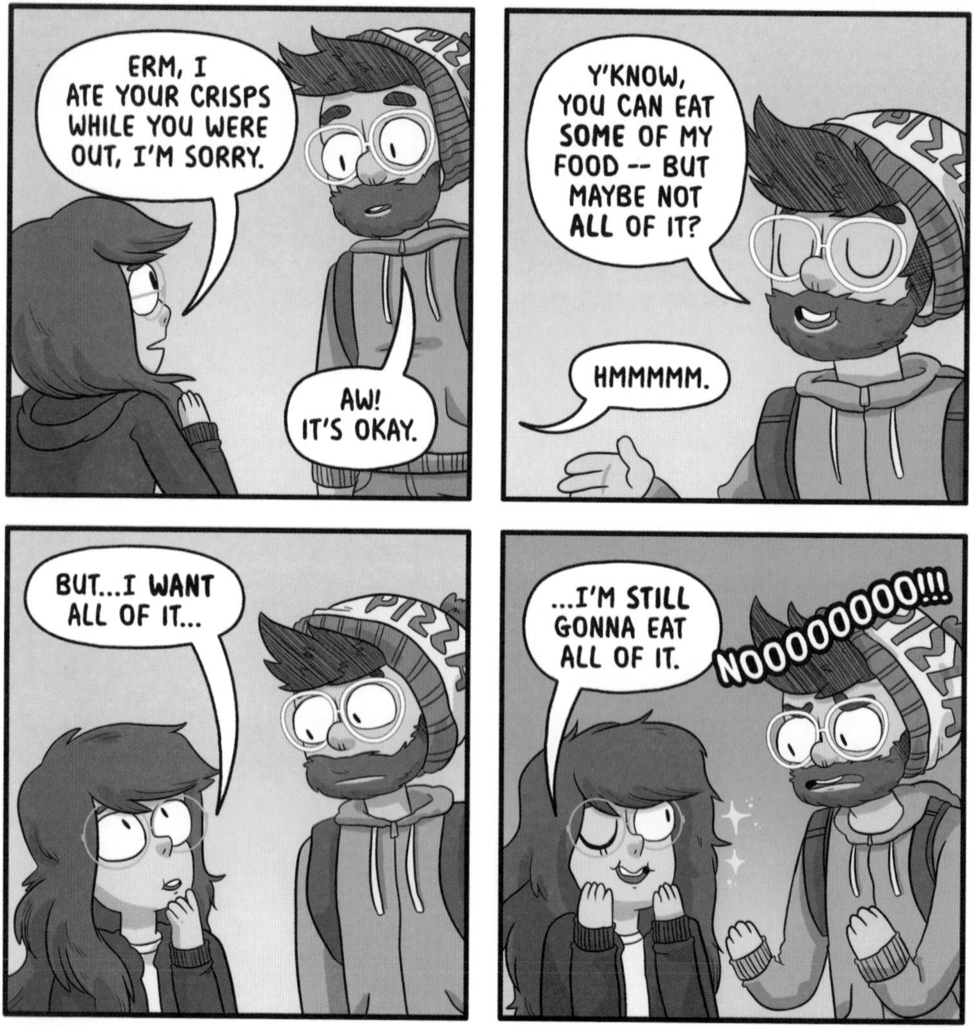
ERM, I ATE YOUR CRISPS WHILE YOU WERE OUT, I'M SORRY.
AW! IT'S OKAY.
Y'KNOW, YOU CAN EAT SOME OF MY FOOD -- BUT MAYBE NOT ALL OF IT?
HMMMMM.
BUT...I WANT ALL OF IT...
...I'M STILL GONNA EAT ALL OF IT.
NOOOOOOOO!!!

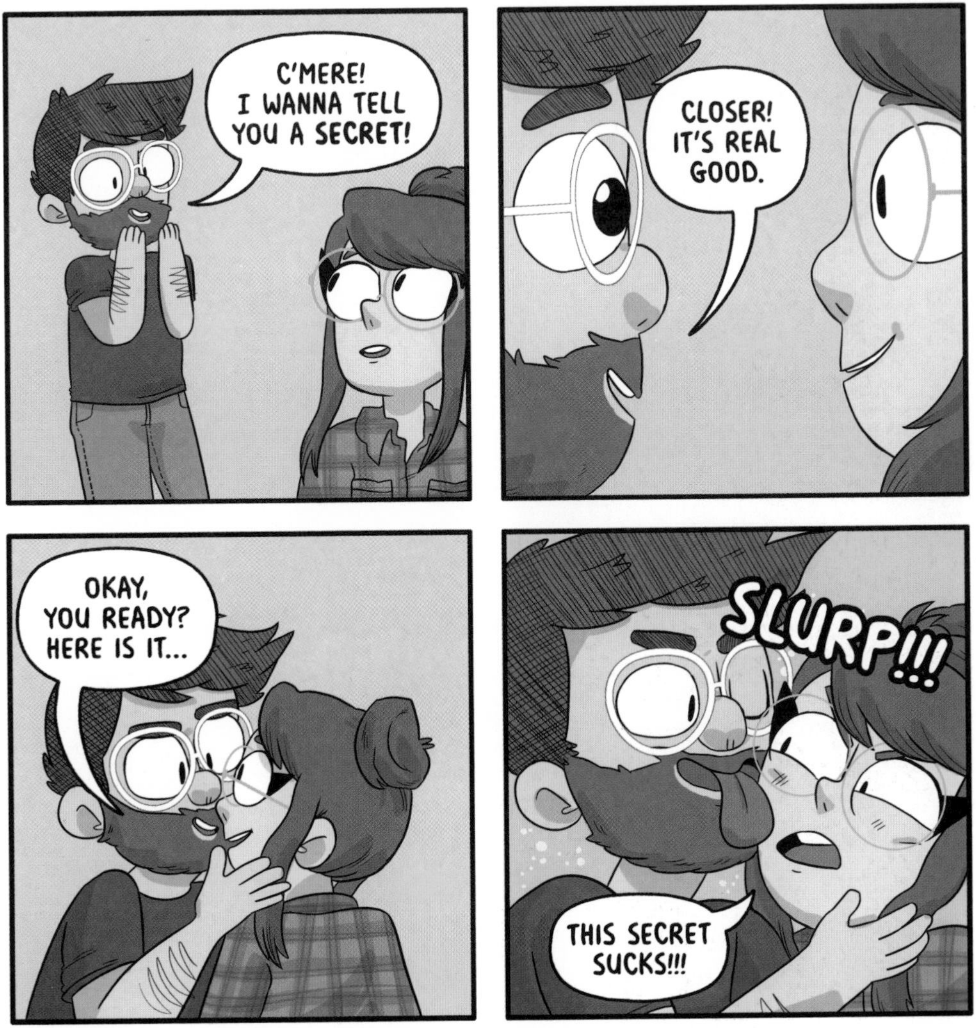
C'MERE! I WANNA TELL YOU A SECRET!
CLOSER! IT'S REAL GOOD.
OKAY, YOU READY? HERE IS IT...
SLURP!!!
THIS SECRET SUCKS!!!

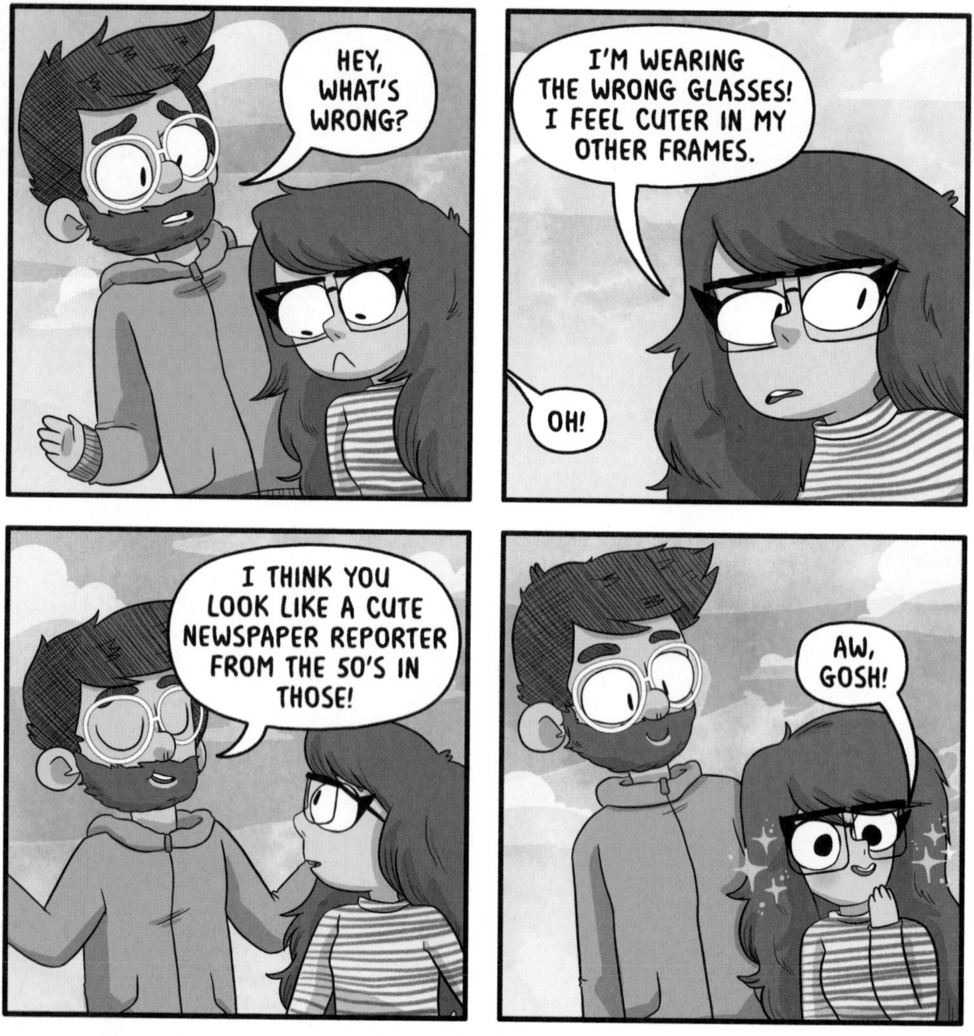
HEY, WHAT'S WRONG?
I'M WEARING THE WRONG GLASSES! I FEEL CUTER IN MY OTHER FRAMES.
OH!
I THINK YOU LOOK LIKE A CUTE NEWSPAPER REPORTER FROM THE 50'S IN THOSE!
AW, GOSH!

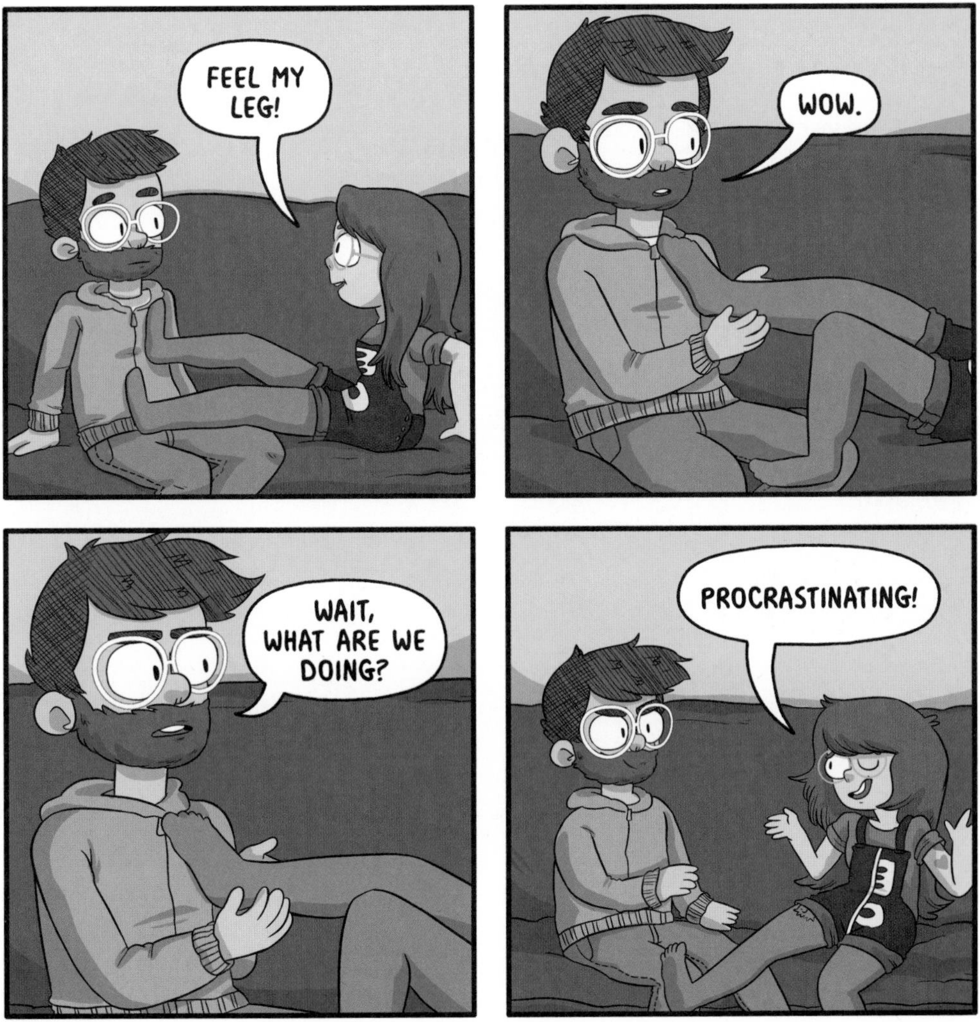
FEEL MY LEG!
WOW.
WAIT, WHAT ARE WE DOING?
PROCRASTINATING!

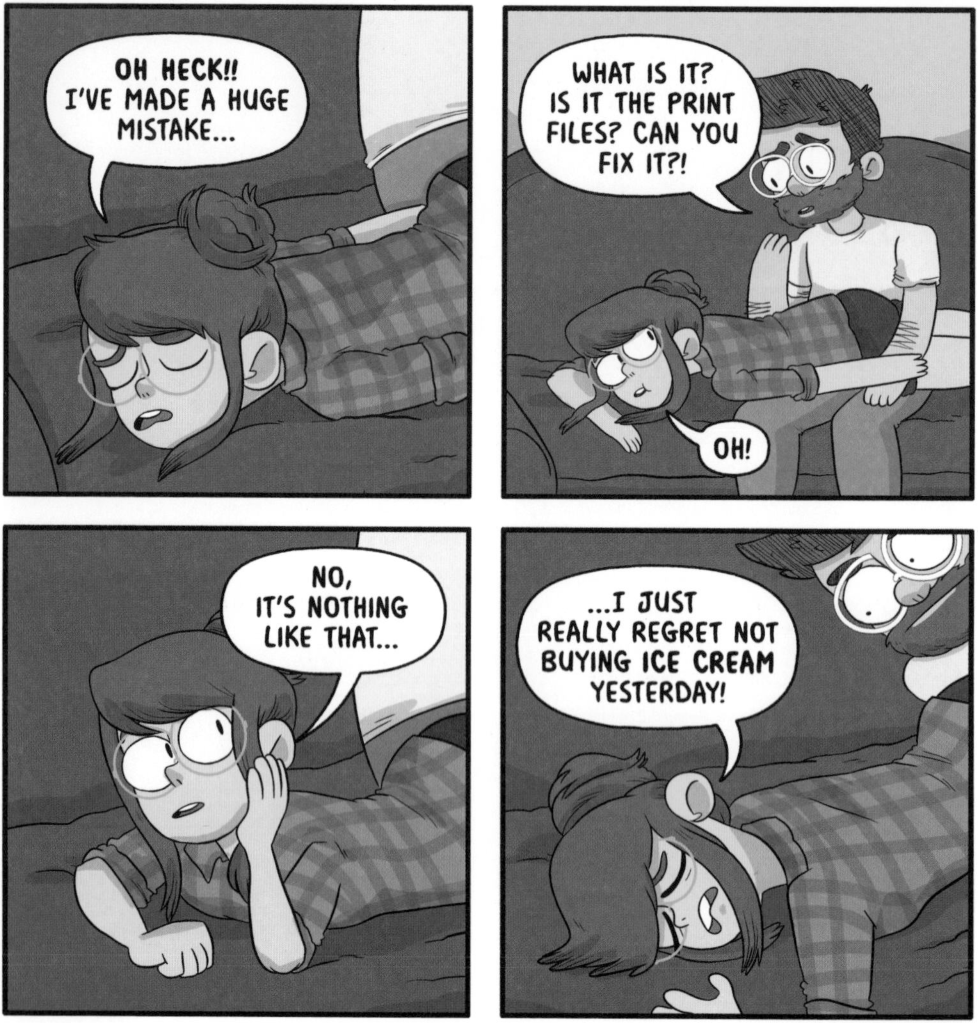
OH HECK!! I'VE MADE A HUGE MISTAKE...
WHAT IS IT? IS IT THE PRINT FILES? CAN YOU FIX IT?!
OH!
NO, IT'S NOTHING LIKE THAT...
...I JUST REALLY REGRET NOT BUYING ICE CREAM YESTERDAY!

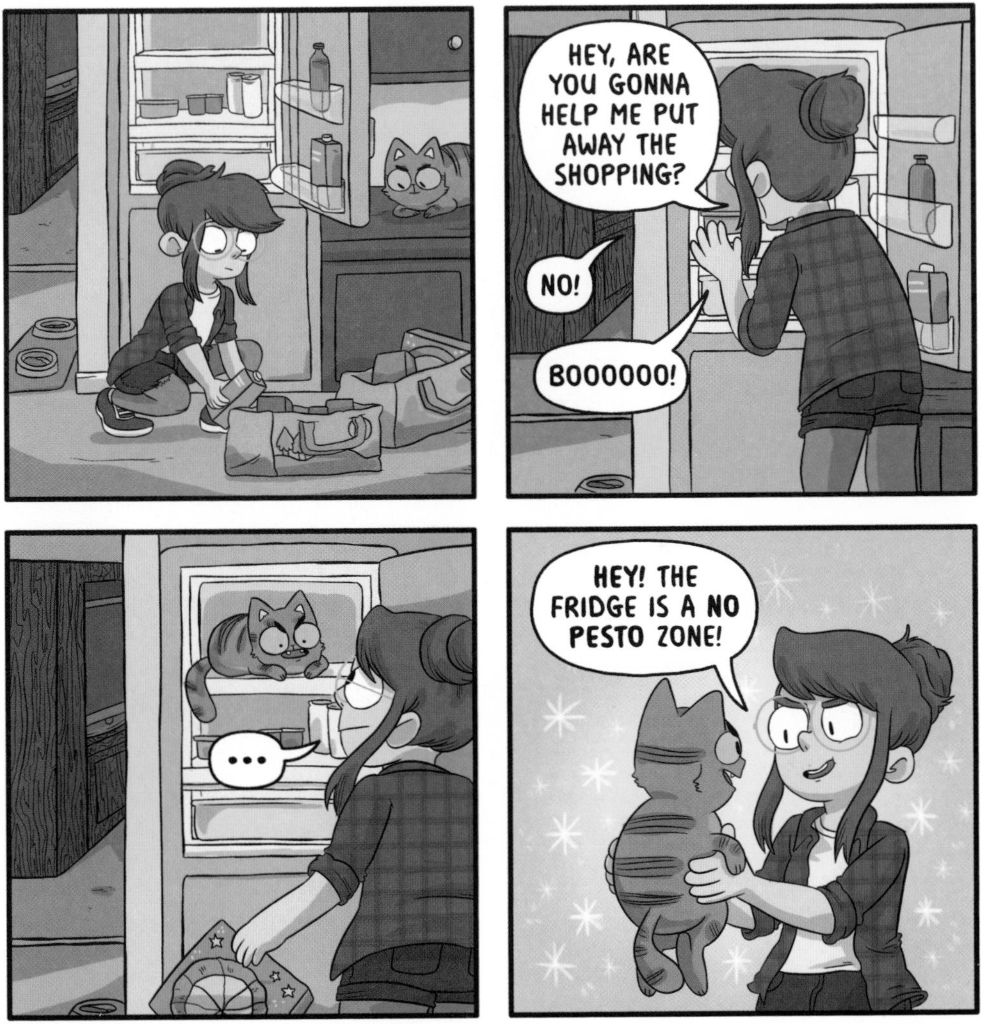
HEY, ARE YOU GONNA HELP ME PUT AWAY THE SHOPPING?
NO!
BOOOOOO!
...
HEY! THE FRIDGE IS A NO PESTO ZONE!

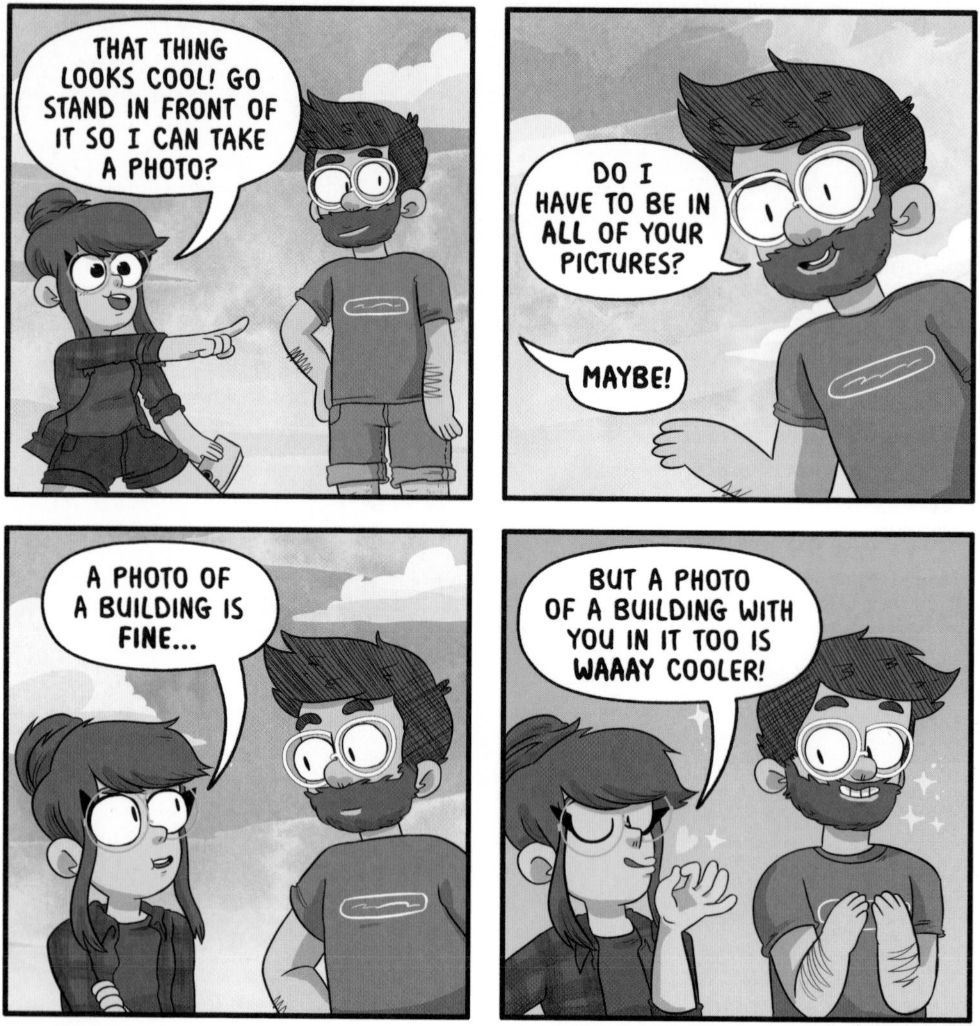
THAT THING LOOKS COOL! GO STAND IN FRONT OF IT SO I CAN TAKE A PHOTO?
DO I HAVE TO BE IN ALL OF YOUR PICTURES?
MAYBE!
A PHOTO OF A BUILDING IS FINE...
BUT A PHOTO OF A BUILDING WITH YOU IN IT TOO IS WAAAY COOLER!

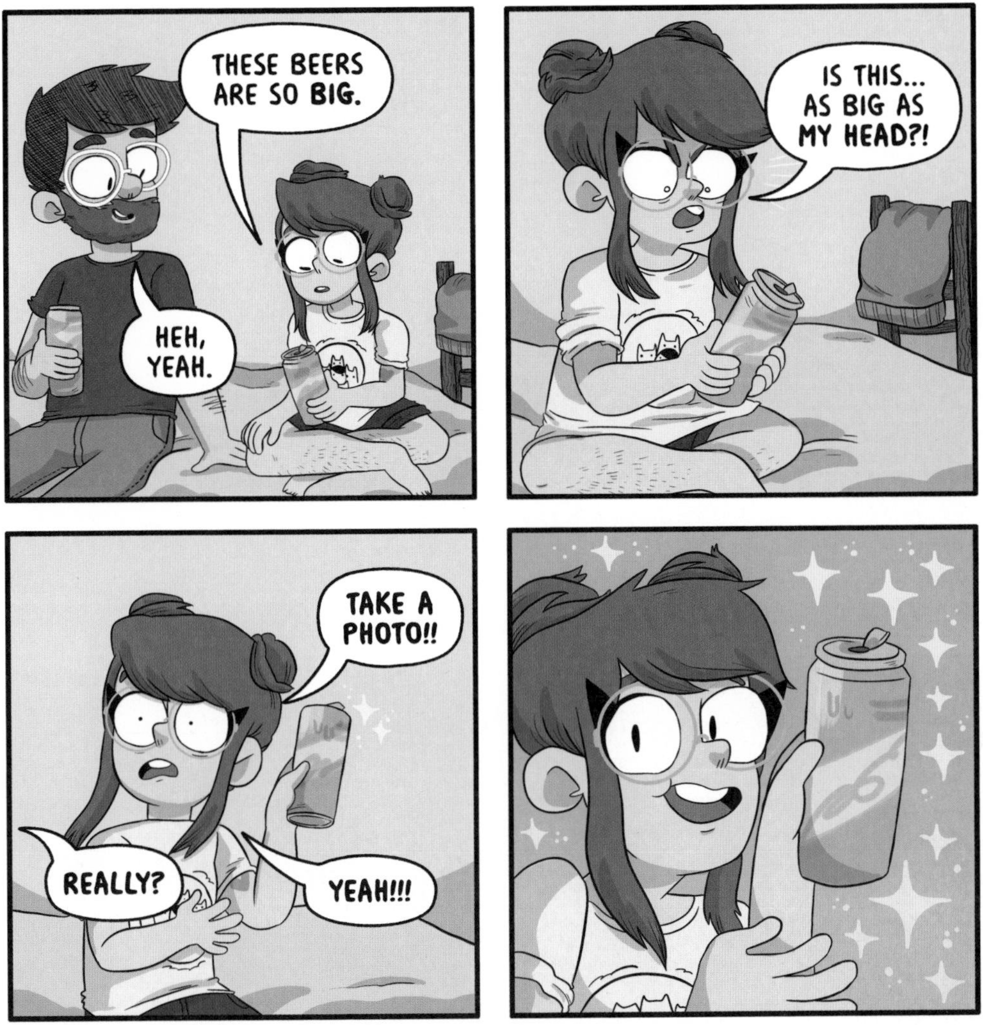
THESE BEERS ARE SO BIG.
HEH, YEAH.
IS THIS... AS BIG AS MY HEAD?!
TAKE A PHOTO!!
REALLY?
YEAH!!!

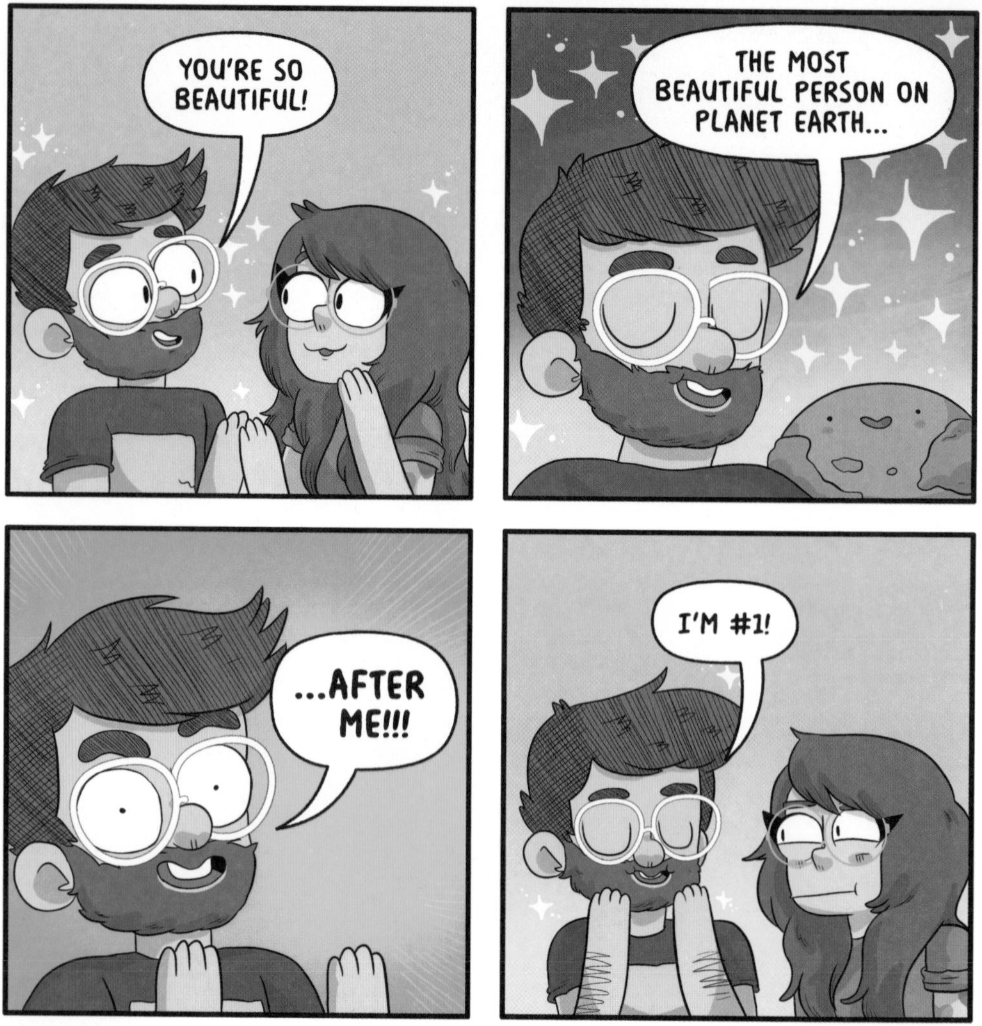
YOU'RE SO BEAUTIFUL!
THE MOST BEAUTIFUL PERSON ON PLANET EARTH...
...AFTER ME!!!
I'M #1!

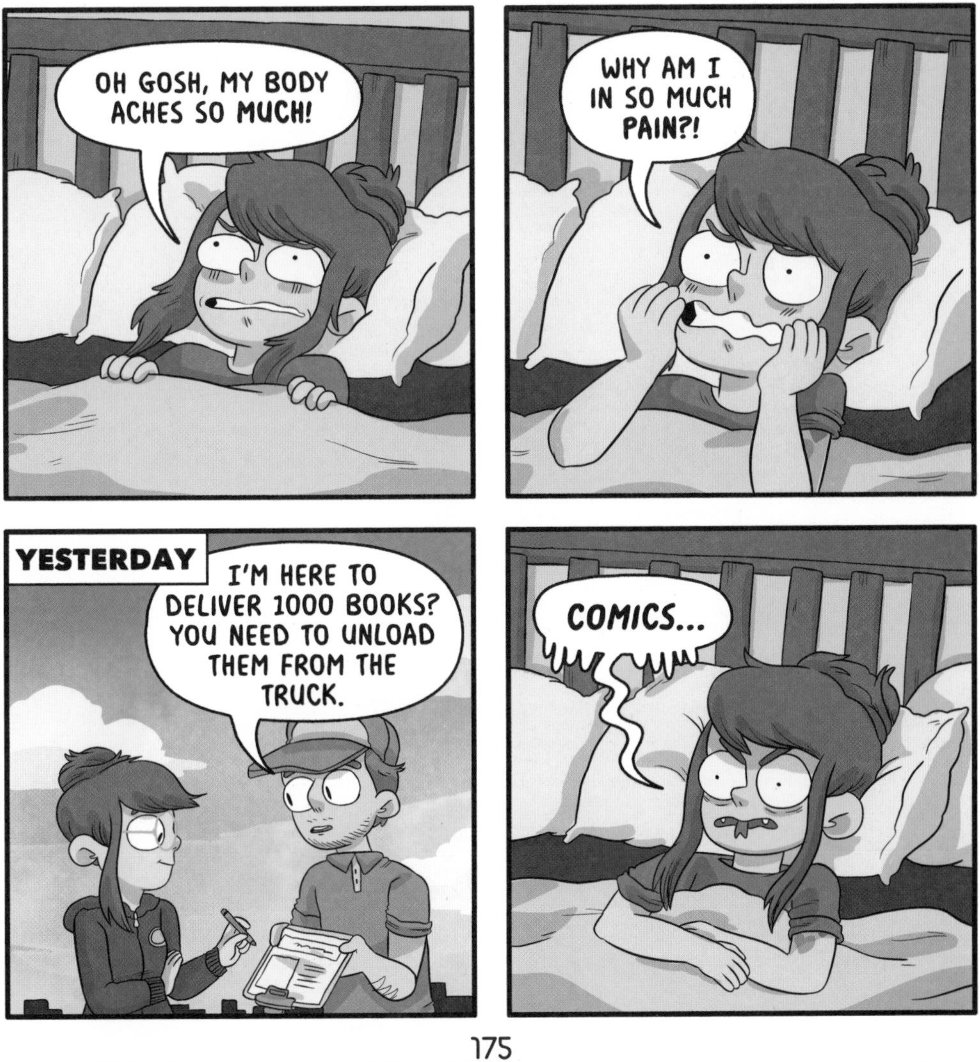
OH GOSH, MY BODY ACHES SO MUCH!
WHY AM I IN SO MUCH PAIN?!
YESTERDAY
I'M HERE TO DELIVER 1000 BOOKS? YOU NEED TO UNLOAD THEM FROM THE TRUCK.
COMICS...

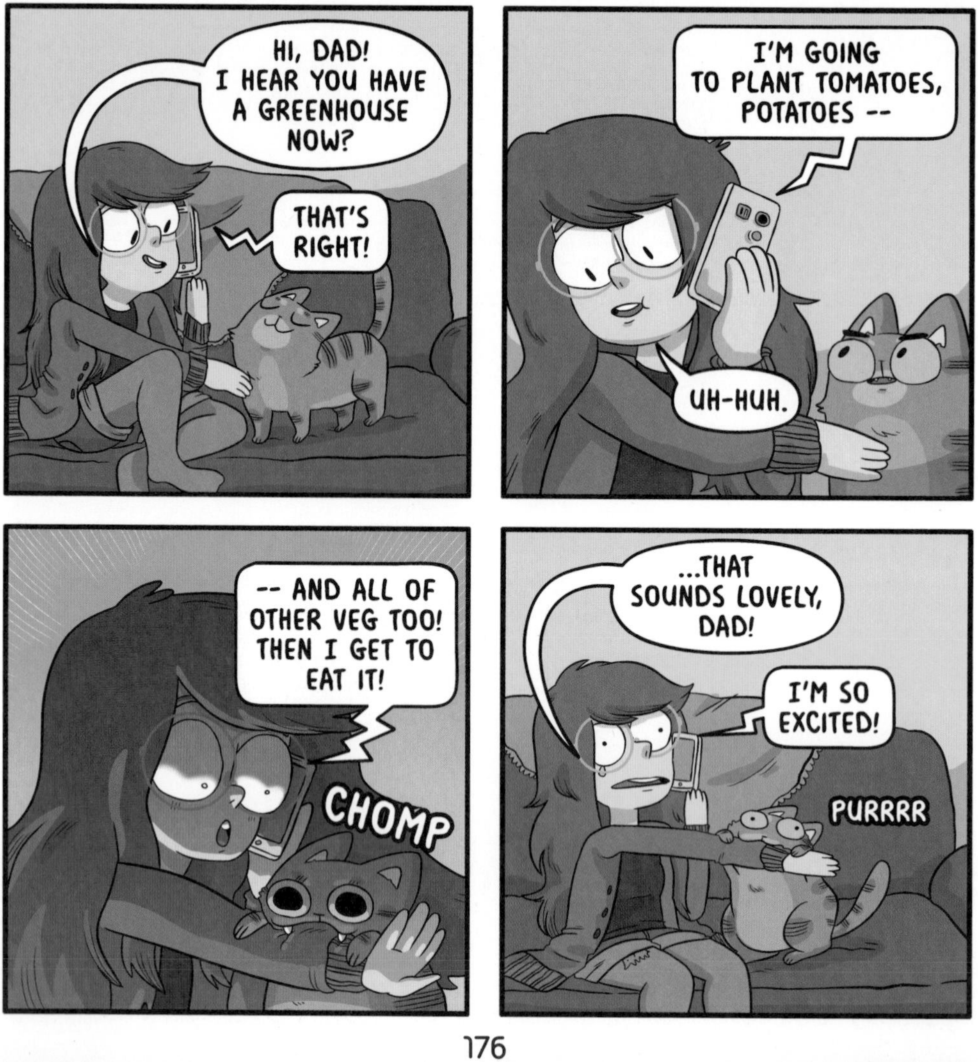
HI, DAD! I HEAR YOU HAVE A GREENHOUSE NOW?
THAT'S RIGHT!
I'M GOING TO PLANT TOMATOES, POTATOES --
UH-HUH.
-- AND ALL OF OTHER VEG TOO! THEN I GET TO EAT IT!
CHOMP
...THAT SOUNDS LOVELY, DAD!
I'M SO EXCITED!
PURRRR

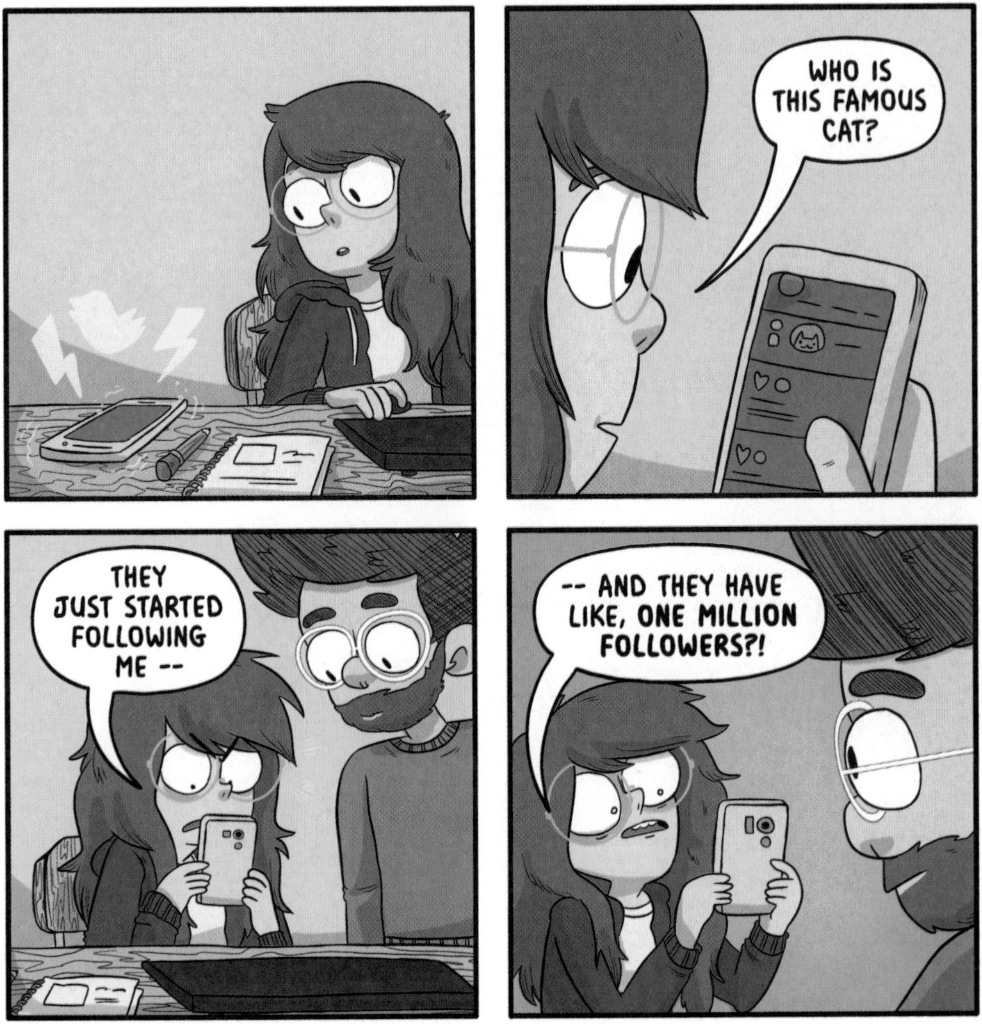
WHO IS THIS FAMOUS CAT?
THEY JUST STARTED FOLLOWING ME --
-- AND THEY HAVE LIKE, ONE MILLION FOLLOWERS?!

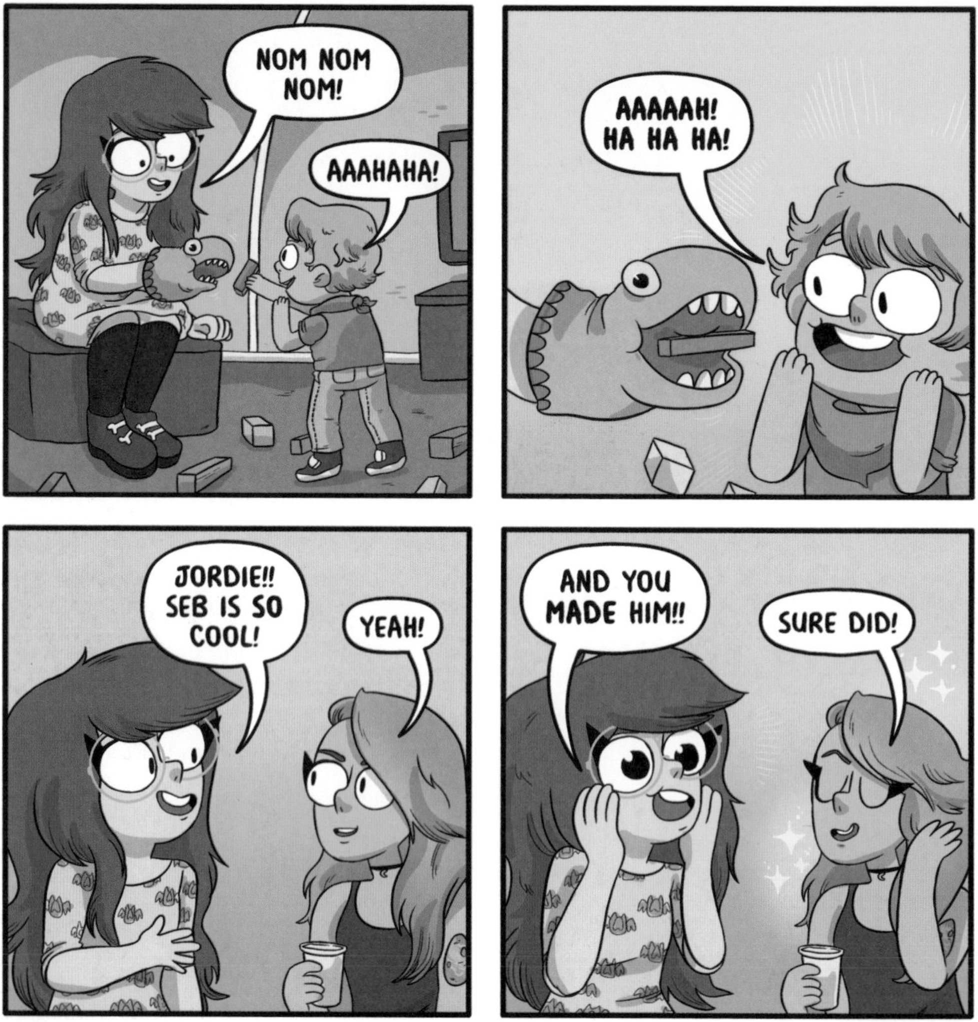
NOM NOM NOM!
AAAHAHA!
AAAAAH! HA HA HA!
JORDIE!! SEB IS SO COOL!
YEAH!
AND YOU MADE HIM!!
SURE DID!

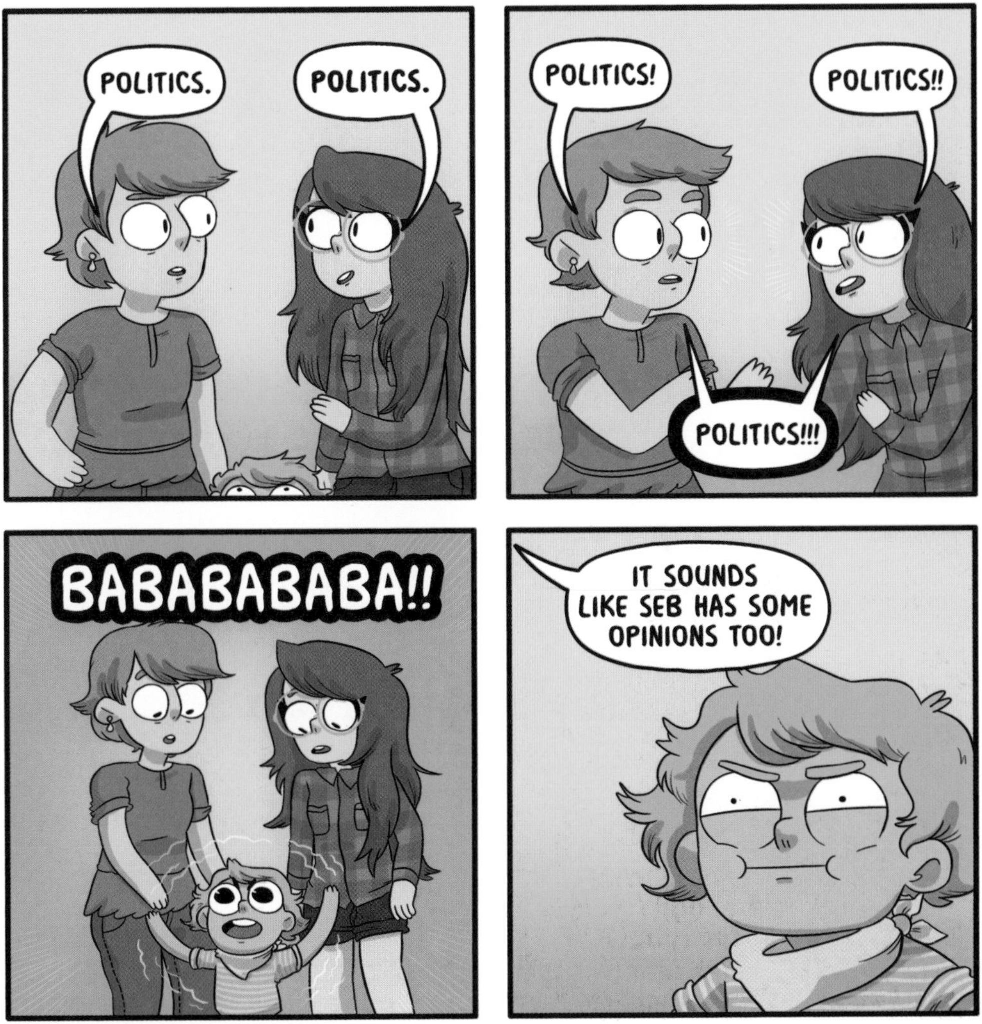
POLITICS.
POLITICS.
POLITICS!
POLITICS!!
POLITICS!!!
BABABABABA!!
IT SOUNDS LIKE SEB HAS SOME OPINIONS TOO!

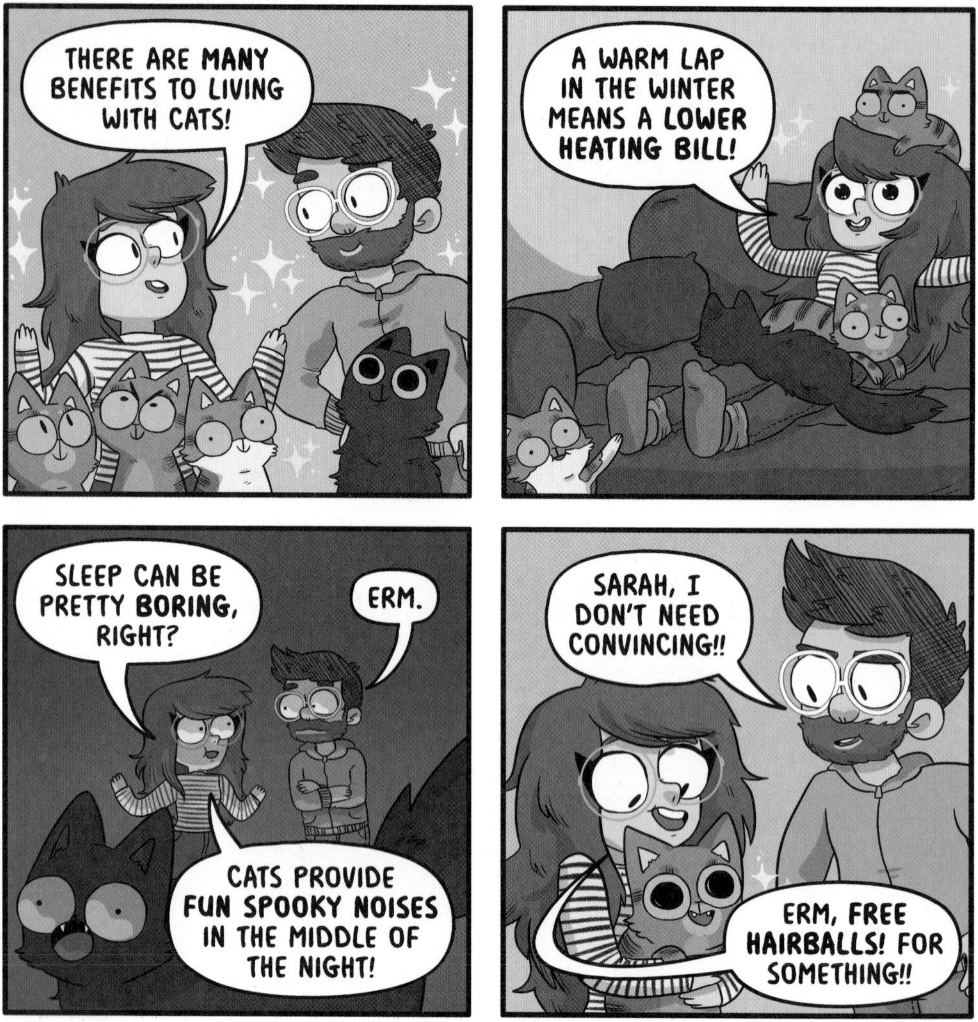
THERE ARE MANY BENEFITS TO LIVING WITH CATS!
A WARM LAP IN THE WINTER MEANS A LOWER HEATING BILL!
SLEEP CAN BE PRETTY BORING, RIGHT?
ERM.
CATS PROVIDE FUN SPOOKY NOISES IN THE MIDDLE OF THE NIGHT!
SARAH, I DON'T NEED CONVINCING!!
ERM, FREE HAIRBALLS! FOR SOMETHING!!

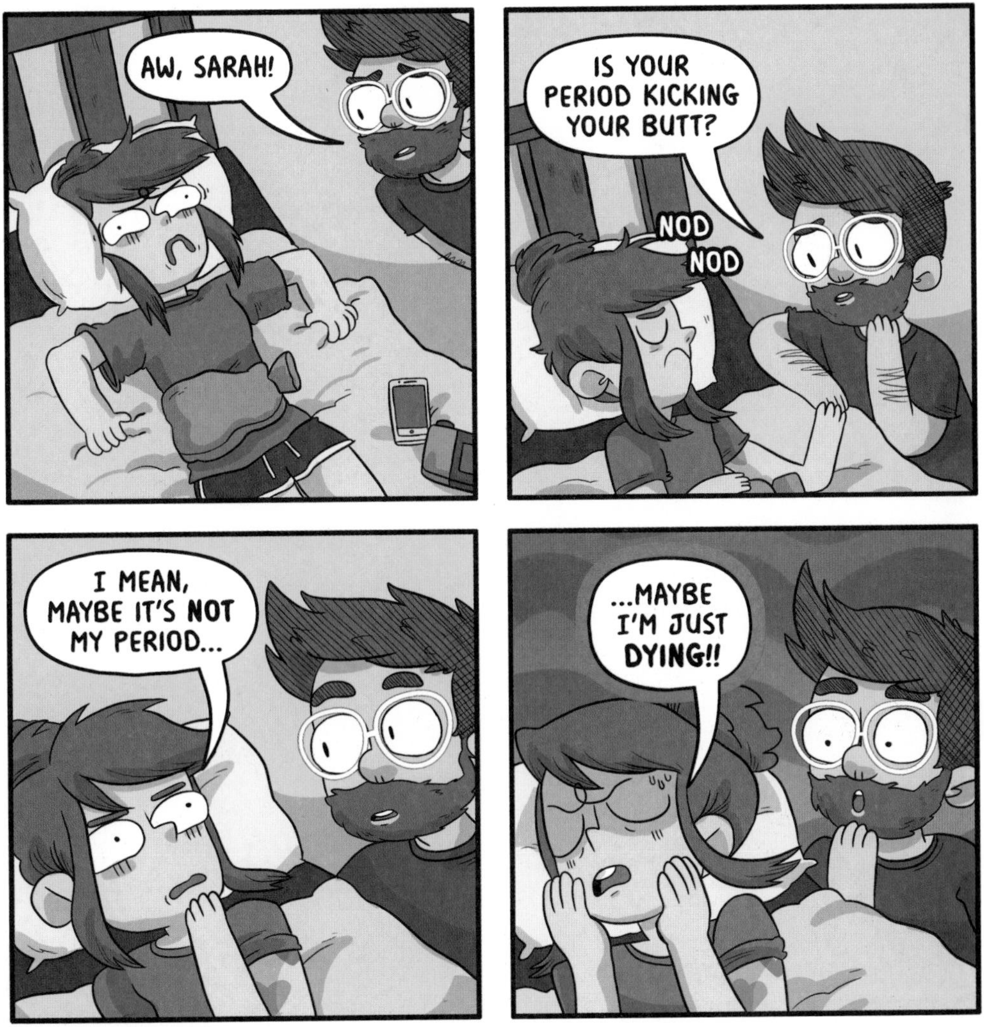
AW, SARAH!
IS YOUR PERIOD KICKING YOUR BUTT?
NOD NOD
I MEAN, MAYBE IT'S **NOT** MY PERIOD...
...MAYBE I'M JUST **DYING!!**

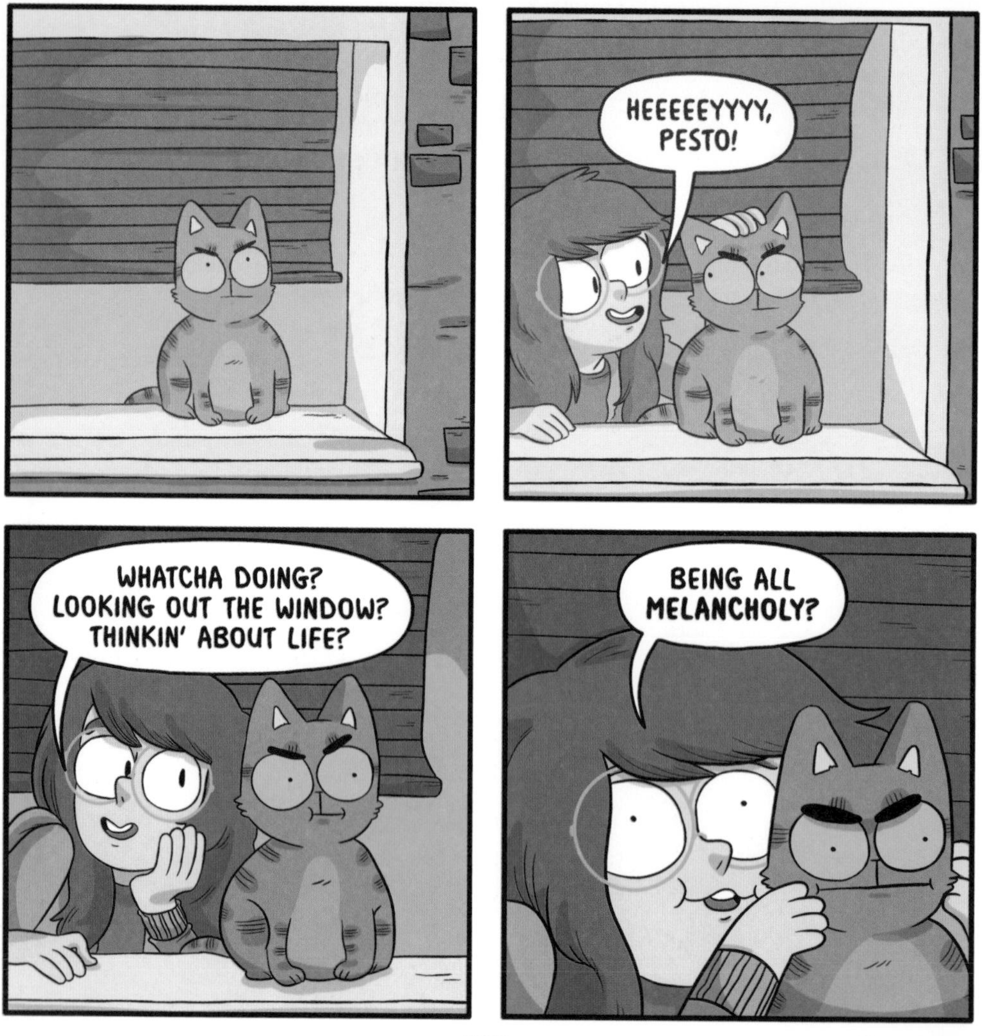
HEEEEEYYYY, PESTO!
WHATCHA DOING? LOOKING OUT THE WINDOW? THINKIN' ABOUT LIFE?
BEING ALL MELANCHOLY?

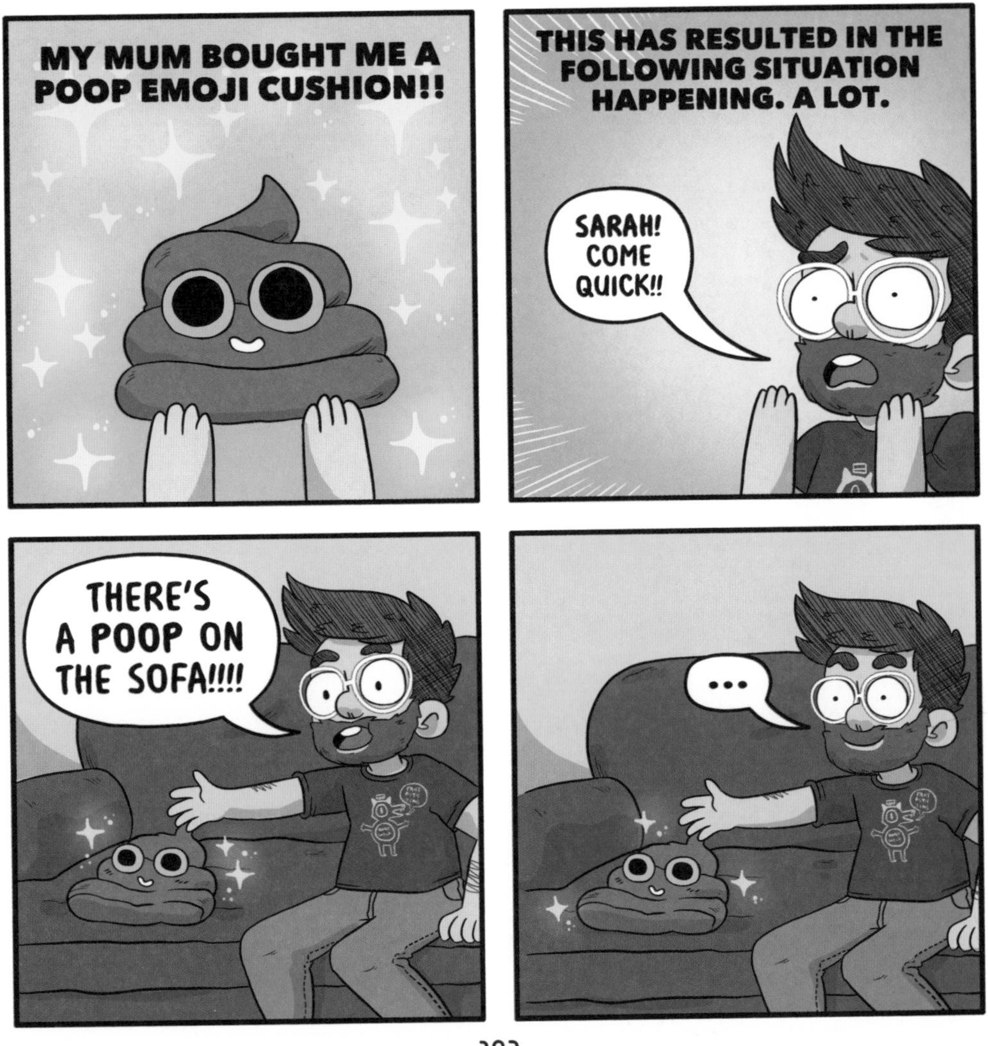
MY MUM BOUGHT ME A POOP EMOJI CUSHION!!
THIS HAS RESULTED IN THE FOLLOWING SITUATION HAPPENING. A LOT.
SARAH! COME QUICK!!
THERE'S A POOP ON THE SOFA!!!!
...

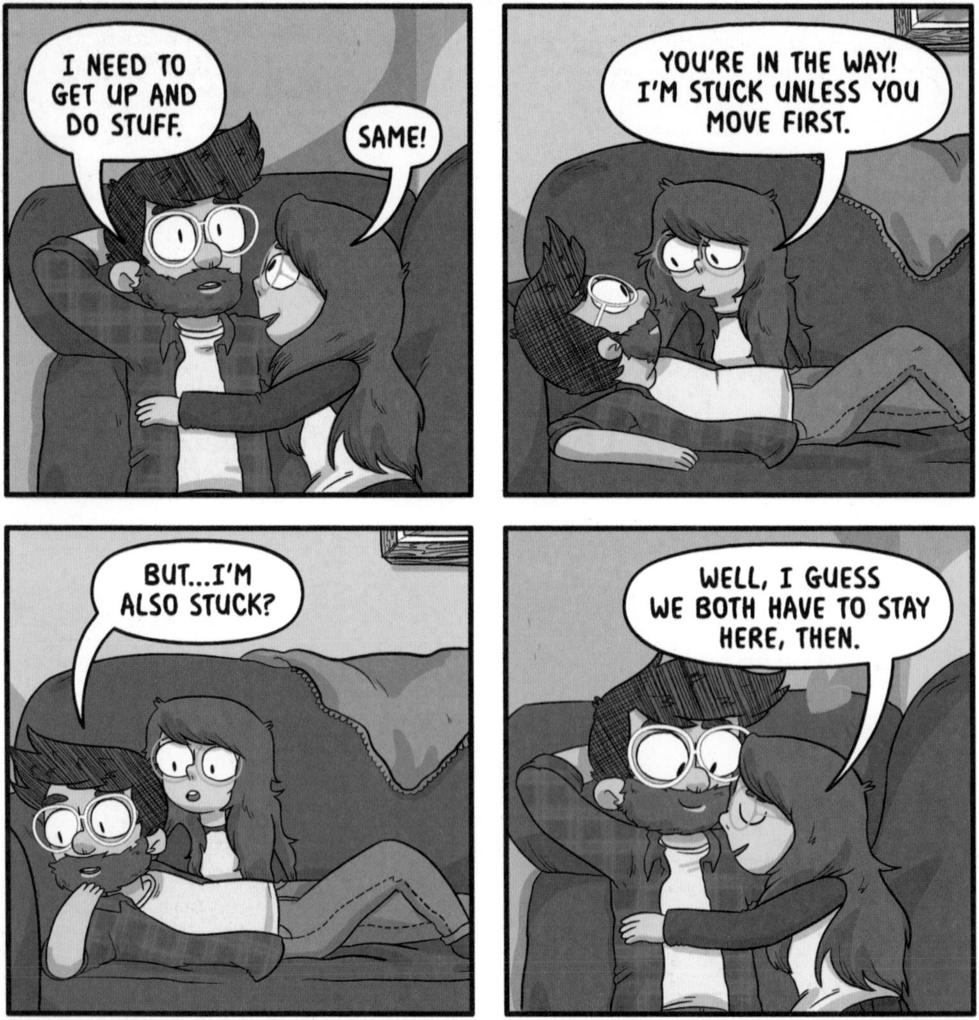
I NEED TO GET UP AND DO STUFF.
SAME!
YOU'RE IN THE WAY! I'M STUCK UNLESS YOU MOVE FIRST.
BUT...I'M ALSO STUCK?
WELL, I GUESS WE BOTH HAVE TO STAY HERE, THEN.

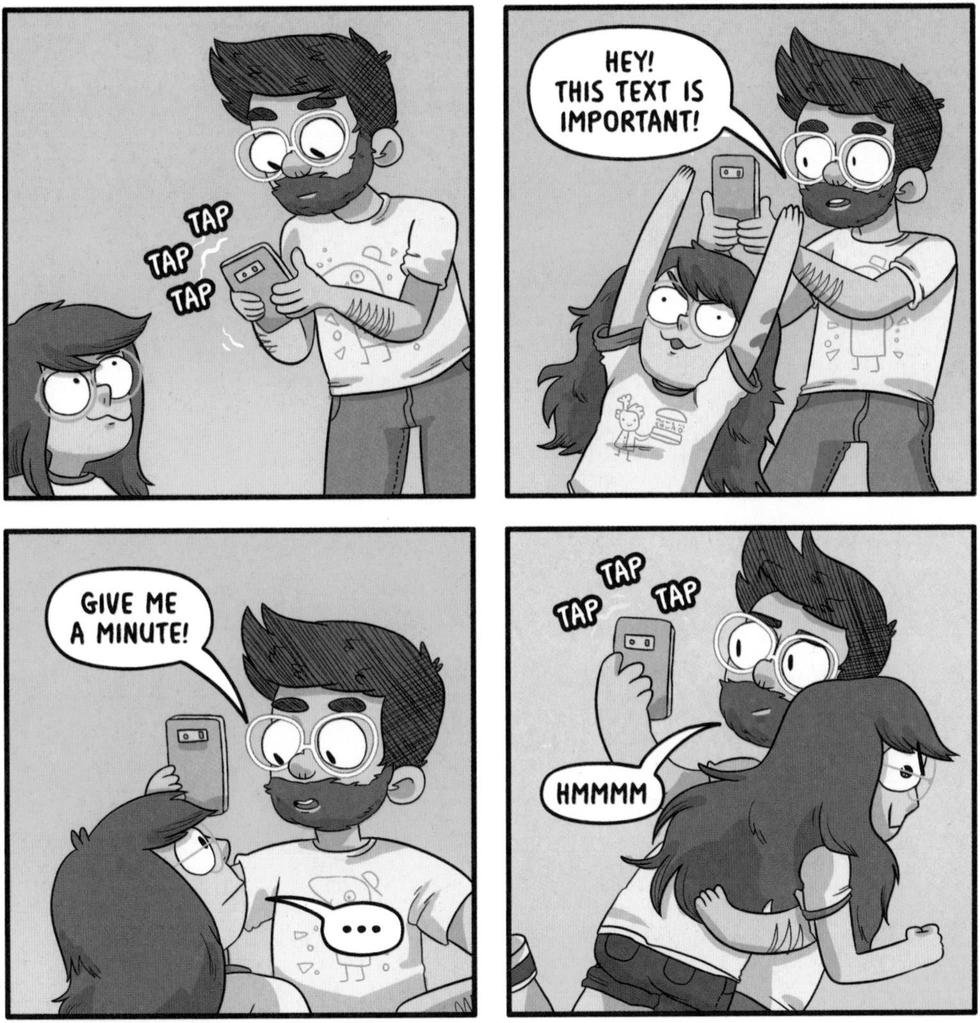
TAP
TAP
TAP
HEY! THIS TEXT IS IMPORTANT!
GIVE ME A MINUTE!
...
TAP
TAP
TAP
HMMMM

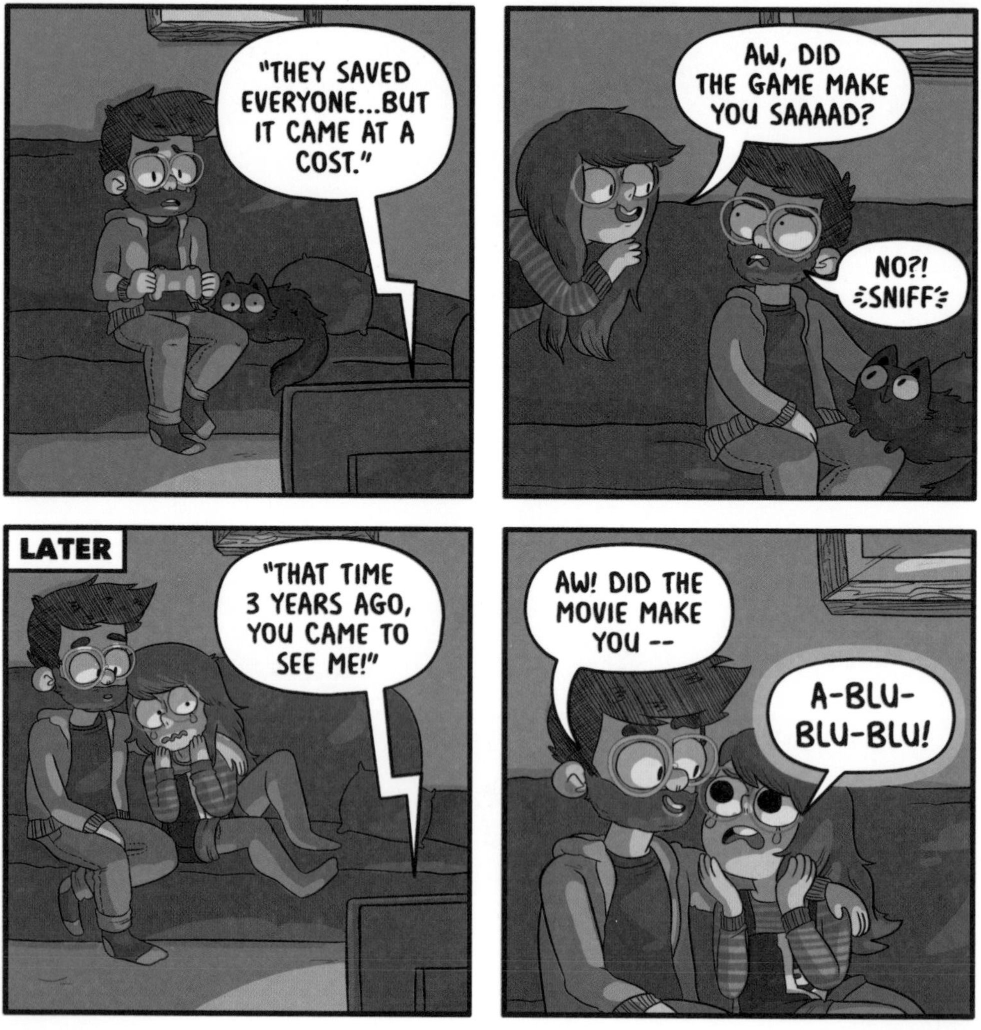
"THEY SAVED EVERYONE...BUT IT CAME AT A COST."
AW, DID THE GAME MAKE YOU SAAAAD?
NO?! SNIFF
LATER
"THAT TIME 3 YEARS AGO, YOU CAME TO SEE ME!"
AW! DID THE MOVIE MAKE YOU --
A-BLU-BLU-BLU!

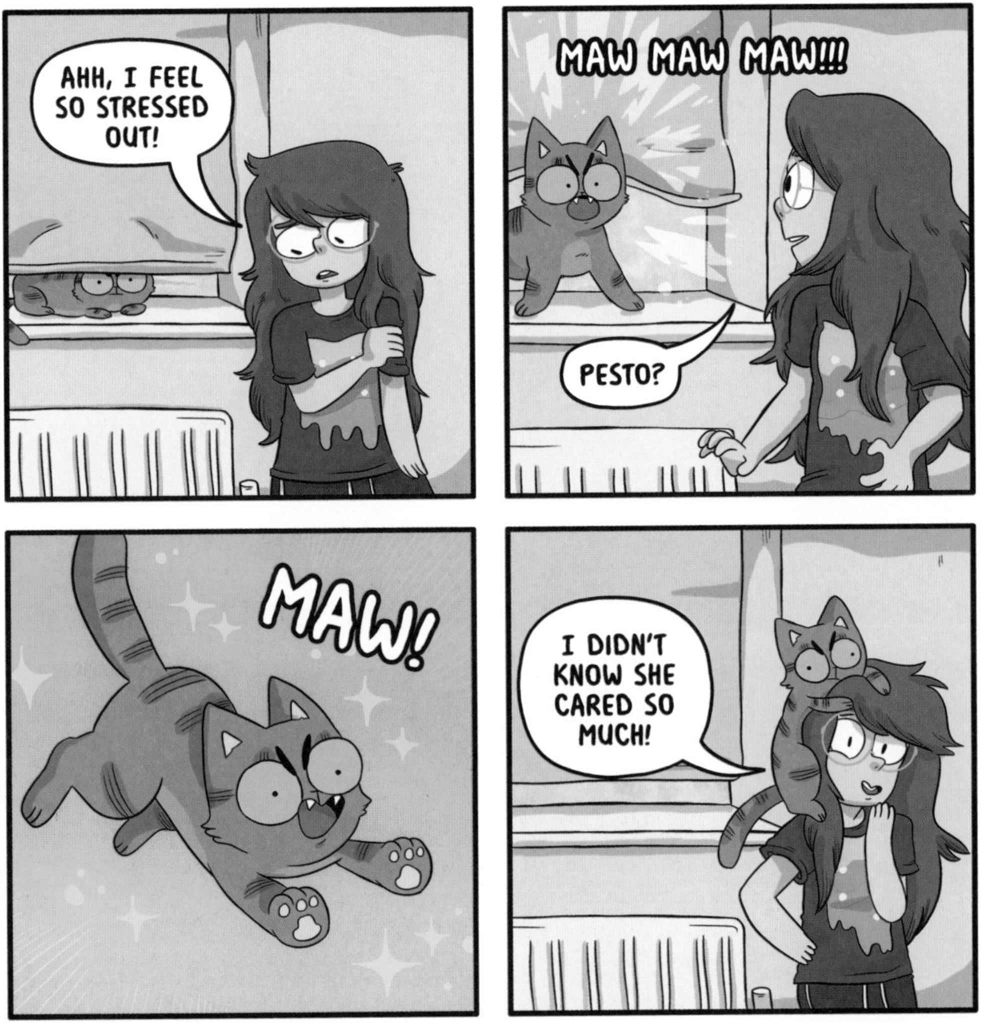
AHH, I FEEL SO STRESSED OUT!
MAW MAW MAW!!!
PESTO?
MAW!
I DIDN'T KNOW SHE CARED SO MUCH!

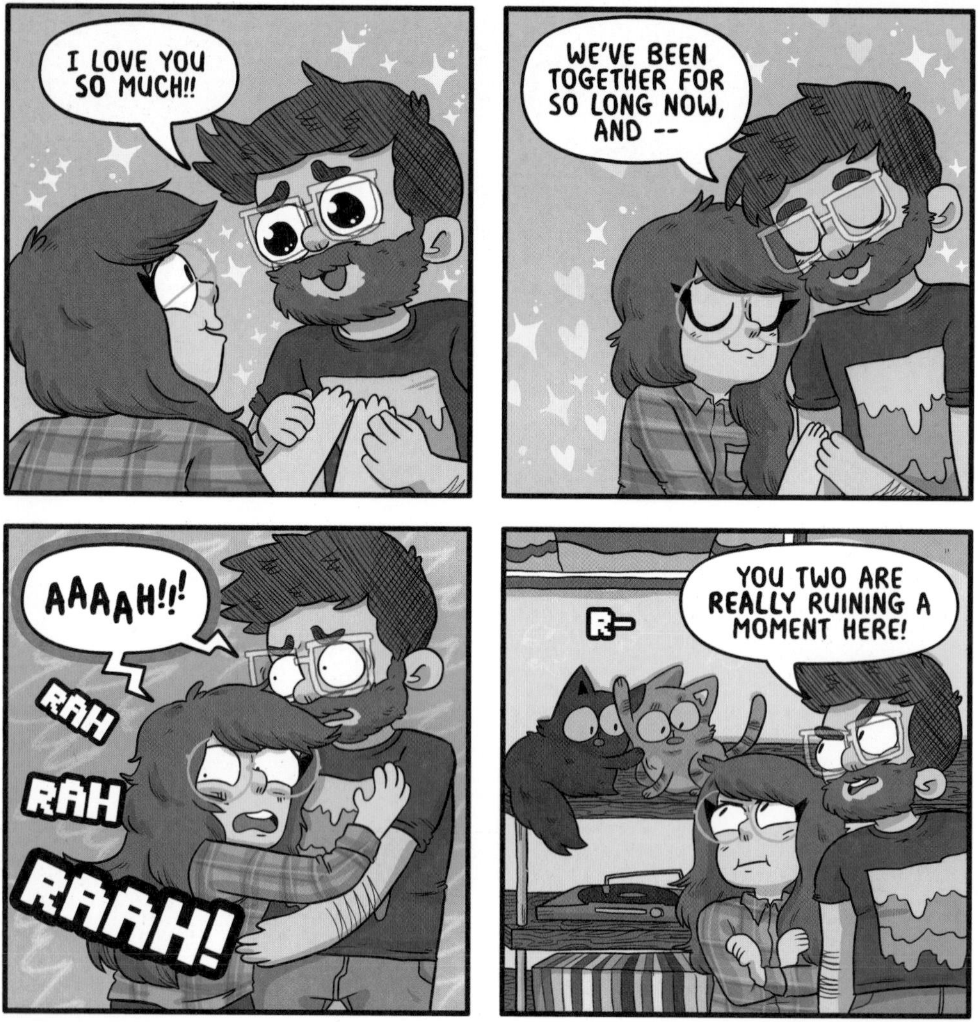
I LOVE YOU SO MUCH!!
WE'VE BEEN TOGETHER FOR SO LONG NOW, AND --
AAAAH!!!
RAH
RAH
RAAAH!
R-
YOU TWO ARE REALLY RUINING A MOMENT HERE!

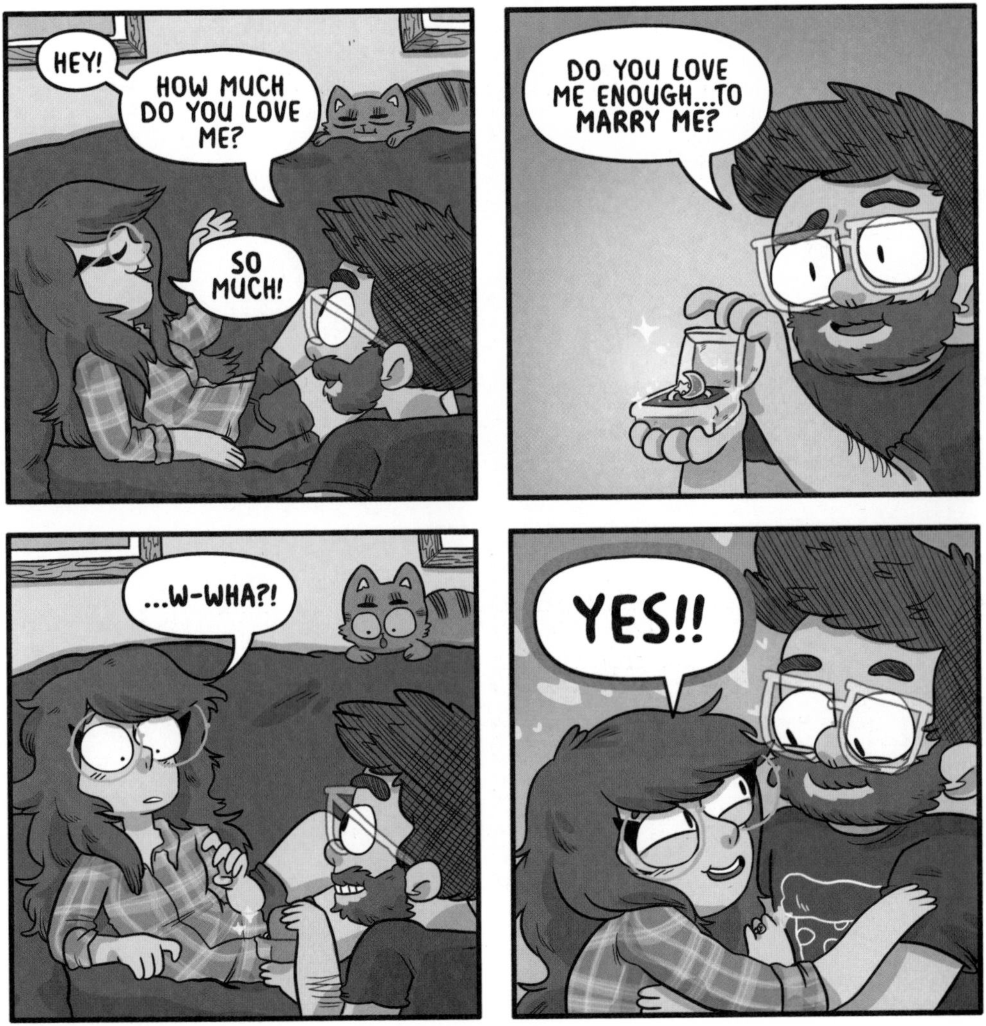
HEY!
HOW MUCH DO YOU LOVE ME?
SO MUCH!
DO YOU LOVE ME ENOUGH...TO MARRY ME?
...W-WHA?!
YES!!

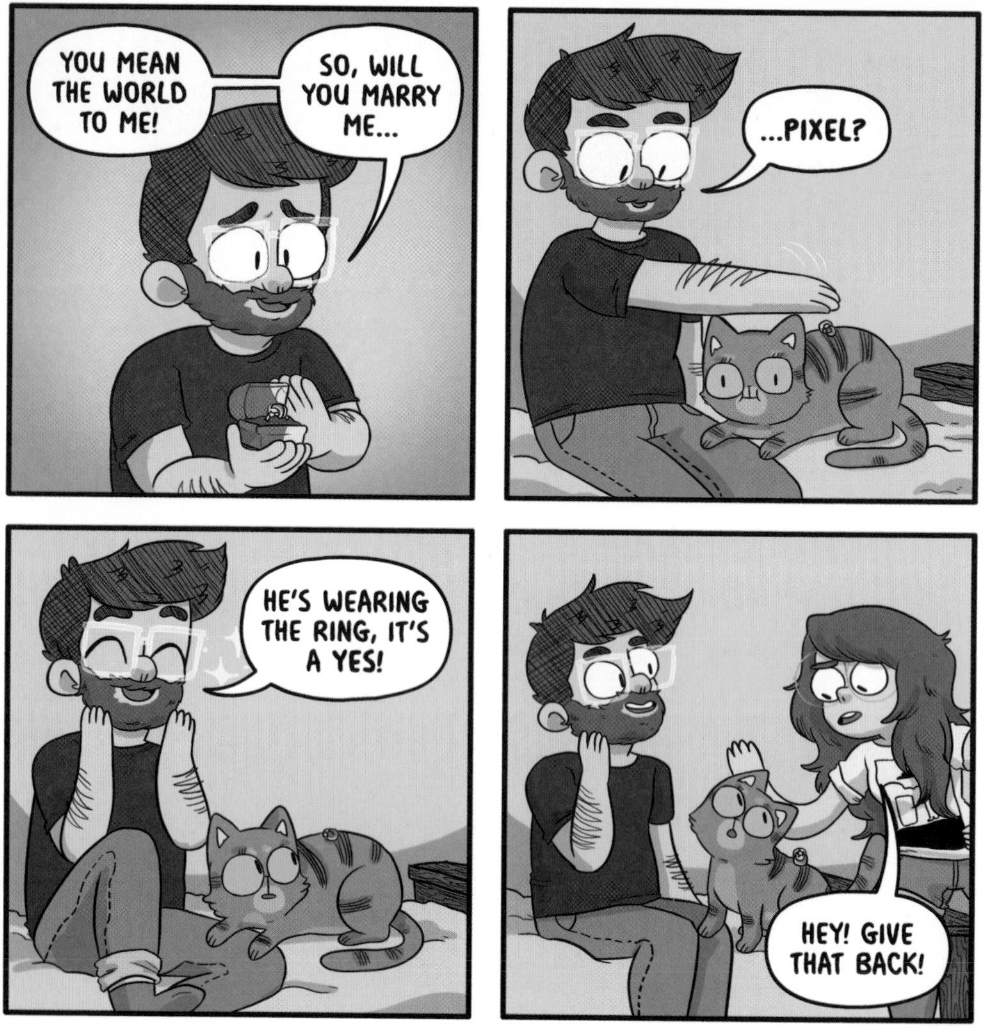
YOU MEAN THE WORLD TO ME!
SO, WILL YOU MARRY ME...
...PIXEL?
HE'S WEARING THE RING, IT'S A YES!
HEY! GIVE THAT BACK!

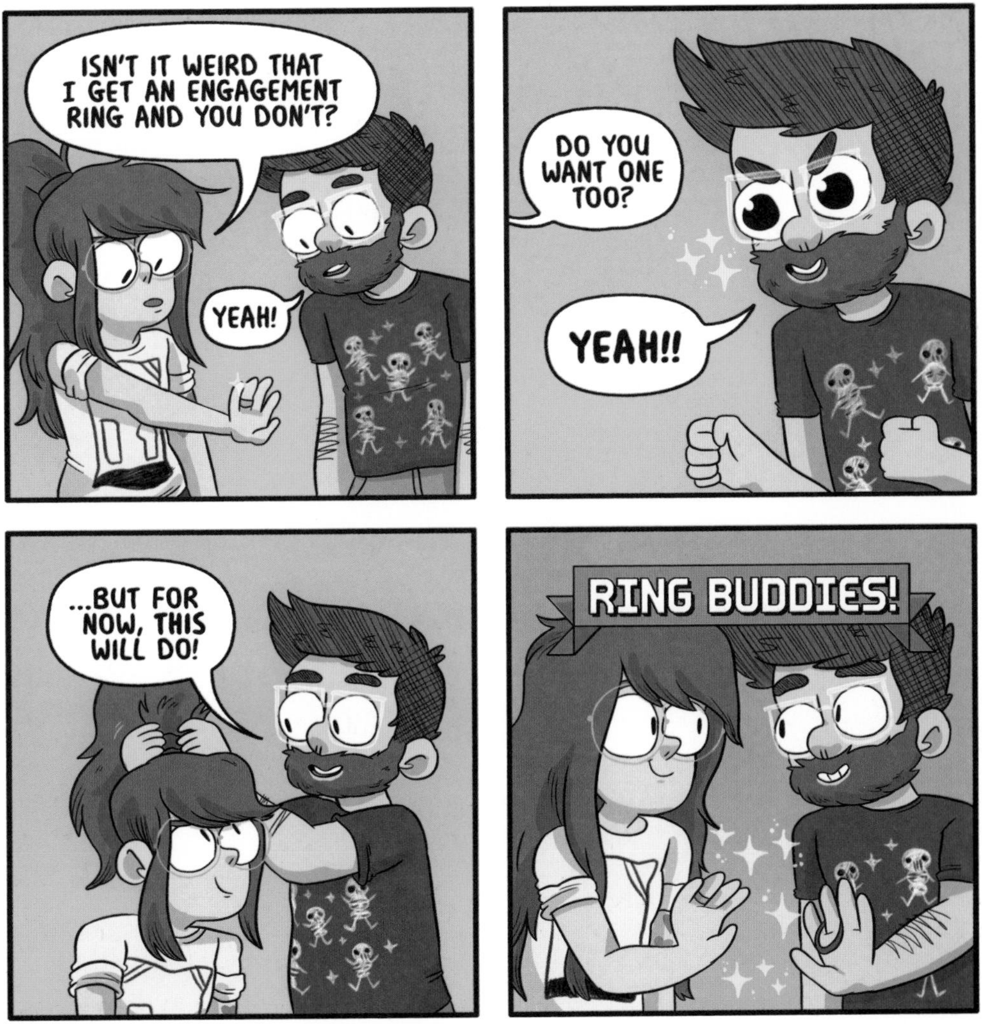
ISN'T IT WEIRD THAT I GET AN ENGAGEMENT RING AND YOU DON'T?
YEAH!
DO YOU WANT ONE TOO?
YEAH!!
...BUT FOR NOW, THIS WILL DO!
RING BUDDIES!

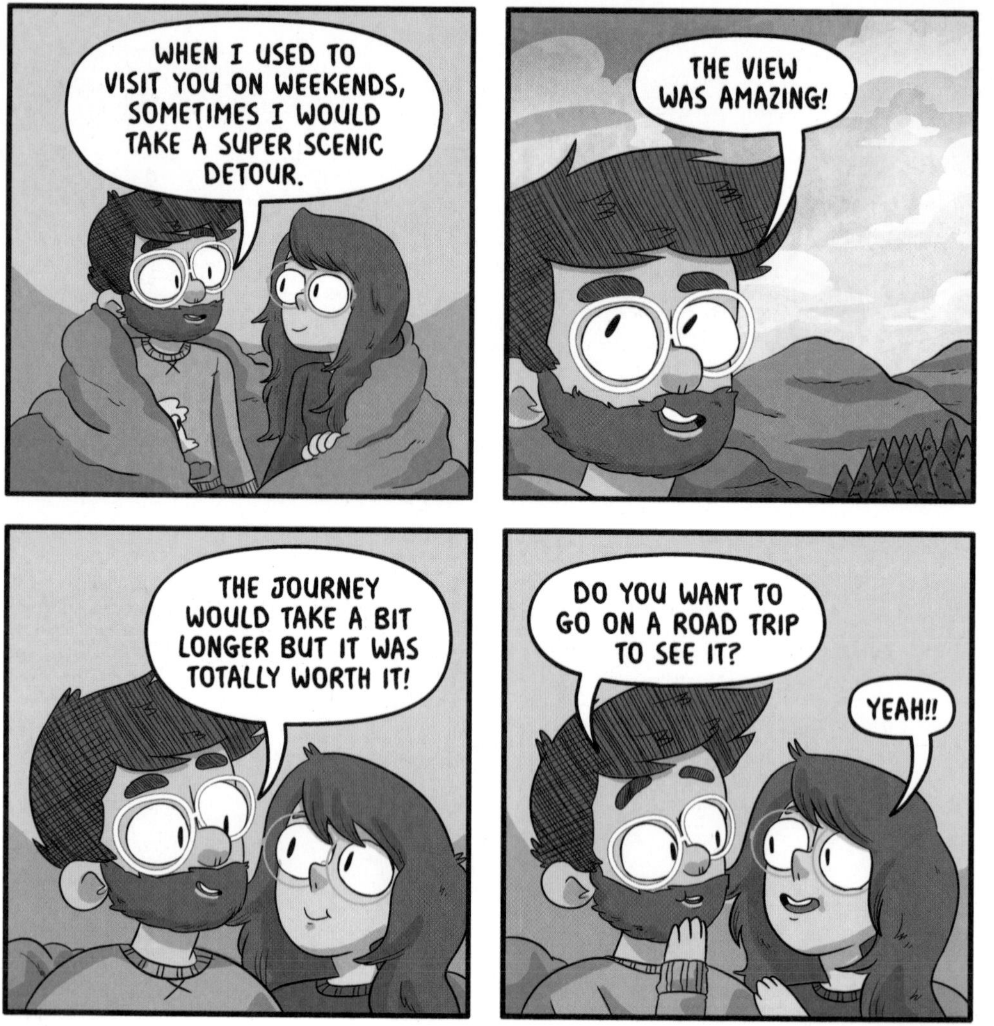
WHEN I USED TO VISIT YOU ON WEEKENDS, SOMETIMES I WOULD TAKE A SUPER SCENIC DETOUR.
THE VIEW WAS AMAZING!
THE JOURNEY WOULD TAKE A BIT LONGER BUT IT WAS TOTALLY WORTH IT!
DO YOU WANT TO GO ON A ROAD TRIP TO SEE IT?
YEAH!!

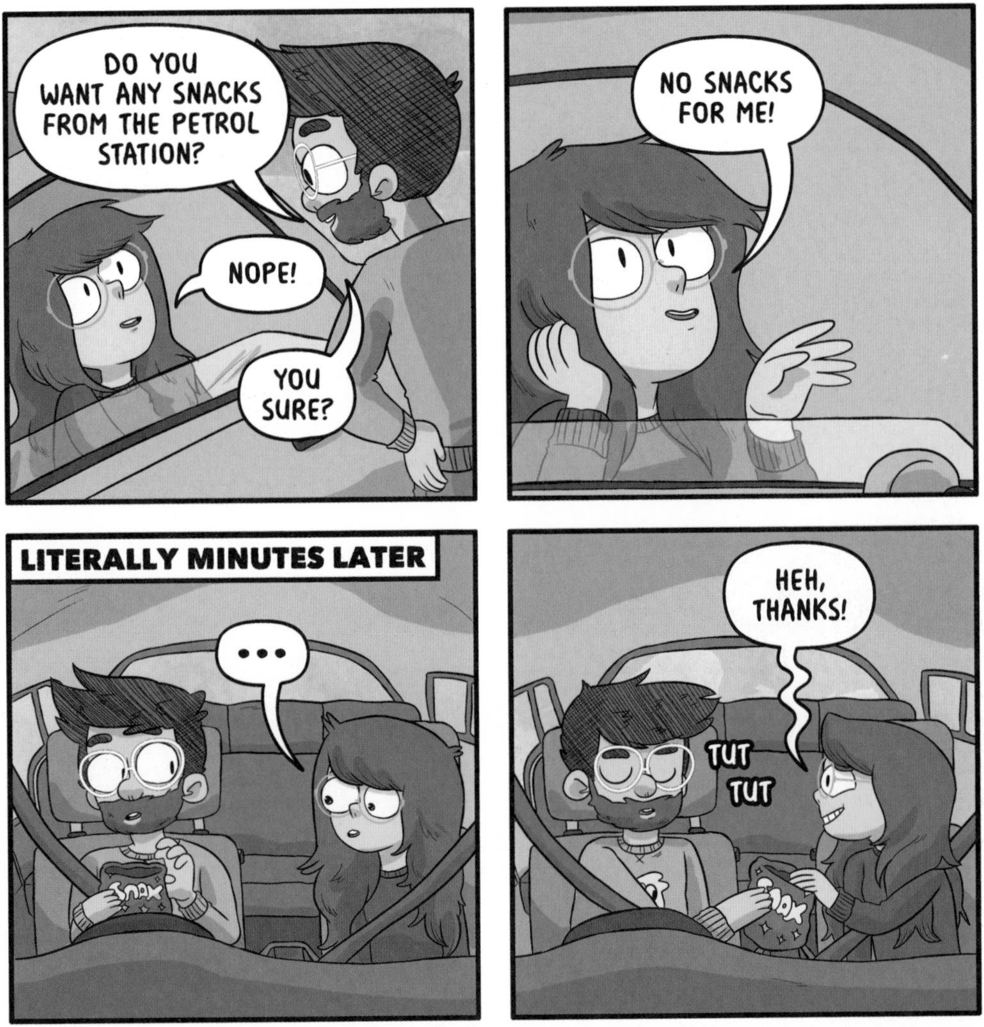
DO YOU WANT ANY SNACKS FROM THE PETROL STATION?
NOPE!
YOU SURE?
NO SNACKS FOR ME!
LITERALLY MINUTES LATER
...
HEH, THANKS!
TUT
TUT

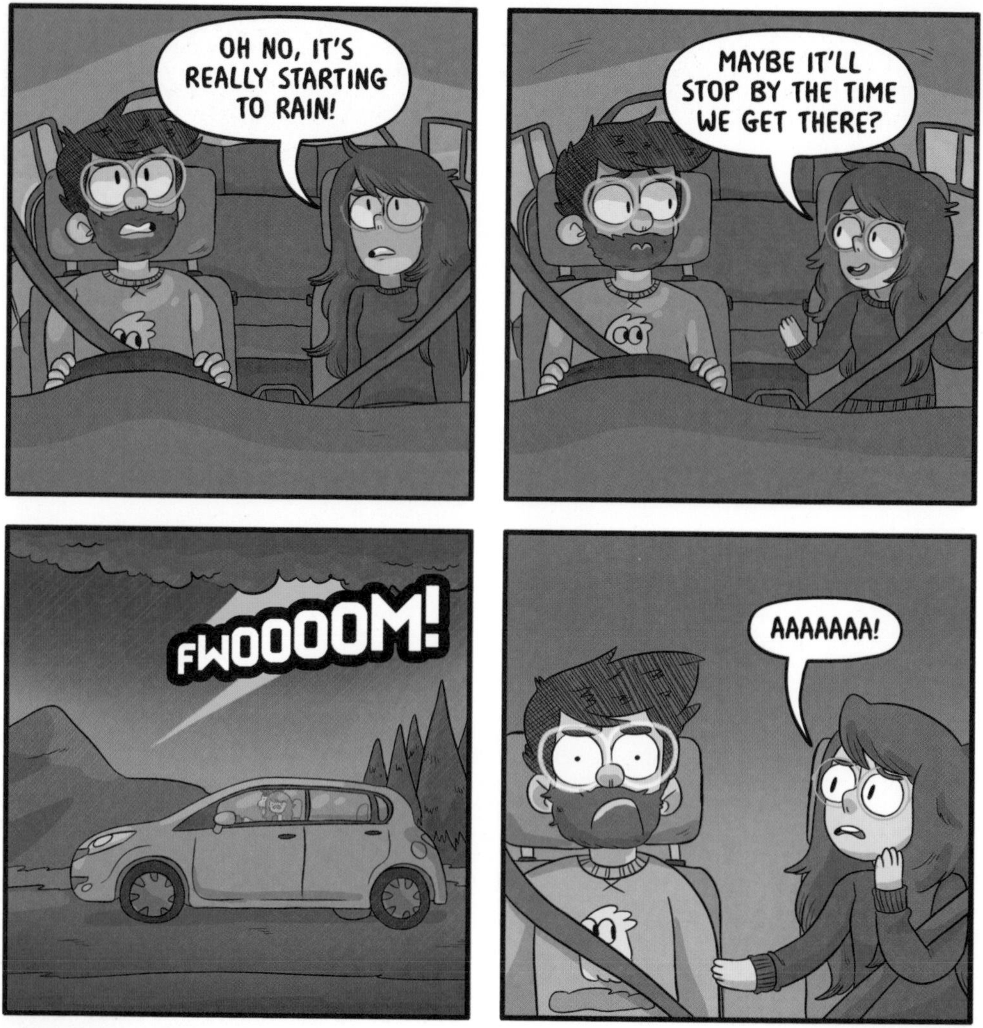
OH NO, IT'S REALLY STARTING TO RAIN!
MAYBE IT'LL STOP BY THE TIME WE GET THERE?
FWOOOOM!
AAAAAAA!

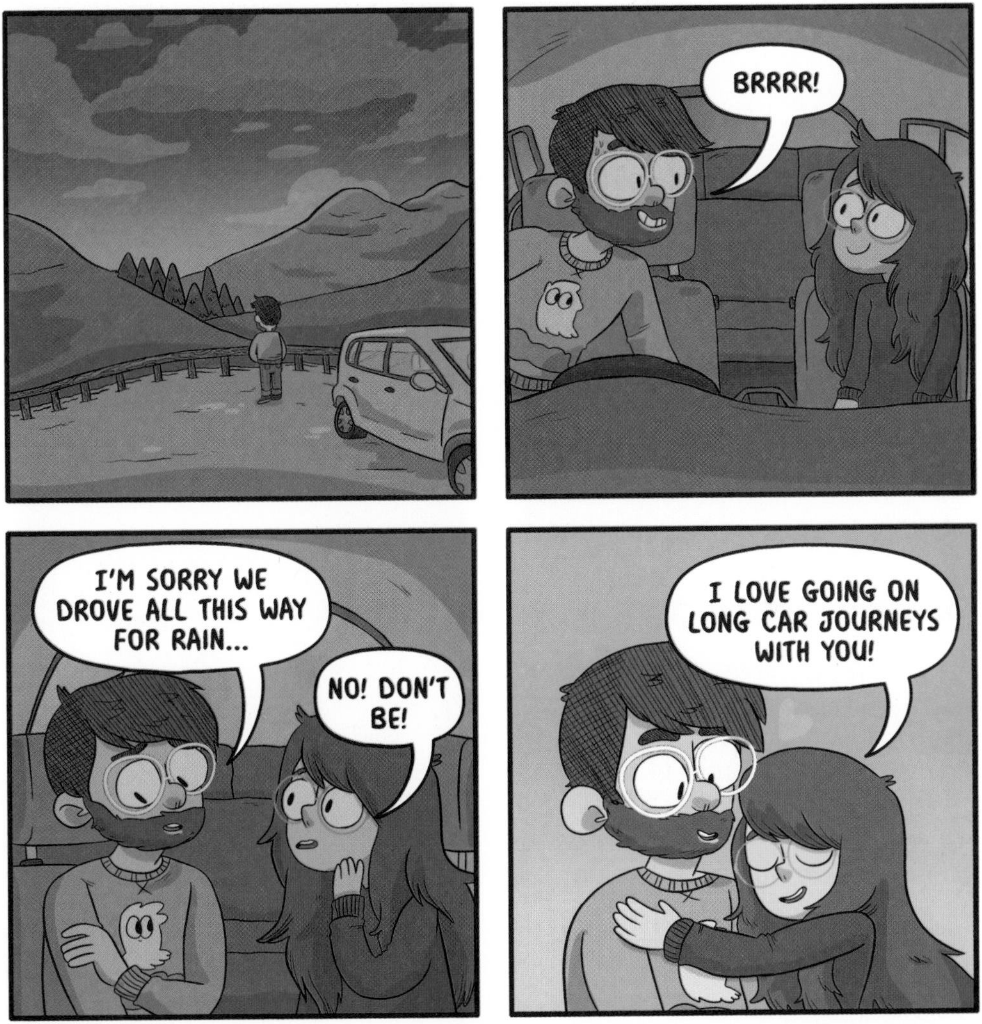
BRRRR!
I'M SORRY WE DROVE ALL THIS WAY FOR RAIN...
NO! DON'T BE!
I LOVE GOING ON LONG CAR JOURNEYS WITH YOU!

OUR SUPER SPECIAL BONUS COMIC BY STEF

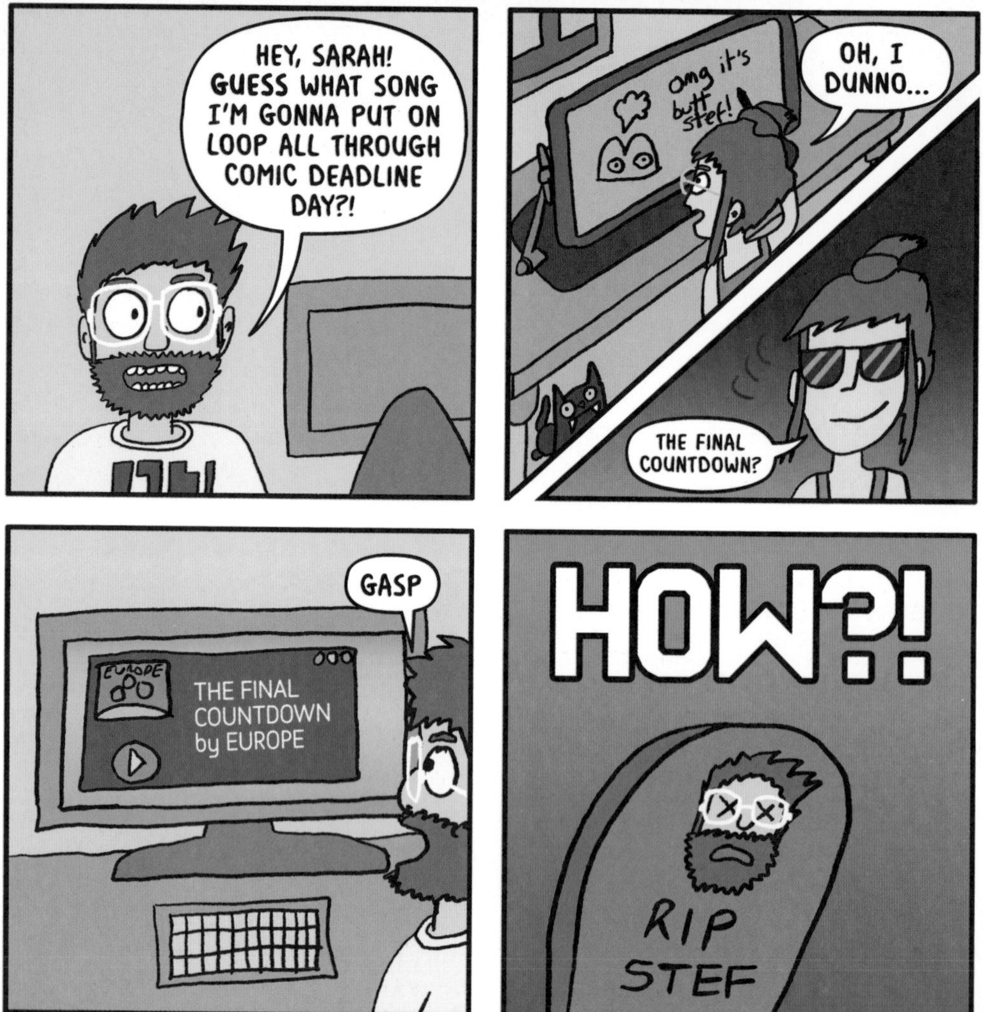
HEY, SARAH! GUESS WHAT SONG I'M GONNA PUT ON LOOP ALL THROUGH COMIC DEADLINE DAY?!
omg it's butt stef!
OH, I DUNNO...
THE FINAL COUNTDOWN?
GASP
EUROPE
THE FINAL COUNTDOWN by EUROPE
HOW?!
RIP STEF

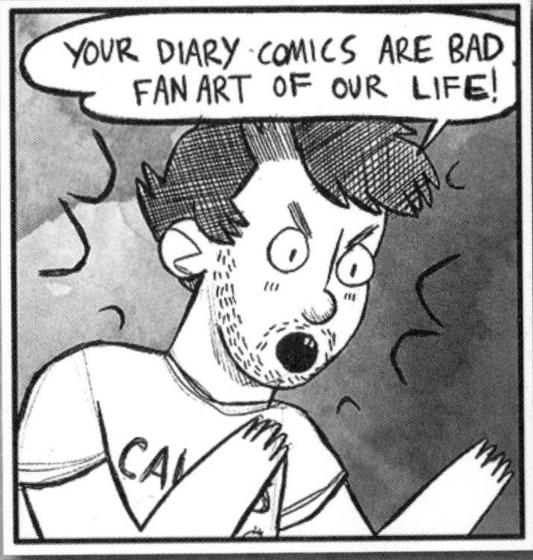
YOUR DIARY COMICS ARE BAD FAN ART OF OUR LIFE!

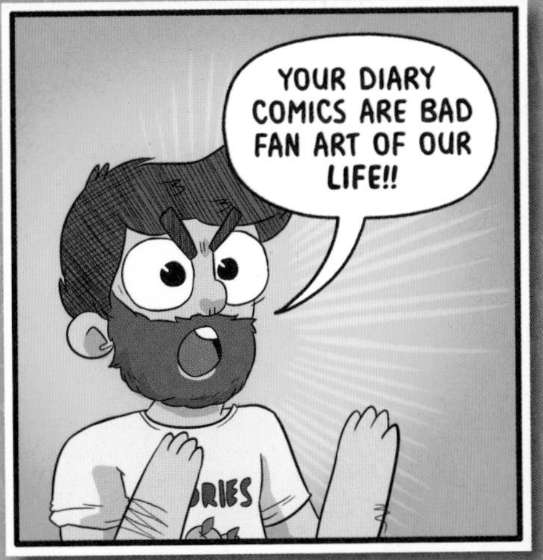
YOUR DIARY COMICS ARE BAD FAN ART OF OUR LIFE!!

REDRAWN COMICS

I made three smaller collections of *Our Super Adventure* back in between 2013 and 2015. These books were in black and white and each one contained about 40-50 comics.

In the first *Our Super Adventure* book, ***Press Start To Begin***, I really enjoyed going back and visiting some of those strips and redrawing them in my current style, and I thought that I would do the same again for book number two!

I hope you enjoy seeing the old art with the new! It's super surreal to see just how much my drawing style has changed over the years!

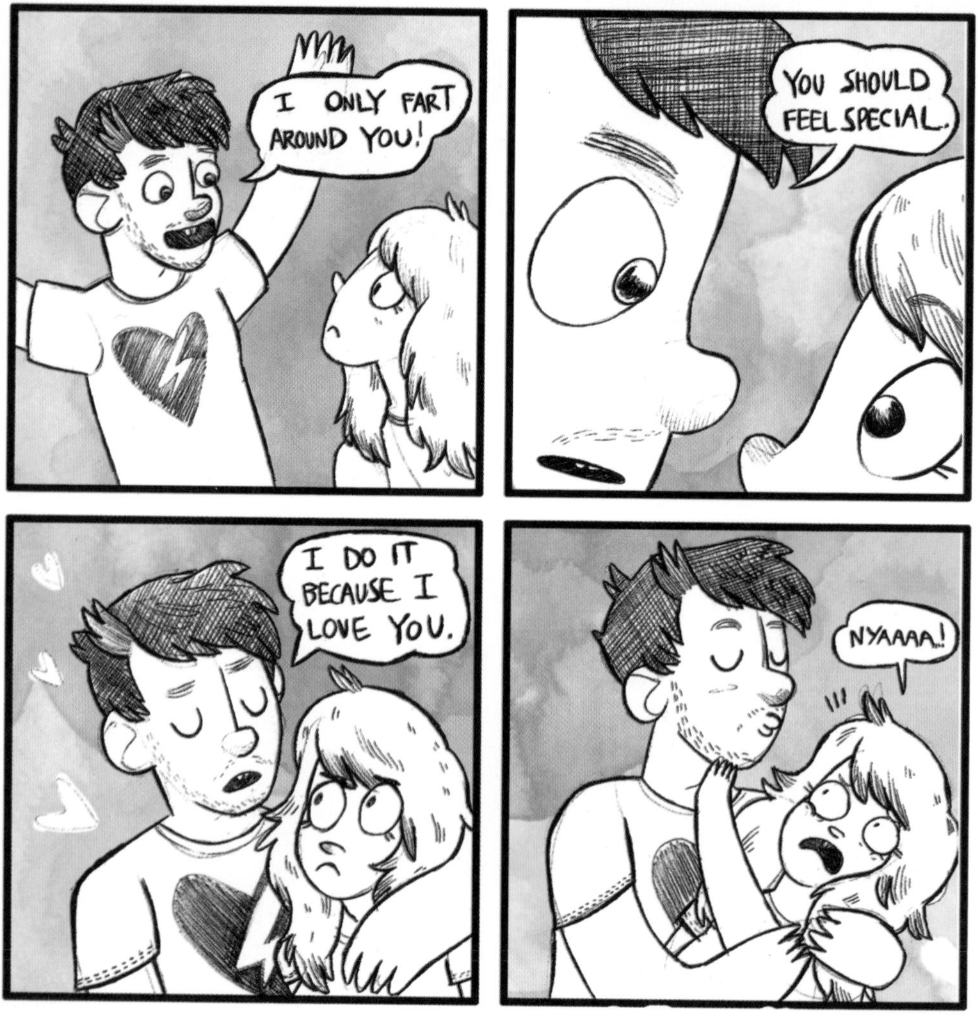
I ONLY FART AROUND YOU!
YOU SHOULD FEEL SPECIAL.
I DO IT BECAUSE I LOVE YOU.
NYAAAA!

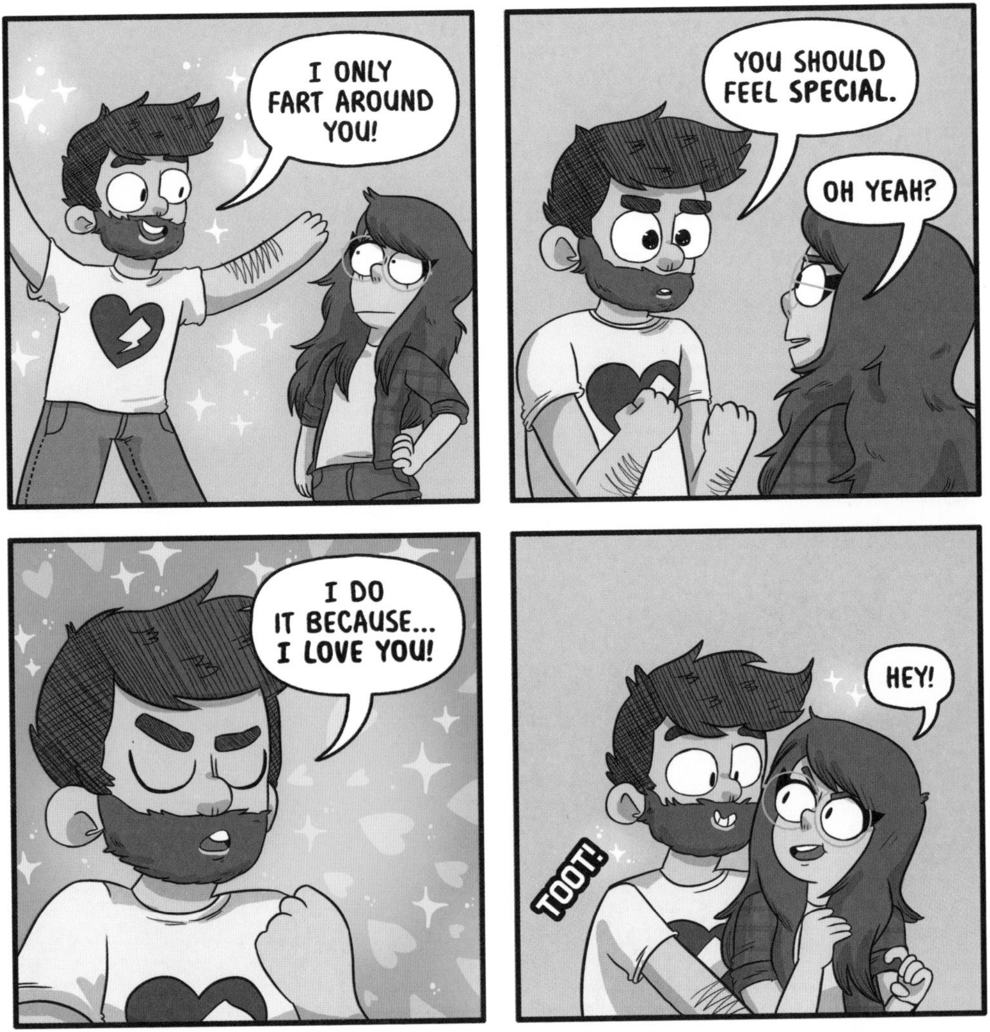
I ONLY FART AROUND YOU!
YOU SHOULD FEEL SPECIAL.
OH YEAH?
I DO IT BECAUSE... I LOVE YOU!
TOOT!
HEY!

CAN I EAT THIS?
COM
NOPE
COMIXX
COM
CAN I EAT THESE?
NOPE

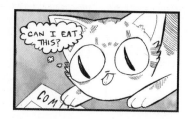

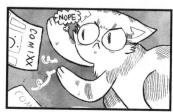

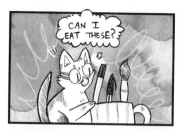

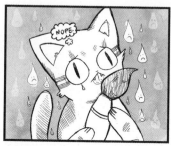

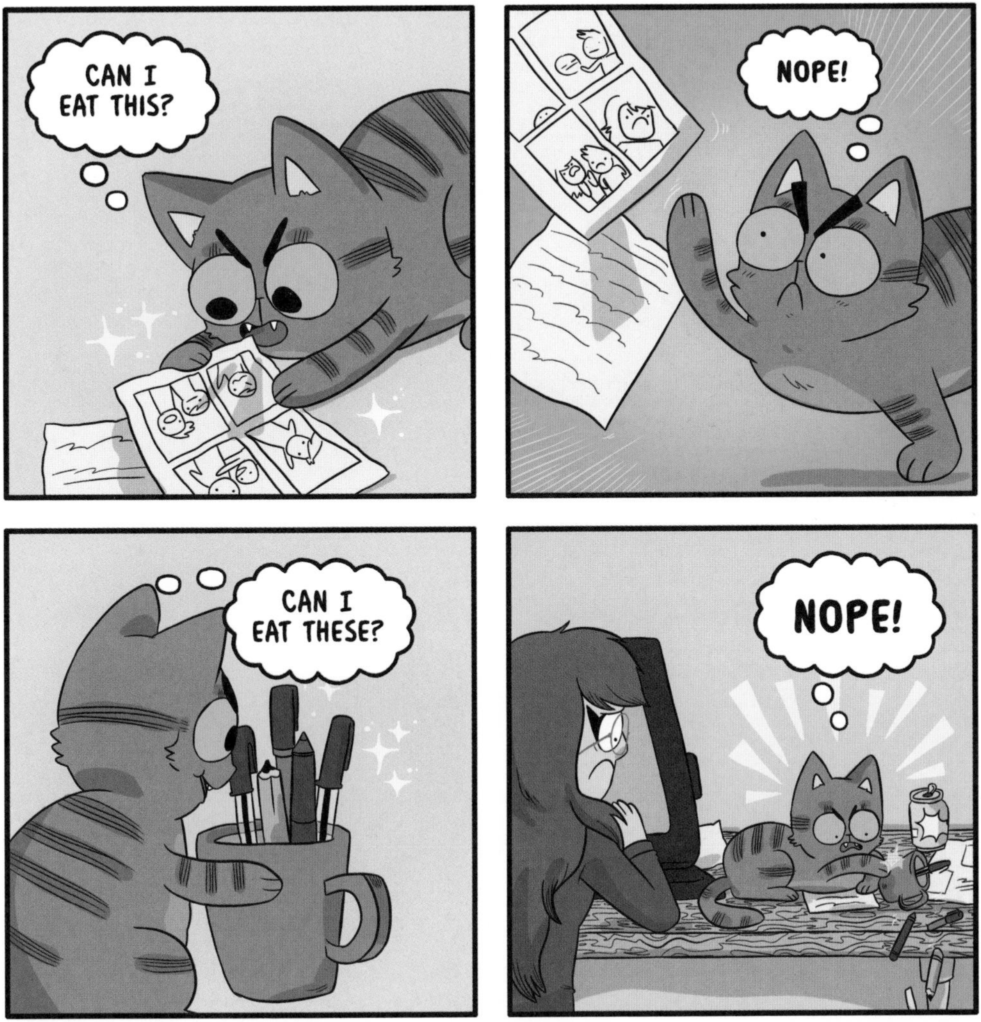
CAN I EAT THIS?
NOPE!
CAN I EAT THESE?
NOPE!

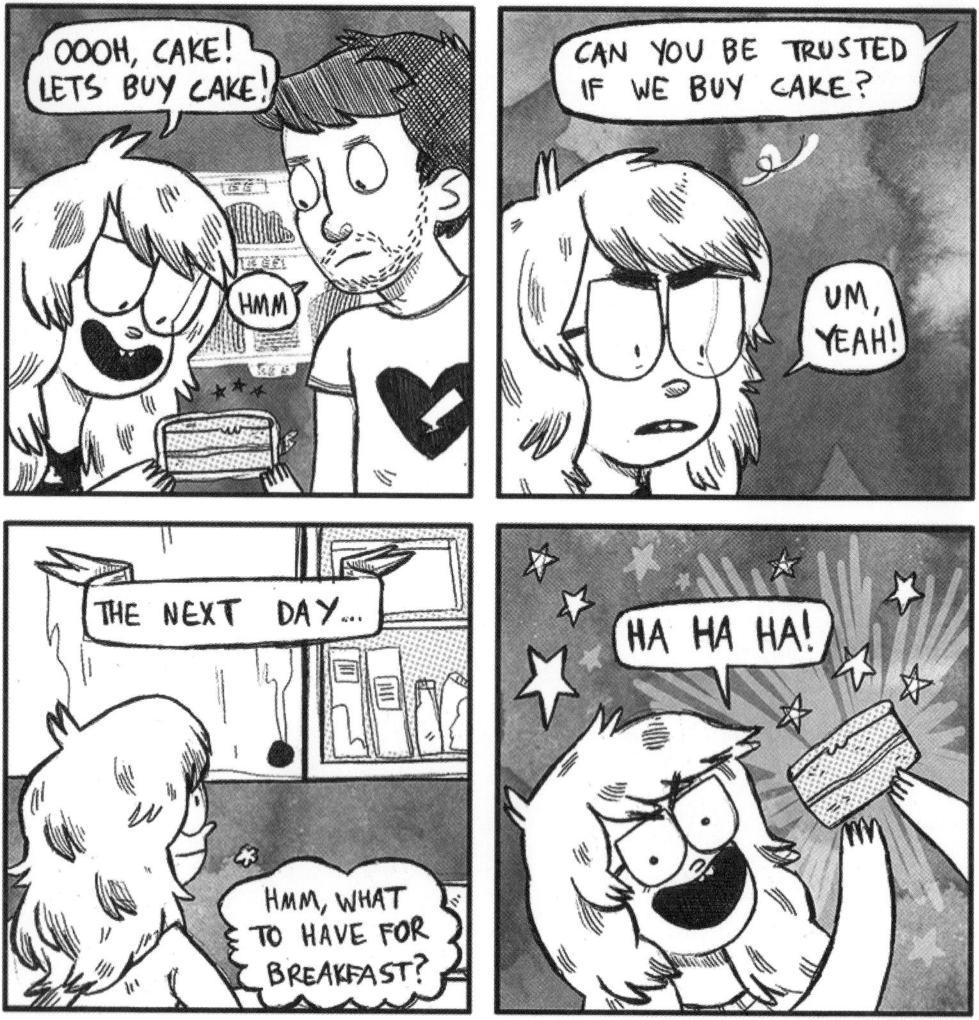
OOOH, CAKE! LETS BUY CAKE!
HMM
CAN YOU BE TRUSTED IF WE BUY CAKE?
UM, YEAH!
THE NEXT DAY...
HMM, WHAT TO HAVE FOR BREAKFAST?
HA HA HA!

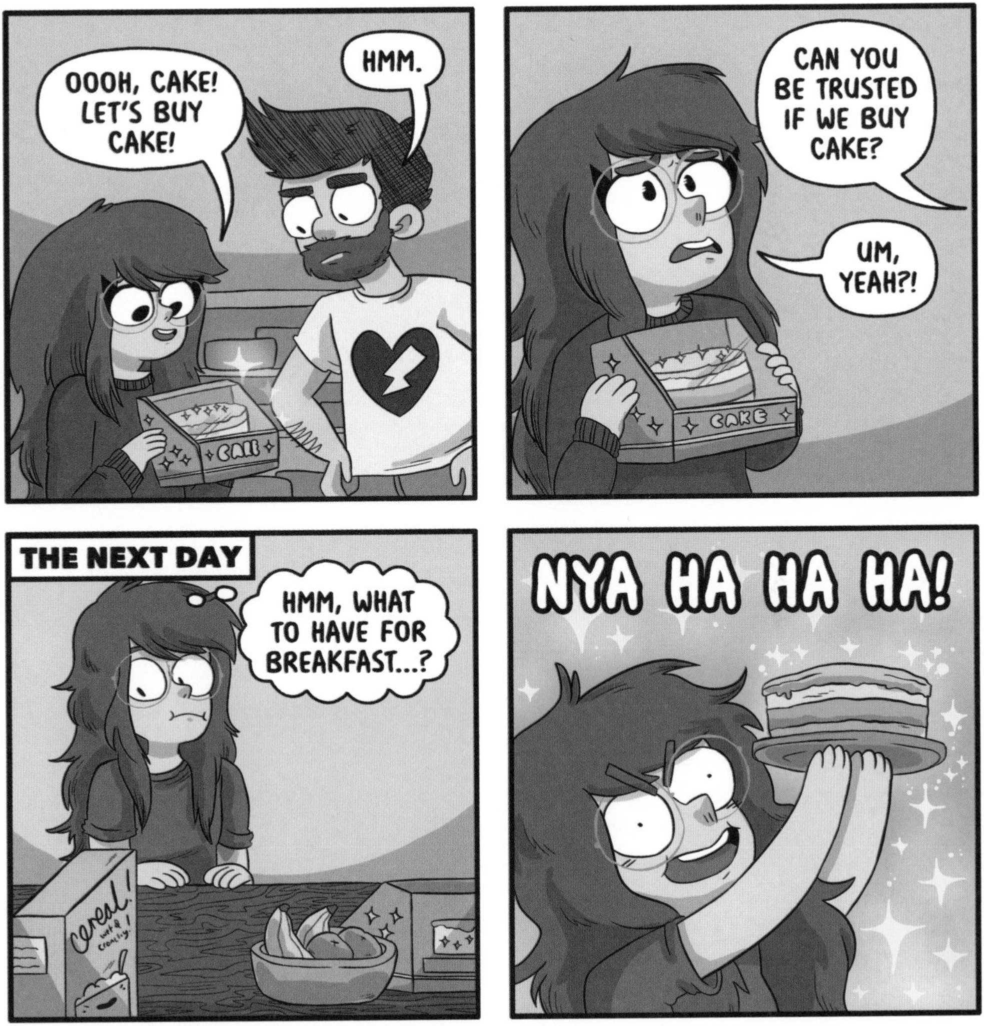
OOOH, CAKE! LET'S BUY CAKE!
HMM.
CAKE
CAN YOU BE TRUSTED IF WE BUY CAKE?
UM, YEAH?!
CAKE
THE NEXT DAY
HMM, WHAT TO HAVE FOR BREAKFAST...?
cereal!
NYA HA HA HA!

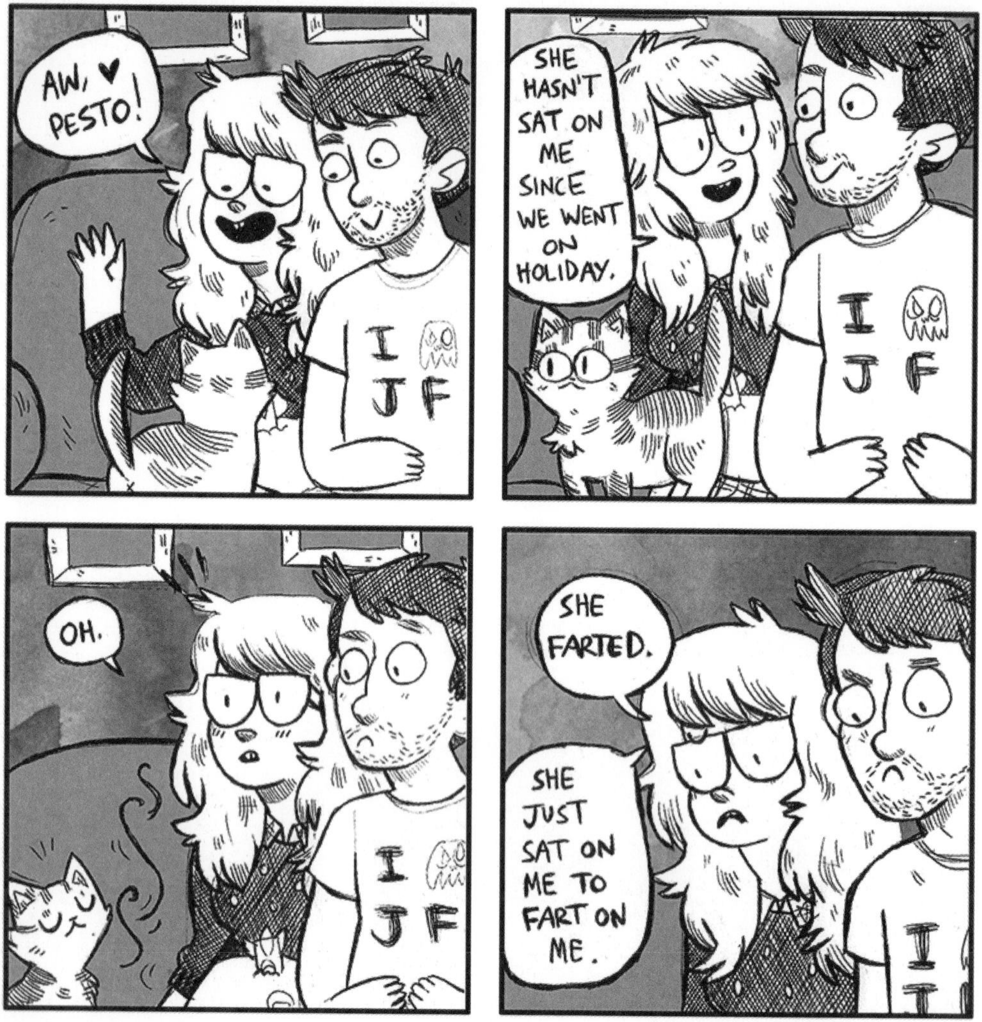
AW, ♥ PESTO!
SHE HASN'T SAT ON ME SINCE WE WENT ON HOLIDAY.
OH.
SHE FARTED.
SHE JUST SAT ON ME TO FART ON ME.

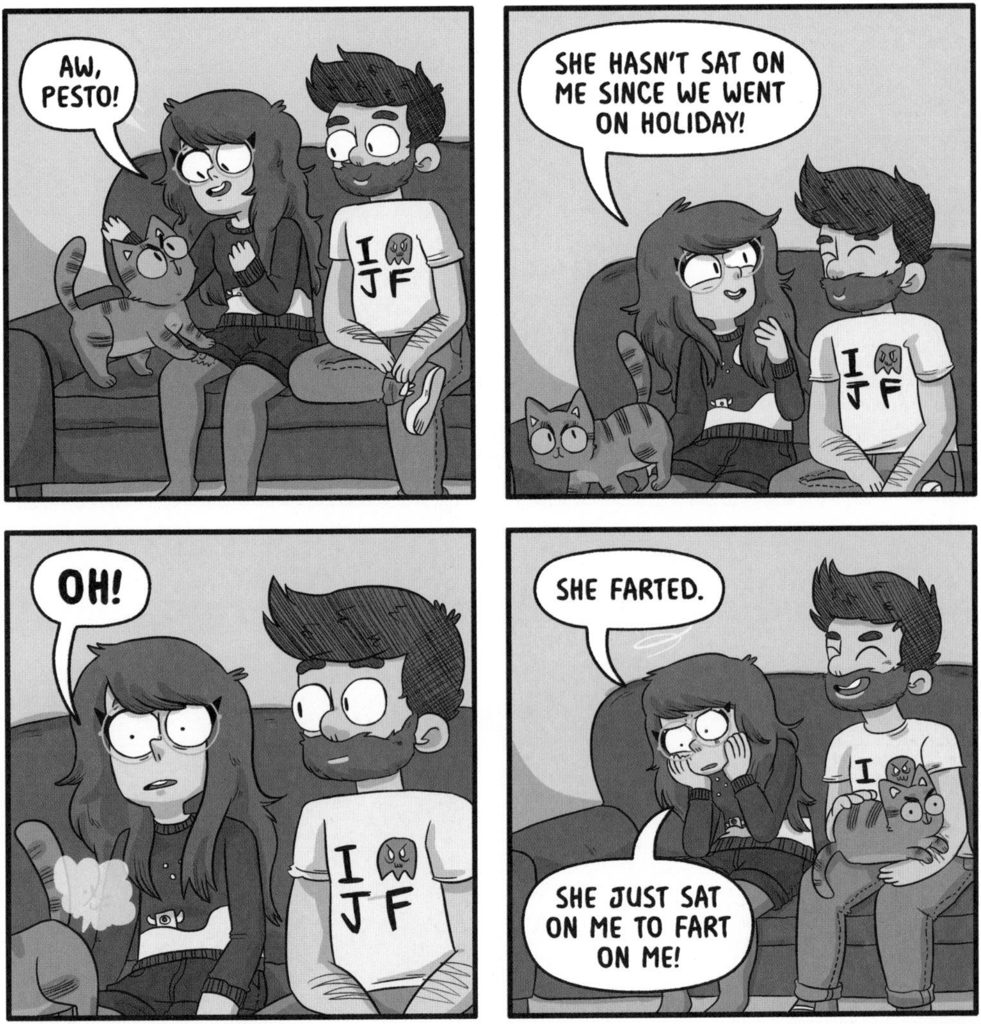
AW, PESTO!
I JF
SHE HASN'T SAT ON ME SINCE WE WENT ON HOLIDAY!
I JF
OH!
I JF
SHE FARTED.
I
SHE JUST SAT ON ME TO FART ON ME!

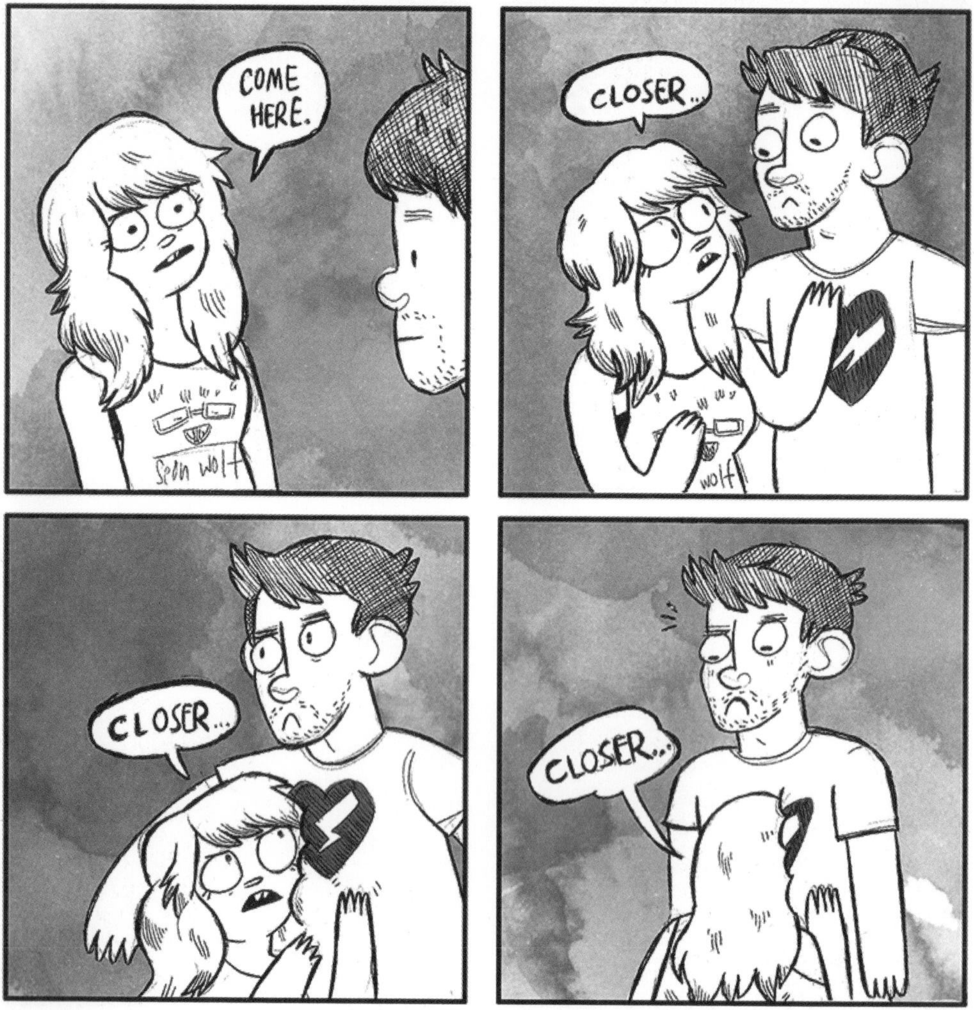
COME HERE.
CLOSER...
CLOSER...
CLOSER...

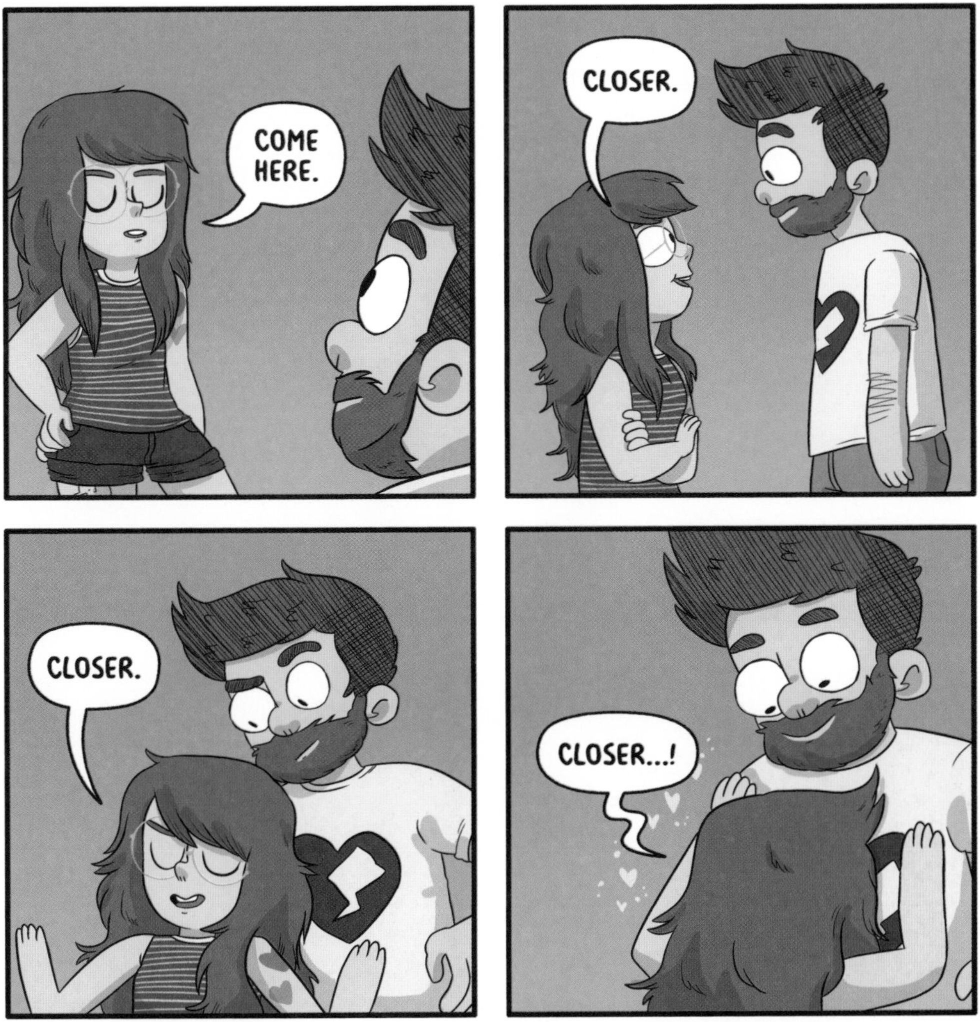
COME HERE.
CLOSER.
CLOSER.
CLOSER...!

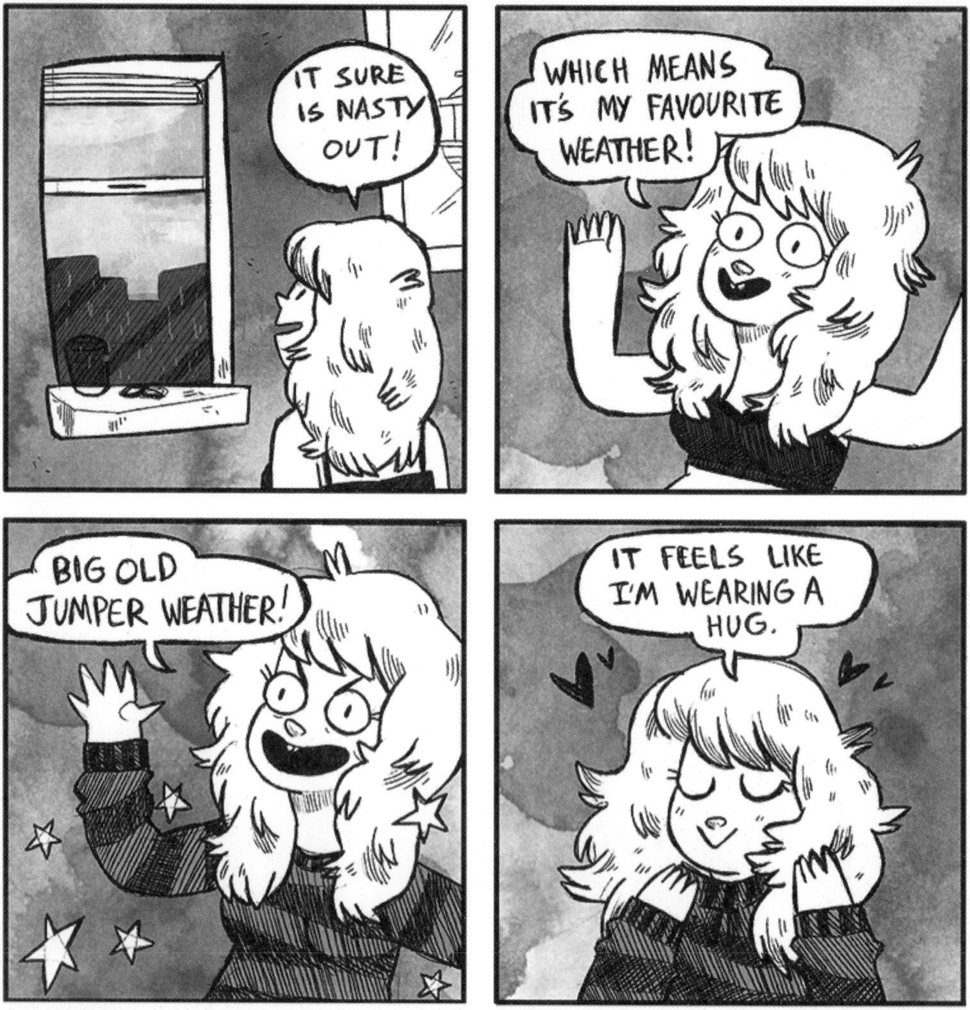
IT SURE IS NASTY OUT!
WHICH MEANS IT'S MY FAVOURITE WEATHER!
BIG OLD JUMPER WEATHER!
IT FEELS LIKE I'M WEARING A HUG.

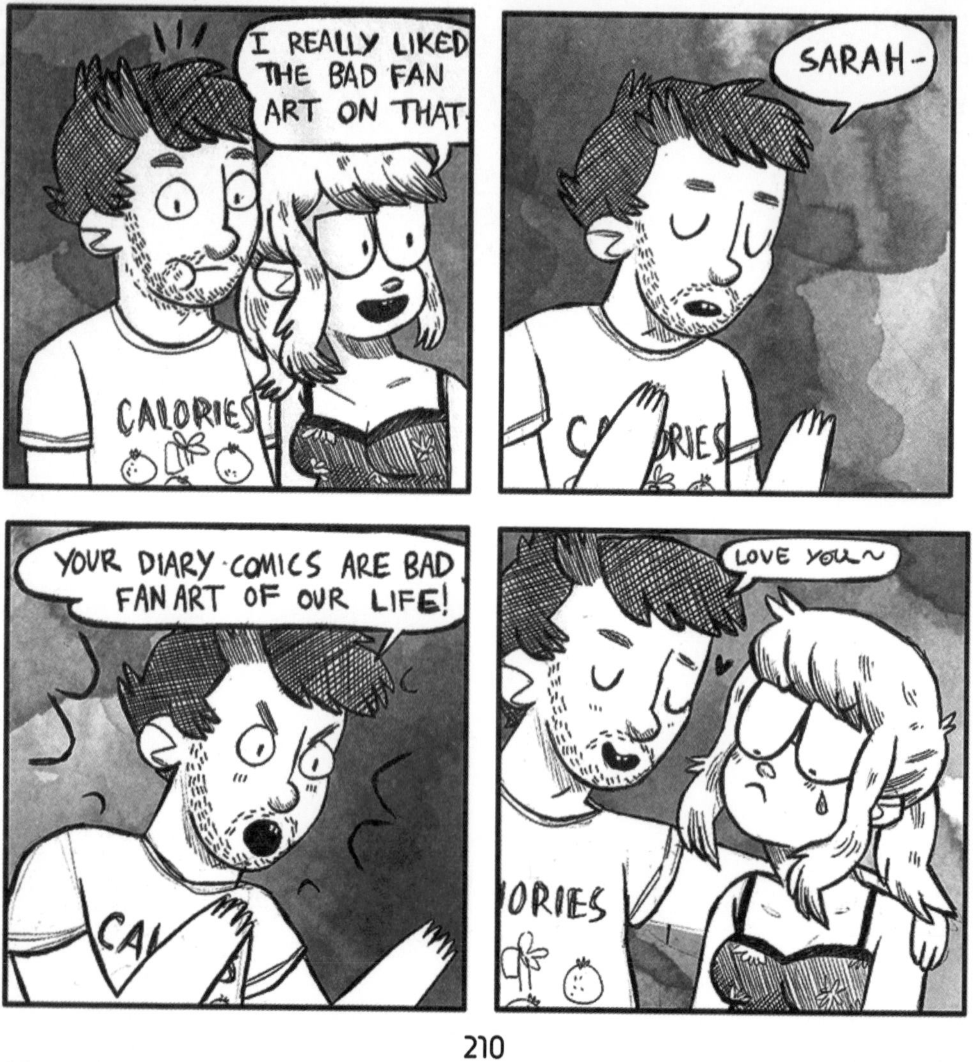
I REALLY LIKED THE BAD FAN ART ON THAT-
CALORIES
SARAH-
YOUR DIARY COMICS ARE BAD FAN ART OF OUR LIFE!
LOVE YOU~

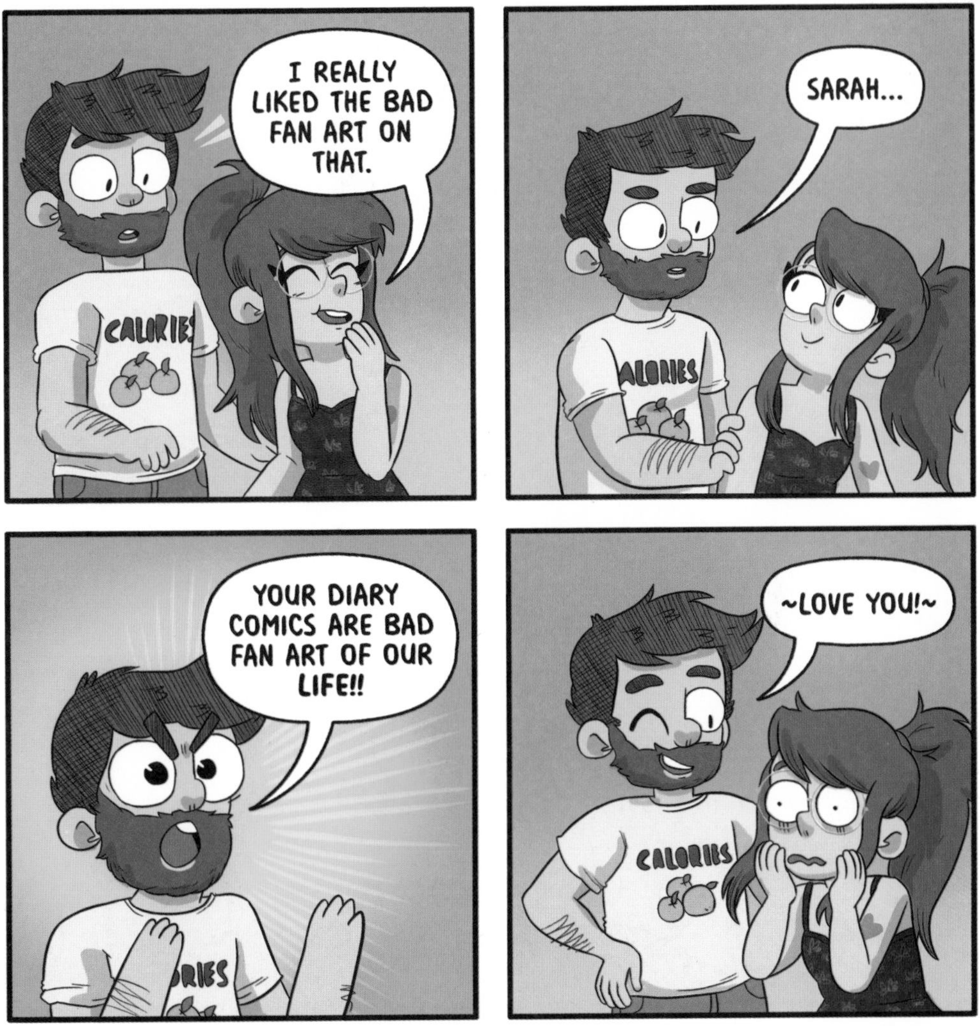
I REALLY LIKED THE BAD FAN ART ON THAT.
CALORIES
SARAH...
ALORIES
YOUR DIARY COMICS ARE BAD FAN ART OF OUR LIFE!!
ORIES
~LOVE YOU!~
CALORIES

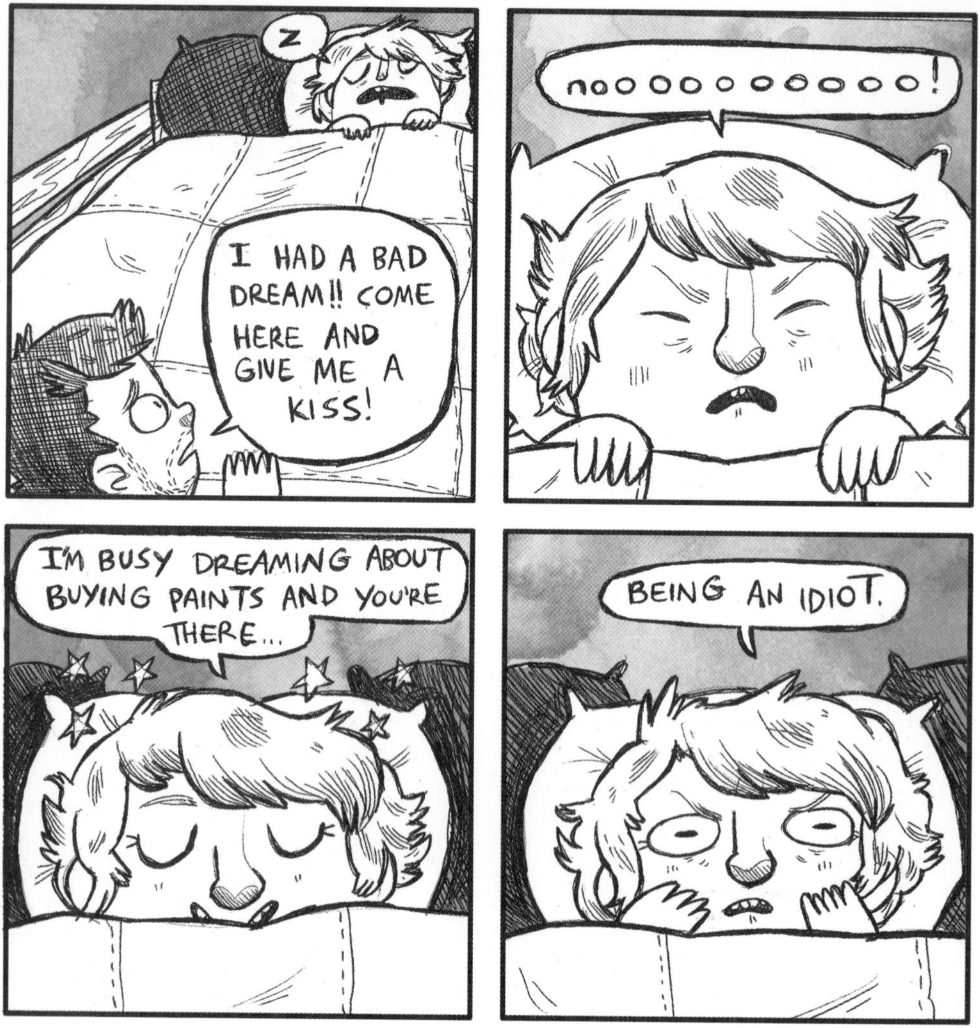
Z
I HAD A BAD DREAM!! COME HERE AND GIVE ME A KISS!
noo ooo o ooooo!
I'M BUSY DREAMING ABOUT BUYING PAINTS AND YOU'RE THERE...
BEING AN IDIOT.

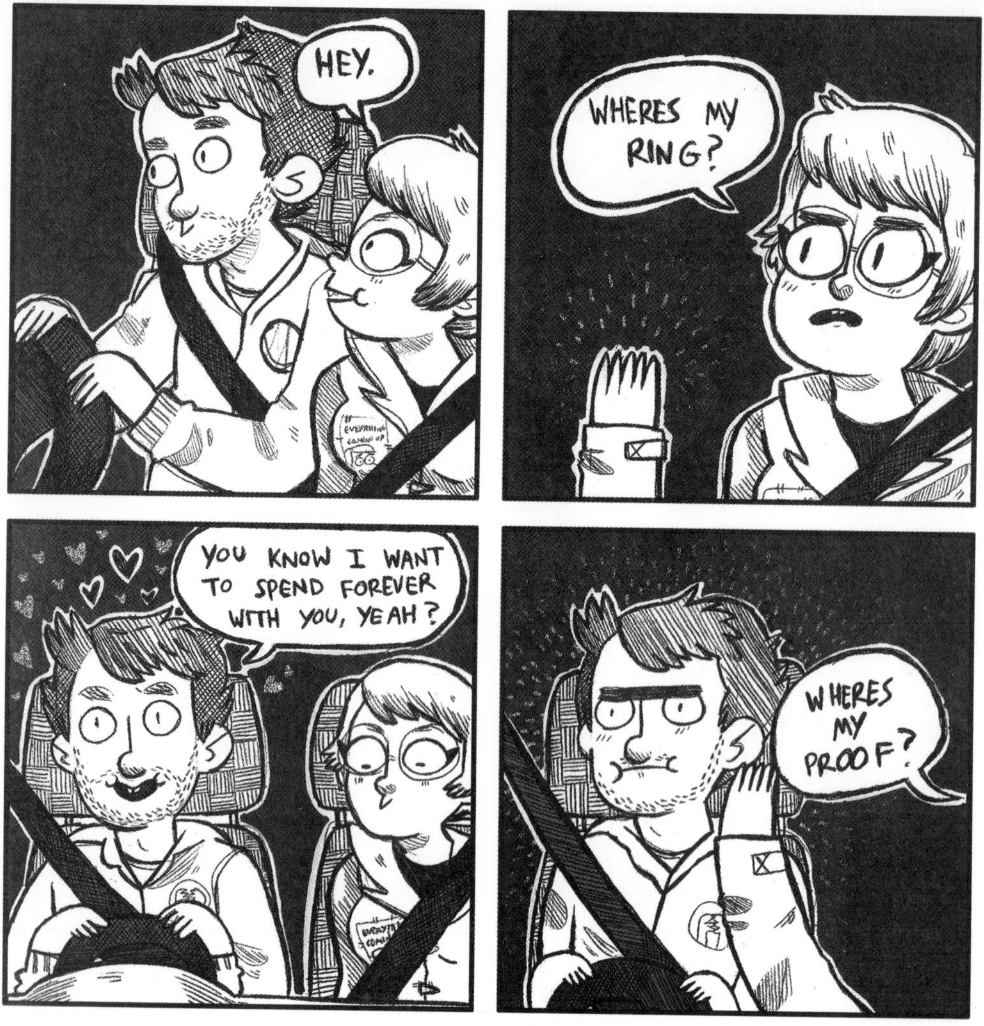
HEY.
WHERES MY RING?
YOU KNOW I WANT TO SPEND FOREVER WITH YOU, YEAH?
WHERES MY PROOF?

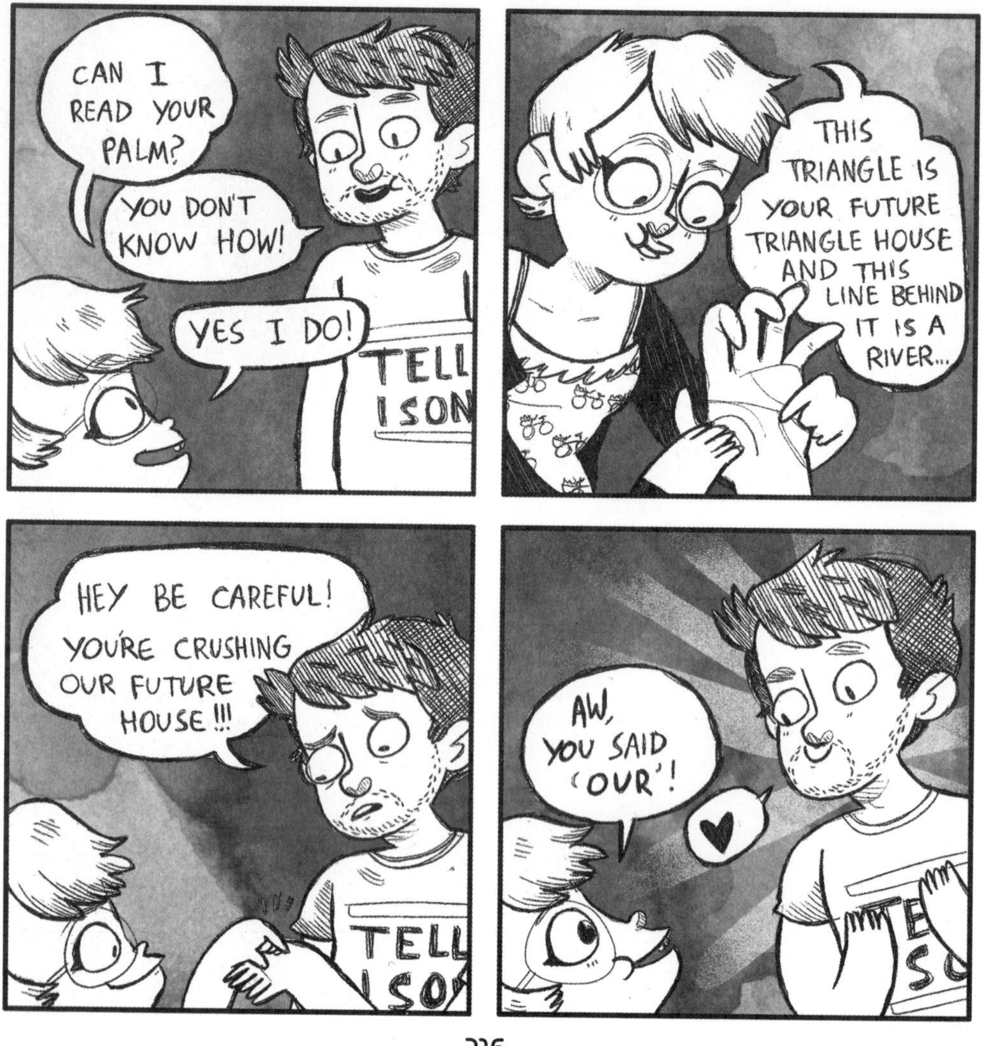
CAN I READ YOUR PALM?
YOU DON'T KNOW HOW!
YES I DO!
TELL ISON
THIS TRIANGLE IS YOUR FUTURE TRIANGLE HOUSE AND THIS LINE BEHIND IT IS A RIVER...
HEY BE CAREFUL!
YOU'RE CRUSHING OUR FUTURE HOUSE!!!
TELL ISO
AW, YOU SAID 'OUR'!

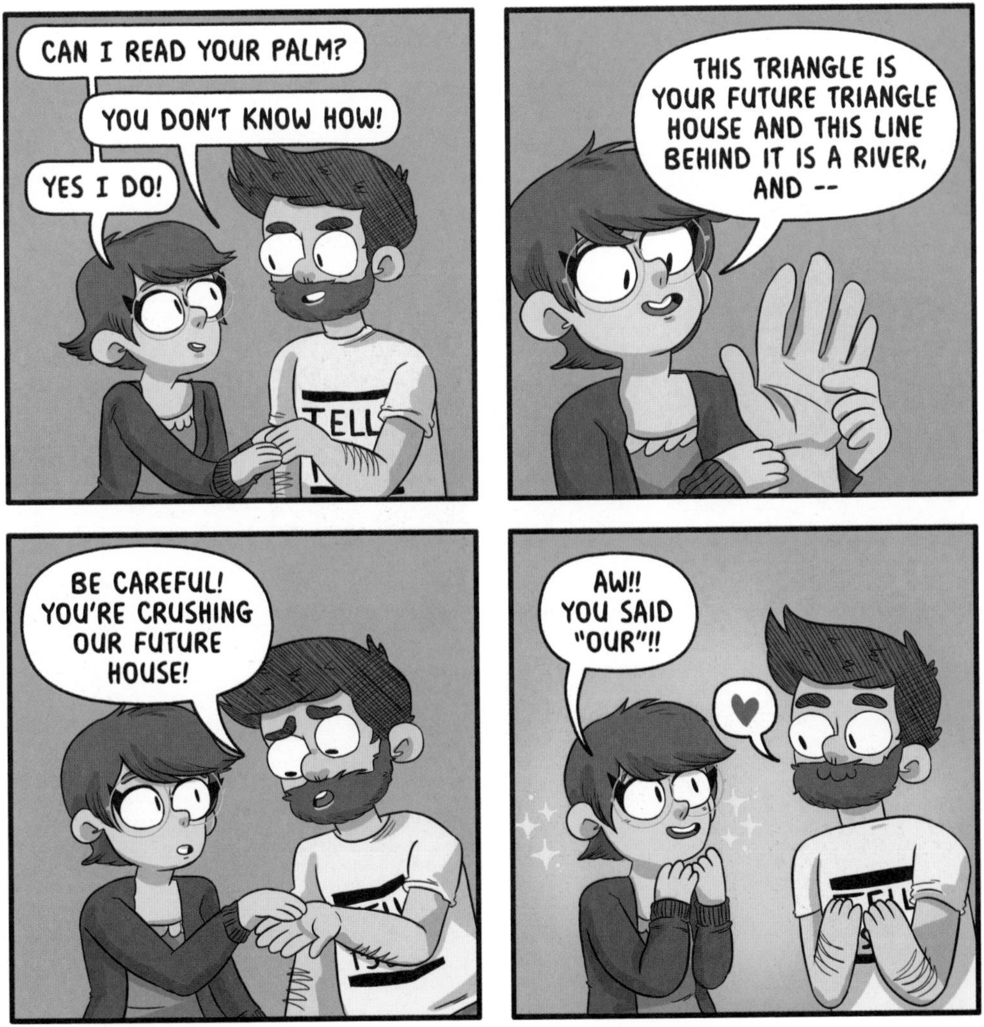
CAN I READ YOUR PALM?
YOU DON'T KNOW HOW!
YES I DO!
THIS TRIANGLE IS YOUR FUTURE TRIANGLE HOUSE AND THIS LINE BEHIND IT IS A RIVER, AND --
BE CAREFUL! YOU'RE CRUSHING OUR FUTURE HOUSE!
AW!! YOU SAID "OUR"!!

PHOTO DIARY 2015-2018

Loads of weird and cool stuff happened between the first *Our Super Adventure* book and this one, so where better to chronicle that stuff than right here and right now!

2015

I was nominated for "Emerging Talent" at the British Comic Awards 2015! I didn't win but I did get this very nice mug!

My first Kickstarter book delivery! They basically filled my old studio room.

2016

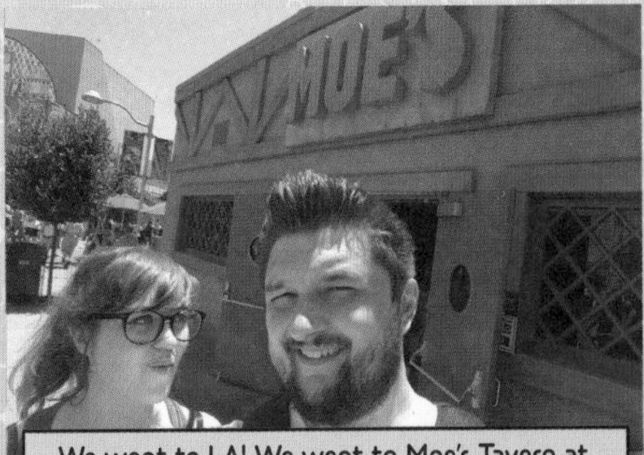
MOE'S

We went to LA! We went to Moe's Tavern at Universal Studios and had a very very expensive Duff beer!

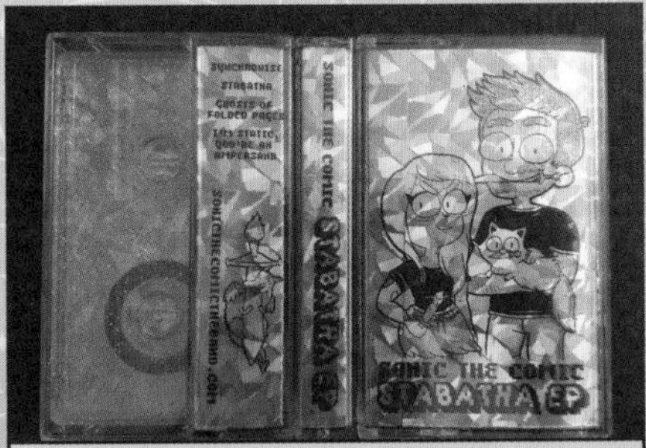
SONIC THE COMIC
STABATHA EP
SONIC THE COMIC STABATHA EP

Me and Stef released a new tape for our band Sonic The Comic! The cover was holographic and the tape was glittery!

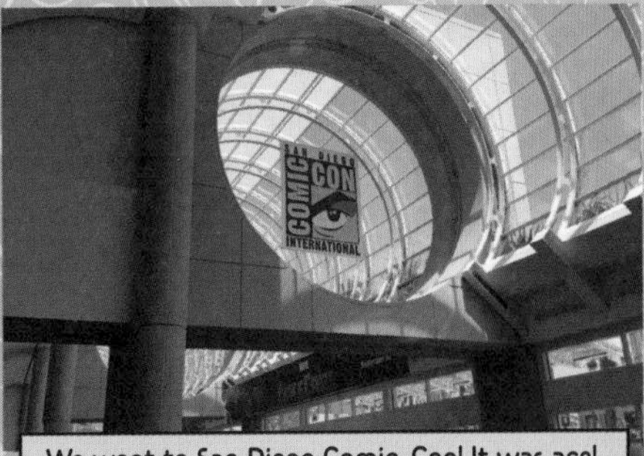
SAN DIEGO
COMIC CON
INTERNATIONAL

We went to San Diego Comic-Con! It was ace! (There's more about it in my book *Our Super American Adventure*!)

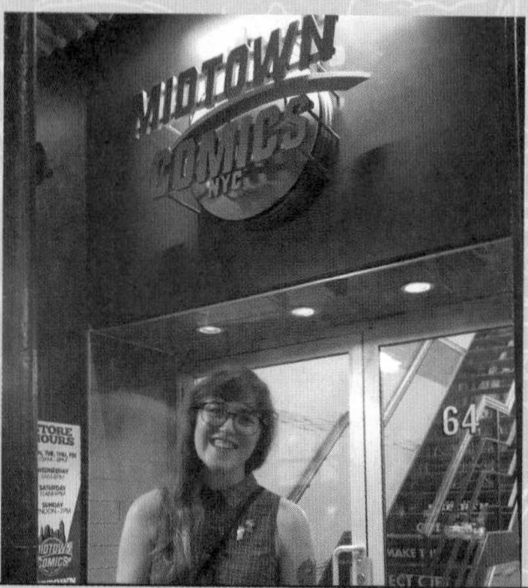
MIDTOWN
COMICS
NYC
STORE HOURS
64
Issue #1 of the *Rick and Morty* comic that I wrote and drew had just been released so I did a signing at Midtown Comics in New York!

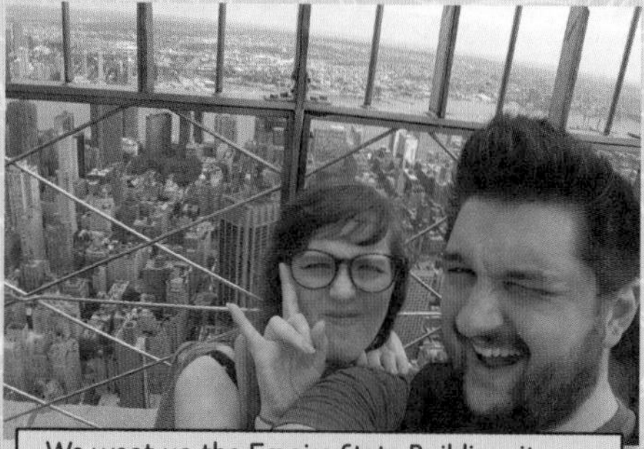
We went up the Empire State Building, it was super high and very windy!

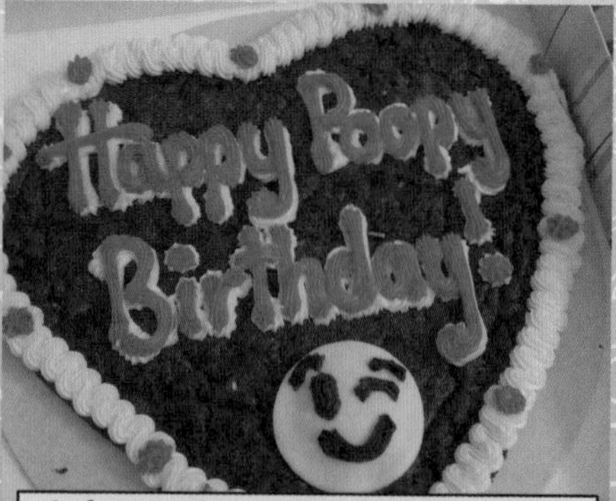
Happy Poopy
Birthday!
Stef got me this very good birthday cookie. 10/10 would eat again!

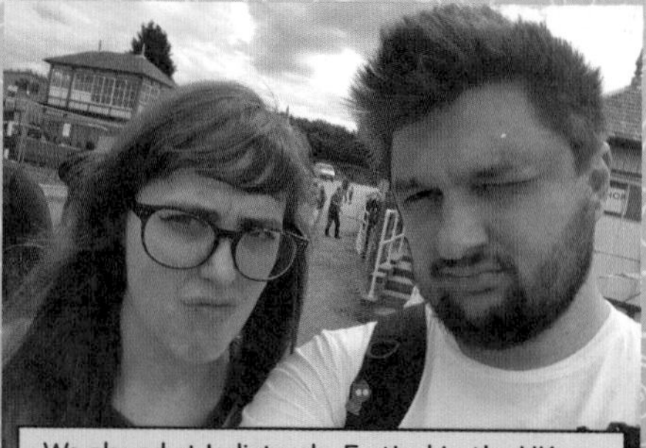
We played at Indietracks Festival in the UK on the day after we got back from America. We were very, very, jetlagged!

2017

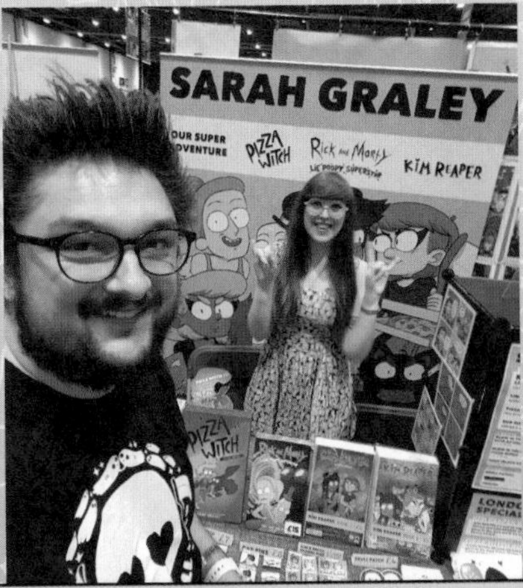
SARAH GRALEY
PIZZA WITCH
KIM REAPER

We tabled at MCM convention in London in May, We've tabled at that show about nine times!

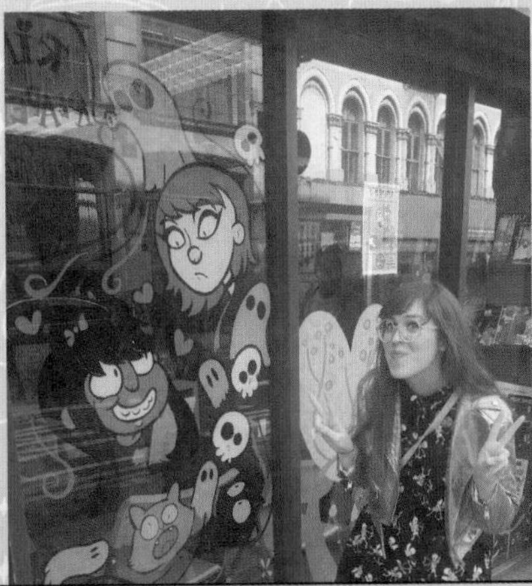

In April, I did a signing tour of all the Travelling Man comic shops to celebrate *Kim Reaper* #1! Manchester had this ace window mural!

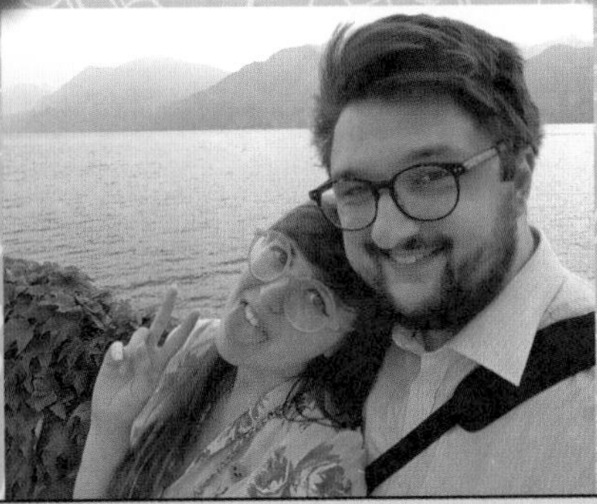

Stef's sister got married in a castle in Italy on Lake Garda. it was super hot and super picturesque! AND in a castle!!!

WASHINGTON D.C. AND SPX

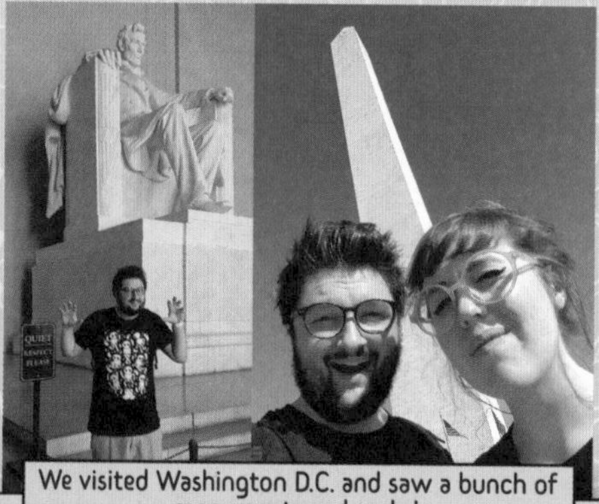

We visited Washington D.C. and saw a bunch of monuments and parks!

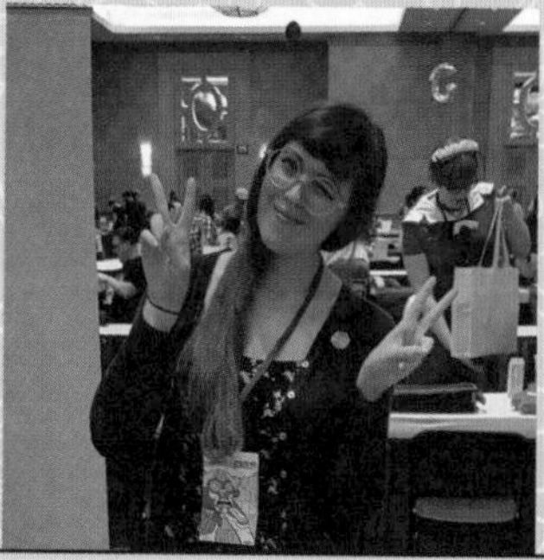

We went to Small Press Expo! (SPX). It was our first time going and it was just a great convention! So many good books!

NEW YORK CITY

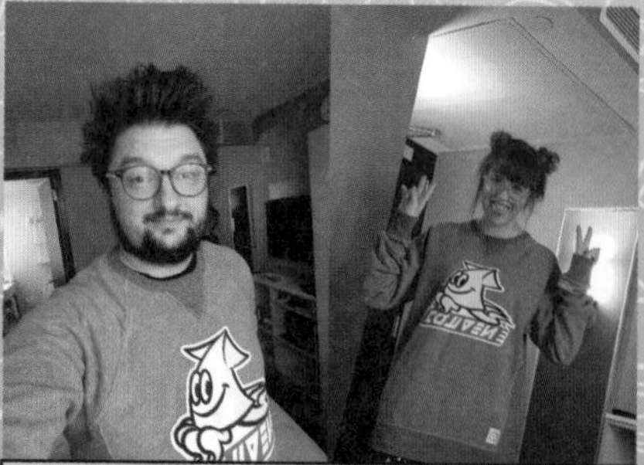

We went to the Nintendo shop in NYC and bought matching *Splatoon* sweaters! (We love *Splatoon 2*! It's such a good game!)

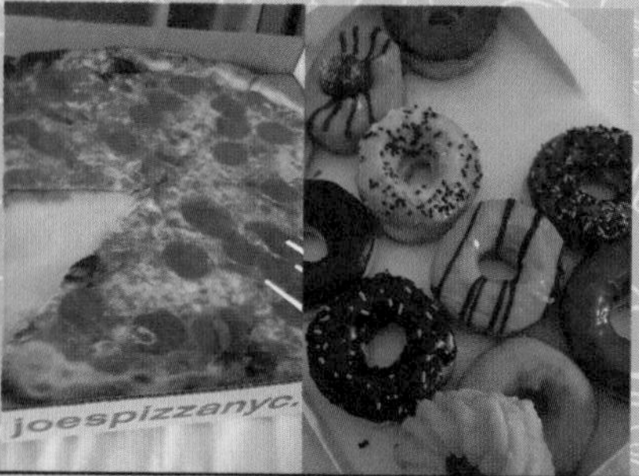
joespizzanyc.

We got some super good food! we went to the famous Joe's Pizza, and got some spooky Dunkin Donuts!

NEW YORK COMIC CON 2017

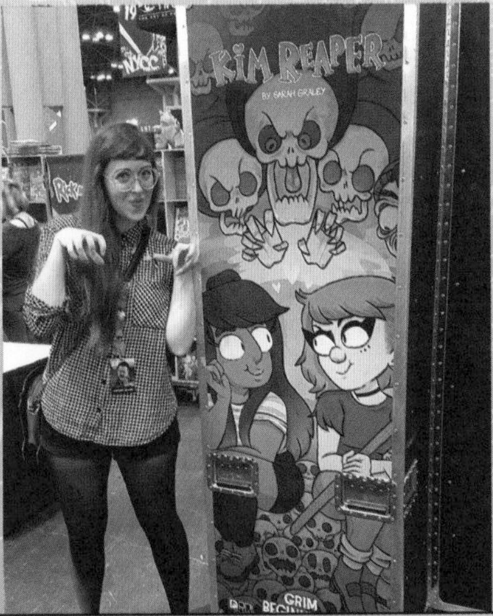
KIM REAPER
BY SARAH GRALEY
NYCC

The Oni Press booth had this amazing life size *Kim Reaper* flight case decal!

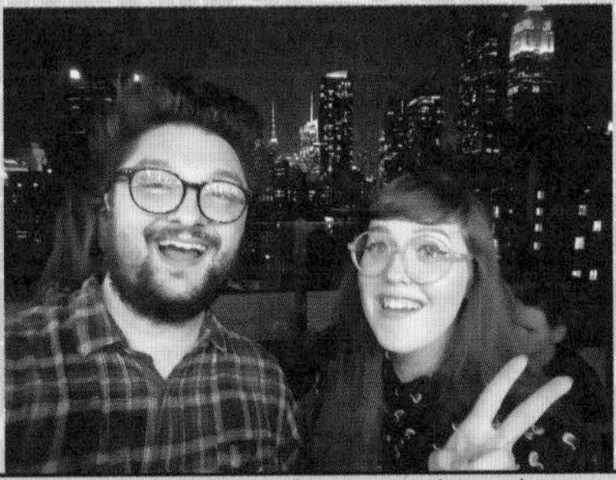

We went to a rooftop party hosted by Webtoon, it was super hot and loud!

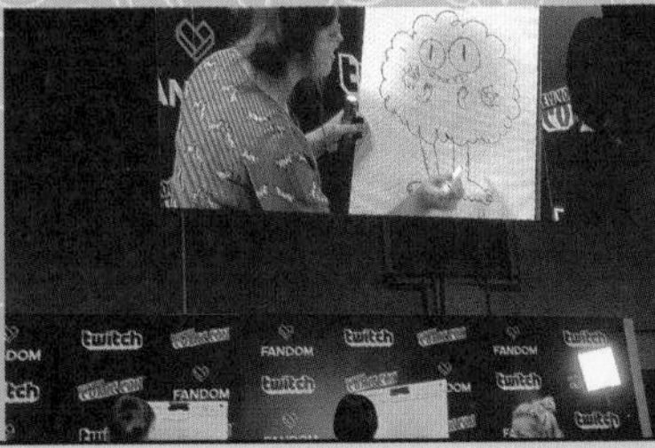
twitch
FANDOM

I was part of a live stage event called Monster Battle Time that was organised by Oni Press! I got to draw a bunch of cool monsters for kids!

SEATTLE AND ECCC 2018

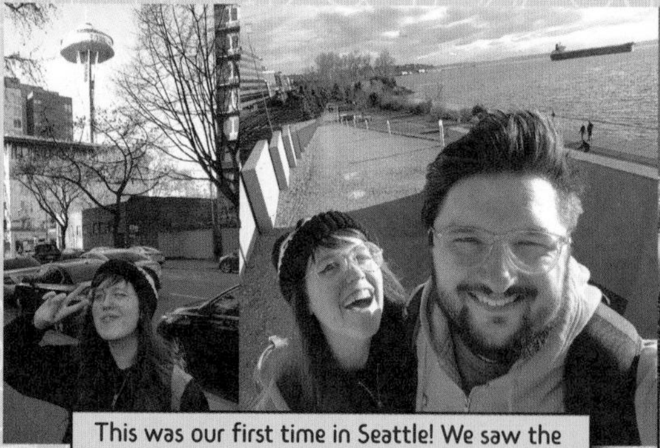

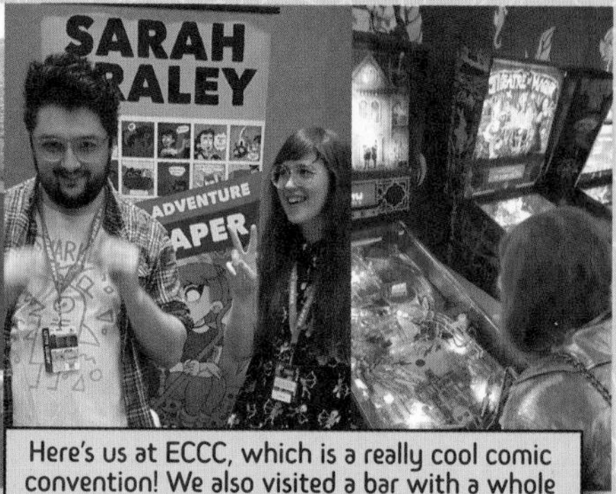
SARAH
ADVENTURE

This was our first time in Seattle! We saw the Space Needle, went to watch Superchunk play at Neumos, and went to MoPOP!

Here's us at ECCC, which is a really cool comic convention! We also visited a bar with a whole room of pinball machines!

CHICAGO AND C2E2 2018

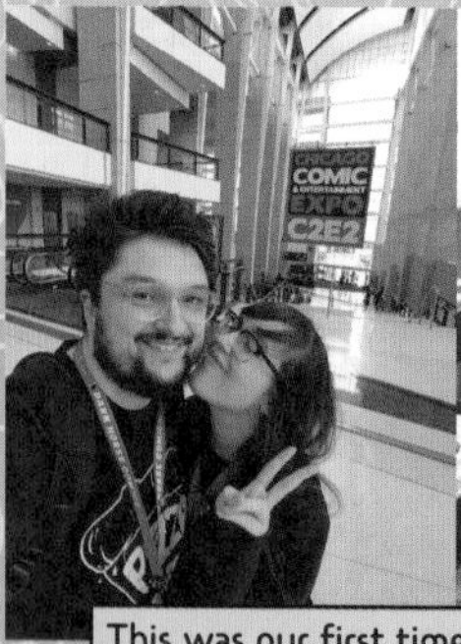
COMIC
EXPO
C2E2

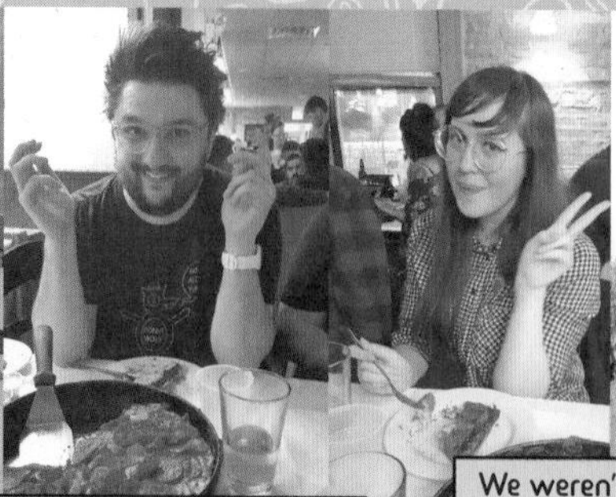

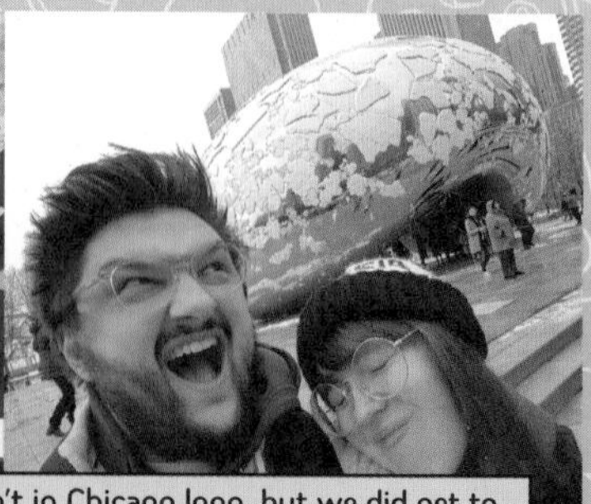

This was our first time in Chicago too! We had a blast at C2E2, and we had some deep dish pizza at Pequod's too! It was so good!

We weren't in Chicago long, but we did get to see The Bean (a.k.a. The Cloud Gate) covered in snow before our flight home!

2018

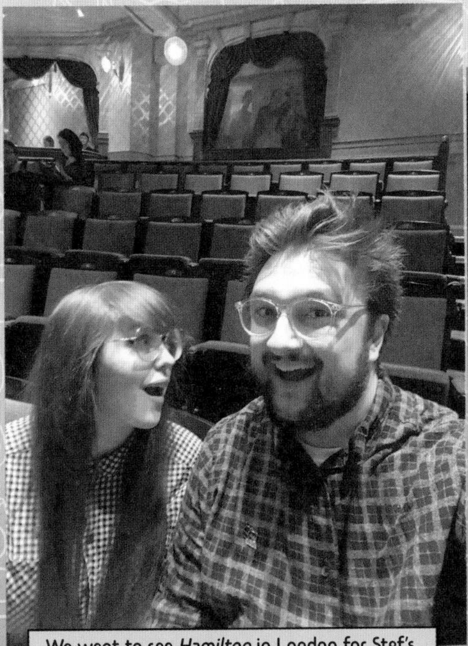

We went to see *Hamilton* in London for Stef's birthday! It's a really wonderful musical and it was incredible live!

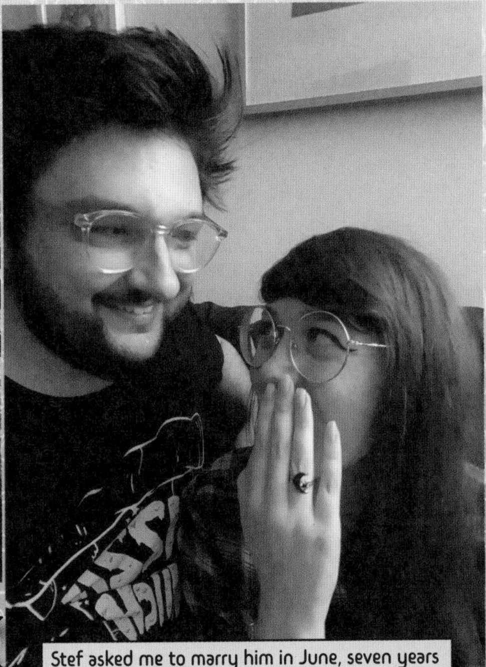

Stef asked me to marry him in June, seven years to the day of our first date! (I said yes!)

THUMBNAIL GALLERY

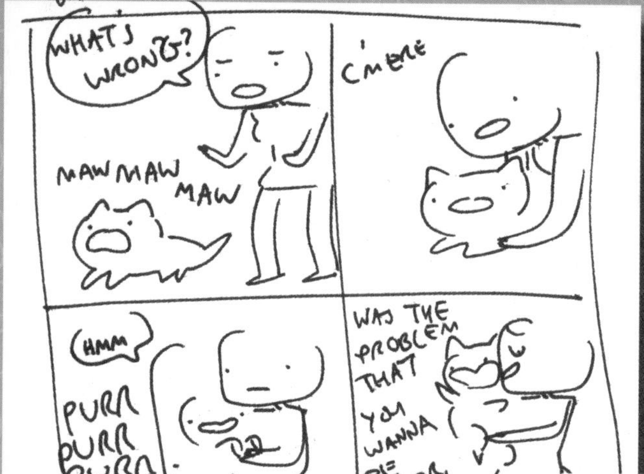
WHAT'S WRONG?
MAW MAW MAW
C'MERE
HMM
PURR PURR PURR
WAS THE PROBLEM THAT YOU WANNA BE TALLER, HUH?

Our Super Adventure comics start off as quickly scribbled down thumbnails, which I'll normally note down shortly after something weird or cute has happened!

I think these rough comics hold a certain kind of weird charm, so here's a small selection of them for some of the comics in this book!

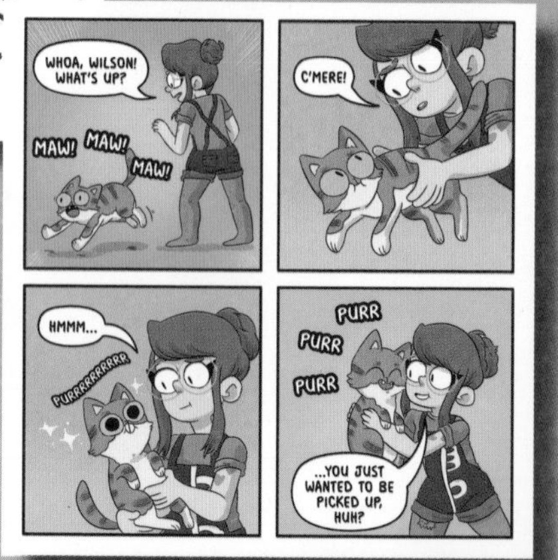
WHOA, WILSON! WHAT'S UP?
MAW! MAW! MAW!
C'MERE!
HMMM...
PURRRRRRRRRR
PURR
PURR
PURR
...YOU JUST WANTED TO BE PICKED UP, HUH?

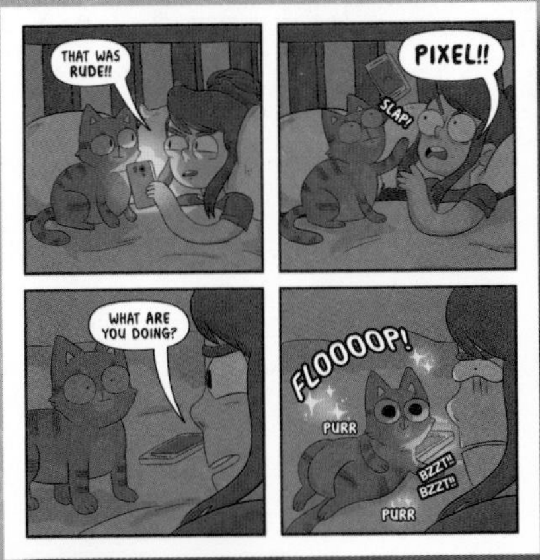
THAT WAS RUDE!!
PIXEL!!
SLAP!
WHAT ARE YOU DOING?
FLOOOOP!
PURR
BZZT!!
BZZT!!
PURR

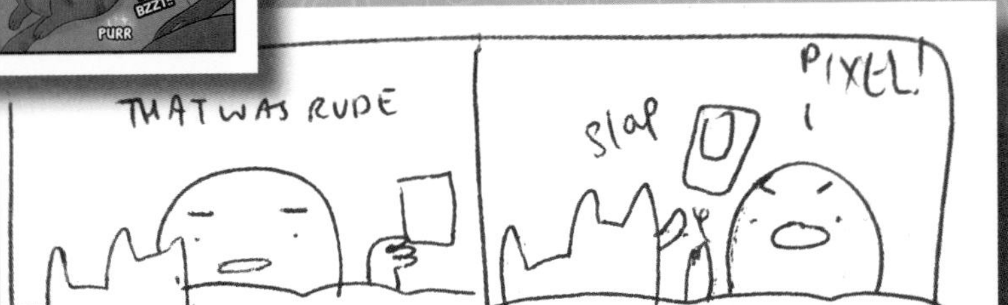
THAT WAS RUDE
PIXEL!
slap
PURR
PURR
WHAT ARE YOU...
GAAAH

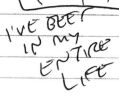

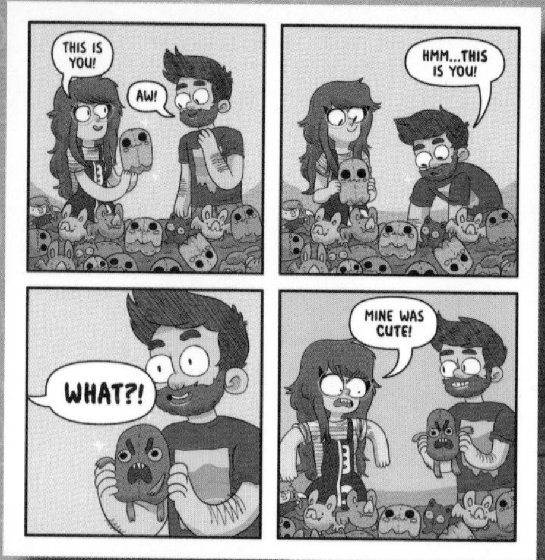
THIS IS YOU!
AW!
HMM...THIS IS YOU!
WHAT?!
MINE WAS CUTE!

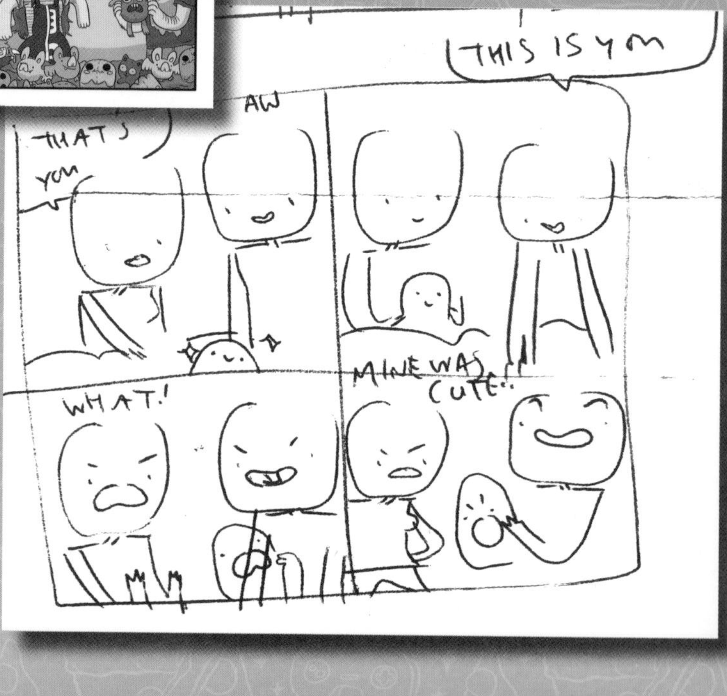
THAT'S YOU
AW
THIS IS YM
WHAT!
MINE WAS CUTE!

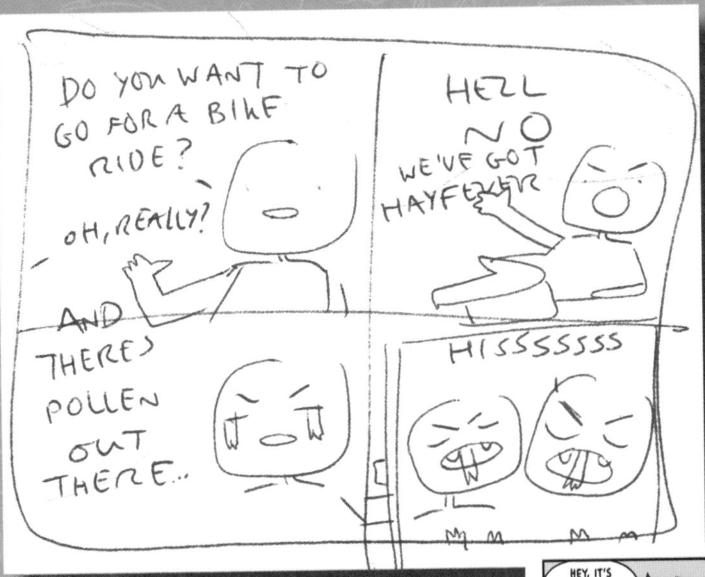
DO YOU WANT TO GO FOR A BIKE RIDE?
OH, REALLY?
HELL NO
WE'VE GOT HAYFEVER
AND THERES POLLEN OUT THERE...
HISSSSSSS

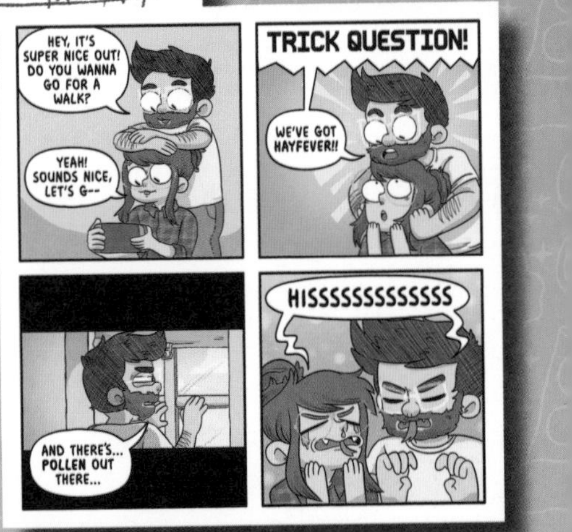
HEY, IT'S SUPER NICE OUT! DO YOU WANNA GO FOR A WALK?
YEAH! SOUNDS NICE, LET'S G--
TRICK QUESTION!
WE'VE GOT HAYFEVER!!
AND THERE'S... POLLEN OUT THERE...
HISSSSSSSSSSSSS

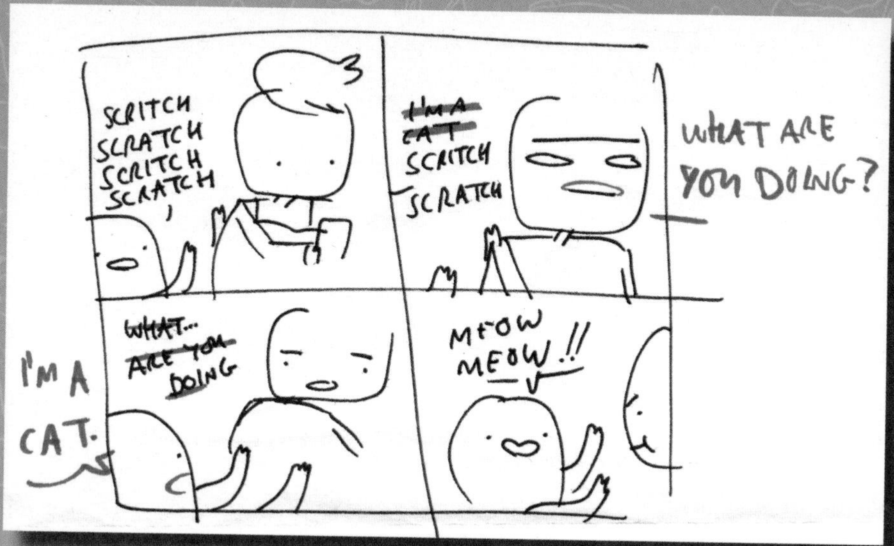
SCRITCH SCRATCH SCRITCH SCRATCH
I'M A CAT
SCRITCH SCRATCH
WHAT ARE YOU DOING?
WHAT... ARE YOU DOING
I'M A CAT.
MEOW MEOW.!!

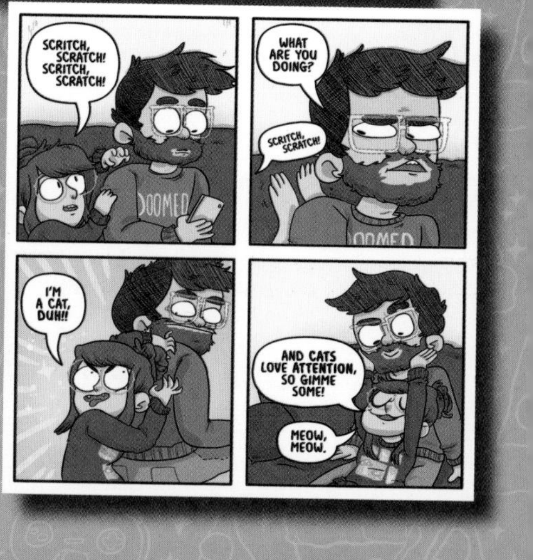
SCRITCH, SCRATCH! SCRITCH, SCRATCH!
DOOMED
WHAT ARE YOU DOING?
SCRITCH, SCRATCH!
I'M A CAT, DUH!!
AND CATS LOVE ATTENTION, SO GIMME SOME!
MEOW, MEOW.

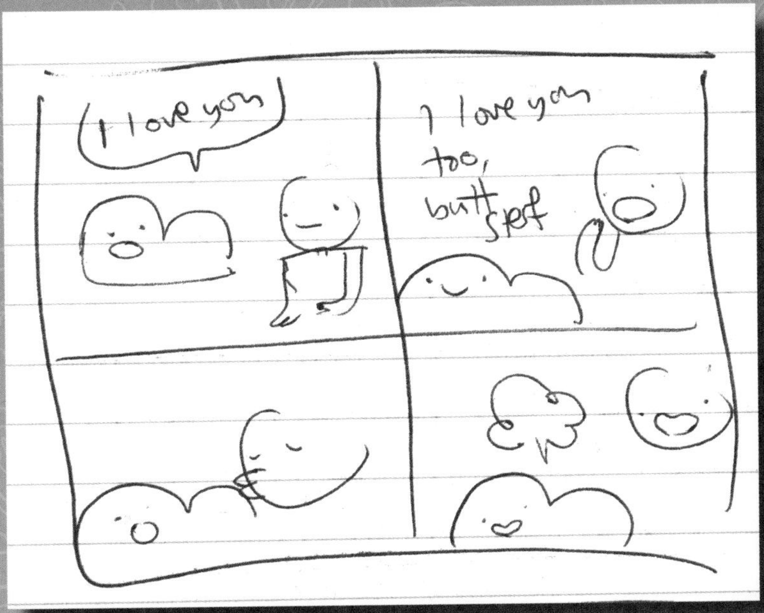
I love you
I love you too, butt Stef

Sometimes comic thumbnails sadly stay as comic thumbnails. I think you'll all agree that the world is a worse place without this stunning rough comic, entitled "Butt Stef".

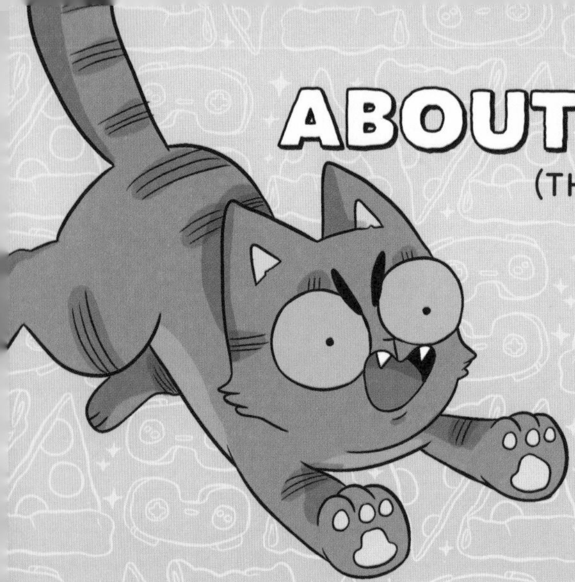

ABOUT OUR CATS

(THE REAL STARS OF THE BOOK)

PESTO aka "Poopo"

- She's the angriest looking cat!
- The mum of Pixel and Wilson.
- Favourite Place To Sleep: Sarah's armpit.
- Special Ability: Secretly really friendly when Wilson isn't around.

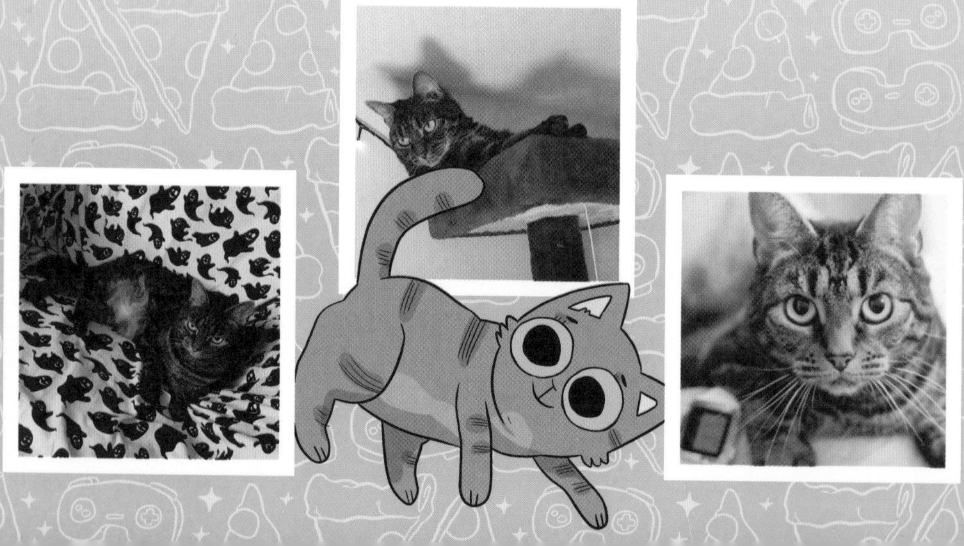

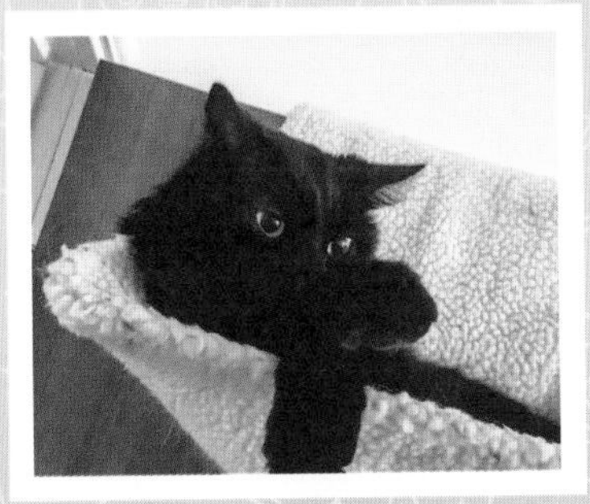

TOBY aka "Tobes"

- She's a fluffy black cloud.
- She is Pesto's sister!
- Favourite Place To Sleep: She has claimed Stef's office chair as her bed, please don't move her.
- Special Ability: Loves Stef a lot and will pat his butt to get his attention.

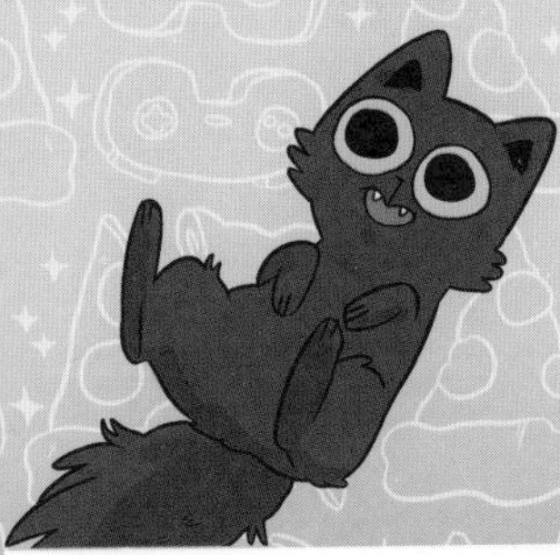

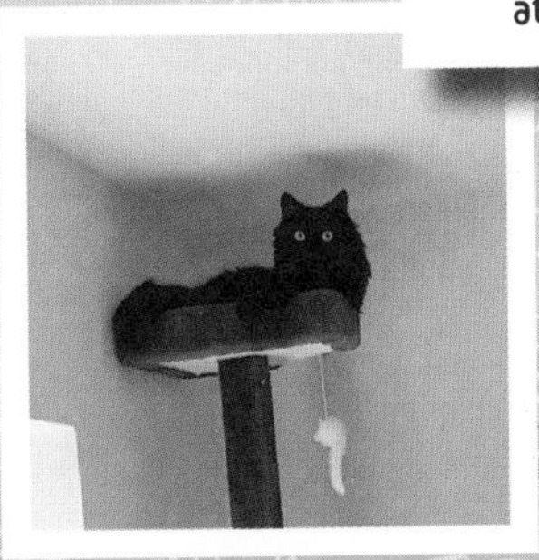

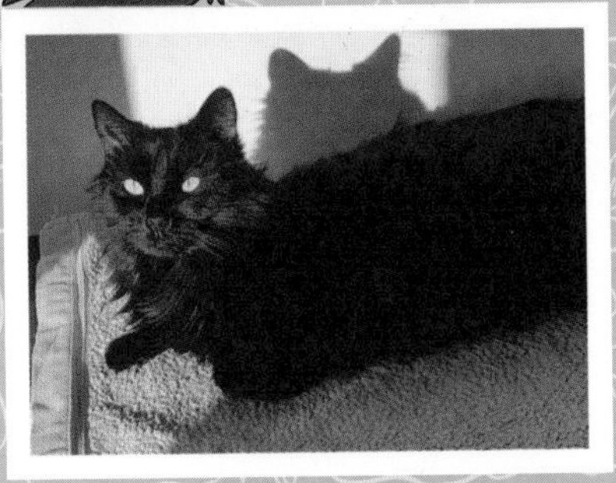

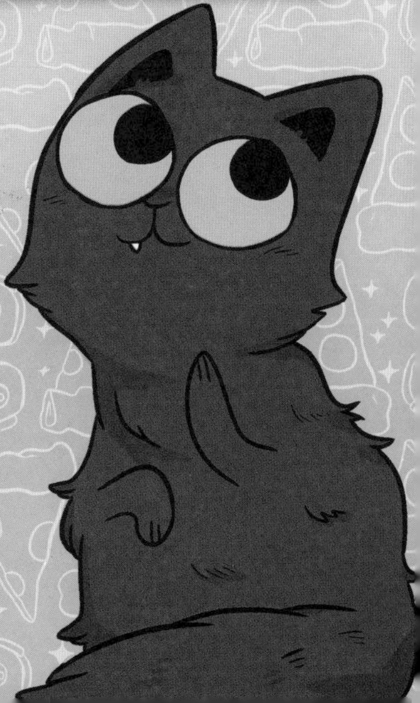

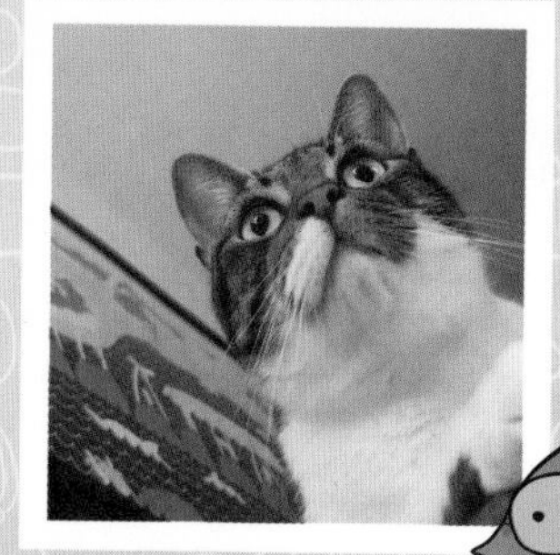

WILSON aka "Willy"

- A friendly troublemaker!
- Wants to play with the other cats more than they want to play back.
- Favourite Place To Sleep: Wherever there is another cat sleeping already.
- Special Ability: Purrs all the time!

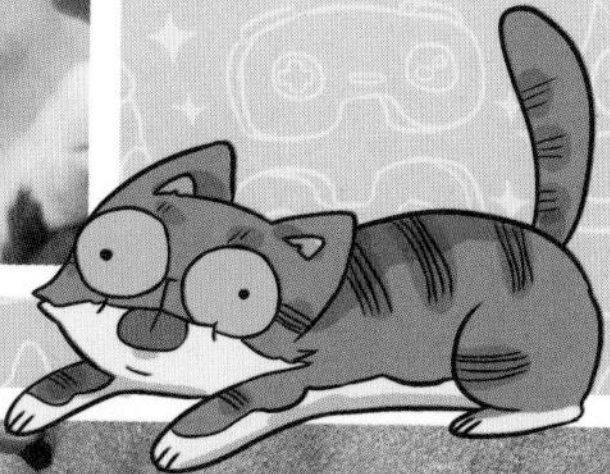

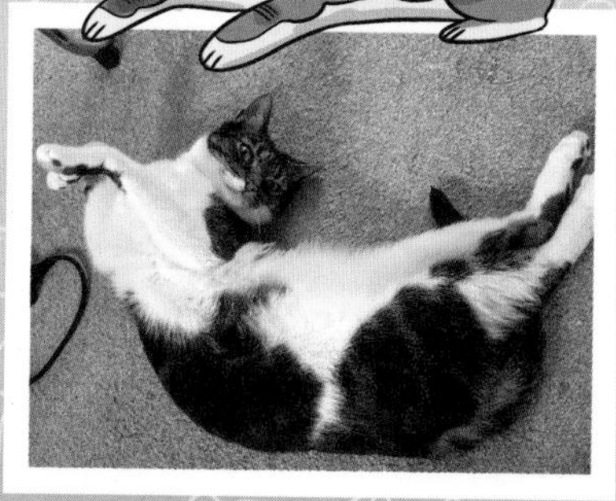

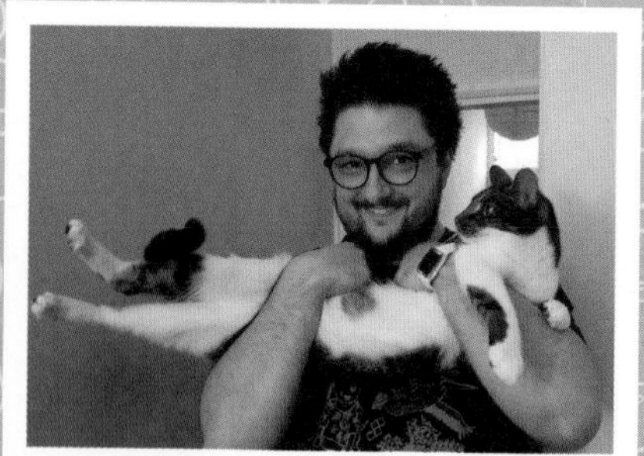

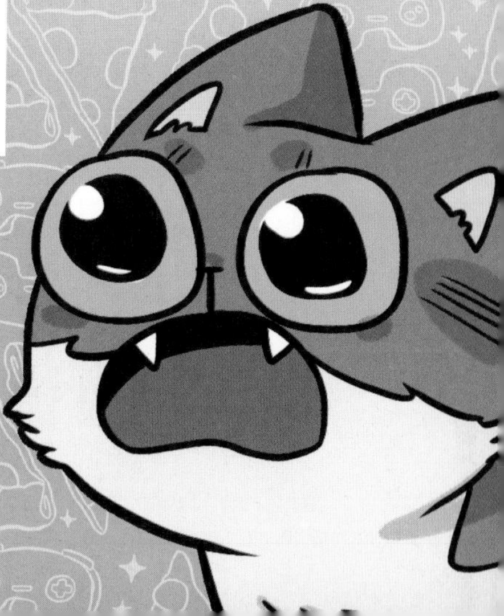

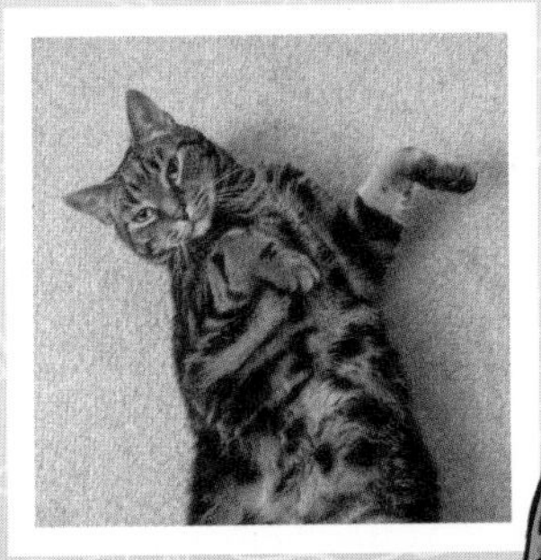
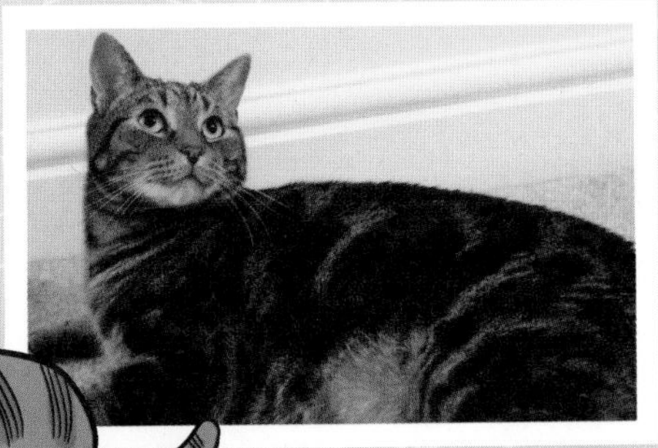
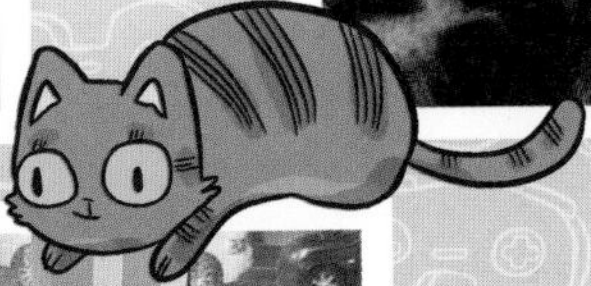
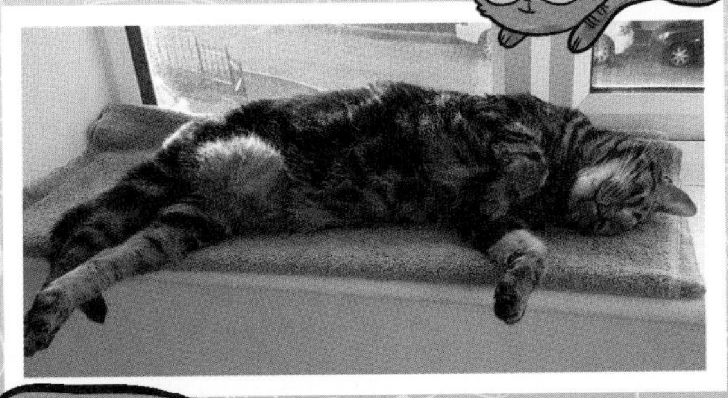
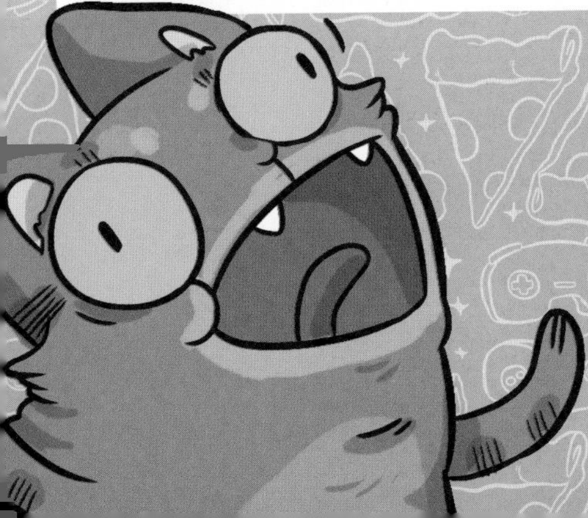

PIXEL aka "Pickle"

- An adorable little sandbag of a cat.
- Known to walk all over Sarah while she's asleep.
- Favourite Place To Sleep: In our bedroom after walking all over Sarah.
- Special Ability: Does incredibly sad meows whenever he wants attention.

THE SUPER ADVENTURERS

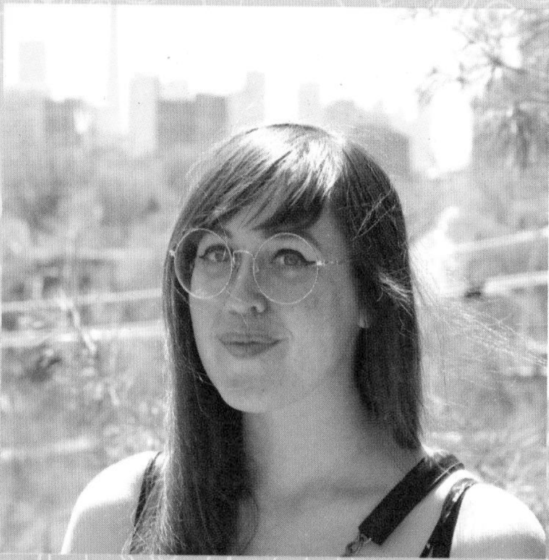

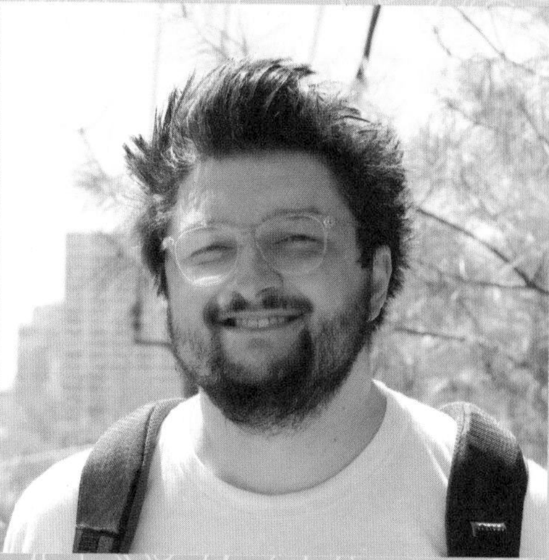

Sarah Graley is a comic writer and artist who lives in Birmingham, UK, with four cats and a cat-like boy. She has been drawing ***Our Super Adventure*** since 2012, alongside other comics such as ***Kim Reaper*** (Oni Press), ***Rick and Morty: Lil' Poopy Superstar*** (Oni Press), ***Glitch*** (Scholastic Graphix) and ***Minecraft Volume One*** (Dark Horse Comics).

You can find out more about her at sarahgraley.com!

Stef Purenins is a cat-like boy who does lettering and colour assisting, as well as helping Sarah out with design stuff and admin and what-not.

He makes video game music over at tinyspells.bandcamp.com!

THANKS & ACKNOWLEDGEMENTS

Special thanks to our families and friends for being a part of our weird little life, even when we're super busy with comics work!

Thank you to our editor at Oni Press, Ari Yarwood, and thank you to everyone else at Oni Press for always taking care of us when we visit the US and for wanting to put out these books to a wider audience!

Thank you to Steven Salpeter for always being an incredibly supportive agent and a fountain of knowledge that we're lucky to have in our lives!

Thank you to all of our comic pals, in both the UK and the rest of the world! We love getting to read all of the cool books that people we know put out!

Lastly, thank you to everyone who has read or picked up this book - or any *Our Super Adventure* book for that matter! Especially those people who backed either of the books on their initial Kickstarter campaigns!

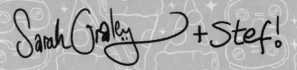

FIND US ONLINE

sarahgraley.com
oursuperadventure.com
@sarahgraleyart & @tinyspells
facebook.com/sarahgraleyart
instagram.com/sarahgraley
sonicthecomic.bandcamp.com

READ MORE OUR SUPER ADVENTURE!

Our Super Adventure: Press Start To Begin

The first volume of diary comics! Contains 200 comics all about cats, pizza, and navigating adult life!

Our Super American Adventure

Travel comics all about our first trip to America! See what we got up to in LA, San Diego Comic-Con and New York!

Our Super Canadian Adventure

Travel comics all about our first trip to Canada! We discover mysterious new foods and see the sights in Toronto, and then get pretty wet at Niagara Falls!

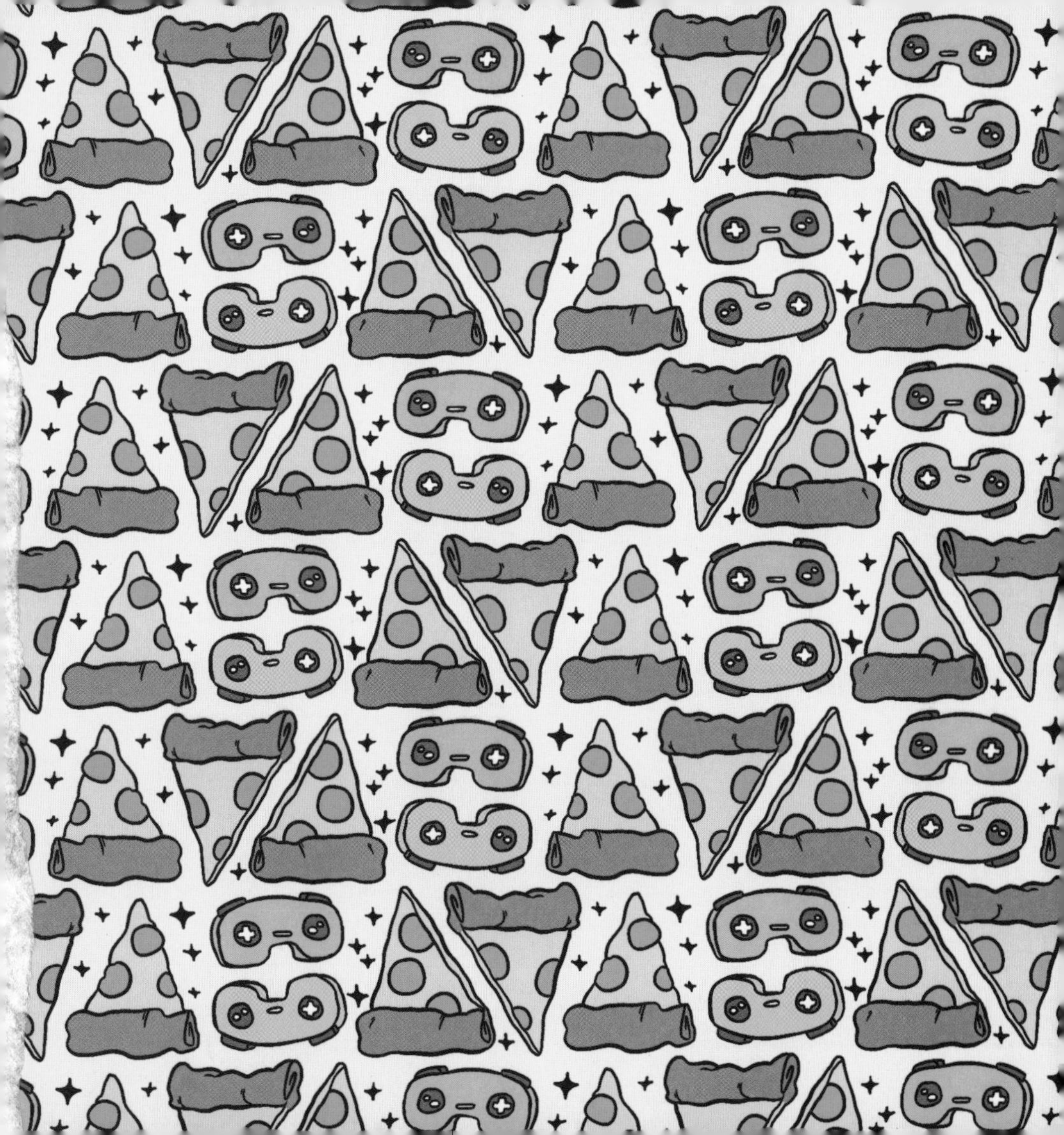

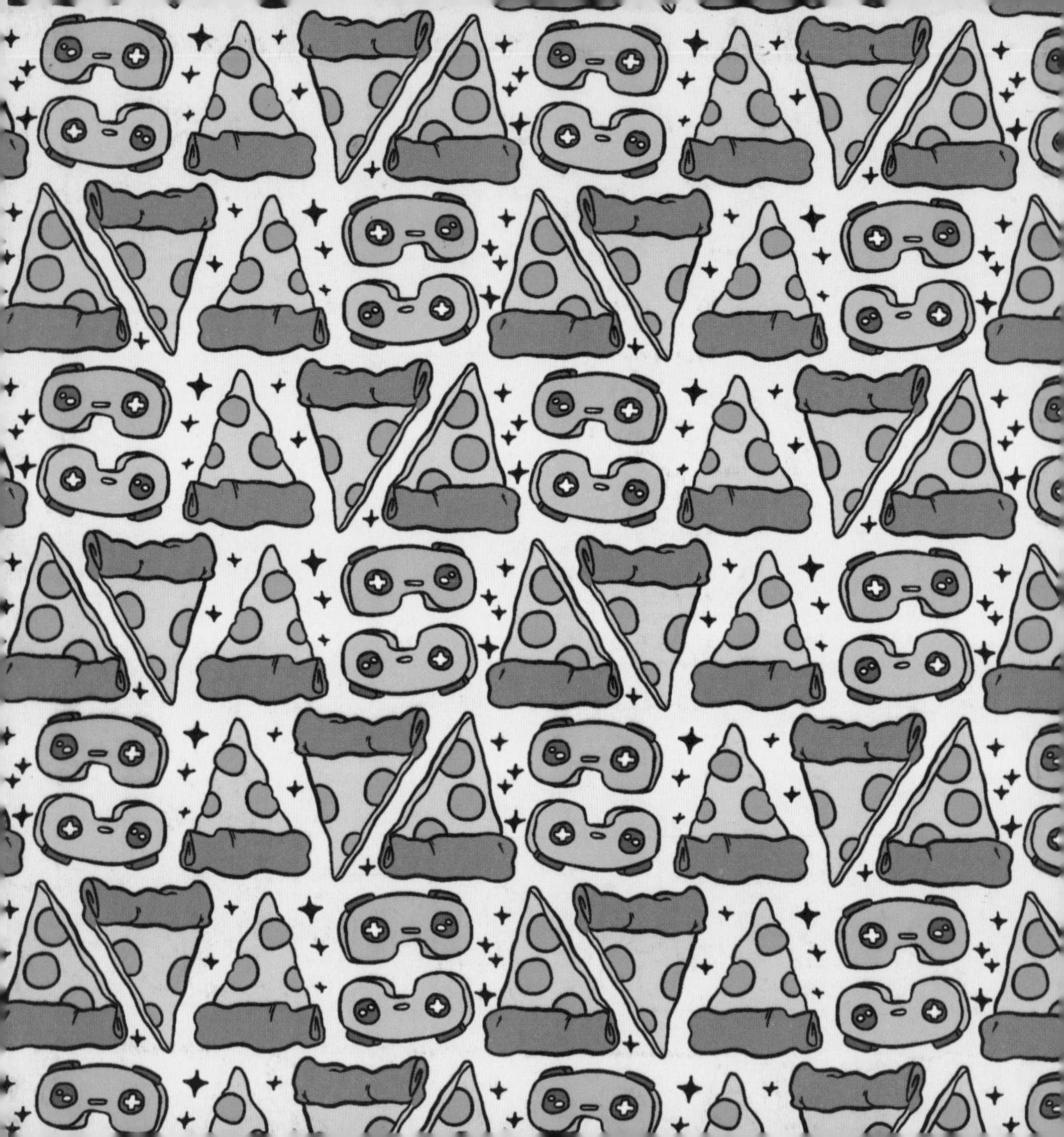